LIFESKILLS HELPING

Helping Others Through a Systematic People-Centered Approach

Richard Nelson-Jones

Royal Melbourne Institute of Technology

Brooks/Cole Publishing Company
Pacific Grove, California

 A CLAIREMONT BOOK

Brooks/Cole Publishing Company
A Division of Wadsworth, Inc.

Printed in the United States of America
10   9   8   7   6   5   4   3   2   1

Library of Congress Cataloging-in-Publication Data
Nelson-Jones, Richard.
    Lifeskills helping : helping others through a systematic people
-centered approach / Richard Nelson-Jones.
       p.   cm.
    Includes bibliographical references and index.
    ISBN 0-534-19674-8
    1. Counseling. 2. Helping behavior. I. Title.
BF637.C6N44 1992
158'.3—dc20   92-29521
                                             CIP

Sponsoring Editor: *Claire Verduin*
Editorial Associate: *Gay C. Bond*
Production Editor: *Penelope Sky*
Manuscript Editor: *Judith Johnstone*
Interior Design: *Anne Draus, Scratchgravel Publishing Services*
Cover Design: *Susan Haberkorn*
Art Coordinator: *Susan Haberkorn*
Interior Illustration: *Matrix Communications, Inc.*
Interior Clip Art Images: *Quick Art™, © 1985–1992 Wheeler Arts*
Typesetting: *Scratchgravel Publishing Services*
Printing and Binding: *Malloy Lithographing, Inc.*

ABOUT THE AUTHOR

Richard Nelson-Jones coordinates the counseling psychology training program at the Royal Melbourne Institute of Technology, where he is Associate Professor. He has written six books, three of which have been published by Brooks/Cole: *Human Relationships: A Skills Approach; Thinking Skills: Managing and Preventing Personal Problems;* and *Group Leadership: A Training Approach.*

 He has written numerous scientific and professional articles for Australian, British, Canadian, and American journals. He is a distinguished psychologist Fellow of the Australian and British Psychological Societies and was the first chairperson of the British Psychological Society's Counseling Psychology Section.

Nelson-Jones is no stranger to North America. He spent five childhood years in the San Francisco Bay Area, obtained his master's and doctorate degrees from Stanford University, and worked in New England and in Canada.

PREFACE

Lifeskills Helping offers a language, model, and skills for becoming a more effective helper. I hope it challenges you to think somewhat differently about how you work and live. I present a systematic people-centered approach not only for managing immediate problems, but also for altering the skills weaknesses, or problematic skills, that sustain problems. The focus of lifeskills helping is not just the present. Clients can acquire self-helping skills that will allow them to prevent or manage problems in the future. I offer a five-stage model for helping clients develop specific lifeskills for assuming responsibility for how they feel, think, and act.

This is a basic text for educators, trainers, and students in the counseling and helping service areas. Courses for which the book is suitable include those in counseling, psychotherapy, psychology, social work, probation work, nursing, rehabilitation, education, career work, youth work, correctional work, welfare work, community relations, pastoral care, and personnel management. The book will also support trainers and students in voluntary agencies (for instance, in marital counseling, migrant counseling, or gay and lesbian counseling).

A number of assumptions underlie the lifeskills helping approach. First, to live effectively clients need to learn and then maintain good lifeskills. Second, although external factors contribute, clients sustain problems because of weaknesses in one or more lifeskills. Third, after helping, clients often repeat problematic behaviors when faced again with the problems that brought them to helping, because helpers may have insufficiently assisted them to learn and maintain relevant lifeskills. Fourth, the aim of helping is to provide clients with self-helping skills for managing not only current problems but future ones as well. People-centeredness involves showing clients how to become their own best helpers.

ORGANIZATION

Part 1 is introductory. Chapter 1 defines terms and presents a theoretical framework for the lifeskills helping model. In Chapter 2, I describe the model. Chapter 3 looks at what students and helpers bring to their helping work.

In Part 2, I systematically present the five stages of the helping model. Chapters 4 and 5 focus on the component skills of Stage 1, which are to develop the relationship between helper and client and to identify and clarify problems. Chapter 6 presents skills for Stage 2: assessing and redefining problems in skills terms. Chapters 7 and 8 describe skills for Stage 3: stating working goals and planning interventions. The next four chapters present the Stage 4 skills for developing the client's self-helping skills. Chapter 9 describes central training skills for delivering interventions. Chapters 10, 11, and 12 review interventions that are focused on thinking skills, action skills, and feelings. Chapter 13 presents skills for Stage 5: how to end helping and consolidate self-helping skills.

The separate *Student Manual for Lifeskills Helping* is available to supplement the text and encourage learning-by-doing.

ACKNOWLEDGMENTS

You will discover that lifeskills helping has its own language and ideas. Nevertheless, my approach owes much to others' work. The emphasis on the importance of supportive helping relationships and on sensitively attending to clients' feelings shows the influence of Carl Rogers' person-centered therapy. The emphasis on thinking skills is derived from the writings of Albert Ellis, Aaron Beck, and Donald Meichenbaum, among others. The emphasis on action skills reflects the behaviorists. The emphasis on personal responsibility and choice has origins in the work of Viktor Frankl, Irvin Yalom, Abraham Maslow, William Glasser, Hobart Mowrer, and Paul Tillich. Henry Stack Sullivan, Gerard Egan, and Robert Carkhuff were forerunners in developing stage models of helping sessions and the helping process. I am grateful to all those writers and to the many others whose names are in the bibliography. I also appreciate the contributions of the following reviewers: David Cross, Houston Community College; Margaret J. French, Pitt Community College; Gloria

Gasparotto, St. Cloud State University; Jean Macht, Montgomery County Community College; and Rich Reiner, Rogue Community College.

I warmly thank the following members of the Brooks/Cole team: Claire Verduin, for commissioning the book and for her continuing faith in my authorship; Gay Bond, for her delightful personal approach to administrative correspondence; Penelope Sky, for efficiently and diligently overseeing production; Judy Johnstone, for her sensitive and literate manuscript editing; and Susan Haberkorn and Anne Draus for their imaginative cover and interior designs.

Richard Nelson-Jones

CONTENTS

❀ ❀ ❀ ❀ ❀ ❀ ❀ ❀ ❀ ❀ ❀ ❀ ❀ ❀ ❀ ❀ ❀ ❀ ❀ ❀

PART ONE

❀ ❀ ❀ ❀ ❀ ❀ ❀ ❀ ❀ ❀ ❀ ❀ ❀ ❀ ❀ ❀ ❀ ❀ ❀ ❀

INTRODUCTION

CHAPTER ONE

FRAMEWORK AND GOALS

Everything should be made as simple as
possible, but not simpler.

—Albert Einstein

CHAPTER QUESTIONS

❀ *What is lifeskills helping?*

❀ *How is lifeskills helping a people-centered
approach?*

❀ *What are lifeskills?*

❀ *What is a psychological-education
theoretical framework?*

❀ *How do people acquire and maintain
lifeskills?*

❀ *How can people change and develop
lifeskills?*

❀ *What are the ultimate and mediating
goals of lifeskills helping?*

❀ *What are some characteristics of
lifeskills helpers?*

The helping skills considered in this book are based on a psychological-education, or "lifeskills," model. Lifeskills helping is a people-centered approach for assisting clients and others to develop self-helping skills. This approach uses a simple, direct educational framework instead of psychological jargon. Geared to the needs of the vast majority of ordinary people, lifeskills helping assumes that *all people* have lifeskills strengths and weaknesses. Ineffective feeling, thinking, and acting reflect one or more lifeskills weaknesses rather than sickness or disease. Lifeskills helpers collaborate with clients in supportive relationships to detect lifeskills weaknesses that sustain difficulties and educate them in developing relevant self-helping skills.

Lifeskills helping always entails learning. As Corsini observes of psychotherapy, lifeskills helping "may be learning something new or relearning something one has forgotten; it may be learning how to learn or it may be unlearning; paradoxically, it may even be learning what one already knows" (Corsini, 1989, p. 5). Common concerns that clients present to helpers include:

"Our marriage seems to be heading for the rocks."
"I feel depressed and apathetic."
"I'm having a hard time making up my mind about my career."
"I get very tense and anxious about exams."
"I'm having trouble adjusting to my new surroundings."
"I feel lonely and find it difficult to make friends."
"I'm very angry a lot of the time."
"My life seems to have no purpose."
"I can't seem to stand up for myself."
"I'm over-stressed and don't know what to do about it."
"I feel guilty about being a mother and having a career."
"Our sex life is practically nonexistent."
"I can't break loose from the hold my parents have over me."

The basic starting point for lifeskills helpers is that each of these statements describes a learning problem. Relevant medical considerations are, of course, taken into account. Nevertheless, almost by definition, educational deficiencies account for most psychological problems.

Lifeskills helping is nothing new. Although they don't necessarily use the same language, most helpers are interested in assisting clients to develop skills of productive living. Furthermore, most parents try to help their children develop the skills for living happily. Lifeskills helping aims to spell out the "common sense" of effective helping. It builds upon the work of numerous theorists, researchers, helper trainers, and practitioners. Why re-invent the wheel when you can help the already-existing wheel to run more smoothly?

A PEOPLE-CENTERED APPROACH

When the term *people-centered* is applied to lifeskills helping, what does it mean? Let's look at some dimensions of people-centeredness.

Goals

The basic question of lifeskills helping is "How can counselors and lifeskills trainers become more effective educators about personal responsibility?" The goals of lifeskills helping have to do with helping people to help themselves. The goal of any helping encounter, however brief, is not limited to helping clients feel better or cope better with an immediate problem. Rather, lifeskills helpers aim to have clients take away some new skills for living. In this "take-away" respect, lifeskills helping resembles McDonald's or Kentucky Fried Chicken! People are viewed as personally responsible for making the most of their lives. The goal of lifeskills helping is to provide them with the confidence and skills for assuming—rather than avoiding—this responsibility. Lifeskills helping aims to empower people not only now but also in the future. The approach seeks to develop clients' self-helping skills so that they become their own best helpers.

Language

Because the goal of lifeskills helping is to nurture permanent self-help skills, the language of helping must lend itself to the client's self-instruction. In any helping situation, there are at least four possible languages operating—namely, helper and client inner and outer speech (Nelson-Jones, 1986). Lifeskills helping is based on a theoretical framework that helpers can use both for inner and outer speech; helpers do not need to speak one language to themselves and another to clients. Lifeskills helpers use their own and their clients' outer speech to develop clients' inner speech, so that the clients can understand their own problems and instruct themselves, through sequences of choices, to cope with them.

Contrast the above idea of people-centered language with the language of so-called person-centered therapy. Person-centered helpers operate out of a theoretical framework that is rarely, if ever, explicitly communicated to clients (Raskin & Rogers, 1989; Rogers, 1951, 1959). Consequently, to a certain extent at least, person-centered helpers may be talking one language to themselves and another to clients. The process of person-centered helping involves helpers' reflecting in their outer responses the outer statements of their clients. No direct attempt is made to influence clients' inner speech so that they can later instruct themselves. Person-centered helping is based on the unfolding of potential rather than a systematic development of competencies. But both are necessary for effective helping, and because of this lopsidedness, person-centered helping falls short of people-centered helping. Approaches like rational-emotive therapy and transactional analysis result in more closely matching helpers' inner and outer speech, and also attempt to train clients in self-instruction (Berne, 1961, 1964, 1972; Dusay & Dusay, 1989; Ellis, 1962, 1980, 1989).

Figure 1.1 provides an illustration of public and private talk in counseling and lifeskills training. Much counseling and training is educationally inefficient. It doesn't focus enough on moving beyond helper and client public talk at B and C. In lifeskills helping, counselors and group leaders use public talk at B and C

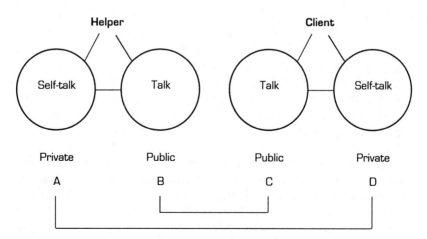

Helping Contact

Figure 1.1 Public and private talk in counseling and lifeskills training

not just to develop a helping relationship, but to work from helper private self-talk at A in order to influence client private self-talk at D. Communicating from an educational framework in relatively simple language, counselors and group leaders can help clients develop private self-talk to monitor, maintain, and develop their own skills. Thus, the language of lifeskills helping becomes the people-centered language of self-helping and self-instruction.

Clienteles

A lifeskills approach takes acquiring and maintaining psychological wellness rather than psychological disturbance as its starting point. Lifeskills helping is people-centered in that all people may benefit at some stage of their lives from contact with skilled helpers. You do not have to be sick or fit into a category of the Diagnostic and Statistical Manual of Mental Disorders— Revised (*DSM-111-R*; American Psychiatric Association, 1987) to benefit from helping! Problems of living are widespread. As Ellis quips, a way to spell life is H-A-S-S-L-E (Ellis, 1977). While growing up, the fortunate acquire many of the needed lifeskills in both developmental and preventive ways. This may include individual and group contact with lifeskills helpers. Those youngsters less fortunate may require considerable remedial help to develop good lifeskills. Even those more fortunate may later wish to work on specific problems and to become more skilled in a number of areas.

The statistics on marital breakdown provide one indication of the pervasiveness of human problems. In the early 1980s the divorce rate for first marriages in the United States was 49 percent (Glick, 1984). Approximately 83 percent of divorced men and 78 percent of divorced women eventually remarry (Wilson & London, 1987). Second divorces are common. It is predicted that 61 percent of divorced men and 54 percent of divorced women who were in their thirties in 1980 and who marry a second time will experience a second divorce (Glick, 1984). The above figures partly reflect the fact that obtaining a divorce has become easier than in earlier generations. Also, there is less disapproval of divorce than there was in the past. Nevertheless the figures underestimate the extent of marital breakdown. If the figures for the separated population were added to those of the divorced population to form a "dissolution index," the statistics for marital breakdown would be considerably higher. In addition, we need to recognize that many couples neither separated nor divorced are unhappy.

Marital breakdown and its distress involves children. In the United States only 68 percent of children live with both biological parents (Bianchi & Seltzer, 1986). There are ethnic differences among children living with both biological parents: The proportions for white, Hispanic, and black children are 73 percent, 67 percent, and 38 percent, respectively. Keeping relationships happy and intact is just one of the many possible examples where large numbers of people need to shift the balance of their lifeskills strengths and weaknesses more in the direction of strengths.

Problems and Potentials

Lifeskills helping not only focuses on helping people cope with their problems, but it also focuses on freeing their potentials. Lifeskills helping is people-centered in that it focuses on the range of competencies that all people require for their survival, maintenance, and enhancement. It is an egalitarian approach that assumes that everyone—regardless of age, sex, race, color, or creed—has the "potential for growth and the right to personal maximization of competence" (Albee, 1984, p. 230). Problems for which people require adaptive feelings, thoughts, and actions to maximize their potentials can occur at all ages of the lifespan and in all areas of life (Egan & Cowan, 1979; Erikson, 1963; Havighurst, 1972; Kohlberg & Gilligan, 1971; Masterpasqua, 1989; Perry, 1970; Sugarman, 1986).

The kinds of problems and potentials for which lifeskills helping is appropriate range from basic thinking and action skills for all stages of the lifespan to developmental competencies that are more life-stage specific (for example, learning intimacy and sexual relating skills for young adults, and coping with aging and dying skills for the old). Lifeskills helping can focus on problems and potentials in all major areas of life (for example, partner relationships, sex, parenting, occupational choice, work, study and test taking, leisure, and health). Furthermore, lifeskills helpers work with many symptoms often more indicative of dis-ease than disease (for example, depression, acute and chronic anxiety, phobias, delinquent behavior, substance abuse, and aggression).

Helping Process

Lifeskills helping is people-centered. Helpers and clients collaborate in such activities as clarifying problems, redefining problems in skills terms, setting goals, choosing interventions, setting session agendas, and evaluating progress. Lifeskills helpers require both good training and good relationship skills. They can hide behind neither a facade of phony expertise nor the mystique of a medical model. The process of lifeskills helping requires much client participation in decision making. If helpers want clients to redefine problems in skills terms, they have to offer clear explanations and negotiate such redefinitions with them. After all, it is their clients' lives they seek to influence, and clients ultimately implement treatment recommendations on their own. Helpers attempt at all times to be psychologically present in interviews as genuine and caring people (May & Yalom, 1989). However, they do not have to accept everything that clients tell them. Lifeskills helpers are frequently more people-centered when they confront and expand upon clients' perceptions than when they simply reflect them. Clients may feel more understood by helpers who expand their awareness than by those who merely stay close to their view of themselves and their problems. Lifeskills helpers are educators who offer training expertise within the context of democratic, supportive relationships. Another way of looking at the client role is as that of trainee. This trainee role reflects Mosak's comment about the psychotherapy of Adler: "Although assuming the role of student, the patient is still an active learner responsible for contributing to his or her own education" (Mosak, 1989, p. 85).

Helpers

Lifeskills helping is people-centered in that many different categories of people are helpers. Earlier the point was made that clients need to learn to be their own helpers in targeted skills areas. Formal helping provides one arena for lifeskills helping. Such helpers are likely to be service professionals and paraprofessionals: counselors, psychologists, social workers, probation officers, nurses, and personnel officers, among others. Many can use the lifeskills helping framework in doing their jobs (for example, clergy, teachers, coaches, managers, and supervisors). Even more people—nonprofessionals—can use lifeskills helping as partners, parents, and friends. Helpers apply the same lifeskills framework to themselves as to their clients. Though helpers may be of differing levels of competence and sophistication, the more widely distributed lifeskills helping becomes, the better.

DEFINING LIFESKILLS HELPING

What Are Skills?

Whether referring to client or helper skills, meanings of the word *skill* include proficiency, competence, and expertise. The essential element of any skill is the ability to make and carry out sequences of choices to achieve objectives. For instance, if clients are to be good at asserting themselves or managing stress, they have to make and implement effective choices in these areas. Similarly, if you are to be good lifeskills helpers, you have to make and implement effective choices in relating to clients, assessing lifeskills strengths and weaknesses, redefining problems in skills terms, offering appropriate interventions, and assisting clients to consolidate self-helping skills.

The concept of skill is best viewed not as an either-or matter in which you either possess or do not possess a skill. It is preferable to think of yourselves and your clients as possessing *skills strengths* or *skills weaknesses,* or a mixture of the two. Positive choices in skills areas are skills strengths. Negative choices are skills weaknesses. Put simply, the criterion for client choices is whether they help or hinder clients in assuming personal responsibility for happiness and fulfillment. The criterion for helper choices is how well they help clients assume personal responsibility.

In all lifeskills and helping areas, people are likely to possess strengths and weaknesses in varying degrees. For instance, in the area of listening, you may be skilled at understanding talkers, but poor at showing your understanding. The object of lifeskills helping is to enable clients to move, in one or more skills areas, more in the direction of skills strengths rather than skills weaknesses. The object of helper training is the same, but in regard to helping skills rather than lifeskills. In both instances, those being trained are helped to affirm themselves and others by becoming *better choosers.*

What Are Lifeskills?

Lifeskills involve *personally responsible choices.* When people are being personally responsible they are in the process of making choices that maximize their happiness and fulfillment (Frankl, 1959; May & Yalom, 1989; Nelson-Jones, 1987; Yalom, 1980). Personal responsibility is a positive concept wherein people are responsible for their own well-being and for making their own choices within the givens of their existence. Lifeskills are the component skills through which people assume—rather than avoid—personal responsibility for their lives. Lifeskills are *self-helping skills* that enable people to help themselves. As such, they empower rather than disempower or weaken people (Hopson & Scally, 1981; Masterpasqua, 1989).

Lifeskills are conducive to *mental wellness*. People who possess inadequate lifeskills are less able to fulfill their potential and meet their needs than those more skilled. Psychological distress both reflects and results from deficiencies in lifeskills. However, this is less true for biologically influenced conditions—for instance, schizophrenia and bipolar depressive disorders (Lazarus, 1989). Lifeskills possess a *psychological component*. Virtually any skill (for instance, cooking) might be viewed as a lifeskill. However, all the lifeskills mentioned in this book have a large mental component in them. Thus, even though many lifeskills are stated as observable actions, usually they heavily involve people's thoughts and feelings as well.

Lifeskills are *processes*. People lead their lives into the future and are always in the process of becoming (Allport, 1955). Throughout their lives, people are choosers who can never escape the mandate to choose among possibilities (Frankl, 1969). People possessing a lifeskill choose to make, and continue making, the choices related to it. To attain their full humanness, people require a *repertoire of lifeskills* in a number of different areas. These lifeskills need be appropriate both to their developmental tasks and to any special problems, challenges, and transitions they may face.

Some of the preceding dimensions are drawn together in this definition of lifeskills: *Lifeskills are personally responsible sequences of self-helping choices in specific psychological skills areas conducive to mental wellness. People require a repertoire of lifeskills according to their developmental tasks and specific problems of living.*

What Is Lifeskills Helping?

Lifeskills helping involves helpers in making choices that assist clients to develop lifeskills. Many of these helping choices are made in one-to-one interviews. However, lifeskills helpers may also work with couples and families. In addition, lifeskills helpers frequently lead groups to train participants in one or more specific skills. In *Group Leadership: A Training Approach* (1992), I review helper skills for leading lifeskills groups. Later on in the present book I present skills for individual lifeskills helping.

Attitude, Knowledge, and Skills

Specific lifeskills can be viewed as comprising three dimensions: attitude, knowledge, and skills. Helping skills comprise the same three dimensions.

Attitude An appropriate attitude to any lifeskill or helping skill is that you assume personal responsibility for acquiring, maintaining, using, and developing it. You may lose some or all of a skill if you fail to work at maintaining it. A personally responsible attitude is the motivational ("wanting to do it") dimension.

Knowledge Each lifeskill and helping skill involves knowledge about correct choices. People who have been exposed to good examples, by parental behavior for instance, may acquire much knowledge implicitly rather than explicitly. People with skills weaknesses often need the knowledge clearly spelled out so that they can instruct themselves. Knowledge is the "knowing how to do it" dimension of a lifeskill or a helping skill.

Skills The skills dimension of a lifeskill or a helping skill entails the application of attitude and knowledge to practice. Skills can be either inner (focusing on feeling and thinking) or outer (focusing on observable actions) or a combination of the two. In appropriate circumstances, you translate "wanting to do it" and "knowing how to do it" into "actually doing it."

A PSYCHOLOGICAL-EDUCATION THEORETICAL FRAMEWORK

The word *education* has a double derivation from its Latin origins. Education is derived from the verb *educare*, "to nurture, to rear." However, the verb *educare* is a variant of the verb *educere*, "to lead out" (Jones, 1990). A psychological-education theoretical framework encompasses both meanings of the word *education*. On the one hand, the framework acknowledges the importance of nurturing. On the other hand, the framework stresses the need for instruction to lead people to develop better lifeskills for themselves.

The term *psychoeducation* has been popularized by writers like Ivey (1976). Ivey acknowledges his debt to Guerney in stressing the educator model of helping (Guerney, Stollak, & Guerney, 1971). Ivey and his colleagues observe: "In the psychoeducational model the counselor or therapist becomes a 'teacher.' "

(Ivey, Ivey & Simek-Downing, 1987, p. 360). The theoretical framework presented here acknowledges that helping, be it parental or professional, requires a combination of nurturing and teaching. In most instances, it is not sufficient to be just a teacher.

Helping practice rests on conceptual or theoretical frameworks. Models of the person guide models of practice. The psychological-education framework underlying the helping skills described in this book attempts to integrate concepts from the existential, humanistic, cognitive, and behavioral positions. Because this book is oriented to practical experience, I will present only an overview, or thumbnail sketch, of its psychological-education framework. Elsewhere I have provided fuller statements of the framework (Nelson-Jones, 1987, 1991).

Assumptions

The underlying assumptions—the building blocks or basic concepts—of the lifeskills approach include the following.

Lifeskills

Apart from such obviously biological functions as breathing, virtually all human behavior is viewed in terms of learned lifeskills. The term *lifeskills* in itself is a neutral concept. Lifeskills may be strengths or weaknesses depending on whether or not they help people to survive and to develop potentials. As mentioned earlier, lifeskills are viewed as sequences of choices that may be well or poorly made.

Interrelationship of Thinking, Feeling, and Action

In varying degrees most lifeskills comprise thinking, feeling, and action elements. Thinking, feeling, and action influence each other. Thinking often accompanies, or results from, feelings at various levels of awareness. Conversely, people may choose to regulate feelings by altering the way they think about themselves, others, and the environment. The connection between thinking and action is also two-way: Thinking influences action and action influences thinking. Likewise, as with Beck's depressed patients, feelings and actions influence each other (Beck, Rush, Shaw, & Emery, 1979). Figure 1.2 depicts the interrelationships between feeling, thinking, and acting.

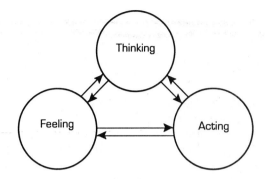

Figure 1.2 Interrelationships between feeling, thinking, and acting

Energizing Drive

Ordinary people may have difficulty understanding terms like "the organism's actualizing tendency" (Raskin & Rogers, 1989, p. 169), or "self-realizing." All people possess an energizing drive toward surviving, maintaining, and developing themselves. However, humans possess weak instinctual remnants (Maslow, 1970). Consequently, people's fortunate or unfortunate experiences tend to determine how they harness their energizing drive to work for or against them.

The goals of the energizing drive may be viewed on at least three dimensions: first, the basic survival dimension; second, the pleasure dimension, or what Ellis calls "short-range hedonism" (Ellis, 1989, p. 209); and third, the higher dimension of socially oriented involvements and commitments. Terms like *self-actualizing* (Maslow, 1962, 1970) and *propriate striving* have been used to describe "the integrity that comes only from maintaining major directions of striving" (Allport, 1955, p. 51). Lifeskills are required for each of the above three ways of expending energy. However, most humans are probably more driven by survival and short-range hedonism (pleasure seeking) than by longer-term and higher-level strivings.

The energizing drive is neither good nor bad. Nature does not operate in such terms. Humans are animals first and people second. People are more likely to operate instinctually in ways that protect themselves and the species. However, the long human learning process and our human ability for symbolic thought offer as much scope for lifeskills weaknesses as strengths. Biologically, both as individuals and as a species, humans have predispositions for both adaptive and maladaptive behaviors. Human fallibility is a biological, as well as a psychological, fact of life.

Survival Anxiety

To existential psychologists, the fear of death, nonbeing, or destruction is the underlying fear from which all other fears are derived (May & Yalom, 1989; Yalom, 1980). I prefer the term *survival anxiety* to "death anxiety." The notion of survival anxiety focuses more than death anxiety on the continual fears of the living. Survival anxiety relates both to people's fear of death itself and to their fear of not being competent to meet survival needs. This view is echoed by Beck, who sees anxiety disorders as characterized by "excessive functioning or malfunctioning of normal survival mechanisms" (Beck & Weishaar, 1989). People with anxiety disorders maximize the chances of negative outcomes and minimize the chances of positive outcomes—instead of realistically appraising situations and having an appropriate level of anxiety. As part of this process, they may distort their sense of competence to bring about desired outcomes or, in more academic terms, their self-efficacy beliefs (Bandura, 1977, 1986, 1989). Virtually all people suffer from higher levels of anxiety than are strictly required to cope effectively with life's challenges. The comedian Mel Brooks is not alone in suffering from high anxiety! High anxiety can be both cause and effect of lifeskills weaknesses.

Threefold View of Self

Our self is what we call "I" or "me." It is the center of our own personal universe. The self has three major components.

1. *The Natural Self:* Each of us has a fundamental biological inner nature, or inner core, of genetic aptitudes, drives, instincts, instinct remnants, and human potentialities. This is our animal nature. Some of this animal nature is shared by the entire human species (for instance, the need for food, shelter, physical safety, belonging, and love). Some of this animal nature is unique to each person; it includes individual aptitudes, inner valuing process, and energizing drive. This inner nature or biological core of personhood is the Natural Self.

2. *The Learned Self:* The Learned Self is the product of the individual's social learning experiences. It reflects the way people have been taught to perceive themselves and their lifeskills strengths and weaknesses. In an ideal world, people's

(like superego)

Learned Selves would be in accord with their Natural Selves. Their Learned Selves would provide them with lifeskills to fulfill their animal natures within the constraints of reality. However, in the real world, most people have acquired misperceptions and lifeskills weaknesses that block attainment of human potential. The Learned Self can be for good or ill; it is usually for both.

3. *The Choosing Self*: Whereas people's Natural Self represents their biological endowment, and their Learned Self reflects their learning history, the Choosing Self represents their capacity to create their lives through present and future choices. Thus people not only *have* selves, but also continuously *create* selves. The Choosing Self provides a mechanism that allows people to discard the misperceptions and skills weaknesses of their Learned Selves that block the fulfillment of their Natural Selves. People can choose aspects of the multipotential Natural Self that they wish to develop. This is particularly important in lifeskills helping, where clients choose to develop specific skills to attain their own personal goals.   (ego)

Personal Responsibility

Focusing on personal responsibility is almost like focusing on your nose. Though it may be right in front of your face, the concept is not always easy to observe (Nelson-Jones, 1987). Lifeskills helping adopts the existential notion of people as responsible for the authorship of their lives (Sartre, 1956; May & Yalom, 1989; Yalom, 1980). Another metaphor is that people are responsible for inventing their lives. Authorship or invention requires a continuous process of choosing. Maslow wrote of this process in terms of a series of two-sided choices. One side represented safety, defense, fear, and regression; the other, progression or growth (Maslow, 1962, 1971).

Personal responsibility is an inner process in which people work from inside to outside. This process starts with people's thoughts and feelings and leads to their observable actions. Furthermore, especially as people grow older, many if not most of the significant barriers to assuming responsibility are internal rather than external. However, both inside and outside of helping, people "differ enormously in the degree of responsibility they are willing to accept for their life situation and in their modes of denying responsibility" (May & Yalom, 1989, p. 377). To assume personal responsibility involves acquiring, maintaining, and developing effective lifeskills. Such lifeskills enable people to affirm their existence despite all inner fears and outer threats.

Acquiring Lifeskills

Here are some factors influencing how people learn lifeskills strengths and weaknesses.

Supportive Relationships

Children require supportive relationships. Bowlby (1979) talks of the concept of a secure base, otherwise referred to as an "attachment figure." He notes accumulating evidence that humans of all ages are happiest and most effective when they feel that they have a trusted person who will come to their aid should difficulties arise. Rogers also stressed the need for supportive parent-child relationships characterized by high degrees of respect, genuineness, and empathic understanding, whereby children can feel sensitively and accurately understood (Rogers, 1951, 1959). Supportive relationships can be provided by many people other than parents (for instance, relatives and teachers). Growing up, most people seem to need at least one primary supportive relationship.

There are many reasons why presence of supportive and absence of unsupportive or hostile relationships help children develop lifeskills. First, supportive relationships provide children with the security to engage in exploratory behavior and risk trial-and-error learning. Such exploratory behavior represents a series of personal experiments in which children collect information about themselves and their environments. Second, supportive relationships help children listen better to themselves. By feeling prized and accurately understood, children can get more in touch with their wants, wishes, and personal meanings. Third, children may feel freer to manifest emerging lifeskills without risk of ridicule. Fourth, instruction in specific skills is frequently best conducted in the context of supportive relationships where the anxiety attached to learning is diminished. Fifth, the presence or absence of supportive relationships can either affirm or deny children's sense of worth. They may either be helped to become confident to face life's challenges or they may become inhibited, withdrawn, and afraid to take risks. Alternatively, they may mask their insecurity by excessive attention seeking.

Learning from Example

Learning from example is a major way in which people acquire lifeskills strengths and weaknesses. How to think, feel, and act can be learned from other people. Frequently parents remain unaware of behaviors they demonstrate to their children. If either or both parents are emotionally inexpressive, children miss opportunities for observing how to express emotions. If parents and others use ineffective thinking skills (for example, blaming and overgeneralizing) children may be quick to do likewise. In addition, children may acquire from parents' examples poor action skills for relationships, work, leisure, and health care. The converse is also true. Lifeskills concerning how to feel, think, and act may be acquired from the role modeling of parents and significant others. Significant others may include peers, teachers, siblings, other relatives, and even media characters.

Bandura considers that an observer is more likely to adopt another's example if the demonstrated behavior is valued by the observer and also brings rewards to the person being observed (Bandura, 1977). However, just as teaching by example is often unintentional, so is learning by example. For instance, the effects of modeling are less direct when thinking skills rather than action skills are involved. Not only are thinking skills not visual (in the sense that action skills are), but they are also seldom clearly verbalized. People may absorb, from example, deficient skills for thinking, feeling, and action and remain unaware that it happened.

Learning from Consequences

Learning lifeskills from observing role models frequently intermingles with learning them from rewarding or unrewarding consequences. For example, parents who are poor at showing emotions themselves may not reward their children for expressing emotion. Rewards are either primary or secondary. Primary rewards have fundamental biological significance, including food, shelter, sex, and human warmth (Skinner, 1971). Much human behavior is governed by secondary rewards that have become associated or conditioned to primary rewards, such as approval or money.

Rewarding consequences play a large part in helping or hindering people from acquiring lifeskills. From birth, humans receive messages about how "good" or "bad" their actions are. Usually with the best of intentions, adults try to reward children for developing the skills necessary to cope with the world. However, often adults provide rewards inadequately. For example, most people learn their relationship skills and thinking skills from a mixture of observing others, unsystematic feedback, and trial and error. Either inside or outside the home, it is rare that people are systematically rewarded as they develop these lifeskills. Furthermore, sometimes children are rewarded for ex-hibiting skills weaknesses rather than strengths. For instance, they may find that they are more likely to get their way if they shout aggressively rather than take a more reasonable ap-proach. In addition, skills weaknesses can be acquired by people becoming too dependent on the need for external rewards rather than trusting their own judgment and skills. Also, skills weak-nesses can be developed by people receiving the message that their whole personhood is bad, rather than a specific behavior being insufficiently skilled. Last but not least, many people ac-quire skills weaknesses through receiving negative feedback be-cause of their sex, race, social class, or culture.

Instruction and Self-Instruction

Psychologists researching animal behavior stress the importance of learning from example and from consequences. However, hu-mans possess the capacity for symbolic thought and communi-cation. Consequently, instruction is a major transmitter of lifeskills. Much lifeskills instruction takes place informally in the home. Some of this instruction is very basic (for instance, asking children to say please and thank you). Children are frequently told by their parents how to relate, how to study, how to look after their health, and so on. Relatives and peers are other pro-viders of instruction outside educational settings.

Much informal lifeskills instruction takes place in schools and colleges. However, systematic attempts to train youngsters in a range of relationship skills are probably still more the exception than the rule (Hatch & Guerney, 1975; Morgan, 1984; Sprinthall, 1980). Nevertheless, lifeskills programs are run in many schools in such areas as career education (Amatea, Clark, & Cross, 1984; Roessler, 1988) and drug and alcohol education (Dorn & South, 1986). In addition, a range of lifeskills programs may be offered in colleges and universities inside or outside the formal curricu-lum. The lifeskills targeted include: relationship skills; study skills; managing test anxiety; career development skills (Swain, 1984); anxiety and stress management skills (Romano, 1984); and effective thinking skills (Barrow & Moore, 1983; Heppner, Neal, & Larsen, 1984). Usually participation in such programs is voluntary.

Instruction can be for better or for worse. Skills weaknesses as well as strengths may be imparted. For various reasons, those instructed may resist instructors. Sometimes instructors are poor at drawing out learners rather than just telling them what to do. Frequently instruction contains sex bias (for instance, teaching only *girls* parenting skills). In addition, lifeskills may not be communicated clearly enough for learners to instruct themselves afterwards. If learners are unable to talk themselves through the sequences of choices, the lifeskills have been inadequately presented and learned. Much instruction falls far short of this self-instructional objective.

Information and Opportunity

People require adequate information to develop lifeskills. For example, keeping children in ignorance about basic facts of sexuality and death impedes self-awareness and emotional responsiveness. Intentionally or unintentionally, adults often relate to their children on the basis of lies, omissions of truth, or partial truths (Steiner, 1974). Furthermore, necessary information may not be readily available outside the home. For instance, schools differ greatly in the adequacy of the career information they provide.

Children, adolescents, and adults alike need available opportunities to try out and develop lifeskills. Ideally such opportunities are in line with their maturation and state of readiness. People may have different opportunities on account of their sex, race, culture, social class, financial position, or schooling—to mention just some barriers. Furthermore, people can be fortunate or unfortunate in having parents who open up rather than restrict learning opportunities. Children and adults also have a role in seeking out information and opportunities. Some have better skills at this than others.

Anxiety and Confidence

Children grow up having both helpful and harmful experiences for developing self-esteem. The fortunate acquire a level of anxiety that both protects against actual dangers and also motivates them toward realistic achievements. Those less fortunate may acquire debilitating anxieties through role modeling, instruction, or provision of faulty consequences. Even parents who communicate carefully can bruise children's fragile self-esteem. Far worse are hostile and defensive parents. Here children's feelings and perceptions are doubly discounted: first by the initial aggression and second by being subjected to further aggression when they react. Deficient behaviors resulting from (as well as manifesting) anxiety include: unwillingness to take realistic risks; tense and nervous rather than relaxed learning; a heightened tendency to say and do the wrong things; unnecessary aggression; excessive approval seeking; and underachieving, with or without overstriving. Inadequate performance in different skills may further raise anxiety and make future lifeskills learning even more difficult. However, people who are helped, or who help themselves, to acquire anxiety management skills may learn lifeskills more easily than those without such skills.

Maintaining Lifeskills Weaknesses

People can maintain both lifeskills strengths and weaknesses. This section focuses only on how people maintain lifeskills weaknesses. Especially for children, *acquiring* lifeskills strengths and weaknesses is more a matter of "what the environment does to me" than "what I do to myself." Young people are frequently at the mercy of their elders. However, *maintaining* lifeskills strengths and weaknesses is a different matter. Here, because lifeskills are maintained into adulthood, there is a shift in the direction of "what I do to myself" rather than "what the environment has done to me." Following are processes that maintain lifeskills weaknesses.

Thinking Skills Weaknesses

Thinking skills weaknesses are a major element of poor lifeskills. Too much anxiety tends to be a common theme in faulty thinking. The following are some thinking skills weaknesses.

Attributional deficiencies   How people look at causality influences the degree to which they maintain lifeskills weaknesses. Assigning responsibility and cause is a way people have of making sense of what happens in their lives. Faulty *attributions* (assignments) explain responsibility and cause inaccurately. People who avoid rather than assume responsibility for their lives are poor candidates for initiating desirable behavior changes. The following are possible attributional errors that may sustain lifeskills weaknesses. These attributional deficiencies tend to convert partial truths into whole truths by overlooking relevant aspects of personal responsibility.

1. *"It's my nature."* Such an attribution fails to acknowledge the large learned component in most lifeskills weaknesses.
2. *"It's my past."* For people who have left home, attributions of unfortunate pasts have little to do with how they maintain their skills weaknesses in the present.
3. *"It's my bad luck."* People can "make" their luck by developing relevant skills.

4. *"It's my poor environment."* Many people have learned to overcome the skills weaknesses contributed to by their poor environments.
5. *"It's all your fault."* Why bother to change when negative events are someone else's fault?
6. *"It's all my fault."* Quite apart from being inaccurate, blaming yourself all the time may erode the confidence required to deal with life's problems.

Unrealistic personal rules Personal rules are the dos and don'ts by which people lead their lives. All of us have an inner rulebook of standards for ourselves and for others. Sometimes these standards are realistic and appropriately flexible. On other occasions the standards may be unrealistic and inappropriately rigid. Ellis has coined the term *mustabation* to refer to rigid internal rules characterized by "musts," "oughts," and "shoulds" (Ellis, 1980, 1989). These unrealistic rules are not only lifeskills weaknesses in themselves, but may also help maintain other lifeskills weaknesses. Below are illustrations of mustabatory personal rules in various lifeskills areas.

1. *Feeling:* "I must never get angry."
2. *Sex:* "I must always perform at a high level."
3. *Thinking:* "Women must not be as smart as men."
4. *Relationships:* "I must always win an argument."
5. *Study:* "I must write the perfect term paper."
6. *Work:* "I must always be stimulated by my job."
7. *Leisure:* "I must not enjoy myself too much."
8. *Health:* "I must always push myself to the limit of my endurance."

Perceiving inaccurately A Chinese proverb states: "Two thirds of what we see is behind our eyes." People erroneously maintain lifeskills weaknesses if they rigidly perceive their skills to be either better or worse than they are. They may find it difficult to accept contrary feedback if they overestimate how intelligent, affectionate, competent at work, or good in bed they are. People may misperceive positive feedback to sustain a negative self-picture as well as negative feedback to sustain a positive self-picture (Rogers, 1959). In both instances, the faulty perceiving contributes to maintaining lifeskills weaknesses as well as being a lifeskills weakness in itself.

"Defense mechanisms," "defenses," or "security operations" are terms for the ways that people operate on incoming information that differs from their existing self-pictures (Arlow, 1989; Clark, 1991; Freud, 1936; Maslow, 1962, 1970; Sullivan, 1953). Defensiveness involves people's reducing awareness for short-term psychological comfort (to avoid pain). Defensive processes range from denying incoming information to distorting it in various ways: for example, rationalizing (making excuses when your behavior causes you anxiety), or projecting (externalizing thoughts and feelings onto others rather than owning them).

Negative self-talk   Negative self-talk may be contrasted with coping self-talk (Meichenbaum, 1977, 1983, 1985, 1986; Meichenbaum & Deffenbacher, 1988). Coping self-talk has two main functions: calming and coaching. A sample calming self-instruction might be "Keep calm." A sample coaching self-instruction might be "Break the task down." Frequently, calming and coaching statements appear together: "Keep calm. Break the task down." Negative self-talk statements keep people from working on a range of lifeskills weaknesses. Such negative statements include: "I'm never going to be able to do it," "I'm starting to feel anxious and things may get out of control," and "The future is hopeless."

Fear of change   Once acquired, lifeskills weaknesses can become well-established habits resistant to change (Ellis, 1985, 1987; Grieger, 1989). Fear of change includes the following dimensions:

1. Fear of the unknown
2. Fear of the discomfort in making the effort to change
3. Fear of losing the payoffs from existing behaviors
4. Fear of inner conflict between the old and the emerging self
5. Fear of conflict with others arising from changing
6. Fear of failure
7. Fear of the consequences of success

All learning involves giving up the safety of the known to develop new skills. Some people are better able to confront fears about change than others. Some of the thinking skills mentioned earlier (for example, perceiving accurately and using coping self-talk) help people manage rather than avoid change.

Unchanged Environmental Circumstances

Lifeskills weaknesses are usually maintained both by how people think and by what the environment keeps doing to them. Most factors mentioned in the section on how people acquire lifeskills can help maintain lifeskills weaknesses. People may continue to have insufficiently supportive relationships. They may still be exposed to examples of poor thinking and action skills. They may continue to receive inappropriate rewarding consequences. They may fail to receive or find adequate lifeskills instruction and thus continue instructing themselves in their weaknesses. In addition, they may still be exposed to insufficient or faulty information and lack suitable opportunities to develop their skills and human potential.

Change and Self-Development

Change in lifeskills helping may entail acquiring new skills strengths, releasing and developing existing skills strengths, relearning previously acquired skills strengths, unlearning and possibly extinguishing skills weaknesses, and learning how to maintain and develop skills after helping. In addition, wherever possible, lifeskills helpers attempt to strengthen people's general level of self-esteem. Here, rather than outline specific helping skills, I will mention some mechanisms of change within a psychological-education framework.

Learning by Supportive Relationships

People do not always require supportive relationships to develop lifeskills (for example, they may learn from skills manuals or computers). Nevertheless, change is more likely to occur if lifeskills learning takes place within the context of supportive relationships. Earlier, I mentioned some of the reasons that children learn best in supportive relationships, where they are understood and prized. They feel confident enough to engage in exploratory behavior. They are better able to listen to themselves and get in touch with wants and wishes. They are better able to take the risks involved in learning new skills. All of these reasons apply to offering clients supportive relationships, both individually and in groups.

In addition, supportive relationships help clients drop some defenses and assume rather than avoid personal responsibility for life and behavior. Sometimes clients arrive at such insights on their own. Other times, they may need assistance from helper challenges and confrontations. Such challenges are best done within the context of supportive relationships, or they risk doing more harm than good. A further reason for offering supportive helping relationships is that many clients need reaffirmation of their faith in human relating. Some clients need a gentle, sensitive, nurturing, and healing relationship prior to a more active skills focus. In their contacts with clients, lifeskills helpers provide rewarding consequences both for relating in general and for developing specific targeted skills.

Learning by Instruction

While helpers can encourage clients to do their own work, frequently clients require instruction as well. Lifeskills helpers are both facilitators and trainers. Conversely, clients are both persons whose potential is unfolding and students requiring specific knowledge and skills to function more effectively. Instruction within helping relationships is not only a matter of initial presentation of concepts and ideas. Much lifeskills instruction takes place as people rework and practice the original concepts and skills. Furthermore, good lifeskills helpers are always on the lookout for ways of presenting material so clearly that clients learn to instruct themselves. In addition, where relevant, lifeskills helpers instruct clients in the skills of information seeking and opportunity creation. Helpers are far from the only sources of instruction. Books, training manuals, self-help cassettes and videos, computer-assisted learning packages, other helpers, and lifeskills group participants can be additional sources.

Learning by Observing

Areas for *observational* learning include feelings, thinking skills, action skills, and action skills with accompanying self-talk. In lifeskills helping, observational learning can take place in many ways. First, helpers are role models of competent helping relationships. Second, helpers may demonstrate specific skills (for example, the verbal, voice, and body messages to make assertive behavior change requests). Third, helpers may arrange that clients observe audiocassette or videotape demonstrations. Such material may have been developed by the helper or purchased from commercial sources. Fourth, thinking skills in particular may be demonstrated in writing (for instance, in self-help manuals). Fifth, helpers may encourage clients between sessions to identify and observe role models who demonstrate targeted skills. Sixth, helpers may encourage visualized demonstration. Here clients imagine themselves or a third party performing the targeted skills competently. Seventh, in lifeskills groups, participants are likely to demonstrate both skills strengths and weaknesses for each other.

Where possible, helpers try to increase the attention level of clients. Strategies for this include demonstrating skills clients want to learn, choosing demonstrators with whom clients can identify, and telling clients what to watch for either in advance or as the demonstration unfolds.

Learning by Doing

Lifeskills helping lays heavy stress on active learning. Supportive helping relationships enable clients to develop the skills of talking about themselves and of breaking down and clarifying problems. Where appropriate, within-session instruction and demonstration of skills is either accompanied by or followed by coached practice. Further behavior rehearsals may take place, possibly incorporating video feedback. Learning by doing is often accompanied by teaching clients how to verbalize, and then subvocalize, appropriate self-instructions. Frequently clients get between-session homework assignments. At the end of a session they play active roles in choosing assignments. At the start of the subsequent session both clients and helpers review progress. This is a time to acknowledge successes and analyze difficulties and setbacks. Homework assignments include: self-monitoring forms, exercises, thinksheets, games, personal experiments in which behavior changes are tried and evaluated, and practice, practice, practice!

Learning by Consolidating Trained Skills

Lifeskills helpers do not rely on the "train and hope" approach to whether or not clients work to maintain their treatment gains (Goldstein & Keller, 1987; Stokes & Osnes, 1989). Because it is not what happens in helping that counts but what happens afterwards, lifeskills helping always pays attention to consolidating trained skills as self-helping skills. From the start, with each client, helpers pay attention to issues of transfer, generalization, maintenance, and development of skills. Helper strategies for consolidating self-helping skills include: providing rationales for helping that emphasize self-helping; developing clients' self-assessment and goal-setting skills; assigning regular homework tasks; rehearsing coping with difficulties and setbacks; helping clients identify and use supports; working with significant others who can help clients in their home or work environments; arranging for follow-up contact with the helper or other appropriate people; identifying peer self-help groups; providing information on further skills-building opportunities; and suggesting further reading and audiovisual material. In addition, helpers can pay attention to thinking skills for maintaining change (for example, attributing cause accurately, knowing how to self-instruct, using self-reward, accurately perceiving feedback, and acknowledging rather than discounting the rewards from maintaining change.

Learning by Self-Development

Ideally, former clients can go beyond maintaining existing skills to develop them to higher levels. They may become self-motivated learners who know and apply the principles of developing lifeskills strengths on their own. Such people are committed to personal development, either in specific skills areas or across a range of skills. All of us need to learn to become our own best helpers. A distinction may be made between difficulties and problems; problems arise when attempted solutions to difficulties are unsuccessful. Thus the attempts at resolving the difficulty become part of the problem. People who have learned the skills of psychological self-helping are much less likely to allow themselves to stay stuck in chronic problems than are those who have not. Well-functioning people are capable of sustaining their own development. Where appropriate, they do use others as resources both for support and for building up specific skills strengths.

GOALS FOR LIFESKILLS HELPING

Parloff (1967) suggests that the goals of counseling and therapy can be better understood if they are divided into two categories: mediating and ultimate. Ellis makes the distinction between inelegant and elegant change as goals for Rational-Emotive Therapy (Ellis, 1980). Whereas inelegant change focuses on symptom removal, elegant change "goes much beyond this kind of symptom removal, and aims at a significant lessening (rather than a complete removal) of clients' *disturbability*" (Ellis, 1980, p. 13). In lifeskills helping, a distinction can also be made between ultimate (or elegant) goals and mediating (or inelegant) goals. In addition lifeskills helping emphasizes preventive goals. For example, attending a friendship skills training program in elementary school may prevent the development of skills weaknesses.

Ultimate Goal: Personal Excellence

Lifeskills helping is a positive and optimistic approach whose goals require stating in the positive. The ultimate goal of lifeskills helping is to see people assume responsibility for personal excellence. Other terms for personal excellence are high-level competence, psychological wellness, and self-actualizing (Maslow, 1970), and assuming personal responsibility (Nelson-Jones, 1987). The term *personal excellence* has been chosen because of its clearly educational connotations. Top educational institutions strive not only to be excellent in themselves, but also to impart to students the skills through which they will continue to strive for excellence after they leave. Similarly, at the elegant end of lifeskills helping, clients work toward broader, higher, and longer lasting levels of skills that go well beyond "just getting by."

Personal excellence is both state and process. The state of personal excellence is that of attaining a high level of competence across a range of skills areas. However, lifeskills are not static, and they have to be reclaimed daily. The process of personal excellence is that of assuming effective personal responsibility for making the choices that maintain and develop the positive aspects of one's human potential. Personal excellence requires the ability and the consistent desire to make and implement life-affirming choices.

Mediating Goals: Specific Lifeskills

Mediating goals in lifeskills helping entail helping clients acquire the processes of effective choosing in specific skills areas. Terms like *symptom removal* are not used because of their medical rather than educational connotations. In *Personal Responsibility Counseling and Therapy* (1987), I grouped lifeskills according to the four R's of psychological well-being: responsiveness, realism, relatedness, and rewarding activity. Another way to view lifeskills is in terms of thinking skills, action skills, and feelings-related skills.

Thinking Skills

Effective people think realistically (Ellis & Harper, 1975; Emery, 1982; Nelson-Jones, 1990a). Thinking skills include: possessing a realistic conceptual and linguistic framework; assuming responsibility for your own choices; coping self-talk; choosing realistic personal rules; perceiving accurately; attributing cause accurately; predicting risk and reward realistically; setting personal goals; using visualizing skills; exercising decision-making skills; and managing problems skills.

Action Skills

Action skills are observable behaviors. They are what you do and how you do it, rather than what and how you feel and think. Action skills vary by area of application. The following are some applied areas (though an incomplete listing) with illustrative action skills.

> *Relationships:* Skills include making initial contact, conversing, disclosing, listening, showing caring, asserting yourself, and managing anger and conflict.
>
> *Parenting:* Skills include the above, especially in rearing children, and also skills like sexual and moral education.
>
> *Study:* Skills include managing time effectively, meeting deadlines, reading effectively, writing term papers and theses, managing achievement and test anxiety, taking tests, participating in groups, and speaking publicly.
>
> *Work:* Skills include job seeking, interviewing, supervising, managing, working as a team, negotiating, handling transitions, making the most of a work setting, and giving and receiving feedback.
>
> *Leisure:* Skills include seeking out rewarding pastimes, being willing to develop skills in specific activities, having the ability for passive relaxation, and taking adequate and enjoyable vacations.
>
> *Health:* Skills include eating nutritionally and in moderation, moderating alcohol consumption, avoiding smoking, avoiding addictive drugs, keeping physically fit, managing stress well, and observing a good balance between work, relationship, family, and recreational activities.
>
> *Social participation:* Skills include being a good neighbor, identifying and participating in community activities, and working for desirable social changes.

Feelings-Related Skills

Effective people are both responsive to their underlying animal natures and emotionally literate. Feelings-related skills include: acknowledging the importance of feelings; awareness of and openness to feelings; awareness of wants and wishes; inner empathy (the ability to tune in to and explore feelings; awareness of bodily sensations; capacity for experiencing sensuality; capacity for experiencing loving and sociable feelings; and being fully aware of existential limitations (for instance, death). Feelings-related skills can be extended to include such composite feeling, thinking, and acting skills as relaxation, anxiety management, and stress management. Feelings-related skills can be viewed in more general terms, such as confidence, self-acceptance (Ellis, 1989), and a broadly based sense of self-efficacy (Bandura, 1977, 1986, 1989).

THE LIFESKILLS HELPER

What Lifeskills Helpers Are

Lifeskills helpers hold humanistic values, whether outside or within religious frameworks. These values include: respect for each individual, acknowledgment of human fallibility, belief in human educability, belief in the human potential for reason and social living, and a sincere desire for a better world. Lifeskills helpers subscribe to a psychological-education theoretical framework, which was outlined earlier. This theoretical framework integrates elements of existential-humanistic and cognitive-behavioral psychology. In both their helping and personal lives, lifeskills helpers are always choosers.

Lifeskills helpers are practitioner-researchers who constantly make, implement, and evaluate behavior-change hypotheses. At least four sources of knowledge enlighten their helping. First, they pay attention to theoretical knowledge. The psychological-education framework requires continuous updating in light of new knowledge about human development. Second, they endeavor to keep abreast of relevant research findings about the processes and outcomes of helping. When they work in a speciality area (for example, vocational counseling or marriage-and-family counseling) they need to keep up with pertinent research findings. Third, they learn from professional experience. They are active seekers about how to operate more effectively. They evaluate their work and, if necessary, modify their helping skills accordingly. Fourth, lifeskills helpers are alive and vibrant human beings who learn from their personal experience outside of formal helping. This kind of reflective learning is especially important for helpers operating within a psychological education framework in which they and their clients require the same lifeskills. If you can acquire, maintain, and develop your own lifeskills, you should be better able to help clients.

Lifeskills helpers are educators. Taking into account the state of readiness, expectations, and skills levels of each client, they flexibly use both relationship and training skills. The focus of helping includes nurturing and healing vulnerable clients, assisting clients with specific problems and decisions, crisis management work, and preventive and developmental lifeskills training. The clientele for helping may be an individual, a group, or an institution. Lifeskills helpers are always conscious of ways to "seed" (disseminate) helping skills to others. Furthermore, they recognize that sometimes "upstream" helping, focusing on organizational policies and practices that create problems, may be necessary instead of or in addition to "downstream" helping with individuals or groups of clients (Egan & Cowan, 1979).

Within an educational framework, lifeskills helpers use a variety of training interventions focusing on feeling, thinking, and action. In individual work, lifeskills helpers do not want to be archaeologists or historians; instead they focus mainly on clients' present and future. In particular, helpers collaborate with clients to identify skills weaknesses that are currently causing difficulties. Then helpers assist clients in shifting the balance of the relevant skills weaknesses and strengths more in the direction of strengths. Lifeskills helpers always heavily emphasize clients' consolidating trained skills as self-helping skills. They always encourage people to become their own best helpers.

What Lifeskills Helpers Are Not

Another way of defining what lifeskills helpers are is to point out what they are not. First, they are no different from other people except that they possess better helping skills. They still have their own struggles, imperfections, and difficulties in affirming their positive rather than negative potentials. Second, they are not superficial manipulators. They genuinely care for the growth and development of their clients and collaborate with them to choose working goals and methods. Where clients require gentle and sensitive nurturing, they attempt to provide it as they move toward more skills-focused training approaches. Third, lifeskills helpers are neither magicians nor snake-oil doctors promising instant cures! People usually come to helping with long-established skills weaknesses (as well as strengths). Helpers emphasize that behavior change usually requires hard work. Clients will need continuing effort and practice to maintain and develop skills.

Fourth, lifeskills helpers cannot do clients' work. They do not encourage dependent relationships. Rather, they quietly and sometimes more forcefully confront clients with the responsibility for making their own lives. At best they can only influence clients to develop better lifeskills. If clients are going to change, they have to demonstrate their own commitment. Fifth, lifeskills helpers do not encourage conformity. Each client is assisted to think through which choices are best in their unique life circumstances. Sixth, lifeskills helpers do not view themselves as having a monopoly on helping skills. Many helping skills are similar to skills needed for other roles (for example, being a partner, friend, parent, or supervisor). In addition, many helping skills can be used for self-help. The more people we have who possess good helping skills, the better.

CHAPTER HIGHLIGHTS

- Lifeskills helping is a people-centered approach for assisting clients and others to develop self-helping skills.
- The language of lifeskills helping is democratic and lends itself to client self-instruction.
- Lifeskills helping focuses on the problems and potentials of people in general. It takes psychological wellness (rather than psychological disturbance) as its starting point.
- Lifeskills are personally responsible sequences of self-helping choices in specific psychological skills areas conducive to mental wellness. People require a repertoire of lifeskills according to their developmental tasks and specific problems of living.
- Lifeskills helping aims to shift the balance of clients' skills strengths and weaknesses more in the direction of strengths.
- The underlying assumptions of a lifeskills psychological education framework incorporate the following basic concepts: lifeskills; interrelationship of thinking, feeling, and action; energizing drive; survival anxiety; Natural, Learned, and Choosing Selves; and personal responsibility.
- Lifeskills strengths and weaknesses are acquired by: supportive relationships; learning from example; learning from consequences; instruction and self-instruction; information and opportunity; and anxiety and confidence.
- Lifeskills weaknesses are maintained by thinking skills weaknesses and by unchanged environmental circumstances.
- Change and self-development take place by learning through supportive relationships, instruction, observing, doing, consolidating trained skills as self-helping skills, and assuming personal responsibility for self-development.
- The ultimate goal of lifeskills helping is personal excellence: attaining a high level of competence across a range of skills areas and consistently making and implementing life-affirming choices.
- The mediating goals of lifeskills helping are specific lifeskills in the areas of thinking, action, and feelings. Applied areas for lifeskills include relationships, parenting, study, work, leisure, health, and social participation.
- Lifeskills helpers hold humanistic values either outside of or within religious frameworks. They are practitioner-researchers who constantly make, implement, and evaluate behavior-change hypotheses. Within an educational framework, they use a variety of interventions focusing on feeling, thinking, and action.
- Lifeskills helpers always encourage people to become their own best helpers.

CHAPTER TWO

OVERVIEW OF THE LIFESKILLS
HELPING MODEL

You're either part of the solution or part of
the problem.

—Eldridge Cleaver

CHAPTER QUESTIONS

❀ *What are the inner and outer games of
lifeskills helping?*

❀ *Why is it important for both helpers and
clients to focus on both inner and outer
games?*

❀ *What is the difference between managing
problems and altering problematic skills?*

❀ *What is DASIE, the five-stage model for
managing problems and altering
problematic lifeskills?*

❀ *What helper skills and client behaviors
illustrate each stage of DASIE?*

❀ *What are issues in applying the lifeskills
helping model?*

THE INNER AND OUTER GAMES OF HELPING

The cognitive-behavioral approach to helping emphasizes cognitions and behaviors. However, terms like *cognitions* and *behaviors* are not everyday language, let alone the language of self-helping. Borrowing and adapting from Gallwey's book *The Inner Game of Tennis* (Gallwey, 1974), the lifeskills approach often talks about *inner-game skills* and *outer-game skills*. Inner-game skills are thinking skills, or how you think. Thinking skills comprise such areas as perceiving accurately, using coping self-talk, possessing realistic personal rules, and attributing cause accurately, among others (Beck, 1976; Ellis, 1989; Nelson-Jones, 1990a). Thinking skills can be used to influence feelings as well as to guide actions. Outer-game skills are action skills, or how you act. Unlike thinking skills, which are mostly covert, action skills are by definition overt. The appropriateness of action skills differs across areas of living (for example, relationships, sex, work, study, or leisure).

You do not ignore feelings when you focus on thinking and action skills. People feel how they feel. Although feelings, thoughts, and actions are interrelated, people cannot alter how they feel unless they alter how they think or act—or both. If they consciously wish to alter how they feel, they must make choices governing thinking and action skills. Even if it is unintended, your choices will influence your feelings.

Lifeskills helping takes a two-pronged approach to both helper and client skills. Effective helpers and clients make effective inner- and outer-game choices. To help you become an effective helper, I need to work not only with your action skills but also your thinking skills. If you are going to help your clients become more effective, you need to work not only with their action skills but also their thinking skills. After formal helping ends, if clients are to help themselves effectively, they need to work on both their thinking and action skills. You may find it useful to tell clients about the inner- and outer-game analogy. The inner- and outer-game distinction is basic to the lifeskills model of helping.

Clients' Inner and Outer Games

Inner Game

Clients' inner games are made up of their thinking skills strengths and weaknesses. Each has a profile of such strengths and weaknesses. Sometimes people can get by in life without activating significant skills weaknesses. However, when people come for help, you may be sure they have activated their thinking skills fault lines. Clients cannot avoid the inner game. There is no taking time out on the touch line. (Just close your eyes for 30 seconds and try to think of nothing. Probably you found that all the time you were conducting an inner dialogue.) You cannot avoid thinking and, consequently, making implicit and explicit choices. Many times these choices position clients for self-defeating feelings and actions.

When it comes to managing and preventing personal problems, clients tend not to think of themselves as possessing thinking skills, let alone thinking skills strengths and weaknesses. At best, most clients have only a partial awareness of their inner-game skills and of how they can use these skills to support rather than oppress themselves. Being insufficiently aware both of the concept of thinking skills and of their own related strengths and weaknesses leaves clients vulnerable to maintaining problems. They may want to change, but have no insight into the hidden choices that hinder them. By making poor thinking choices, clients may become their own worst enemies. During helping sessions, clients may remain unaware that some thinking skills weaknesses (for example, an unrealistic rule about the need for helper approval) may hinder rather than assist change.

Outer Game

Clients' outer games comprise their action skills strengths and weaknesses. As with thinking skills, clients possess profiles of action skills. Both inside and outside helping, people act on the environment with varying degrees of success, sending verbal, voice, body, touch, and action messages (Nelson-Jones, 1990b). Clients are more likely to use skills language when describing actions than thoughts. Nevertheless, most clients probably do not conceptualize in skills terms what they do in the important areas of their lives such as relationships or parenting. For example, while a client might talk of the need to become more assertive, few would go the next step to talk about assertion skills. And probably no client would go further, to break assertion skills down into their verbal, voice, body, touch, and action message components.

Helpers' Inner and Outer Games

Inner Game

Helpers' inner games comprise their thinking skills strengths and weaknesses and how they use them. Like clients, helpers cannot avoid using thinking skills; they cannot *not* think. Helpers use their thinking skills strengths and weaknesses in their private and working lives, and this may impact on how they perform with clients. For example, helpers may bring unfinished private business into helping. They can also exhibit thinking skills weaknesses in regard to helping. For example, helpers who are unclear about the theoretical basis of their work may confuse their clients. Helpers who either consciously or unconsciously want to create dependence may exhibit one or more thinking skills weaknesses (for example, unrealistic needs for approval or power, coupled with failure to attribute to clients sufficient responsibility for change). Helpers may also misperceive clients and their problems (for example, either projecting their own difficulties onto clients or exaggerating the degree to which clients have sexual problems). Always remember that how well you play your inner game is central to your ability to help others.

Outer Game

Helpers are senders of observable messages in both their private and working lives. To date, most counseling texts have been much stronger on training helpers in action rather than in thinking skills. For helpers, basic action skills—"tools of the trade"—include attending (for example, eye contact), using openers and continuation messages, reflecting, helpful questioning, challenging and confronting, and summarizing. Additional action skills with a clearer educational focus include assessing, redefining problems in skills terms, stating working goals, instructing, demonstrating, arranging structured activities, and assigning homework. Each stage of helping challenges helpers to use both thinking and action skills.

Helpers and clients use inner-game and outer-game skills in their outside lives as well as during helping. To the extent that helpers use good thinking and action skills in their outside lives, they are effective people; to the extent that they use such skills in helping, they are effective helpers. Effective helpers work to develop clients thinking and action skills for use "outside." Clients all exhibit different levels of thinking and action skills during helping sessions. The skills clients exhibit in helping offer valuable clues about how they think and act outside.

PROBLEMS AND PROBLEMATIC SKILLS

Lifeskills helping has preventive and developmental as well as problem-management goals. As an educational approach, it lends itself to both individual and group interventions. In addition to managing immediate problems, lifeskills helpers assist clients to change underlying patterns. Beyond the immediate problem, skills weaknesses can manifest themselves both *horizontally*, across a range of current situations, and *vertically*, in future situations. Many problems occur in repetitive cycles. For example, individuals may not only require assistance in finding employment, but also in identifying and developing job-seeking skills for future use. A further example is that of people who relate poorly to colleagues in one setting and change jobs, only to have similar troubles in the new settings. Indeed, such people's relationship problems may extend far beyond work. Helping clients deal with relationship difficulties in one work setting is desirable. Helping the same clients develop skills to prevent future difficulties with work colleagues is even better. Best of all is to help the clients to develop relationship skills for use across a range of settings, both now and in the future.

Mary was a divorced woman who had custody of her 15-year-old son Rick. For over a year she had been dating George, who was also divorced and had custody of his two sons, ages 8 and 10. For several months Mary had been planning a camping vacation. Repeatedly she tried to talk Rick into having George and his two children join them on the trip. Rick adamantly refused. Mary was very reluctant to tell George because she thought he might be hurt and react angrily. The date for the proposed vacation was getting nearer and nearer. When asked, Mary told the counselor that she had difficulty bringing up sensitive issues with anyone and that she disliked any form of conflict. The counselor pointed out to Mary that she could not only manage a problem by discussing Rick's refusal with George, but also use this problem to build skills for future relationship issues. Mary agreed that she needed to develop her skills both for now and for the future. It would help her not only with George but also with Rick and with others.

Table 2.1 depicts the relationship between working to manage a problem and working to manage an underlying pattern of skills weaknesses. Ideally the object is to avoid repetitive cycles of the same problems. Frequently practical considerations (for example, heavy caseloads or clients content with short-term problem solving) limit helper contact with individual clients. However, helpers who only aim to help clients manage immediate and specific problems, when they could work to alter problematic skills, do clients a disservice. Where possible, the focus in lifeskills helping is on developing skills for life—not just for the present. In reality, helpers and clients frequently compromise on the amount of time and effort they address to underlying patterns of skills weaknesses.

Table 2.1 Managing problems and changing problematic skills weaknesses into self-helping skills strengths

Period	Event
Period 1: Pre-helping	Problematic skills patterns are either inadequately dealt with or goes unnoticed by client.
Period 2: Request for helping	Client recognizes problems and is willing to seek help.
Period 3: During helping	Helper and client focus on developing client's self-helping skills for managing immediate problems and future similar problems.
Period 4: Post-helping, short term	Client uses new self-helping skills to manage immediate problems better.
Period 5: Post-helping, longer-term	Client maintains and consolidates self-helping skills strengths to prevent recurrences of problematic skills weaknesses and to better manage future problems.

DASIE: THE FIVE-STAGE MODEL

DASIE is a five-stage model for helping clients manage problems and alter problematic lifeskills. The model provides a set of guidelines for helper choices. The acronym can be a useful memory device to helper trainees when faced with the anxiety of working with clients for the first time. Figure 2.1 depicts DASIE's five stages. Table 2.2 overviews the central task, illustrating helper thinking and action skills and desired client behaviors for each stage of the model.

Stage 1: Develop the Relationship, Identify and Clarify Problems

Stage 1 covers various pre-helping contacts by clients. Even though helpers may not be directly involved, making appointments and being greeted at reception desks are two important preliminaries that can be handled well or poorly. If initial phone inquiries are fumbled, no further contacts may transpire. If clients perceive they are mechanistically treated at reception desks, such perceptions create negative climates for meeting helpers. A

D   DEVELOP the relationship, identify and clarify problem(s).

A   ASSESS problem(s) and redefine in skills terms.

S   STATE working goals and plan interventions.

I   INTERVENE to develop self-helping skills.

E   END and consolidate self-helping skills.

Stage 1
DEVELOP the relationship, identify and clarify problem(s).

Stage 2
ASSESS problem(s) and redefine in skills terms.

Stage 3
STATE working goals and plan interventions.

Stage 4
INTERVENE to develop self-helping skills.

Stage 5
END and consolidate self-helping skills.

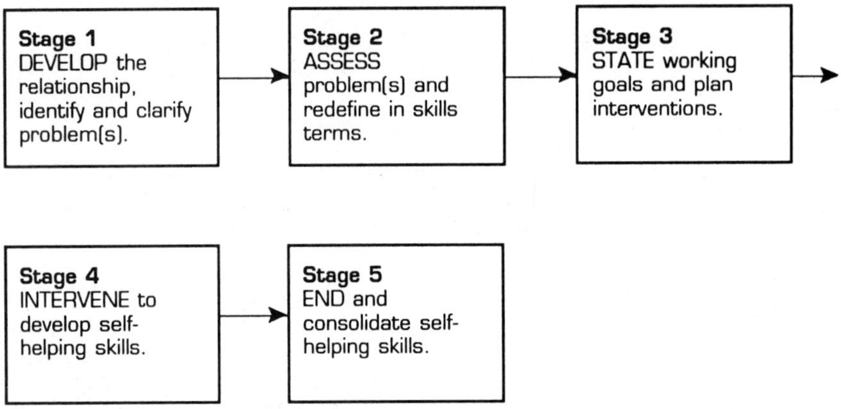

Figure 2.1   DASIE: The five-stage lifeskills helping model

further important preliminary is how helpers meet, greet, and seat clients. Developing the helping relationship starts from the moment of first contact. When meeting clients in waiting areas, you may be perceived as more friendly and competent if you go over to them and show them into your office rather than just stand at the door. Clients are often threatened at the prospect of meeting helpers and you need to show empathy for their feelings of vulnerability. Furthermore, initial impressions are important. Early negative judgments about helpers are hard to retrieve.

On reentering your office, politely show clients to their seats and help them to feel safe. At an appropriate moment, possibly in the waiting area, greet them by saying "Hello, I'm _____, a (helper) here." The issue of what you and your clients call each other can be handled during the initial or subsequent sessions according to the wishes of both parties and the rules of the social context in which helping occurs. Always pay attention to your voice and body as well as to your verbal messages. The old saying "It ain't what you say, but how you say it" applies for

Table 2.2   DASIE: A five-stage model for managing problems and altering problematic lifeskills patterns

Stage	Task	Illustrative Helper Skills	Client Behaviors
Stage 1 DEVELOP the relationship, identify and clarify problem(s)	Build rapport and help clients to reveal, identify, and describe problem(s).	*Thinking skills:* coping self-talk, perceiving accurately *Action skills:* structuring, permission to talk, continuation messages, empathic responses, establishing agendas, helpful questioning, encouraging self-talk, confronting appropriately, summarizing	Identify problem areas, specify details, share thoughts, feelings, and personal meanings
Stage 2 ASSESS problem(s) and redefine in skills terms	Elicit relevant information to define problem(s) in skills terms.	*Thinking skills:* accurately perceiving, accurately attributing cause, forming explanatory hypotheses, analyzing and evaluating information *Action skills:* relationship skills plus active empathy, focused information gathering, formulating and discussing working definitions	Collaborate to identify skills weaknesses; develop "handles" for working on problems and problematic skills.
Stage 3 STATE working goals and plan interventions	State working goals and negotiate self-helping interventions to attain them.	*Thinking skills:* making realistic rules, predicting, goal setting *Action skills:* Translating skills redefinitions into goal statements, choosing and discussing educational interventions, answering questions, designing programs to attain goals	Collaborate in setting goals; acknowledge need to work actively on problems and problematic skills patterns; collaborate in discussing interventions and plans.

(continued on next page)

Table 2.2   *(continued)*

Stage	Task	Illustrative Helper Skills	Client Behaviors
Stage 4 *INTERVENE* *to develop* *self-helping* *skills*	Work to develop self-helping skills strengths in problem areas.	*Thinking skills:* making realistic rules, accurately attributing cause, accurately perceiving, evaluating and possibly reformulating hypotheses *Action skills:* relationship skills plus implementing self-helping interventions; establishing session agendas; instructing; demonstrating; arranging structured activities; setting homework; discussing and evaluating progress; encouraging and supporting self-helping; reverting to earlier stages of model as necessary	Work to acquire thinking and action self-helping skills strengths; develop self-instruction skills; do homework; review progress; work through difficulties and setbacks.
Stage 5 *END and* *consolidate* *self-helping* *skills*	Terminate helping contact and consolidate self-helping skills.	*Thinking skills:* predicting realistically, accurately attributing cause, goal setting, developing managing problem strategies *Action skills:* anticipatory structuring for termination reviewing progress and goal attainment, consolidating learnings, developing maintenance and relapse prevention strategies, getting feedback, handling affective and relationship issues, saying goodbye	Share in reviewing progress, anticipate difficulties; develop coping strategies; summarize learnings; work on problem(s) and problematic skills.

both helpers and clients. Helpers can undercut good verbal messages by sloppy voice and body messages. From the start, observe clients' verbal, voice, and body messages so that you can respond appropriately. In addition, start formulating your working model about what clients' problems really are and what thinking and action skills weaknesses sustain them.

Stage 1 has two overlapping functions: developing helping relationships with clients and working with them to achieve fuller descriptions of problems. Lifeskills helping places heavy emphasis on building supportive working relationships with clients. Supportive relationships go beyond showing empathy, nonpossessive warmth, and genuineness (Rogers, 1957) to the more active fostering of client self-support. Helpers support clients both emotionally and technically. Emotionally, they encourage clients as they tell their stories, gain insight into their skills weaknesses, and strive to manage problems and develop skills strengths. Technically, helpers support clients in analyzing skills strengths and weaknesses, setting realistic goals, planning for change, and implementing interventions. The nature of the supportive relationship differs according to the stage of the DASIE model you are in. In stage 1, the primary emphasis is on providing emotional support as clients tell their stories and share their frame of reference. In subsequent stages, while still offering emotional support, helpers show support by supplying specific expertise as psychological educators.

When clients are seated, begin by explaining such matters as how much time you have together, any limitations on confidentiality, and how you work. You are establishing the structure within which you will be working together. At this stage you want to find out "Why is the client here?" "What is going on that causes and sustains the problems?" and "Am I going to be able to work with this client?" The sorts of questions that clients seek to answer are: "Can I trust this helper not to hurt me?" "Will I get relief from my distressing feelings?" "Is my problem solvable?" and "Can this helper do anything for me?" If clients have had previous unsuccessful contacts with other helpers, a further question for them may be "In what way is this helper different from the others?"

End your initial structuring by giving clients permission to tell their stories. Encourage them to share their frame of reference about their problem areas. At first you give clients space to tell their stories in their own way. Many of your early questions may be open-ended, as you don't want to curtail their response at this early stage. Often it is helpful and less jarring if your questions build on what clients have just said, rather than seeming to come from "outer space." You can request examples, greater specificity, and elaboration of feelings and personal meanings. If you intersperse empathic reflections with questions, clients are less likely to feel they're getting the third degree. Together you and your clients build fuller descriptive pictures of problem areas. Sometimes you may need to refrain from exploring a problem area more fully to check that there are not other more important agendas. If it is unclear, you can ask your clients what areas are important for them to work on.

What of the inner game of helping? At each stage of the model, helpers' thoughts influence how they behave. Helpers subscribing to the theoretical framework offered here can still possess thinking skills weaknesses that significantly interfere with their effectiveness. Helpers need to acknowledge that throughout the helping process they are always choosers. How helpers send verbal, voice, and body messages is one area of choosing. How helpers choose to think about their clients is another area. Ideally helpers are practitioner researchers who make sound hypotheses both about how to respond to clients' communications and about how to form working definitions and interventions. Helping is a continuous process of hypothesis making and testing on the part of both helpers and clients (Kelly, 1955). Part of being a practitioner-researcher entails awareness of relevant research literature. However, a large part of a research or scientific approach rests on how helpers make moment-by-moment and case-by-case decisions. Helpers require sensitivity both to the processes of clinical hypothesis making and testing and to how they might invalidate these processes.

The following is a cautionary tale about a practitioner-researcher who failed to resist labeling clients prematurely. Judy is a 20-year-old student client. In the following (highly hypothetical) excerpt, each time Judy says something more about herself, the helper labels her problem differently—all within the first five minutes of the initial session! Imagine a cartoon format, with each "client says" and "helper thinks" pair being represented by balloons.

Judy: I'm very tense about my upcoming exams.
Helper thinks: *This is a test anxiety problem.*
Judy: I haven't been studying efficiently for some time now.
Helper thinks: *Aha. Her test anxiety is because of poor study skills. Judy has a study skills problem.*
Judy: I wonder if I'm taking the right courses.
Helper thinks: *Perhaps this is really an educational choice problem.*

Judy: My parents are always pressuring me to do it their way. I just want to be my own person.

Helper thinks: *Judy has a young-adult identity problem. Also, she needs to assert herself more with her parents.*

Judy: I was doing all right until my relationship with Bill broke up. Since then I've been feeling very depressed.

Helper thinks: *Judy must have a reactive-depression problem.*

Judy: I think I drove Bill away by being too aggressive. Now I regret the way I acted.

Helper thinks: *This is now a managing anger and conflict problem. Help, I've got a problem too. I'm confused!*

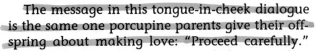

The message in this tongue-in-cheek dialogue is the same one porcupine parents give their offspring about making love: "Proceed carefully." Especially at the start of stage 1, helpers need to remember that they are practitioner-researchers, and thus need to base their hypotheses on careful collection and assessment of information.

Helpers' thinking skills are also related to their ability to listen and respond with understanding. For example, beginning helpers are often very anxious. Even experienced helpers may be anxious with new clients. When anxiety gets above a certain level it debilitates rather than facilitates (Alpert & Haber, 1960). Helpers may contribute to their own anxiety by negative self-talk, where they focus on their shortcomings, make catastrophic predictions, and overemphasize what might go wrong. Excessive helper anxiety interferes with both inner listening (helpers' capacity to listen to what goes on in themselves), and outer listening (helpers' capacity to hear and understand clients). Helpers may also bring unrealistic personal rules regarding need for approval and achievement to their work. Such rules distort listening if helpers focus too much on themselves rather than their clients.

Inaccurately attributing responsibility for clients' lives is another potential helper (thinking skills) weakness. Helpers may be unclear about the boundaries of their own and their clients' responsibilities. Consciously or unconsciously helpers may create dependency and fail to build client self-helping skills adequately. For instance, they may selectively listen for evidence of client weakness and need for help, rather than for evidence of client strength and ability for self-support. Also, helpers may leap in with suggestions as to how clients might behave, rather than help clients to make their own choices.

Helpers can misperceive clients in numerous ways. You may find it hard to perceive clients accurately if they exhibit certain emotions (for instance, anger or self-pity), remind you of significant others in your own life, or are skilled at manipulating you (for instance, through flattery). In addition, there may be basic differences between helpers and clients (for example, age, sex, social class, and culture) contributing to misperceptions. Helpers and clients relate to each other on the basis of "personifications" (Sullivan, 1954). *Personifications* are mental constructions that people make of each other. An important helper task of stage 1 is to start making accurate personifications of clients. However, a poor base for effective helping is when "my picture of me" needs to distort "my picture of you" to stay intact. All helpers possess anxieties and defenses that interfere with their effectiveness to a greater or lesser degree. Will (1954) observes, in his introduction to Sullivan's *The Psychiatric Interview*, "Thus both psychiatrist and patient, while strongly motivated to meet, are also driven by anxiety to withdraw from each other. This interplay of movements—multiple variations of advance and retreat—is characteristic of the field of the interview" (p. xii). Stage 1 of lifeskills helping, where both parties have the anxiety of meeting for the first time and helpers have the added anxiety of the expectation to help clients, is a particularly fertile breeding ground for distorted personifications and communications, for advances and retreats.

I will provide a summary of the same case at the end of the discussion of each stage of the lifeskills helping model. Only the bare bones of the case will be presented. All cases do not fit themselves so neatly into the five-stage lifeskills helping model as this one.

Rob, a married man in his mid-forties, decides to see a counselor, Sue Clark, because he is afraid his marriage may break up due to his temper outbursts. Sue starts the initial session by telling Rob that this is an exploratory interview to find out what concerns him and to see if together they can identify possible options and skills for dealing with his problems. She encourages Rob to say why he has come and to describe his concerns more fully. Sue's verbal, voice, and body messages convey both person-orientation and task-orientation. Within the context of a supportive relationship, this is a working session.

Early in the session Rob reveals that his wife Betty knows he has come for counseling and approves, but does not wish to come herself. Rob and Betty are the parents of three girls, aged 15, 13, and 11.

The precipitating crisis was that Rob struck his oldest daughter Ruth, whom he has always found hard to handle. Rob cares deeply for family life and is scared that the family may disintegrate unless he gets control of his temper. Sue encourages Rob to describe how he and

Ruth relate, including focusing on the recent physical violence. Rob also shares his perceptions of how he and the other family members relate. He expresses mixed feelings about his wife, who dislikes trouble at home and does not always support his discipline attempts.

Rob has a short fuse—people get to him. He has had trouble outside the home too, including rows with employers and colleagues. Rob recalls that his father was very strict and had a bad temper. Sue facilitates Rob's description of his problem and of how he and others think and behave. She is alert for clues concerning Rob's thinking and action skills weaknesses. For instance, when Rob says that people get to him he gives the impression that he has no choice over how he reacts.

As the initial stage proceeds, Rob becomes aware that Sue is helping him to develop a fuller picture of his problem. After a series of exploratory questions, interspersed with empathic reflections, Sue summarizes the content of the interview so far and checks out Rob's reactions to the summary. By now, not only does Sue have a greater knowledge of Rob and his problem, but Rob has also broadened his perspective. Nevertheless, Sue is aware that further work remains to be done in moving beyond a descriptive to a skills definition of Rob's problem.

Stage 2: Asses Problems and Redefine in Skills Terms

The object of this stage is to build a definitional bridge between *describing* and *actively working* on a problem and its underlying skills weaknesses. In stage 1, problems have been described, amplified, and clarified in everyday language. The description of clients' problems represents an expansion of their internal viewpoints but does not yet provide them with new insights. In stage 2, helpers build upon information collected in stage 1 to explore hypotheses about how clients think and act that causes them difficulties. Helpers add to and go beyond clients' present perceptions to look for "handles" on how to work for change. They collaborate with the client in the detective work of breaking down problems into their component skills weaknesses. Whereas stage 1 might end with descriptive summaries of problems in everyday terms, stage 2 ends with redefining problems in skills terms.

Helpers offer clients supportive relationships in stage 2. In stage 1, helpers support clients in telling their stories in their own terms. In stage 2, helpers support clients in making sense of their stories. A distinction can be made between *reflective* empathy and *active* empathy, each of which may help clients expand their perceptions. In reflective empathy, helpers understand clients' existing perceptions. Clients are provided with psychological space to explore and experience their thoughts, feelings, and personal meanings. Helpers are mirrors that allow clients to see their reflections and then, when ready, to go further in self-understanding. In active empathy, helpers use their psychological skills and insights, not only to understand where clients are, but also to provide insights on how clients can get to where they want to be. Clients who come for initial interviews may feel more understood by helpers who give them tools with which to work on problems than by helpers who offer only reflective empathy. Skilled helpers offer both reflective and active empathy. The explanations that helpers offer as part of active empathy are likely to be more accurate if they are based on information clients shared because of their reflective empathy.

A critical ingredient of stage 2 is for helpers to maintain a skills focus. Maintaining a skills focus does *not* mean that helpers immediately translate everything clients say into skills language. However, the question at the back of helpers' minds in stage 2 is always "What skills weaknesses sustain this client's problems?" Especially for beginning helpers, another question is "If I identify skills weaknesses, do I possess the interventions to deal with them?" Many neophyte helpers possess very restricted repertoires of practical interventions, thus limiting their capacity to formulate working definitions and follow through on them. Most clients do not think of their problems in skills language, so helpers require sensitivity about when and how they convey to clients that they may have specific thinking and action skills weaknesses.

What are helper action skills for assessing problems and redefining them in skills terms? The ability to maintain supportive relationships is fundamental. Basic facilitation skills (attentive body messages, reflective responding, and sending verbal, voice, and body continuation messages) are very important. Helper facilitation skills sustain the emotional aspect of supportive relationships.

However, supportive relationships also have more technical, or task-oriented, aspects. The emphasis in helpers' questions differs in stage 2. In stage 1, helpers ask questions to clarify clients' existing frames of reference. In stage 2, helpers are likely to question as much from their own as from their clients' frame of reference. Much of their questioning is based on information provided by clients, clues, hunches, how things are said, what is left unsaid, and overt and subtle indications of what underlying thought patterns might be. While the major focus is on pinpointing skills weaknesses, attention is also paid to identifying skills strengths and resources. Strengths reviews, or what Ivey and his colleagues call "positive asset search" (Ivey, Ivey, & Simek-Downing, 1987), both identify skills for coping with problems and prevent the tone of assessments from becoming negative.

A distinction exists between clients' acknowledging that they have problems and acknowledging that certain of their behaviors may sustain them. In stage 2, helpers go beyond helping clients acknowledge that they have problems to assisting them in taking personal responsibility for what they do or fail to do that perpetuates them. Clients can err in the direction of over-externalizing or over-internalizing the causes of their problems. Accurate attribution of cause and responsibility is desirable. For example, Craig externalizes his marriage problems. He plays the victim and launches into a long description of what Mary does to him, without mentioning how he behaves toward Mary. Sometimes getting clients like Craig to provide information about their own behavior helps them to acknowledge responsibility more accurately. Within the context of supportive relationships, helpers may need to confront clients like Craig with challenges of varying degrees of strength to their existing perceptions. Sometimes helpers ask personal responsibility questions that help clients confront themselves with their roles in sustaining problems. Such questions include "How is your behavior helping you?" and "Is there anything different you could be doing from what you are doing now?"

Cindy is an example of someone who attributes too much responsibility to herself. She contributes to her anxiety and depression by thinking that everything that goes wrong is her fault. She is just as much in need of help as Craig in learning how to attribute responsibility accurately for her problems. Some clients need help in overcoming a passive stance to life. Tania, a bored housewife in her mid-forties whose children have grown up, has been waiting for change to come from outside herself rather than acknowledging her own responsibility for making changes occur. Tania's helper needs to share this observation with her. In stage 2, helpers not only assist clients in pinpointing skills weaknesses, but also encourage them to have the motivation and commitment both to acknowledge their own roles in sustaining problems and to change.

Helpers need to develop good skills at redefining problems in skills terms and communicating these working definitions to clients. A good redefinition clearly points out the client's main skills weaknesses and shows how they are sustaining the problems. Helpers need to distinguish what is important material. Redefinitions that are too comprehensive confuse people. Helpers can explain that it is valuable to break problems down into the component skills weaknesses that underlie them. This could be a good time to introduce clients to the distinction between thinking skills and action skills, possibly using the analogy of the inner and outer games.

Often it helps to write redefinitions in skills terms on whiteboards. Visual communication makes it easier for clients to retain what you say and, if necessary, suggest alterations. Helpers may use a simple T diagram to present the thinking and action skills weaknesses that sustain each problem (see Table 2.3). Redefinitions of problems in skills terms, otherwise known as T redefinitions, need to be negotiated with clients. Helpers require good questioning and facilitation skills when checking redefinitions with clients. If helpers, in stages 1 and 2, have competently gathered information, skills redefinitions should flow logically from this material. Clients who share their helpers' conceptualizations of problems are more likely to commit themselves to developing needed self-helping skills than clients who resist helpers' conceptualizations. Redefinitions of problems in skills terms are essentially hypotheses, based on careful analysis of available information, about clients' thinking and action skills weaknesses. As hypotheses, they are open to modification in light of further or better information.

Redefining problems in skills terms can be difficult. Mistakes in redefinition not only lead to wasted time and effort, but may contribute to clients' being even less able to manage problems.

Table 2.3 Simple T diagram for presenting redefinitions of problems in skills terms

Problem	
Thinking Skills Weaknesses	**Action Skills Weaknesses**
1.	1.
2.	2.
3.	3.
4.	4.

Lee was a Chinese-Malaysian foreign student repeating the first year of an engineering course that he was obviously going to fail. Lee was afraid of how his parents would react to his failure and also undecided about whether he wanted to be a production engineer. Instead of helping Lee develop skills to handle these areas, his helper, a counselor trainee, defined his problem as lack of assertive skills in seeking help from faculty members. Lee himself had reservations about this way of viewing his situation. Despite this feedback, the helper persisted in spending time in trying to build up Lee's academic help-seeking skills. Thus, the helper's faulty working definition blocked Lee from working on more pertinent skills weaknesses.

What thinking skills weaknesses can block helper effectiveness in stage 2? Helpers require good memories and powers of reasoning to analyze and evaluate relevant information. The process of formulating redefinitions in skills terms may create anxiety in some helpers, over and above the anxiety of relating to new clients. Helpers need to tolerate ambiguity as they search for handles to clients' problems. Especially for beginning helpers, the combination of their own lack of experience and lack of clarity as they strive to formulate client problems in skills terms may be daunting. Coping self-talk, possessing realistic rules and expectations, and being clear about the boundaries of their own and their clients' responsibilities can ease their anxieties. Other helper thinking skills weaknesses are that they may not perceive clients' communications accurately or may have a tendency to fit clients to their pet hypotheses, despite contradictory evidence.

Here is a summary of how the counselor and Rob proceeded in stage 2 of their helping contact.

The counselor, Sue Clark, after checking her descriptive summary with Rob, said she would now like to explore some specific areas of Rob's thoughts and actions to see if they could find ways that he could improve his situation. Sue observed that some things Rob said indicated he thought he had little choice over how he behaved. Rob agreed that he had little control over his temper. He had always been that way and wondered if it were his "nature." Sue also explored what Rob said to himself when faced with provocations, such as the time his daughter Ruth came home later than agreed after being out with her boyfriend. Rob's self-talk appeared to fire him up rather than calm him down. The realism of his rules concerning family behavior was another thinking skills area that Sue explored with Rob. Because the action skills concerning how Rob communicated to his family had already been covered in stage 1, Sue did not repeat this exploration.

Using the whiteboard, she then suggested a tentative T redefinition of Rob's anger problem in skills terms. Sue's T redefinition included the following thinking skills weaknesses: (1) inadequately acknowledging that he was always a chooser and responsible for his thoughts, feelings, and actions; (2) using anger-provoking self-talk when faced with provocations; and (3) possibly having rigid and unrealistic personal rules concerning standards of behavior in the family. Action skills weaknesses included: (1) poor listening skills, especially when angry; (2) poor assertion skills, for instance in how he stated his wishes about his daughter's behavior; and (3) poor skills at working through conflicts with others.

Sue checked each part of this working definition with Rob, to see both whether he understood it and whether he agreed with it. Rob expressed relief when the redefinition in skills terms was explained to him. For the first time, he thought he could do something about his temper.

Stage 3: State Working Goals and Plan Interventions

In stages 1 and 2, you and your clients moved from descriptive definitions to skills redefinitions of problems. In these early stages, you attempted to answer the questions "What is or are the problems?" and "What thinking and action skills weaknesses sustain them?" Stage 3 builds on your redefinitions in skills terms, to focus on the question "What is the best way to manage problems and develop requisite skills?" Stage 3 consists of two phases: stating goals and planning interventions.

Stating Goals

Goals can be stated at different levels of specificity. First, goals can be stated in overall terms such as "I want to feel less depressed," "I want to improve my marriage," or "I want to come to terms with my disability and get back into life." Such overall statements of goals have value in giving clients a vision about what they want out of helping. However, overall goal statements refer more to ends than to means.

Second, goals can be stated in terms of the broad skills required to attain the desired ends. This is the level of specificity required for stage 3. Assuming you succeed in redefining problems in skills terms, stating goals becomes a relatively simple matter. Working goals are the flip side of your redefinitions—positive statements of skills strengths to replace existing skills weaknesses. For instance, if part of the skills redefinition of Pedro's problem is that he has poor job-seeking skills, developing job-seeking skills becomes his working goal.

Third, goals can be stated still more specifically. For example, Pedro's job-seeking skills could be broken down into such sub-skills as how to telephone prospective employers, develop a resume, conduct newspaper searches, handle interviews, deal with being turned down, and so on. Helpers have to decide the level of detail for sharing goals in early sessions. Each case must be treated on its own merits. Clients can only cope with so much information at any one time. A risk of getting into too much detail in an initial session is that clients retain little if anything.

If necessary, restate and check clients' overall goals. State working goals clearly and succinctly. If using whiteboards, you can alter skills redefinitions to become working goals. T redefinitions of skills weaknesses become T statements of goals. Check with clients that they understand and agree that working goals truly represent skills required to manage problems better.

How helpers think influences how well they set working goals. Goals must be stated clearly, realistically, and, where appropriate, with a time frame. Helpers need to be realistic about what is attainable. Helpers' own needs for achievement and for results may interfere with such realism. Stating goals realistically implies predicting how attainable they are for clients. Risks are attached to stating goals that are either too high or too low.

Planning Interventions

Having stated goals, helpers' next set of choices concerns how best to help clients attain them. Interventions are actions on the part of helpers designed to help clients attain goals. Helpers tend to state goals in terms of their repertoire of interventions. For example, helpers knowledgeable about thinking skills tend to include thinking skills in statements of working goals. Consequently, when stating goals, you already have ideas about how to attain them.

There is no single best way to plan interventions, since clients' problems and underlying problematic skills vary so much. Try to involve clients as much as possible. For example, you might say "Given that these are your goals, how might you best attain them?" You can still add to clients' suggestions. You can outline ways of attaining each skills goal, but remain flexible as to when and how to use different interventions. For example, you might schedule interventions to build on current specific issues.

Then, at different stages of helping, you can negotiate with the client what goals and interventions are important.

Another approach is to design more formal plans focused on one or more specific skills. Here helpers and clients trade off flexibility for program clarity. Still another approach is to use a standard treatment package; for example, a cognitive-behavioral program for insomnia (Morawetz, 1989).

Here are two final points concerning plans. First, even though plans may entail helpers' offering interventions (for example, teaching relaxation skills), their purpose is always that these become self-helping interventions. Second, plans are hypotheses about how to attain working goals. Both working goals and plans are open to modification in light of feedback.

Here is a summary of how the helper handled stating working goals and planned interventions in stage 3 of the case study about Rob.

The counselor, Sue Clark, clarified with Rob that his overall goal was to improve his relationship with Ruth and, hence, improve his marriage. Now Sue turned the previously agreed-upon redefinition of Rob's anger problem into a T statement of working goals. Rob's thinking skills goals were: (1) to acknowledge that he was a chooser and responsible for his thoughts, feelings, and actions; (2) to use coping self-talk when faced with provocations; and (3) to develop realistic personal rules concerning standards of family behavior. Rob's action skills goals included developing : (1) good listening skills; (2) assertion skills, particularly as to how he stated his wishes about his daughter's behavior; and (3) conflict negotiation skills.

Sue realized that Rob's objective was to develop some skills as quickly as possible, rather than to have a long-term helping relationship. Instead of designing a step-by-step training plan, Sue suggested the best way to proceed was to help Rob develop skills in relation to material he brought into each session. She required homework, including listening to audiocassettes of sessions. Sue asked Rob to monitor how he communicated to Ruth and other family members and to report back next session. Also, Sue requested that Rob keep a log of his thoughts and feelings before, during, and after specific anger provocations.

Stage 4: Intervene to Develop Self-Helping Skills

The interventions stage has two objectives. First, to help clients manage their presenting problems better. Second, to assist clients in working on their problematic skills patterns and developing skills strengths. The emotional climate throughout the intervention stage is collaborative. Within the context of supportive relationships, helpers assist clients in assuming responsibility for managing problems and altering problematic skills. Good relationship skills are important during this stage. One use of facilitation skills is to understand clients both for their sake and yours. Clients feel more supported if they think helpers understand what they go through, both in having problems and in trying to cope with them. Also, good helping relationship skills enable you to understand clients better and, if necessary, to adjust your working definitions and goals accordingly. Another use of facilitation skills is to support training interventions (described more fully in Chapters 9 to 12). You may need to process clients' thoughts and feelings about engaging in specific interventions (for instance, role-plays or muscular relaxation). Also, helpers require relationship skills for clients to learn maximally from skills demonstrations (for instance, checking out their learnings and showing understanding as they try out demonstrated skills).

Throughout lifeskills helping there is a tension between helpers' being person-oriented and task-oriented. A risk in the intervention stage is that helpers become too task-oriented. For instance, with clients coming to sessions after very difficult weeks, helpers may decide it is premature to work directly on problems and problematic skills until clients have had the opportunity to share and process their thoughts and feelings about what currently bothers them. Of course, there are risks in the other direction: namely, becoming too person-oriented, so that the training focus of sessions gets lost.

Sometimes another tension in lifeskills helping can be that between focusing on problems and focusing on problematic skills. Realistically, what many clients want is to deal with problems as quickly as possible rather than focus on underlying problematic skills. For instance, what bothers Erica is containing her anxiety sufficiently to pass a test in two weeks' time, rather than developing anxiety management skills for future tests. Another example is that of Ern, who wants to cope with an upcoming job interview rather than subsequent job interviews. Helpers too may operate under time and resource limitations militating against their intervening as thoroughly as they might like. Furthermore, both helpers and clients work within an overall culture that is more problem-oriented than problematic skills–oriented. Skills are for fixing motor cars and playing sports rather than for managing psychological problems. Even though the focus may not be as thorough as desirable, helpers require creativity in maintaining a skills focus in all helping contacts.

What are some helper action skills for the intervention stage? When helpers provide rationales for interventions, they emphasize both skills language and client responsibility for skills development. Clients are clearly encouraged to own both problems and problematic skills. Helpers need to develop a repertoire of interventions. Such interventions must encompass both thinking skills and action skills. Thinking skills interventions tend to be generic across most problem areas. Action skills interventions are usually, though not always, more specific to problem areas. Helpers need to develop a repertoire of action skills interventions that are relevant to the problems of their target populations: for example, career choice helpers require interventions that support clients' acquiring career decision-making, job-seeking, and interviewing skills; marital and family helpers require interventions that support relationship skills such as listening, self-disclosing, and managing anger and conflict. Helpers should keep abreast of relevant theoretical and research literature on how best to intervene for specific problems and skills weaknesses.

Helpers are psychological educators. They require good training as well as good assessment and helping relationship skills to intervene effectively. It is insufficient to know *what* interventions to offer without also being skilled at *how* to offer them. Table 2.4 depicts modes of psychological education or training and modes of learning in lifeskills helping. Helpers work much of the time with the three training modes of "tell," "show," and "do." They require special skills for each. "Tell" entails giving clients clear instructions concerning the skills they wish to develop. "Show" means offering demonstrations of how to implement skills. "Do" means arranging for clients to perform structured activities and homework tasks.

Table 2.4 incorporates the notion of consolidation, thus highlighting the importance throughout helping of focusing on issues of transfer, development, and maintenance of skills. As much as possible, helpers train skills as self-helping skills. For example, helpers can train relaxation skills in either helper-centered or people-centered ways. The main difference is that people-centered training emphasizes more how clients can relax themselves through self-instruction and how they can use relaxation as a coping skill. In this vein, Goldfried and Davison have advocated teaching systematic desensitization, which incorporates relaxation skills, as a self-control procedure (Goldfried, 1971; Goldfried & Davison, 1976).

Table 2.4 Modes of psychological education or training and of learning

Psychological Education or Training Mode	Learning Mode
Facilitate	Learning from self-exploring and experiencing self more fully
Assess	Learning from self-evaluating and self-monitoring
Tell	Learning from hearing
Show	Learning from observing
Do	Learning from doing structured activities and homework tasks
Consolidate	Learning from developing self-helping skills in all the above modes

Like overall helping contacts, individual sessions in the intervention stage may be viewed in four phases: preparatory, initial, working, and ending. These session phases overlap. The preparatory phase entails helpers thinking in advance how best to assist clients. Helpers ensure that, if appropriate, they have available the following: session plans; training materials (for instance, handouts); and audiovisual aids (for instance, whiteboards and audiocassette-recorders).

The initial phase consists of meeting, greeting, and seating, then giving permission to talk. Beginning early in the process, helpers may wish to establish session agendas. Session agendas can be both explicit and implicit. For instance, without verbalizing session agendas, helpers may go from checking out how clients feel, to reviewing the past week's homework, to focusing on one or more problematic skills or problems in clients' lives. On other occasions, helpers and clients may openly negotiate session agendas. Once you establish session agendas, you can still alter them if more pressing business arises.

The working phase focuses on specific interventions designed to help clients manage problems and develop lifeskills. While being sensitive to the client's need to focus on describing problems, helpers should maintain a skills focus. There are three main approaches to the working phase. First, you may adapt your skills training to material clients bring into sessions. Second, you may follow pre-arranged skills training plans. Third, you may both work with clients' material and complete specific training plans. During the working phase, you use helping relationship skills both to encourage self-disclosure and self-exploration and to support specific activities.

The ending phase lasts from a time near the end of one session to the beginning of the next. This phase focuses on summarizing the major session learnings, negotiating homework, strengthening commitment to between-session work, and rehearsing and practicing skills outside helping. Consolidating learned skills into self-helping skills takes place at the end of, and between, each session. Frequently clients are asked to write down their homework assignments. Writing down homework assignments serves the following purposes: It gives a message that homework is important, clarifies what is required, helps clients' memories, and provides something in writing that can be posted as a reminder.

What thinking skills can help or hinder the intervention stage? Helpers require accurate perception and, where necessary, flexibility in being able to discard or reformulate working goals and definitions. Highly rigid and defensive helpers may deny or insufficiently acknowledge the ineffectiveness of certain interventions. Helpers require the ability to attribute responsibility and cause accurately. For instance, helpers need to help clients own both their problems and their responsibility for developing skills strengths. However, helpers have responsibilities too—for instance, to perform competently. They need to beware of falsely attributing cause for slow or nonexistent progress to clients without examining the adequacy of their helping behaviors. As always, helpers' unrealistic personal rules regarding such matters as making mistakes, needing clients' approval, and getting quick and impressive results may interfere with effective performance. Furthermore helpers can use self-talk for good or ill (for example, calming themselves down and staying task-oriented when faced with angry and manipulative clients, rather than giving way to negative self-talk about themselves and their clients).

The following is a continuation of the case study of Rob at stage 4, where we intervene and develop client self-helping skills.

The counselor, Sue Clark, saw Rob for a total of seven sessions over a two-and-a-half-month period. The intervention stage lasted from the second to the sixth session. At the start of each session, Sue checked whether Rob had any pressing concerns and how he had progressed with homework. She approached each session flexibly within the context of the agreed-upon skills redefinition and working goals. Sue's considerations in establishing session agendas included both where Rob wanted to focus and how best to develop Rob's self-helping skills.

Sue trained Rob in the thinking skills goal that he was a chooser, partly by articulating this as a skill, partly by encouraging Rob to become more aware of the consequences of his choices, partly by reframing his language (for example, "Ruth made me so angry" was reformulated into "I chose to get very angry with Ruth"), and partly by reflective responses that continuously and unobtrusively emphasized personal responsibility. Sue trained Rob in coping self-talk skills by spending part of an early session teaching him directly by instruction, demonstration, and coached practice. In subsequent sessions, Sue checked out how well Rob used his coping self-talk skills outside counseling. Sue trained the skill of choosing realistic personal rules by getting Rob to identify and examine his rules regarding his own and Ruth's behavior in specific situations that Rob brought to the session. Sue then helped Rob reformulate inappropriate rules.

In regard to attaining action skills goals, Sue taught Rob some simple listening skills (for instance, not interrupting, and checking out how well he understood his daughter's position). Sue trained Rob in the action skills of being more assertive in stating wishes and negotiating conflicts. She reviewed with him different ways of acting in specific family situations and their consequences. She paid attention to voice and body as well as verbal messages when rehearsing Rob in assertion and negotiating conflict skills. Sue made extensive use of the whiteboard for working on both thinking and action skills.

Sue ended each session by summarizing the main learning points and negotiating homework assignments. Rob listened to the cassettes of preceding sessions as part of his homework. Since Rob was surrounded by his family, Sue encouraged him to start using his skills at home and to "learn on the job." His wife and daughters appreciated Rob's efforts to work on his temper. Even early on, Rob's efforts were rewarded by decreased family tension.

Stage 5: End and Consolidate Self-Helping Skills (Termination)

The end of lifeskills helping is built into its beginning. From start to finish, helpers and clients develop skills for self-helping. Though longer contact may be warranted, much lifeskills helping is relatively short-term (say up to ten sessions). Sometimes helpers have to work in even tighter time frames of one or two sessions. Reasons for very brief helping include clients' personal deadlines (for instance, upcoming meetings with estranged spouses or imminent tests). Also, even when seeing skilled helpers, some people do not like the client role. Furthermore, reluctance to continue with helping may be heightened where either clients or third parties pay for it.

Sometimes ending is formalized by fixed-term contracts, but in most instances ending is more open-ended. Ideally, ending is based on both parties' perceiving that clients have made not only appreciable gains in their ability to manage their problems, but have also consolidated their gains into self-helping skills for use afterwards.

Usually either helpers or clients bring up the topic of ending before the final session. This allows both parties to work through the various task and relationship issues connected with ending the contact. A useful option is to "fade" contact with some clients by seeing them progressively less often. Certain clients may appreciate the opportunity for booster sessions, say one, two. three, or even six months later. Booster sessions provide both clients and helpers with the chance to review progress and consolidate self-helping skills. Scheduling follow-up telephone calls can perform some of these functions too.

Lifeskills helping seeks to avoid the "train and hope" approach (Goldstein & Keller, 1987; Stokes & Osnes, 1989). For instance, prior to the ending stage, helpers structure realistic expectations when discussing working definitions and goals with clients. Also, helpers attempt to build client self-observation and assessment skills. Transfer and maintenance of skills is encouraged by such means as developing clients' self-instructional abilities, working with real-life situations during helping, and using between-session time productively to rehearse and practice skills.

Strategies that helpers may use during the final (ending and consolidating) self-helping skills stage include encouraging clients to assume the primary responsibility for reviewing their progress (Ward, 1984). Clients can summarize their managing problems skills. These summaries may be recorded for later playback and revision. A strategy for clients who experience difficulty acknowledging gains is to listen to a recording of an early session. Helpers can work with clients to identify difficulties and setbacks, then together they can develop and rehearse coping strategies for dealing with them. Sometimes clients require help in identifying people to support their efforts to maintain skills. Helpers may also provide clients with information about further skills-building opportunities.

Helpers need strong thinking skills to conduct the ending and consolidating stage. They need to be accurate in perceiving their clients' progress in acquiring skills. Assuming clients do not make the decision for you, knowing when to end entails predicting realistically how well clients will use skills on their own. Helping may either be ended prematurely or allowed to drag on too long.

When ending, you may attribute cause and responsibility inaccurately (for instance, you may overestimate your responsibility for clients' lives and be reluctant to let go of them). Helpers need to use their skills at formulating realistic goals to assist clients in maintaining and developing skills. In addition, helpers can use their skills at managing problems to assist clients in developing managing problems strategies to maintain skills.

Here is a summary of stage 5, the ending and consolidation of self-helping skills, in the case study of Rob.

Throughout helping, his counselor, Sue Clark, worked to consolidate Rob's managing anger skills as self-helping skills. During the sixth session, Sue and Rob decided that they would probably have one more session in four weeks' time when Sue came back from an overseas trip. In this session, Rob mentioned that he felt he had lost some of his influence in the family by adopting a more reasonable approach to provocations. Using the whiteboard, Sue developed with Rob a balance sheet of positive and negative consequences of using his skills. As a result, Rob perceived the balance to be heavily in favor of maintaining them.

Rob started the seventh and final session by stating that his life was going much better. Sue helped Rob provide specific evidence for this assertion. Together Rob and she explored each of Rob's main relationships to see how well Rob was using his skills and with what consequences. Rob was definitely attaining his initial goal of an improved relationship with his oldest daughter Ruth. Rob affirmed his decision to end counseling. Sue helped him to review his learnings from the sessions. Rob mentioned how he was more prepared to think first, talk things over, and play the game of life with his head. Rob thought that there were still problems in his marriage, but he did not wish to work on them at present. Sue Clark left it open for Rob to return for helping if necessary.

APPLYING THE MODEL

Here are some considerations in applying the lifeskills helping model. The underlying theme throughout is that helpers, in the best interests of clients, need to apply the model flexibly.

Sequencing

DASIE (Develop relationship-Assess-State goals-Intervene-End) is intended to provide some guidelines rather than be a straight-jacket. Though your roles differ, the model assumes a degree of collaboration between you and your clients. Remember that managing problems and altering problematic skills rarely proceed according to neatly ordered stages. The stages tend to overlap (for instance, your clients' descriptions of problems contribute to how you jointly assess them). Also, there may be reversion to earlier stages (for example, as more information or new problems arise during the intervention stage, working definitions and goals may be refined). Helping can be messy. You operate on the basis of hypotheses about yourself, your clients, and the helping process. You require flexibility to incorporate either new or previously overlooked information into your hypothesis making and testing. A further point is that the five-stage model requires adjusting not only to individual clients, but also to the setting and social context in which you work. For example, a priest helping a parishioner is likely to operate in a much more informal way than a counseling psychologist in private practice.

Brief Helping

The following assumptions underlie the DASIE model. First, much helping is relatively short-term, say 3 to 10 sessions, and second, it tends to be focused on one or two major problem (or problematic skills) areas. As such DASIE is a model of central tendency. However, helping can also be very brief, say one or two sessions, or more extended, say 11 to 20 sessions or more. Often very brief helping contacts take place because clients have immediate agendas that require attention (for example, a test, a job interview, or an unexpected crisis). In such instances, helpers require flexibility in choosing how person-oriented or task-oriented to be. For example, an early skills focus may be inappropriate with recently bereaved clients needing space to tell their stories and experience their feelings. On the other hand, an early skills focus may be highly appropriate with clients anxious about upcoming job interviews. Here, based on tailor-made T definitions, helpers may provide clients with "crash training courses" in anxiety management and job interview skills.

Extended Helping

Even with competent helpers, numerous reasons exist why helping may last longer than 10 sessions. For example, clients may come from emotionally deprived backgrounds in which, along with learning poor lifeskills, their confidence has been badly undermined. Clients may have multiple problems and skills weaknesses. Also, clients may differ in the severity of a problem (for instance, shyness or tendencies to irrational thinking). In addition, clients may possess resistances to change (Ellis, 1987) or feel that change is being forced upon them by others. Furthermore, some clients' personal and social environments may not support change.

Since different reasons exist for extended helping, there are no simple answers for how best to go about it. With highly vulnerable clients, helpers may need to spend more time establishing trusting relationships. Also, vulnerable clients may require more gentle and nurturing relationships than robust clients. Furthermore, such clients may take longer to get to the point where they possess insight into how they sustain problems. However, it is possible to overgeneralize. Some vulnerable clients may benefit from helpers' confronting their skills weaknesses. Also, right from the initial session, some vulnerable clients may appreciate working on one or two specific skills.

Helping may go more slowly where clients' starting points are low in specific skills areas. Helpers may have to break down skills more, spend more time on instruction and demonstration, and offer clients more support as they rehearse and practice skills. In extended helping, much session time is spent on working through the application of targeted skills to specific issues in clients' lives, including their fears about using the skills. Where clients possess multiple problems and skills weaknesses, helpers and clients face the issue of prioritizing those skills most in need of attention. In extended contacts, helpers and clients also have to prioritize between initial and emerging problems and problematic skills areas. Emerging problems may arise through clients personally changing, or through changes in their environments. Working definitions and goals may require reformulation. Clients' progress may be slowed down by others in their environments, such as teachers, parents, or spouses. If so, helpers need to consider whether it is worth broadening helping to include them.

CONCLUDING COMMENT

Beginning helpers are likely to find that it takes time to become proficient in the lifeskills helping model. This training model requires helpers to go beyond offering good relationship skills to offering good assessment and didactic skills. Also, the model requires helpers to possess effective inner-game (thinking) skills as well as effective outer-game (action) skills. Many beginning helpers experience difficulty in making the transition from *talk-ing* relationships, based on good facilitation skills, to *training* relationships, based on assessment and specific interventions designed to assist clients as they manage problems and problematic skills patterns. The lifeskills helping model requires helpers to step outside their everyday language to conceptualize problems in skills terms. Some beginning helpers do not find this congenial and take much time to make the transition, if they ever do. Also, the lifeskills helping model requires helpers to develop a range of specific interventions related to clients' problems and problematic skills. Again, it takes time to build up a repertoire of interventions. In fact, there is always room for improvement. It is a lifetime challenge to stay proficient in, and to develop further, your lifeskills helping skills.

 ## CHAPTER HIGHLIGHTS

- Lifeskills helping focuses on both client and helper inner games, or thinking skills, and outer games, or action skills.
- A distinction exists between problems and the problematic skills that sustain problems. Lifeskills helping focuses on both problems and problematic skills.
- Beyond a presenting problem, problematic skills can manifest themselves both horizontally, across a range of similar current situations, and vertically, in future similar situations.
- DASIE is a five-stage model for helping clients manage problems and alter problematic lifeskills patterns.
- In stage 1, helpers develop supportive relationships with clients and work with them to identify and clarify problems.
- In stage 2 (assess problem(s) and redefine in skills terms), helpers and clients collaborate to build definitional bridges between describing and actively working on problems and problematic skills.
- In stage 3, helpers translate skills redefinitions into working goals and plan interventions to attain them.
- In stage 4, within the context of supportive relationships, helpers intervene to develop clients' self-helping skills. Helpers require a repertoire of thinking skills and action skills interventions about which they are both knowledgeable and skilled in applying.
- In stage 5, the helping contact ends, with further attention paid to consolidating clients' self-helping skills.

- Helpers should apply the DASIE lifeskills helping model flexibly (for instance, the sequencing of stages may overlap).
- Helpers also require flexibility in adapting DASIE to very brief, as well as extended, helping contacts.
- Beginning helpers are likely to take time to become proficient in the lifeskills helping model. It is a lifetime challenge to stay proficient and to develop your lifeskills helping skills still further.

CHAPTER THREE

WHAT YOU BRING TO
TRAINING AND HELPING

I am simply a human being, more or less.
                                        —Saul Bellow

CHAPTER QUESTIONS

❀ *What are your motives for helping?*

❀ *What helping skills have you learned?*

❀ *How do you think about helping?*

❀ *How emotionally responsive are you?*

❀ *How confident are you?*

❀ *What anxieties and fears do you have about helping?*

❀ *How might your sexuality influence helping?*

❀ *What sex-role identity and expectations do you possess?*

❀ *What are your values?*

❀ *What are your ethics?*

❀ *What culture and cross-cultural skills do you bring?*

❀ *What race are you and what racial attitudes do you possess?*

❀ *To what social class do you belong?*

INTRODUCTION

Nobody starts helper training from scratch. Each brings various skills, characteristics, and attributes to the task. Lifeskills helping is not the mechanistic application of a set of techniques. Helpers work within the context of person-to-person relationships to develop clients' self-helping skills. The personhood of both helpers and clients is central to the approach. This chapter focuses on you—what you bring to helper training and to helping. Some characteristics (for instance, your biological sex) you cannot change. Other characteristics (for instance, cross-cultural sensitivity) you can improve. In all instances, your personal characteristics influence how you help.

Helping differs from most other occupations in that the tools are *people*, who use various people skills to help people help themselves. Contrast this with dentists who use tools to work on teeth or with car mechanics who use tools to work on cars. In helping, the self is the tool. The lifeskills model of helping is not independent of the people who apply it. The self that you bring to helper training possesses both strengths and weaknesses. Skilled helpers both enhance their strengths and try to overcome personal blocks. Helpers and clients are made from the same human clay. Yalom, in his book of case studies, *Love's Executioner* (1989), provides excellent illustrations of how helpers' humanity can permeate helping.

Just as helper characteristics influence helping, so student characteristics influence helper training. Here is an illustration.

Sandra was a highly sensitive counseling Master's student in her late thirties. She successfully completed a first-semester practicum course focused on helping relationship skills. The second semester practicum course, in addition to helping relationship skills, focused on assessing and redefining clients' problems (identifying at least one thinking skill weakness and one action skill weakness). Sandra was one of 10 students in a practicum taught by the course leader, who used instruction, modeling, and coaching. In addition, students received three individual supervisions by another experienced counseling psychologist of interview cassettes made with volunteer undergraduate "clients." At the end of the semester, the course leader failed Sandra's assessment cassette because she listened inadequately to her client. She kept jumping in, offering explanations and interpretations from her internal viewpoint. She had panicked when requested to go beyond helping relationship skills to formulate a working definition of her client's problem.

Sandra became highly anxious at failing her assessment cassette at the first attempt. She considered dropping out of the course and even suing her supervisor. Given the discrepancy between her performance and his perceptions of her counseling potential, the course leader offered Sandra some individual coaching to bring her up to passing standard. In the first coaching session, the supervisor suggested that he and Sandra take turns in offering each other 15-minute counseling sessions that emphasized basic facilitation skills.

Sandra used her 15 minutes to explore why she became so control-ling when interviewing. She started by attributing this to her earlier social-work training. Then she acknowledged that she put herself un-der tremendous pressure to get quick results, especially when assessed. She became aware of feeling highly anxious and vulnerable when interviewing. She put this in the context of being one of two daughters who, when her father died when she was 6, was brought up by a single mother. Sandra's mother always encouraged her sister, but actively discouraged all Sandra's scholastic and professional endeav-ors. Sandra hated this side of her mother and was terrified that any lack of performance on her part would prove her mother was right all along in disparaging her.

In her assessment cassette, Sandra did not just work with the cli-ent, but also fought an inner struggle against her mother's "voices in her head." The mental tapes Sandra brought to helper training helped neither her nor her clients. Sandra needed to work on her inner game (her thinking skills weaknesses), as well as on her outer game (how she related to clients).

The case of Sandra illustrates many points in helper training. First, students are influenced by their past and not just by their current training. Second, trainers need to take into account the individual circumstances of each student. Third, an important paradox exists in helper training and helping. Qualities like sensitivity and vulnerability that can be huge assets in helping can also be huge liabilities, unless students and helpers use them for, rather than against, clients. The personal characteristics that make students good can make them bad. A less sensitive and vulnerable person than Sandra might not have flubbed up so badly, yet might have lacked Sandra's helping potential.

Some Starting Points for Helping

Helping interviews are ever-changing processes between two people who influence each other. Helpers and clients bring many characteristics into interviews and experience many thoughts and feelings during interviews. What helpers and clients bring to interviews are not only matters of fact, but also matters of per-

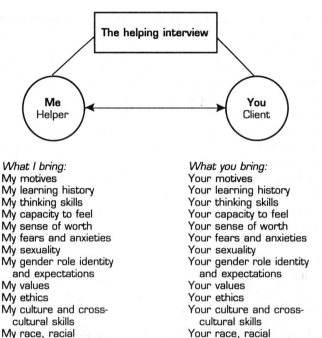

The helping interview

Me
Helper

You
Client

What I bring:
My motives
My learning history
My thinking skills
My capacity to feel
My sense of worth
My fears and anxieties
My sexuality
My gender role identity
   and expectations
My values
My ethics
My culture and cross-
   cultural skills
My race, racial
   attitudes and skills
My social class

What you bring:
Your motives
Your learning history
Your thinking skills
Your capacity to feel
Your sense of worth
Your fears and anxieties
Your sexuality
Your gender role identity
   and expectations
Your values
Your ethics
Your culture and cross-
   cultural skills
Your race, racial
   attitudes and skills
Your social class

Figure 3.1 Some characteristics both helpers and clients bring to helping

ception. For example, helpers may perceive their own race positively, but their clients may perceive it negatively. Figure 3.1 shows some of the characteristics that both helpers and clients bring to interviews. Though this chapter focuses on helper characteristics, part of their significance lies in the ways such characteristics may be perceived by clients. In turn, part of the significance of clients' characteristics rests in how they are perceived by helpers.

The remainder of this chapter encourages you to become more aware of, and to explore the significance of, personal characteristics you bring to helper training and helping.

YOUR MOTIVES

The area of people's motives for helping is complex and provides fertile soil for self-deception. Apart from the obvious requirements for professional recognition, many applicants give vague reasons for wanting to join helper training courses. Such reasons include "I like helping people" and "People find me a good person with whom to talk over problems." Beginning students can hardly be expected to have the diamond-hard commitment of effective and experienced helpers. Nevertheless, some soul searching concerning reasons for entering helping may highlight beneficial motives and unearth harmful motives. The criterion for a beneficial motive is whether its consequences are in the best interests of clients. Needless to say, the categories of beneficial and harmful motives overlap. Specific motives may be both beneficial and harmful. Helpers' own profiles include both beneficial and damaging motives. Furthermore, helpers' profiles of motives can change over time, and also as they interact with individual clients.

Possible Beneficial Motives

What are some of the rewards and values that motivate helpers to pursue clients' best interests? Following are some suggestions.

Altruism   Altruism means unselfish concern for the welfare of others. It entails "viewing and pursuing another person's welfare as an ultimate goal" (Batson, 1990, p. 336). A debate exists as to whether people are capable of altruism, where helping others is an ultimate goal, or only of social egoism, where the primary purpose of helping others is what is in it for you. Helper altruism resembles the concept of *agape* (unselfish love). Clients are prized for themselves and helped to unfold their unique potentials. Helping is genuinely people-centered, rather than a means to pursuing helper self-interest. Some writers view altruism as a fragile flower (Batson, 1990) and a weak instinctual remnant (Maslow, 1970). Maslow makes the further points that the capacity for a wide identification with the human species is a characteristic of self-actualizing people and that many people repress altruistic instincts. Even helpers possessing altruism require "tough minds" to accompany their "tender hearts" (King, 1963, p. 13).

(humanist view to help others)

Humanism   Here humanism is defined as a belief in the possibility that reason can overcome anxiety, fear, and destructive tendencies. Individuals can find the courage to affirm the self "in spite of the elements of nonbeing threatening it" (Tillich, 1952, p. 120). Helpers espousing humanistic values are likely to gain strength from their belief in the possibility for human improvement. Such a belief does not mean ignoring human fallibility and destructiveness. Instead humanism allows helpers to commit themselves to the struggle to make themselves and others better people for the sake of a better world. Many helpers find that religious faiths provide strength to strive for personal improvement and others' welfare.

(social scale)

People orientation Holland's theory of personality types asserts that the special heredity and experiences of people lead to the characteristics of six main personality types: realistic, investigative, artistic, social, enterprising, and conventional (Holland, 1973). The social personality type in particular is found in the helping professions. Illustrative characteristics of the social personality type include: responsibility, helpfulness, friendliness, idealism, femininity, insightfulness, and kindness. People may be attracted to helping when there is a good match between the demands of the role and their personality type. Holland acknowledges that a simple six-category scheme of personality types is unrealistic and talks in terms of profiles of personality types. Nevertheless the social personality type is likely to predominate in helpers' personality-type profiles.

Intellectual curiosity Effective helpers tend to have a great interest in "what makes people tick." They enjoy the challenge of making and testing hypotheses about human behavior. They are constantly in the process of revising their models of the person and of helping practice. They are creative people who continue learning. As such, they acknowledge mistakes. Effective helpers experience excitement from developing their knowledge and competence. Yalom observes that ideological schools of therapy tend to assuage the therapist's, rather than the patient's, anxiety. He states that "the creative members of an orthodoxy, any orthodoxy, ultimately outgrow their disciplines" (Yalom, 1989, p. 36).

Worked-through emotional pain Many people enter helping having experienced significant emotional pain. This pain may be associated with relationships in their families of origin or any of a number of specific circumstances: divorce, sexual abuse, racial discrimination, or physical disability, to mention some. Emotional pain can be for good or ill. Helpers who have worked through their pain and attained some distance from it may have extra sensitivity to the needs of others. In addition, they may have acquired some useful helping skills and insights from being in the client role.

Commitment to competence Effective helpers like to do things well and are prepared to work at it. They take pride in their work and resist taking shortcuts that are not in their clients' best interests. Egan observes that "competence in helping is not a goal to be achieved: it is a lifelong pursuit" (Egan, 1990, p. 63). Helper trainees and trained helpers differ in the extent to which they are prepared to work at *being*, as contrasted with *seeming*, competent. Helper competence has many dimensions: honestly evaluating your helping processes and outcomes; keeping abreast of the literature; being prepared to work on professional and personal problems; and, where necessary, obtaining and learning from supervision. Professional integrity is another term for a commitment to competence.

The preceding are only some potentially beneficial helper motives. You may be able to think of others. Some motives (for instance, money and client goodwill) may help or hinder depending on how pursued.

Possible Harmful Motives

Harmful motives have the common thread that, in varying degrees, they lead to clients' being treated as objects for helpers' gratification rather than respected as unique human beings. Helpers may make inadequate distinctions between "me" and "you." Emotional boundaries can get blurred, to clients' detriment. Though the issues are rarely black and white, potentially harmful motives include the following.

Unresolved emotional pain Many helpers require counseling themselves before they can be fully effective. Without acknowledging it, some enter helping as a way of working on their own concerns at one remove. Their underlying agenda is seeking help rather than providing it. Their sensitivity toward nurturing others stems from their own needs to be nurtured. A possible consequence of unresolved emotional pain is that helpers provide clients with the kinds of help that *they*—rather than their clients—need. The attraction of helping for people with problems seems widespread. For instance, Yeo observes, "When the Samaritans of Singapore first started advertising, they had an overwhelming response. Soon after the selection and screening process was complete, it was discovered that about half the people who volunteered actually needed help with their problems" (Yeo, 1981, p. 24).

Do-gooding Do-gooding may be contrasted with altruism. With altruism, the ultimate agenda is another's welfare. With do-gooding, the ultimate agenda is my own feelings of satisfaction at what a good person I am. Do-gooders need others in dependent roles. They may wish to take charge and, in so doing, treat clients as objects and infantilize them. Though not alone in this tendency, do-gooders may over-concern themselves with obtaining clients' approval and appreciation for their good works.

Seeking intimacy Some are attracted to helping because it provides opportunities for psychological closeness that they find difficult to obtain otherwise. Afraid to take the risks of authentic living, they find the limited nature of the helping role attractive. In addition, some see helping as a way of spending time with sexually attractive people, even though they may stop short of meeting them outside helping or having sexual relations with them.

True believerism True believers are those who enter helping rigidly committed to causes. True believerism implies lack of openness to conflicting evidence and to the specific needs of individual clients. For example, true believers in the rights of minority groups may view individual clients in terms of larger political agendas (for instance, gay rights) rather than as individuals. Once in helping, some become true believers in terms of theoretical positions (for example, hard-line rational-emotive or gestalt therapy advocates). Then, whether appropriate or not, clients risk getting pigeonholed in terms of the concepts of the theoretical position.

Expediency Some people enter helping out of expediency rather than from genuine commitment. An example might be physical-education teachers who are tempted to become school counselors once their joints start aching. Some are motivated towards helping as an easy way of making a living. Unfortunately, some helper trainers fall into this category too. In addition, some people may be thrust by managers into helping roles because they have underperformed in positions regarded as more sensitive.

As with beneficial motives, these suggestions of possible harmful motives are not exhaustive. You may be able to think of others. What are your motives for entering or being in helping? Which beneficial and harmful motives apply to you? Are you satisfied that your motives for helping will always work for, rather than against, your clients' best interests?

YOUR HELPING SKILLS LEARNING HISTORY

Because helping skills are broken down in much greater detail elsewhere, this discussion is brief. People entering helper training all have learning histories of observing others trying to help. In addition, all have learned from the consequences of both their own and others' helping behaviors.

Learning from observing Throughout your life, you have observed a variety of helping relationships. Without always being aware, you have acquired helping skills strengths and weaknesses from observing others. Your parents or surrogate parents provided you with your primary helping relationships. They were important models of both how to and how not to help. Some of this modeling related to how they acted, their outer game (verbal, voice, body, and touch messages). For instance, either or both of them may have used poor verbal and nonverbal skills when trying to understand what upset you. In addition, your parents modeled how they thought, their inner game. For instance, either or both of them may have thought it showed weakness to admit problems and that people should be able to stand on their own two feet.

    Others have also demonstrated various kinds of helping behaviors; these people might include brothers and sisters, grandparents, aunts and uncles, friends, teachers, supervisors, coaches, physicians, ministers, and community leaders. Some of you may have learned as counseling clients from how your helpers behaved. Also, once you enter helper training, the modeling provided by your trainers can be powerful. What do you think has been the influence of others' modeling on the skills strengths and weaknesses that you bring to helping?

Learning from consequences You learn from the consequences of both others' and your own helping behaviors. At different stages in life you have been the recipient of others' attempts to help you. You may be able to recall specific examples of people providing helpful or harmful responses to your help-seeking behaviors. For instance, when Luke, aged 18, mentioned to his uncle his feelings of depression, he was told not to be such a wimp. Janis, aged 14, was more fortunate. When she told her school counselor how upset she was by her parents' splitting up, she met with a warm, interested, and accepting response. You may be aware of others' responses to your help-offering behaviors. Which of your helping behaviors do you think have been useful or harmful and how do you know?

YOUR THINKING SKILLS

Already I have emphasized the importance of the inner game of helping. As a helper you do not just help others, you also think about how to help and always think when you help. However, you may remain unaware of some of your underlying assumptions and thinking skills strengths and weaknesses. Though not covered here, helpers also use thinking skills in their outside lives in ways that later impact their helping effectiveness. Important thinking skills for helping include the following.

Using coping self-talk People bring their styles of self-talk into helping. Beginning helpers are especially inclined to make anxiety-engendering and task-irrelevant self-statements (Kendall & Hollon, 1989; Meichenbaum, 1977; Meichenbaum & Deffenbacher, 1988). They may make remarks to themselves like "I can't cope," "I'm inadequate," "What's going to happen next?" and "The client knows I'm no good." Helpers need to develop the skills of coping self-talk. Coping self-talk consists of the ability to make calming and coaching self-statements (Nelson-Jones, 1990a). Examples of calming self-statements are "Relax," "Calm down," "Take it easy," and "Breathe slowly and regularly." Examples of coaching self-statements are "Make sure to arrive on time so I do not feel rushed at the start of a session," "I need to concentrate on what the client is trying to tell me," and "I need to speak at a moderate rate and be clearly audible." Often calming and coaching self-statements can be joined (for example, "Calm down. I need to concentrate on what the client is trying to tell me."

Choosing realistic helping rules Each person has a rulebook of personal rules for living. Your personal rules are the standards and beliefs by which you live (Beck, 1976; Ellis, 1989). You bring to helping a chapter in your rulebook entitled "My Rules for Helping." These rules can either blight your helping through their rigidity and irrationality or provide you with realistic and flexible guidelines for behavior. The skill of choosing realistic helping rules includes becoming aware of when your rules may oppress rather than support you and clients. In such instances you need to either discard the unrealistic rules altogether or reformulate them into more rational standards. In general, unrealistic helping rules are overgeneralizations that convert partial truths into untruths. Below are examples of unrealistic helping rules that may be held by both beginning and experienced helpers.

"I *must* be the sole source of wisdom and expertise in my helping relationships."

"I *must* be in control of my interviews at all times."

"I *must* never make mistakes."

"I *must* always have my clients' approval."

"I *must* always maintain a professional facade."

"I *must* pressurize clients to self-disclose, whether they want to or not."

"I *must* always have an explanation or interpretation for everything."

"My clients *must* always improve."

"I *must* always get quick results." *"Should" – you want would to operate accord. to you*

In addition, some students possess unrealistic training rules, including the following:

"Learning *must* always be easy and effortless."

"Mistakes and setbacks *must* be avoided all costs."

"I *must* develop effective helping skills immediately or I will never be any good."

Attributing responsibility accurately Beginning helpers bring their attributional styles to helping. Often they experience difficulty in accurately attributing responsibility. If anything, beginning helpers attribute to themselves too much rather than too little responsibility. Some helpers have difficulty in accepting clients' responsibility for their own lives. At best helpers can only influence clients. Ways in which helpers take too much responsibility for helping processes and outcomes include: asking too many questions and insufficiently allowing clients space to tell their stories; making premature suggestions rather than collaborating with clients to formulate working definitions of problems that have meaning for them; insufficiently helping clients to develop self-helping skills; and engaging in excessive self-blame when progress is slow. Conversely, sometimes both beginning and experienced helpers attribute too little responsibility to themselves. They attribute difficulties they experience with clients to "resistances," and fail to acknowledge the contribution of their own poor helping skills.

Perceiving yourself and clients accurately   Two people in a help-ing relationship do not just relate to each other. Instead, they relate to their perceptions of themselves, each other, and the relationship. These perceptions may be of varying degrees of accuracy. In Chapter 2, I mentioned that in helping relation-ships each person develops a personification of themselves and of the other person (Sullivan, 1953). These personifications—literally meaning making up or constructing a person—are men-tal maps of self and others.

You bring to helper training and helping your skills of per-ceiving yourself and your clients accurately. Central to this is the ability to distinguish fact from inference. Your perceptions are subjective facts, but they are not necessarily objective facts. They may contain many inferences of varying degrees of realism in terms of the available facts. Furthermore, you bring to helping the extent of and nature of your defensive processes (Clark, 1991). Defensive processes are *security operations* (Sullivan, 1953) by means of which you may deny and distort information con-tradicting your self-picture.

Other thinking skills are important for your helping effective-ness. Fundamental is the skill of assuming responsibility for ac-quiring, maintaining, and developing your helping skills. Re-lated to this you need a conceptual framework that allows you to think of helping in skills terms and identifies which skills are important. The challenge to work on your helping skills requires specifying them. Other important thinking skills include: assess-ing clients' problems and redefining them in skills terms; setting clear and realistic goals; predicting consequences; using visualiz-ing; making plans; and assisting clients' decision making, and making realistic decisions yourself.

YOUR CAPACITY TO FEEL

You bring to helping your capacity to experience your feelings. Dictionary definitions of feelings tend to use words like physical sensation, emotions, and awareness. All three words illustrate dimensions of feelings. Feelings as *physical sensations* represent your underlying animal nature. The word *emotions* implies movement. Feelings are processes. You are subject to a continual flow of biological experiencing. *Awareness* implies you can be conscious of your feelings. However, you may also deny and distort some of them. Furthermore, you may have learned some unexamined personal rules with their related feelings from your parents and others. Thus, some of your feelings may be based more on their standards than on your own valuing process. To the extent that you are out of touch with your feelings, you are alienated from the core of your personhood. Rogers, in particular, stressed that a feature of modern life is that all people, in varying degrees, are out of touch with their inner valuing process (Rogers, 1961, 1980).

There are many reasons why it is important for helpers to be responsive to their flow of feelings. These reasons include being genuine, spontaneous, and able to resonate and respond appropriately to clients' feelings. In helping you are continuously required to listen to your own, as well as to clients', feelings. Your feelings are good guides to issues in your relationships with clients that may be similar to issues they experience outside helping. For instance, if you feel bored and distant from clients, they may have the same effect on others. You then have the opportunity to analyze the skills weaknesses that create distance.

YOUR SENSE OF WORTH AND ANXIETIES

You bring to helping your feelings of security and insecurity, your pain and unfinished business, and your fears and anxieties. Vulnerability can be an attractive quality in helping relationships. Acknowledging your vulnerability to yourself can make you more understanding of clients' vulnerabilities. Furthermore, appropriate disclosure of vulnerability to clients may be viewed as a token of caring and that you too are a part of the human race.

Your Sense of Worth

Confidence and self-esteem are general traits and also vary across specific situations people face. Some people find difficulty in acknowledging that they lack confidence. Others admit it all too readily. Sometimes, by disclosing underconfidence, they seek to manipulate the environment to look after them. Insecurities and fears, if not confronted and managed, can be the breeding ground for distorted communication. Nobody's upbringing is perfect. In varying degrees you have learned to feel Not-OK as well as OK even though sometimes these Not-OK feelings are difficult to acknowledge.

Intentionally or unintentionally, when people communicate they send two broad categories of messages. One set is specific, having to do with the ostensible purpose of the communication. The other set of messages may be more general and less intentional. These messages send information to receivers pertaining to their worth as persons as well as to how high or low the senders value themselves. Children need the security of positive messages about their unique lovableness. Unfortunately, many parents fail to realize that they often send messages that undermine the tender self-esteem of those they love. Even though their need for understanding may be much greater, the pain of children whose parents often send damaging messages is less likely to be heard than that of children whose parents mostly send positive messages.

In varying degrees, all helpers possess some unresolved pain and unfinished business from their families of origin. Many have overcome significant obstacles to become more confident and effective people. As a helper, related to how confident you feel, you may send to clients either positive and affirming or negative and damaging messages. Effective helpers send many more affirming messages than ineffective helpers. Were you helped to feel confident when you were growing up? How confident a person are you now? How do you think your level of confidence influences the messages you send to clients about their worth?

Your Fears and Anxieties

Both helper and client anxiety is always present in helping encounters (Sullivan, 1954). Part of it comes from being human, part from starting as strangers, part from clients' problems, and part from work undertaken in helping. The words *anxiety* and *fear* are interchangeable. Anxiety may be defined as your fears about your capacity to cope adequately with the future. Anxiety may be viewed either as a 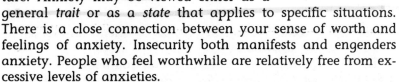 general *trait* or as a *state* that applies to specific situations. There is a close connection between your sense of worth and feelings of anxiety. Insecurity both manifests and engenders anxiety. People who feel worthwhile are relatively free from excessive levels of anxieties.

Beginning helpers bring their general level of anxiety to helping as well as their specific fears and anxieties about it. Helper anxiety may be either facilitating, debilitating, or both (Alpert &

state anxiety - will go away
trait   "   - all the time

Haber, 1960). Excessive levels of anxieties tend to be associated with unrealistic helping rules. For example, the rule "I must always have my clients' approval" leads to oversensitivity to cues of rejection.

Specific fears and anxieties   Following is a list of just a few of the fears and anxieties that people bring to helping. These fears represent subjective rather than objective reality. However, often they are exaggerated and result in unhelpful feelings and actions. Sometimes you may be more afraid of getting what you want than not getting it. Consequently, I group fears into three categories: fear of failure, fear of success, and fear of change.

Fear of Failure

Fear of rejection
Fear of losing clients
Fear of being incompetent
Fear of being seen through
Fear of silences
Fear of not formulating a satisfactory skills redefinition of a
    problem
Fear of not knowing what to do next
Fear of clients' making no progress
Fear of certain client feelings (for instance, anger)
Fears about coping with certain kinds of clients (for instance,
    clients in crisis)
Fears that certain clients may highlight unfulfilled areas in
    your life
Fear of what your supervisor thinks

Fear of Success

Fears about attaining psychological closeness
Fear of not being able to maintain success
Fears about dealing with expressions of gratitude and appre-
    ciation

Fear of Change

Fear that you may be touched deeply by clients and forced to
    reexamine how you live
Fear that you may have to change how you help
Fear of practical changes (for example, the consequences of
    building up a caseload)

Some consequences of helper anxiety Anxiety can have both positive and negative consequences. Helpers able to experience and cope with their own anxieties may be more sensitive to clients' anxieties. A certain degree of anxiety is necessary to tone helpers up and motivate them to give skilled performances. Also, when helpers feel anxious in relation to specific clients or helping events, this anxiety can serve as a signal to explore certain issues regarding themselves, their clients, or their helping relationships.

Many negative consequences flow when helper anxiety becomes debilitating rather than facilitating. Helpers may cease to listen accurately. They may perceive and relate to clients in terms of their own needs and fail to maintain adequate psychological boundaries between "me" and "you." The psychoanalysts call this phenomenon *countertransference*. Helpers may assume too much responsibility both for the content of helping sessions and for their clients' lives. In addition, helpers may use their defensive processes both to distort feedback from clients and also to misperceive the extent of client progress. Some specific behaviors that may result from excessive helper anxiety include asking too many questions, offering superficial reassurance, and being too directive in telling clients how to behave.

Personal counseling How can helping students become more aware of their levels and cues of anxiety and of what might be the consequences for clients? Also, what can students do to overcome excessive anxieties? Some of the anxiety may dissipate with experience, practice, and good supervision. In addition, the lifeskills approach to training includes, where possible, teaching skills in self-referent ways. For instance, a good way to learn how to use thinking skills with clients is to use them with yourself. However, the question remains whether students still require the more intense focus on their skills and anxieties provided by personal counseling. Excessive anxieties affect beginning helpers to varying levels of intensity and in many different ways. Assuming the availability of skilled counselors, most students probably profit from individual work on their sense of worth, anxieties, and lifeskills weaknesses. Lifeskills helping does not assume that a single course of helping is necessarily enough. During their careers, helpers may supplement their self-helping by focused work with other helpers on problematic issues and skills. Also, there is much to be said for seeking peer support, possibly in support groups.

YOUR SEXUALITY

All helpers are sexual beings. However, you have a choice as to how much of your sexuality you bring into helping. Despite the strength of their sexual urges, people differ in the extent to which they experience themselves as sexual beings. Undoubtedly genetic differences exist for libido strength. However, much of the variation in ability to experience sexuality reflects learned inhibitions and prohibitions. Helpers possess thoughts and feelings about their own and their clients' sexuality. I hope that your attitude toward your sexuality is healthy and loving and, where appropriate, this gets transmitted to clients. However, sexual ignorance and poor thinking skills may interfere with helpers' effectiveness in their personal and professional lives. Furthermore, many helpers experience great difficulty avoiding dual relationships and sexual intimacy with clients (Corey, Corey, & Callanan, 1988; Egan, 1990; Yalom, 1989). Professional codes for psychologists and counselors clearly state that such relationships are unethical (American Psychological Association, 1990; Australian Psychological Society, 1986; British Association for Counselling, 1990).

Helpers are of differing sexual preferences. The world is not divided into heterosexuals and homosexuals. Pioneering studies on sexual behavior were conducted in America in the late 1940s and early 1950s by Kinsey and his colleagues (Kinsey, Pomeroy, & Martin, 1948; Kinsey, Pomeroy, Martin & Gebhard, 1953). They found that in the large, predominantly white, middle-class population they surveyed, 4 percent of males and between 1 and 3 percent of females were exclusively homosexual. However, by age 45, half the males and about a quarter of the females had responded homosexually by either arousal or orgasm at some point during their lives. The Kinsey studies are outdated and based on an unrepresentative sample. Nevertheless, they indicate that many helpers are confronted with choices in their personal lives about how to handle homosexual feelings, whether to engage in homosexual sex, and whether openly to admit to homosexual feelings. Kinsey and his colleagues considered that, if social constraints had not been so strong, there would have been a much higher incidence of homosexual response.

Helpers have attitudes about clients' sexual preferences, whether they be the same or different from their own. Furthermore, they possess varying degrees of knowledge about the psychology and behavior of people with different sexual preferences.

Especially if you plan to work in such areas as marital counseling, sexual dysfunction counseling, or counseling gay and bisexual people, you need to review the adequacy of your knowledge and attitudes about sexuality and sexual preference.

Your Sex-Role Identity and Expectations

The following are stipulated definitions of terms relevant to your
exploring the sex-role identity and expectations that you bring
to helper training and helping.

- *Sex:* In this context, sex refers to biological differences between
  males and females (for instance, differences in genitals, repro-
  ductive functions, bone structure, and size).
- *Gender:* Gender refers to the social and cultural classification
  of attributes, attitudes, and behaviors as "feminine" or "masculine."
- *Sex-role identity:* Your sex-role identity is how you view yourself
  and behave on the dimensions of "masculinity" and "femininity."
- *Sex-role expectations:* These are your thoughts and feelings
  about how you and others should think, feel, and behave on
  account of differences in biological sex.
- *Gender awareness:* Gender awareness relates to how aware you
  are of the processes of and consequences of gender scripting
  on both males and females.
- *Sexism:* Individual sexism relates to any feelings, thoughts,
  and actions that assume the superiority of one sex over the
  other. Institutional sexism relates to institutional structures
  that discriminate and devalue a person on the grounds of sex.

Masculinity, Femininity, and Androgyny

In Western societies, certain psychological characteristics have
traditionally been viewed as either feminine or masculine. Feminine characteristics have included being affectionate, gentle,
sensitive to the needs of others, tender, and warm. Masculine
characteristics have included being aggressive, ambitious, assertive, analytical, and dominant (Bem, 1974). Sex-roles based on
gender learning influence social behavior. Argyle (1984) states
that the research evidence suggests that there are a number of
areas where females may be more socially competent than
males. These areas include being better at sending and receiving body language, being more rewarding and polite, disclosing

more, and forming closer relationships. However, he notes that assertion is an area in which women appear to have more problems than men. Both masculine and feminine gender roles may have costs. The traditional feminine sex-role has created problems for many women in such areas as expressing anger, being autonomous, and obtaining power and status (DeVoe, 1990). The traditional masculine role has created problems for many men through over-concern with success, power, and competition, emotional restriction, and restricted affectionate behavior between men (Good, Dell, & Mintz, 1989).

Underlying the femininity–masculinity discussion is the issue of nature versus nurture. The consensus among social scientists seems increasingly to be that humans have weak instinctual remnants toward either a male or female sex-role identity and that such biological predispositions may be easily overwhelmed by the strength of their learning experiences (Oakley, 1972). Related to the importance of nurture over nature has been the growing popularity of the concept of psychological androgyny. The androgynous male or female "is flexible masculine or feminine as circumstances warrant" (Bem, 1981, p. 362). Thus, females and males can be brought up to express a range of characteristics, independent of whether they have traditionally been viewed as masculine or feminine. Possibly in time masculinity and femininity may become outmoded concepts.

The ways in which you learned your current sex-role identity are many and varied. Your gender scripting started at the cradle– with pink for a girl and blue for a boy. You may have observed your parents undertaking different household tasks (for instance, mending clothes or looking after the car). Probably your parents and significant others gave you different toys according to your sex and rewarded different behaviors and characteristics. The books you read showed boys and girls in different roles, as did the films and television programs you watched. When you went to school, you may have been treated differently according to your sex. Furthermore, the subjects you were encouraged to study and the occupations thought appropriate for you also varied by sex. Though not all ways of scripting apply to everyone, nobody can grow up in Western society without a considerable amount of gender brainwashing. Your current sex-role identity is the internalized sum of this brainwashing plus any modifications from countervailing experiences and from thinking for yourself.

Your Sex-Role Expectations

Based on your gender socialization and sex-role identity, you bring sex-role expectations to helping. Also your sex-role identity influences behavior. For example, a consistent research finding is that female therapists are more oriented toward their clients' affect than male therapists (Mintz & O'Neil, 1990). Female therapists experience and express more feelings in interactions with clients than male therapists (Maracek & Johnson, 1980). Sex-role identity and its associated behaviors can also provide a way of categorizing helpers, for example as nonsexist-humanist, liberal feminist, or radical feminist (Enns & Hackett, 1990). Good and his colleagues have proposed gender-aware therapy. They state, "counselors must not only be nonsexist in their work with clients, but they must also understand clients' difficulties within a gender perspective" (Good, Gilbert, & Scher, 1990, p. 377).

Sex-role expectations can permeate helping in a number of ways. You may assess clients differently according to whether or not they fit into traditional sex-roles (Robertson & Fitzgerald, 1990). You may bring to helping inflexible and sexist assumptions for appropriate behavior in dating, marital and partner relationships, and parenting. Your attitudes to sexual harassment, rape, and domestic psychological and physical violence may be sexist. You may also possess unexamined sexist assumptions about the place of males and females in the home or workforce and about jobs and careers appropriate for each sex. In addition, you may engage in simplistic overgeneralizations about the characteristics of males and females and insufficiently acknowledge within-group differences. Some students bring to helping such strong feelings about sex-role and gender issues that they interfere with their ability to formulate accurate working definitions of clients' problems.

YOUR VALUES

The earlier section on motives explored some values underlying your choice to be a helper. However, you bring many other values too. Your values influence how you work with clients. Also, in helping, you may be subject to value conflicts both within your own values and between yours' and your clients' values.

Perhaps the most prominent measure of American values is the Rokeach Value Survey (Rokeach, 1967). Rokeach was influenced by Kluckhohn's (1951) definition of values as "conceptions of the desirable means and ends of action" (p. 395). The Rokeach Value Survey makes a distinction between *terminal values,* or the ultimate end-goals of existence, and *instrumental values,* or the behavioral means for achieving such end-goals. Between 1968 and 1981, there was a high degree of stability in American terminal values (Rokeach & Ball-Rokeach, 1989). In 1981 the six most highly ranked terminal values were a world at peace, family security, freedom, happiness, self-esteem, and wisdom. Rokeach last surveyed instrumental values in 1971, when the six most highly ranked values were honesty, ambition, responsibility, forgiveness, broadmindedness, and courage (Rokeach & Ball-Rokeach, 1989).

The Rokeach Value Survey data relate to national values. However, you bring your individual values to helping. For instance, you may place a low value on materialism, yet be working with a highly materialistic client. Helpers need to be aware of significant values they bring to helping. Then they can be in positions to choose how to handle them (for instance, by consciously trying not to influence clients' values or by self-disclosing your values). One way of viewing your values is, like Rokeach, to place them in a hierarchy ordered by importance. Another way is to view yourself as possessing a profile of values. This profile is composed of your values and the weight you attach to them. Following are some values that people consider, consciously or otherwise, when forming a philosophy of life (Allport, Vernon, & Lindzey, 1960; Holland, 1973; Maslow, 1970).

- *Survival:* The primary instinctual value, though other values sometimes override it (for example, patriotism or religious belief).
- *Love:* Loving and being loved; appreciating others for what they are and not just for what they do.
- *Friendship:* Being joined to others outside your family by mutual intimacy and interests.
- *Family life:* Having and being part of a family; valuing parenthood.
- *Religion:* Acknowledging the need for connectedness to some ultimate and superhuman power.
- *Materialism:* Valuing the accumulation and control of money.
- *Aesthetics:* Appreciating beauty and good taste, with special reference to arts such as music, literature, and painting.
- *Intellect:* Valuing analytical and rational pursuits.
- *Social consciousness:* Helping others; showing social concern.
- *Hedonism:* Valuing fun, pleasure, and having a good time.

- *Career:* Valuing having a career and the work entailed.
- *Practical orientation:* Valuing practical pursuits and, where practical matters are concerned, self-reliance.
- *Nature:* Appreciating and valuing being outdoors and in communion with nature.
- *Autonomy:* Valuing independence, thinking for yourself, and personal enterprise.
- *Convention:* Appreciating tradition; valuing obedience and conformity to the status quo.
- *Self-actualization:* Being committed to personal growth and development.

Value Conflicts

Helpers bring their value conflicts to helping. For instance, a helper may feel conflict about wanting to help others and then charging fees for it. Helpers experience many value conflicts similar to those of clients (for instance, between home and career or between religious teachings and secular values on issues such as abortion).

The values you bring to helping may put you in conflict with clients. Sexual behavior constitutes a potential area of value conflict (Corey, Corey, & Callanan, 1988). For instance, what are your attitudes toward premarital sex? Extramarital sex? Casual sex? Group sex? Teenage sex? Homosexuality? For Roman Catholic helpers, issues of contraception, abortion, divorce, and intentional single parenting create value conflicts. Value conflicts are not restricted to personal counseling. For instance, in academic counseling, how might you feel about clients' consciously choosing not to try when their parents sacrifice to keep them in college? In vocational counseling, how might you feel about clients' drawing unemployment benefits for as long as possible?

You may bring to helping a style of handling value conflicts. For instance, some helpers may want to push their own values regardless of their clients' wishes. Other helpers may consider that the way to handle severe value conflicts is to refer clients to helpers with more similar values. Yet another option is to keep quiet about your values. A further option is to declare your values as your own and, possibly, use this as a springboard for helping clients to clarify their values.

Questioning Your Values

There are many questions you may ask about your values. When I interview applicants for helper training, many experience difficulty answering the question "What are your core values?" How might you answer that question? Would you find it helpful to formulate either a hierarchy or a profile of your values, or both? Other questions that you might ask yourself are "How did I acquire my values and to what degree do they represent my inner valuing process rather than those of others?" "What are my key areas of value conflict?" "In what areas, if any, do I anticipate having significant value conflicts with clients?" and "To what degree are my values open to modification and how might they influence my work with clients?"

YOUR ETHICS

Your ethics and values are interrelated. Numerous ethical issues are connected with helping. Such issues include confidentiality, putting undue pressure on clients, false advertising, financial exploitation, and sexual relationships. I will not deal with such important issues of helper practice here. Rather, I focus on the ethical orientation you bring to helper training in two overlapping areas: learning helping skills and personal integrity.

Learning helping skills   Ethical issues abound in learning helping skills. Though not an either-or matter, students differ in the extent to which they approach helper training with high ethical standards. Probably most students would say their approach to learning helping skills was highly ethical. Unfortunately, students have varying degrees of commitment to competence as well as varying abilities to explore the adequacy of their learning behaviors. Below are a few examples of less-than-ethical student behavior.

- As part of the contract in a counseling skills practicum, Ken is required to confirm that he has done 30 hours of independent interview practice. Ken does only 10 hours, but confirms that he has done 30 hours.
- Lucia is required to read up on different approaches to working with depressed clients, prior to having such clients referred to her. Lucia fails to do most of her reading homework.
- Julie has been told by her supervisor that she intrudes too much by pushing her own values onto her clients. Julie thinks that she knows better than her supervisor and just becomes more subtle as to how she goes about altering her clients' values.

• In a helping skills practicum, there is a clear requirement that students attend all sessions. Paul misses a number of sessions and each time makes excuses, claiming pressure of other business.

Just as a commitment to competence is the hallmark of an ethical helping practitioner, so a genuine commitment to becoming competent is essential for helping students. Issues of professional ethics start with practitioner training. Though obtaining helping degrees and certificates is important, acquiring the knowledge and skills that go with the qualifications is even more important. To what extent are you open to learning and working on your helping skills? How committed to helping competence are you?

Personal integrity   Allied to working on helping skills is the area of working on potentially damaging aspects of yourself that you bring to helping. Helping students vary in the degree to which they acknowledge that their own fears, insecurities, anxieties, and lifeskills weaknesses interfere with effectiveness. Furthermore, helping students vary in the extent to which they realistically acknowledge their strengths and assets. An ethical commitment to helping entails not just working on your outer game (action skills), but also having the courage to confront your inner game (thinking skills) weaknesses. As mentioned earlier, methods of confronting personal deficiencies range from learning helping skills in self-referent ways, self-helping, good supervision, and personal counseling. An ethical commitment to helping entails dealing with specific tendencies you have to nonethical helping behavior, be it breaking confidentiality for the sake of telling a good story or taking a prurient interest in clients' sexual lives. Awareness of areas of fallibility is the first step in preventing ethical lapses.

YOUR CULTURE AND CROSS-CULTURAL SKILLS

You bring your cultural rules and assumptions to helping. Culture pervades every aspect of living: values, ethics, language, food, table manners, music, religion, attitudes toward democracy, sporting activities, family structures and relations, social relations, and body language—to mention only some aspects. Examples of cultural differences abound. Ho (1985) observes that

important Western values include emphasis on youth, asser-
tiveness, independence, and competition, whereas the corresponding Eastern values are emphasis on maturity, compliance,
interdependence, and cooperation. Argyle (1986) studied common rules in 22 social relationships in four different cultures:
Britain, Hong Kong, Japan, and Italy. He found: "In Japan virtually all highly endorsed rules were conflict-regulating ones. In
contrast, Italy endorsed intimacy-reward rules more, especially
compared to Japan" (p. 313). Cultures differed on both verbal
and nonverbal dimensions. Addressing the other person by first
name was highly endorsed in only three Japanese relationships,
a much lower figure than in the other three cultures. Looking the
other person in the eye during conversation was highly endorsed
in virtually all British and Italian relationships, but in less than
half of Japanese and Hong Kong relationships. Yet another example is that eye contact by young people is a sign of disrespect
among some Native American groups (Ivey, 1988).

Your Cultural and Ancestral Roots

What are your cultural and ancestral roots? The 1980 U.S. census found that 83 percent of U.S. residents identified with at least
one ancestral group. The four largest groups, in descending order, claimed some English, German, Irish, or African descent
(Robey & Russell, 1984). Cultural, racial, and ethnic diversity is
on the increase in North America. Between 1980 and 1990,
blacks increased from 11.7 to 12.4 percent of the total U. S. population, while Hispanics increased from 6.4 to 7.9 percent (Allen
& Turner, 1990). During the 1980s, the number of Americans of
"other" races (Asians, Pacific Islanders, Native Americans, Eski-
mos and Aleuts) grew by 65 percent, primarily the result of
Asian immigration. "Other" races share of the U.S. population
rose from 2 to 3 percent (Waldrop & Exter, 1990). Allen and
Turner observe: "In the twenty-first century, one quarter to one
third of all Americans will belong to racial or ethnic minority
groups" (Allen & Turner, 1990, p. 34).
　　Cultural diversity exists not only between, but also within
racial and ethnic groups. For example, the Hispanic group includes 12 million Mexicans, 2.5 million Puerto Ricans, 2 million
Central and South Americans, and 1 million Cubans. Furthermore, each of these groups has its own cultural and linguistic
differences (Swenson, 1990). Canada, historically populated by
English and French Canadians, is also becoming more culturally
diverse. A major reason for this is an increase in Asian immigration (Pryor & Norris, 1983). In both the United States and

Canada, Asians are represented in many different cultural groupings: Vietnamese, Taiwanese, mainland Chinese, Indochinese, Chinese-Malaysians, Japanese, Filipinos, and former residents of Hong Kong.

Your Cross-Cultural Awareness, Sensitivity, and Skills

You bring your degree of cultural awareness to helping. Helpers differ in the extent to which they are aware that how they think, feel, and behave has been conditioned by their cultural upbringing. You may possess cultural tunnel vision without knowing it. Some helpers gain knowledge of other cultures through relatives, friends, and acquaintances. Also, overseas travel may have heightened your awareness of cultural differences and increased your sensitivity to migrants' experiencing culture shock and disorientation.

You also bring your cultural assumptions to helping. A useful distinction is that between culture-deficit and culture-sensitive assumptions. The culture-deficit helping model assumes that the rules and values of the dominant or mainstream culture are normal. Variations observed in minorities are deficits (Rogoff & Morelli, 1989). The culture-deficit helping model incorporates oppression even by those "trying to help" minorities. For example, patronizing attitudes and missionary zeal are two kinds of majority group helper insensitivity experienced by many Native Americans (LaFromboise, Trimble, & Mohatt, 1990). The culture-sensitive helping model avoids the assumption that dominant group practices are proper and superior. Respect is shown for cultural differences, and positive features of cultural variation may be emphasized. Furthermore, helpers show sensitivity to minority group members' differing levels of and wishes for acculturation (LaFromboise, Trimble, & Mohatt, 1990).

You also bring your cross-cultural skills to helping. How good are you at helping people from different cultures to share their cultural differences with you? For instance, if you show interest and give people from different cultures permission to talk about the role of culture in their problems you may be perceived as more empathic (Poon, Nelson-Jones, & Caputi, 1991) and culturally competent (Pomales, Claiborn, & LaFromboise, 1986) than if you are culture-neutral or culture-blind. Such culture-sensitive behaviors also help you to get more within the frames of reference of clients culturally dissimilar from you. Ivey has been a prominent advocate of the need for helpers to develop cultural empathy (Ivey, 1987, 1988; Ivey, Ivey, & Simek-Downing, 1987).

Cultural empathy consists of various components: knowledge about clients' cultures, yet acknowledging individual differences within them; understanding the cultural meaning of verbal, voice, and body messages; allowing clients to reveal the cultural context of problems; helping clients to work through cross-cultural mistrust; and responding in ways appropriate to clients' cultures (for instance, by varying amount of eye contact). Both beginning helping students and experienced helpers vary in their degree of cultural empathy with clients.

YOUR RACE, RACIAL ATTITUDES, AND SKILLS

You also bring your race to helping—whether you are white, black, Asian, or of another racial grouping. Axelson observes: "Race as a subdivision of a species simply implies a degree of inbreeding among the ancestors of the group during their evolution within a specified region of the world. It also implies the ability to adapt to the surrounding physical environment" (Axelson, 1985, p.132). In the United States, most intimate relationships are between people of the same race. Interracial marriages were prohibited in 20 states until the U.S. Supreme Court invalidated such legislation in 1967. Although the United States is a great cultural melting pot, there has been relatively little interracial marriage to make it also a racial melting pot (Wilson, 1984). Currently, Canada also is not a racial melting pot, though for different reasons. There the proportion of nonwhites has traditionally been small, a gradually changing situation.

You bring your attitudes toward your own and other races to helping. Ideally all helpers subscribe to the fundamental value of racial equality. However, helpers have racial learning histories in which they may have acquired negative thoughts and feelings about either their own or other races, or both. In Western societies, the predominant kind of racism is the belief in white genetic superiority over other racial groups. White stereotypes of other races abound. Helpers from minority races are especially likely to have been the victims of racism on both individual and institutional levels. Racist assumptions and behaviors by members of the white majority can lead to second-order racism, whereby members of oppressed minority groups react with simplistic racial stereotypes of whites. Racial differences are often highlighted by cultural differences. Much behavior labeled racist stems from cultural and socioeconomic (rather than solely racial) differences.

Whether members of racial majority or minority groups, helpers possess different levels of awareness about the impact of race on their own and others' identity and life chances (Christensen, 1989). Furthermore, they possess different levels of racial mistrust and attraction. In addition, helpers possess different skills at demonstrating racial empathy. In multiracial societies, it is important that you possess race-sensitive as well as culture-sensitive skills (for instance, giving clients permission to comment both on seeing a racially different helper and also on the racial context of their problems).

YOUR SOCIAL CLASS

Income, educational attainment, and occupational status are three of the main ways social class is measured in North America. Other indicators of social class include how you speak, your table manners, how you dress, the suburb in which you live, and what schools and colleges you attended. The social class in which you were born and reared influences your chances of surviving at birth, your educational and occupational opportunities, whom you are likely to meet and to marry, how much money you are likely to make, how well your health is looked after, and the quality of your funeral. The same holds true for your clients.

Each of you brings your social class to helping. A common stereotype is a middle-class helper who lacks the language, life experience, and skills to relate to lower-class clients. You also bring your sensitivity to the effects of others' social class on you and of your social class on them. Furthermore, you bring your skills at understanding people from different social classes and at forming helping relationships with them. One skill may be handling resistances and negative messages resulting from others' social class insecurities. Another skill is that of using language appropriate to your client group. If you possess feelings of either inferiority or superiority on account of your social class, you should work to eliminate them. Being an effective helper is difficult enough without the intrusion of avoidable social class agendas.

CHAPTER HIGHLIGHTS

- Helping differs from most other occupations in that its main tools are people.
- Your motives for helping can be beneficial or harmful. Beneficial motives include: altruism, humanism, people orientation, intellectual curiosity, worked-through emotional pain, and commitment to competence. Harmful motives include; unresolved emotional pain, do-gooding, seeking intimacy, true believerism, and expediency.
- You are influenced by your learning history, including observing others and learning from the consequences of your own and others' attempts to help.
- You bring thinking skills strengths and weaknesses to helping in such areas as: coping self-talk, choosing realistic helping rules, attributing responsibility accurately, and perceiving yourself and your clients accurately.
- You bring to helping your capacity to feel and to be emotionally responsive and spontaneous.
- Depending on your sense of worth, you may send either negative or positive messages to clients about their worth.
- You may lessen your helping effectiveness through debilitating fears and anxieties. Most helping students can benefit from personal counseling.
- Your sexuality and sexual preference influence how you help.
- Your sex-role identity may be feminine, masculine, or androgynous.
- Your sex-role expectations may liberate or restrict clients' identity and choices.
- You need to become aware of your values in order to handle value issues and conflicts in helping.
- Commitment to competence and personal integrity are ethical issues for helping students.
- You bring your culture, cultural awareness, sensitivity, and skills to helping. In multicultural societies, helpers require cultural empathy.
- You bring to helping your race, experiences of racism, attitudes to race, and skills at relating to racially different people.
- Your social class may make it hard for you to understand and work with clients whose life experiences are very different from yours. In addition, you may have to cope with your own and your clients' social-class insecurities.

❀ ❀

PART TWO

❀ ❀

STAGES AND SKILLS OF THE LIFESKILLS HELPING MODEL

STAGE

1

DEVELOP THE RELATIONSHIP,
IDENTIFY AND CLARIFY PROBLEMS

Chapters 4 and 5 present some skills for stage 1 of the lifeskills helping model. Chapter 4 focuses on using rewarding listening skills to develop the helping relationship. Chapter 5 presents a range of skills for assisting clients in identifying and clarifying their problems.

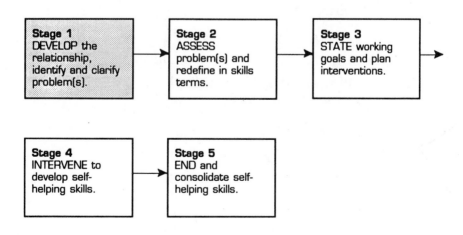

| Stage 1 DEVELOP the relationship, identify and clarify problem(s). | → | Stage 2 ASSESS problem(s) and redefine in skills terms. | → | Stage 3 STATE working goals and plan interventions. | → |

| Stage 4 INTERVENE to develop self-helping skills. | → | Stage 5 END and consolidate self-helping skills. |

CHAPTER FOUR

HOW TO DEVELOP HELPING RELATIONSHIPS

It is as though he [she] listened
and such listening as his [hers] enfolds us
  in a silence
in which at last we begin to hear
what we are meant to be.

—Lao-Tse

CHAPTER QUESTIONS

❀ *What is a helping relationship?*

❀ *What messages do helpers and clients send and receive?*

❀ *Why are perceptions of messages important?*

❀ *What is rewarding listening?*

❀ *Why is rewarding listening important?*

❀ *What are the component skills of rewarding listening?*

Clients come to helping in pain, with problems, with decisions, in crisis, and in need of support. They need to relate to (become connected to) helpers as a means of working on their concerns. Throughout all five stages, the lifeskills helping model heavily emphasizes the quality of the helper-client relationship. However, although the helping relationship is considered both necessary and sufficient for client change to occur in the person-centered approach (Rogers, 1957), for the lifeskills helping model I consider it necessary, but for the most part insufficient.

Though a simplification, a useful distinction in helping exists between a relationship orientation and a task orientation. However, relationship and task orientations are not opposite ends of a continuum. Effective helpers focus both on the relationship and on the task of helping clients develop lifeskills. They go beyond *talking* relationships, where the relationship overshadows the task, to supportive *working* relationships, where the relationship facilitates the task. Though it overstates the point, an analogy may be made with school teaching, where good teacher-student relationships must not be viewed as a substitute for teaching and learning. In stage 1 of the lifeskills model, helpers use relationship skills to form bonds with clients and to elicit information to clarify problems. Throughout DASIE's five stages, helpers use relationship skills both to support helper-client bonding and to support the tasks of each stage. Helping relationships are tools to support clients as they learn self-support. As such, they contain the seeds of their own destruction.

HELPERS AND CLIENTS AS SENDERS AND RECEIVERS OF MESSAGES

Messages are encoded by senders and decoded by receivers (Argyle, 1983). There are five important ways that helpers and clients send messages.

- *Verbal messages:* These are messages expressed in words (for example, what you say when you respond to clients).
- *Voice messages:* These messages relate to how you talk (for example, loudly or softly).
- *Body messages:* Sometimes called *body language,* these are the messages you send with your face and other parts of your body.
- *Touch messages:* Touch is a special kind of body message involving physical contact with another.

- *Action messages:* Action messages are what you do as contrasted with what you say or how you say it (for example,
keeping your appointments and starting on time).

Helpers and clients are not only senders of messages, but they
are also perceivers of how they send messages. For instance,
helpers may rightly or wrongly perceive that they send supportive messages to clients. Furthermore, they are perceivers of each
other's reactions to their messages. For instance, helpers may
consider that clients misunderstand their supportive messages.
In addition, since helpers and clients can send messages in so
many different ways, genuineness is important. For example,
how something is said needs to be congruent with what is said.

Helpers and clients are also receivers of each others' messages.
Furthermore, they perceive the messages they receive with varying degrees of accuracy. The focus of this chapter is on how to
develop relationships by receiving, and showing that you have
received, your clients' messages accurately. Good listening skills
are at the heart of developing effective helping relationships.

Effective listening involves helpers in both receiving and sending messages. On the surface, a client communicates–helper responds unit of interaction may seem simple. However, this is not
the case. As depicted in Figure 4.1, at each of the four points of
the cycle—client sends, helper receives, helper sends, client receives—communication difficulties, which impede effective helping relationships, can arise.

REWARDING LISTENING AND DEVELOPING
HELPING RELATIONSHIPS

Defining Rewarding Listening

A distinction may be made between hearing and listening. *Hearing* involves the capacity to be aware of and to receive sound.
Listening involves not only receiving sounds but, as much as
possible, accurately understanding their meaning. As such, it
entails hearing and memorizing words, being sensitive to vocal
cues, observing body language, and taking into account the personal and social context of communications. However, you can
listen accurately without being a rewarding listener. *Rewarding
listening* entails not only accurately understanding speakers'
communications, but also rewarding them by showing you have
understood. Rewarding listening involves both receiver and
sender skills.

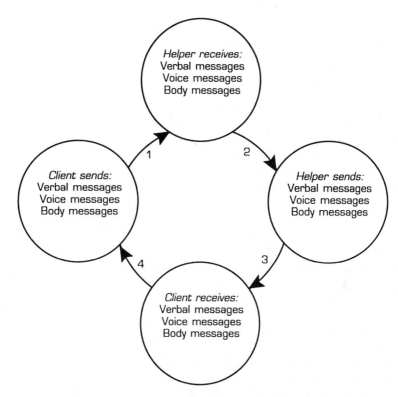

Figure 4.1   Diagrammatic representation of a basic client communicates–helper responds interaction cycle

You may wonder why rewarding listening is so important when there are so many opportunities for people to be listened to in everyday life. Here, it is possible to distinguish between social and helping conversations. *Social* conversations are geared toward meeting the needs of both participants; they have facetiously been described as "two people, taking turns exercising their egos." Listening (let alone rewarding listening) becomes lost along the way. *Helping* conversations primarily emphasize meeting clients' needs. As such they place a high premium on rewarding clients by listening and showing that you understand them.

Four kinds of listening take place in any helping relationship. Listening does not just take place between helper and client, it also takes place within each (Gendlin, 1981). Indeed, the quality of your *inner* listening, or being appropriately sensitive to your own thoughts and feelings, may be vital to the quality of your *outer* listening. Furthermore, if you listen well to others, this may help the quality of their inner listening. Conversely, if you listen either poorly or too much to yourself, you listen less well to others.

Importance of Rewarding Listening

Rewarding listening is probably the central skill in developing and maintaining helping relationships. Rewarding listening by helpers has a number of important consequences.

Establishing and maintaining rapport   You are more likely to develop effective working relationships with clients if they feel understood by you. For example, a study of helpful and nonhelpful events in brief counseling identified eight kinds of events perceived as helpful by clients (Elliott, 1985). These helpful events were grouped into two superclusters corresponding to interpersonal and task aspects of counseling. Understanding was predominant in the interpersonal grouping.

Helping clients disclose   Clients are often shy and anxious. They may be divulging highly sensitive information. Trust and disclo-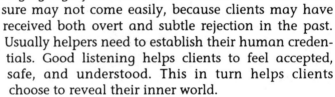sure may not come easily, because clients may have received both overt and subtle rejection in the past. Usually helpers need to establish their human credentials. Good listening helps clients to feel accepted, safe, and understood. This in turn helps clients choose to reveal their inner world.

Helping clients experience and express their feelings   Many clients have been inadequately listened to in their pasts. Consequently, they may have relinquished, temporarily at least, some of their capacity for emotional responsiveness (Rogers, 1959, 1961, 1975). Rewarding listening can help clients acknowledge the inner flow of their emotions. The message some clients may require is that it is OK to experience and express feelings.

Creating a knowledge base   A facetious remark about a psychologist colleague was that he had to ask everyone whether they were male or female, since he was incapable of gathering information without asking questions. If you listen well, most clients collaborate in providing relevant information about themselves. You do not have to interrogate them. Together you build a working model of their problems and problematic skills patterns. Also, at later stages of helping, clients provide you with knowledge about how they use self-helping interventions and about other important life events. Many beginning helpers use questions too much and rewarding listening too little. Some students, however, have the reverse problem.

Creating an influence base   The lifeskills helper is a psychological educator actively influencing clients to develop self-helping skills. Rewarding listening is one way you can build your influence base so that clients are more likely to listen to you. It contributes to clients' perceiving you as competent, trustworthy, and attractive (Strong, 1968, 1978). Also, showing understanding to clients from different cultural groups contributes to your ascribed status and credibility (Sue & Zane, 1987).

Helping clients assume responsibility   Clients who are listened to sharply and supportively are more likely to assume responsibility for working on their problems and problematic skills than those who are not. One reason is that rewarding listening may reduce defensiveness. Another reason is that rewarding listening provides a base for offering well-timed confrontations that encourage clients to assume rather than to avoid responsibility.

Reflective Responding

Rewarding listening requires helpers not only to understand clients' communications accurately, but also to make verbal responses showing accurate understanding. Helpers provide the gift of their listening so that clients genuinely feel understood. Sometimes, responding as if within clients' internal viewpoints is called empathy (Rogers, 1957, 1962, 1975, 1980). Rogers describes empathy likewise: "To sense the client's inner world of private personal meanings as if it were your own, but without ever losing the 'as if' quality, this is empathy. . ." (Rogers, 1962, p. 419). Rogers emphasizes the importance of helpers "communicating your sensings of his/her world as you look with fresh and unfrightened eyes at elements of which the individual is fearful. . ." (Rogers, 1975, p.4). Furthermore, clients need to perceive that helpers empathically understand them, or at the very least communicate the intent to understand (Barrett-Lennard, 1962, 1981; Rogers, 1962).

In Rogers' person-centered helping empathic reflections are the helper's major tool. Rogers' use of empathy particularly focuses on the construct of experiencing (Gendlin, 1962). He attempts to improve the quantity and quality of his clients' inner listening to the ongoing flow of experience within them. This flow is a referent to which clients can repeatedly turn to discover the meaning of their experience, so that they can move forward in it. One study showed that over 53 percent of Rogers' verbal responses fell in the reflection/restatement category, whereas

Lazarus, a more eclectic and task-oriented helper, had only 10 percent of responses in this category (Lee & Uhlemann, 1984).

In lifeskills helping the term *reflective responding* is shorthand for "responding with understanding as if in the client's internal viewpoint." Reflective responding entails tuning into and mirroring with your own verbal, voice, and body messages the crux of the meaning contained in your clients' verbal, voice, and body messages. In lifeskills helping, reflective responding is just  one of the skills (albeit extremely important) that helpers use to help clients manage problems and problematic skill patterns. Helpers use reflective responding not only to build relationships, but also to develop clients' specific skills. The term *reflective responding* is preferred to "empathy" or "empathic responding" for two reasons. First, the word *reflection* more closely describes the process. Second, the term avoids confusion with Rogers' use of empathy. Rogers preferred not to think of empathy as a skill, but as an attitude (Rogers, 1951) or way of being (Rogers, 1975). Rogers' therapeutic goal was to help people become more in touch with their inner valuing process rather than to develop specific lifeskills. Before discussing some component skills of reflective responding, here are a few examples:

> **Patient:** When I first heard I had terminal cancer, my world fell apart. I'm still reeling and frightened at the thought of death.
> **Nurse:** You still feel shaken and scared by the diagnosis of terminal cancer.

> **Woman:** With the children nearing the end of their education, I want to build more of a life for myself. I don't want to hang around the house all the time.
> **Career counselor:** You're determined to carve something for yourself outside the home and not keep brooding over an empty nest.

When helping students are first introduced to the skill of reflective responding, many express reservations.

> "It's so unnatural."
> "Clients will just think I'm repeating everything they say."
> "It gets in the way of my being spontaneous."
> "It makes me too self-conscious."

When learning any new skill (driving a car, or swimming), at first you have to concentrate extra hard to make the correct sequence of choices that constitute the skill. Ultimately, if you work and practice at reflective responding, you are likely to gain fluency in it. Then reflective responding will both appear and feel "natural."

Reflective responding should not be something you use all the time; instead you need to be flexible about incorporating such responses into your helping skills repertoire. Reflective responses may help on many occasions:

- When creating a safe emotional climate for clients to tell their stories
- When you need to show that you have understood
- When you need to check out that you have understood
- When clients struggle to get in touch with thoughts and feelings
- When clients need to experience their thoughts and feelings as valid
- When you want to ensure that clients assume responsibility for their thoughts and feelings independent of what you may think
- When clients need a reward or emotional stepping-stone to continue talking
- When you check out clients' understanding of specific points

REWARDING LISTENING: A 10 SKILLS APPROACH

The remainder of this chapter describes 10 key skills of rewarding listening. Each of these skills entails choices on the part of helpers. How well you implement these skills has consequences for both you and your clients. As a practitioner-researcher you need not only become aware of your rewarding listening choices, but also evaluate their consequences. Many of the following skills overlap:

Skill 1: Know the difference between you and me.
Skill 2: Possess an attitude of respect and acceptance.
Skill 3: Send good body messages.
Skill 4: Send good voice messages.
Skill 5: Use openers, small rewards, and open-ended questions.
Skill 6: Reword.
Skill 7: Reflect feelings.
Skill 8: Reflect feelings and reasons.
Skill 9: Avoid unrewarding don'ts.
Skill 10: Avoid poor thinking skills.

Skill 1: Know the Difference between You and Me

Don't judge any person until you have walked
two moons in their moccasins.

—Native American Proverb

For clients to feel you receive them loud and clear, you need to develop the ability to "walk in their moccasins," "get inside their skins," and "see the world through their eyes." At the heart of rewarding listening is a basic distinction between "you" and "me," between "your view of you" and "my view of you," and between "your view of me" and "my view of me." Your view of you and my view of me are both inside (internal) viewpoints, whereas your view of me and my view of you are both outside (external) viewpoints. The skill of listening to and understanding another person is based on your choosing to acknowledge the separateness between "you" and "me" by getting inside the other's internal viewpoint rather than remaining in your own external viewpoint.

If you respond to what clients say in ways that show accurate understanding of their viewpoints, you respond as if you are inside their internal viewpoints. Such responses do not mean you agree with them, simply that you acknowledge that what they say is their subjective reality. If, however, you choose not to show understanding of your clients' viewpoints or lack the skills to understand them, you are responding from your external viewpoint. In short, if you respond to clients as if inside their internal viewpoints, you respond to them from where they are. If you step outside your clients' internal viewpoints, you respond either from where you are or where you think they should be. Here are some helper comments from an external viewpoint:

"What can I do for you?"
"I think you should always respect your parents."
"Why don't you drop him/her? He/she is not helping you get
   better."
"You are going to be all right."
"I think you have paranoid tendencies."
"You should consider taking tranquilizers during your exam
   week."

Responding from your clients' internal viewpoints entails understanding what they say on their terms. You need to listen carefully and allow clients the psychological space to tell their own stories. Understanding their internal viewpoints also entails decoding clients' messages, especially when they are not clearly sent. The following are examples of internal viewpoint comments by helpers:

> "You're elated at passing your math test."
> "You feel that often people don't look beyond your blindness to discover what sort of a person you are."
> "You find getting fired in a recession a terrifying prospect."
> "You have mixed feelings about your in-laws."
> "You've found immigration a much bigger adjustment than anticipated."
> "You feel really good that your daughter phoned on your birthday."

Think of a three-link chain: client statement–helper response–client statement. If helpers respond from clients' internal viewpoints, they allow them either to continue on the same path or to choose a change of direction. However, if helpers respond from the external viewpoint, they influence clients to divert from paths they would have chosen on their own. Sometimes such external influence is desirable, but frequently it is not. In all instances, helpers need to make conscious choices about whether to respond from the clients' internal viewpoints.

Skill 2: Possess an Attitude of Respect and Acceptance

An accepting attitude involves respecting clients as separate and unique human beings with rights to their own thoughts and feelings independent of yours. Carl Rogers, the founder of person-centered therapy, which heavily emphasizes helpers' being accepting, grew up afraid that if he said anything significant to his mother she would judge it negatively (Heppner, Rogers, & Lee, 1984). An accepting attitude entails suspending judgment on people's goodness or badness. All humans are fallible and possess lifeskills strengths and weaknesses that may have good or bad consequences for themselves and others.

Barriers to an Accepting Attitude

As a helper you need to be psychologically present to clients. This entails an absence of defensiveness and a willingness to allow clients' expressions and experiencing to affect you. Ideally, you should be "all there"—with your body, your thoughts, your senses, and your emotions. Psychological accessibility entails your possessing an accepting attitude not only to clients, but also to yourself. Put simply, a confident person's acceptance of self translates into acceptance of others, whereas the reverse is also true.

Barriers to an accepting attitude manifest themselves both in how you think and how you act. They manifest themselves internally in that helpers may operate on, distort, and filter out certain parts of clients' messages. At worst, you may deny or block out the whole of an incoming message. Barriers operate externally in subtle and not-so-subtle verbal, voice, and body cues to clients, indicating that they should edit what they say. The following are some barriers likely to influence how you listen.

Anxiety-evoking feelings   Clients can express feelings that helpers find hard to handle (for instance, feeling very depressed or even very happy). Helpers may feel threatened by feelings directed toward them (for instance, hostility or liking). Alternatively, helper anxiety may be evoked by the intensity of clients' feelings about others (for instance, envy of a sibling or grief over a bereavement).

Nina, 25, a beginning helper, listened to Stan pour out his resentment over his girlfriend Eva's behavior. Nina was uncomfortable when people became angry. Even though none of Stan's anger was directed toward her, she started feeling very anxious and wondered whether the interview would get out of control.

Anxiety-evoking clients   Helpers may find themselves feeling threatened by certain categories of clients: for example, clients of the opposite sex, seriously disturbed clients, highly successful clients, very intelligent clients, and clients who hold strong feelings with which the helper disagrees.

Penny, 29, a trainee counselor, became uncomfortable when faced with Hank, a sexually active homosexual client. Her discomfort stemmed not from prejudice about gays, but from feeling out of her depth in relating to his life experiences. She was aware that her anxiety about coping made it even harder to empathize with Hank.

Anxiety-evoking situations   Anxiety and threat are present in all helping situations. The following are some common situations where helpers may feel vulnerable, and so their own agendas may preclude their fully listening to clients.

- The first few minutes of an initial session
- Concentrating on developing new skills as well as on their clients

- Finding difficulty formulating a working definition of a problem
- Feeling that progress is too slow
- A client coming late for an appointment
- Recording an interview for supervision

Trigger words, phrases, and attitudes Trigger words, phrases, and attitudes raise a red flag for you. Each helper has his or her own emotionally charged triggers. For example, some helpers are triggered by sexist comments, some by prejudice against gays, some by cross-cultural put-downs, and some by racist comments. Trigger phrases can also be "You" messages from clients to helpers (for example, "You screwed up," "You don't understand," or "You're not helping me enough."

Abe, 31, a Jewish helper, has to work hard to listen to anyone who expresses racist attitudes. Recently Abe had a client, Wayne, who started using the term nigger. *Abe became so angry that, for some moments, he lost sight of his client's vulnerability.*

Sarah, a trainee group therapist who had been raped, allowed herself to be triggered by Carlos, an advanced cancer patient who was a new entrant to her group. Carlos belittled the experiences of rape victims and ended by saying he would welcome a rape attempt by any woman in the group. At this last remark, Sarah said, "If you believe that, you're fucking ignorant!" (Yalom, 1989, p. 70).

Positive words and phrases can also trigger feelings that interfere with your listening (for example, flattery like "Gee, you're wonderful, Ms. Murgatroyd").

Being prejudiced Helpers are not immune from varying degrees of prejudice. For reasons connected with your upbringing, you may tune out people different from you because of their age, sex, sexual preference, culture, race, social class, physical disability, or intelligence level, among other possible differences.

Dale, 27, dislikes working with elderly clients. He not only tries to avoid seeing them, but also withdraws from forming close helping relationships with them. He rationalizes his behavior by saying that he is much more used to spending time with younger clients.

Unfinished business Unfinished business can interfere with your being open to clients. For instance, if you have just come from an argumentative staff meeting, you may be less ready to listen and accept your next client. If you have rushed to get to a session, you may not listen adequately until you have calmed down. You may suddenly think about something said in an earlier helping session and fail to attend to the present. In addition, you may have brought intrusive personal worries with you to helping.

Presenting a professional facade   Genuineness is an important characteristic for helpers (Rogers, 1957, 1975). A difference exists between being genuine and seeming genuine. Some helpers are too concerned with maintaining a smooth professional facade. Their concern with how clients perceive them may interfere with perceiving their clients accurately. Such helpers are too busy listening to their own needs to accept clients fully. Maintaining a professional facade is especially difficult when clients directly challenge your professional adequacy.

Danny, 26, a psychology student on placement at his university's student counseling service, worries that clients will see he is not yet fully competent. He puts on an act by being too friendly and trying to appear too expert. He takes control rather than forming collaborative working alliances with clients.

Emotional exhaustion and burnout   Helpers often possess a combination of difficult environments, demanding clients, and poor skills at setting limits on their involvement. Freudenberger (1980) defines burnout: "To deplete oneself. To exhaust one's physical and mental resources. To wear oneself out by excessively striving to reach some unrealistic expectation imposed by one's self or by the values of society" (p. 17). Emotionally exhausted helpers may be less accepting of clients than when they feel well. Their energy level and sense of personal accomplishment are low. Helping relationships, instead of being positive challenges, can become endurance tests.

Patricia, 43, is a social worker with a heavy caseload. She is highly conscientious and worries a lot about what happens to her clients. Recently she has been feeling depressed, irritable, and very tired. Patricia has to drag herself to work and feels anxious much of the time. She is not doing her best work.

Insufficient administrative support   Helpers in institutions may spend much time securing budgets, ensuring their role is understood, and dealing with other administrative matters. Frequently they lack adequate secretarial support. Insufficient administrative support can undermine morale, increase caseloads, and involve helpers in routine secretarial and administrative chores. A casualty can be how accepting helpers are of clients.

Physical barriers Physical barriers may contribute to your being less accepting of clients than desirable. For example, you may be too hot or too cold, you may lack privacy, your room may be dreary, your chair may be uncomfortable, the lighting may be poor, or there may be too much noise.

Helen is a counseling trainee who is required to interview high school "clients" assigned to her. There is a shortage of suitable interview rooms. On some occasions the only room available is one that has glass windows facing the corridor. Though the room is quiet, Helen feels distracted by the lack of privacy for herself and her clients.

So far we have discussed 10 barriers and filters to your adopting an attitude of respect and acceptance for your clients. Some of the barriers stem solely from you. Some originate in the environment. In both cases, helpers can choose how to react. The list is far from exhaustive. You may think of other barriers and filters applicable to you.

Skill 3: Send Good Body Messages

Helpers always send messages to clients. To be a rewarding person with whom to talk you need to convey your receptiveness and interest physically. Often this is referred to as attending behavior (Ivey, 1988; Ivey, Ivey, & Simek-Downing, 1987). Body messages are the main helper responses *during* a client's verbal utterances. A simple example may highlight the point. Imagine a helper looking out of the window at the start of a session as the client describes a sensitive personal problem. Congruence, both within your body messages and among your verbal, voice, and body messages, increases the chances of rewarding listening. The following are some of the main body messages that demonstrate interest and attention. In varying degrees they provide nonverbal rewards for talking.

Availability Helpers may sometimes (rightly or wrongly) be perceived as insufficiently available to the client. You may be overworked. You may be poor at letting your availability be known. Intentionally or unintentionally you may send messages that create distance. For instance, teachers may physically edge away from pupils who wish to discuss personal concerns. You need to be clear about the messages you convey to clients and others as to your availability.

Relaxed body posture   A relaxed body posture, without slumping or slouching, contributes to the message that you are receptive. If you sit in a tense and uptight fashion, your clients may consciously or intuitively feel that you are too bound up in your personal agendas and unfinished business to be fully accessible to them.

Physical openness   Physical openness means facing speakers with both your face and body. Trainers such as Carkhuff and Egan recommend sitting square to clients, your left shoulder opposite their right shoulder (Carkhuff, 1983; Egan, 1990). However, another option is to sit at a slight angle. Both of you can still receive all of each other's significant facial and bodily messages. The advantage is that each of you has more discretion in varying the directness of your eye contact. Highly vulnerable clients may especially appreciate this seating arrangement.

Slight forward lean   Whether you lean forward, backward, or sideways is another aspect of your body posture. If you lean too far forward you look odd and clients may feel you invade their personal space. If you lean too far back, clients may find this distancing. Especially at the start of helping, leaning slightly forward can encourage clients without threatening them.

Gaze and eye contact   *Gaze,* or looking at people in the area of their faces, is a way both to show interest and to receive facial messages. Women are usually more attentive than men on all measures of gaze (Henley, 1977; Argyle, 1983). Gaze can give you cues about when to stop listening and start responding. However, the main cues used in synchronizing conversation are verbal and voice messages, rather than body messages (Argyle, 1983). *Eye contact* means meeting your clients' eyes. Good eye contact entails arriving at a comfortable level of contact for each client. Staring threatens clients: They may feel dominated or seen through. Some clients even feel threatened at seeing their reflections in shop windows! Clients may perceive you as tense or bored if you look down or away too often.

Appropriate facial expressions   Your face is probably your main vehicle for sending body messages. Ekman, Friesen, and

Ellsworth identified seven main expressions of emotion: happiness, interest, surprise, fear, sadness, anger, and disgust or contempt (Ekman, Friesen, & Ellsworth, 1972). Much facial information is conveyed through the mouth and eyebrows. A friendly, relaxed facial expression, including a smile, usually demonstrates interest. However, during clients' communications, vary your face to show that you understand their emotions (for example, look concerned at bad news).

Appropriate gestures   Perhaps the most common gesture in helping is the head nod. Each head nod can be viewed as a reward to clients, signifying interest. On the negative side, selective head nodding can also control clients. Unconditional acceptance becomes conditional. Arm and hand gestures can also be used to demonstrate responsiveness. However, helpers using expressive arm gestures too much or too little can be off-putting. Other negative gestures include tightly crossing arms and legs, clenching hands, drumming fingers, fiddling with hair or eyeglasses, keeping a hand over your mouth, tugging an ear, and scratching yourself.

Sensitivity to physical proximity and height   Rewarding listening entails respecting clients' personal space. Helpers can be too close or too far away. Perhaps a comfortable physical distance for helpers and clients is sitting with their heads about 5 feet apart. In Western cultures clients might perceive any less distance as too personal (Hall, 1966; Pease, 1981). On the other hand, if helpers are physically too far away not only do clients have to talk louder, but they may perceive you as emotionally distant. The most comfortable height for helping conversations is with heads at the same level. This fact is forgotten by some helpers who sit in higher and more elaborate chairs than clients.

Appropriate use of touch   Use of touch may be appropriate in helping, though care needs to be taken that it is not an unwanted invasion of personal space (Bacorn & Dixon, 1984). For example, demonstrations of concern may include touching a client's hands, arms, shoulders, and upper back. The intensity and duration of touch should be sufficient to establish contact yet avoid discomfort and any hint of sexual interest. Touch is an area in which helpers need to proceed with great caution.

Clothing and grooming   Helpers' clothes send messages that may influence how much and in which areas clients reveal themselves. These messages include social and occupational standing, sex-role identity, ethnicity, conformity to peer group norms, rebelliousness, and how outgoing you are. While maintaining your individuality, you need to dress appropriately for your clientele (for example, delinquent teenagers probably respond better to informally dressed helpers than do stressed business executives). Your personal grooming also provides important information about how well you take care of yourself (for instance, you may be clean or dirty, neat or tidy). In addition, the length and style of your hair sends messages about you.

The concept of rules is very important for understanding the appropriateness of body messages (Argyle & Henderson, 1985; Argyle, 1986). For example, I have mentioned differing physical proximity rules depending on whether you are in a personal or helping relationship. Relationship rules also differ across cultures. For instance, Arabs and Latin Americans stand very close by Western standards. You require sensitivity to the body message rules of the social and cultural contexts in which you work as well as to your own and clients' individual needs.

Helpers require flexibility in making rewarding listening choices. As your helping relationships develop, clients get to know whether and when you are receptive to them. For instance, clients may know from experience that when you lean back you still attend. Sometimes it is better to withdraw message cues of interest and attention. Occasions where such withdrawal may be desirable include: needing to check out your understanding of clients' messages, keeping clients focused on agendas relevant to their problems, and thinking it important that clients receive input from you.

most Common-speaking too quickly

Skill 4: Send Good Voice Messages

Your voice messages can greatly enhance the emotional atmosphere when you listen. When supervising beginning counseling students, I pay great attention to how they use their voice to frame verbal responses to clients. The two most common faults are speaking too quickly and too softly; both indicate anxiety. Your voice can speak volumes about what you truly feel and how emotionally responsive you are to clients' feelings. Helpers may use verbal messages very little during clients' verbal utterances, perhaps restricting them to "uh-hmms." However, voice messages always accompany verbal responses; they are an integral part of rewarding listening. The following are five dimensions of voice messages. They form the acronym VAPER (Volume, Articulation, Pitch, Emphasis and Rate).

Volume Volume refers to loudness or quietness. You need to respond at a level of audibility that is comfortable and easy to hear. Some helpers have the bad habit of fading, letting their voices trail away at the end of sentences. Sometimes helpers unnecessarily quiet their voices to match those of clients. While a booming voice overwhelms, speaking in too quiet a voice may make you appear weak.

Articulation Articulation refers to the distinctness and clarity of speech. Helpers may speak with adequate loudness, but still be difficult to understand. You must enunciate words clearly. Helpers possessing excessively nasal, guttural, or throaty voices might consider speech therapy. Some helpers need to modify strong regional or foreign accents.

Pitch Pitch refers to the highness or lowness of voice. An optimal pitch range includes all the levels at which a pleasing voice can be produced without strain (Kruger, 1970). Errors of pitch include being either too high-pitched or too low-pitched. Helpers' voices may be higher pitched when anxious than when calm.

Emphasis It is important that your voice is expressive in picking up the major feelings and feeling nuances of speakers. Helpers may use emphasis in the wrong places. Additionally, you may use too much emphasis, and seem melodramatic, or too little emphasis, and seem wooden.

Rate Speech rate is often measured in words per minute. Speech rate depends both on how quickly words are spoken and on the frequency and duration of pauses between them. A rapid helper speech rate may contribute to keeping clients anxious rather than calming them down. Often it is a good idea for beginning helping students to speak more slowly. A slower speech rate helps them appear less nervous and also provides more time to think of what to say.

Your use of pauses and silences can also enhance your capacity to be a rewarding listener. If you want to make it easier for clients to tell their stories, you can pause each time they cease speaking before responding, to see if they wish to continue. Good use of silences can also allow speakers more psychological space both to think things through before speaking and to get more in touch with feelings. Some helping students find silences threatening; they have to work on tendencies to speak too soon.

Skill 5: Use Openers, Small Rewards, and Open-Ended Questions

Openers, small rewards, and open-ended questions tend to require using few words, as well as sending voice and body messages. They make it easier for clients to talk.

Openers

Lifeskills helping always starts with checking where the client is. Helpers are not all-knowing. Openers, or permissions to talk, are brief statements indicating that helpers are prepared to listen. Often helpers start initial sessions with a brief opener that encourages clients to share why they have come. Helpers may leave until later in the session a fuller statement of how they work. Openers give clients the message "I'm interested and prepared to listen. Please share with me your internal viewpoint." Examples of openers that might be used in initial helping sessions include:

Hello, I'm _____. Please
    tell me why you've come.
    tell me why you're here.
    tell me what's concerning you.
    tell me what's the problem.
    put me in the picture.
You've been referred by _____. Now, how do you
    see your situation?

Sometimes helpers make opening statements in response to client body messages.

"You seem upset. Would you care to say what's bothering
    you?"
"You seem very nervous."

The statement "You seem very nervous" gives clients the opportunity to talk either about a problem they bring to helping or about how they feel here-and-now in the interview. Helpers can sometimes give permission to talk by body messages alone (for instance, a look, possibly accompanied by an arm gesture).

Some helpers have contacts with clients outside formal interviews (for instance, correctional officers in facilities for delinquents, residential staff in half-way houses for former drug addicts, or nurses in hospitals). You may use "permissions" to talk when you sense that someone has a bothersome personal agenda but needs a bit of encouragement to share it. Openers for use in informal helping include:

"Is there something on your mind?"
"You seem tense today."
"I'm available if you want to talk."

Small Rewards

Small rewards are brief verbal and nonverbal expressions of interest designed to encourage clients to continue speaking. The message they convey is "I'm with you. Please go on." Wrongly used small rewards can encourage clients to respond to their helpers rather than to themselves. For instance, you may say "Tell me more" whenever clients talk about topics of interest to you. Many small rewards are body rather than verbal messages (for example, facial expressions, head nods, and good eye contact). The following are examples of verbal small rewards, though perhaps the frequently used "Uh-hmm" is more a voice than a verbal message.

"Uh-hmm"	"Sure"
"Please continue"	"Indeed"
"Tell me more"	"And . . ."
"Go on"	"So . . ."
"I see"	"Really"
"Oh?"	"Right"
"Then . . ."	"Yes"
"I hear you"	"You're not kidding"

Another kind of small reward is to repeat the last word a client has said:

Client: I'm feeling nervous.
Helper: Nervous . . .

Open-Ended Questions and Cues

Helpers may use questions in ways that either help clients to elaborate their internal viewpoints or lead them out of their viewpoints and possibly into yours. Open-ended questions or cues allow clients to share their internal viewpoints without curtailing their options. A good time for open-ended questions is when, in the initial session, you wish to assist clients to tell their stories. In subsequent sessions too, you are likely to find open-ended cues useful. They include: "Tell me about it"; "Please elaborate"; and, slightly less open-ended, "How do you feel about that?" Open-ended questions and cues may be contrasted with closed-ended ones that curtail speakers' options (for example, "Tell me whether or not you like your boss"). Open-ended questions may be contrasted to leading questions that put answers into clients' mouths (for example, "How do you feel about her? She's a great person, isn't she?").

Skill 6: Rewording

Visualize a helping session between a client and a parrot. The parrot repeats precisely everything the client says. It is important to reword or paraphrase, because you drive speakers crazy if you parrot them. Rewording focuses on the verbal content of what clients say. Sometimes rewording is termed *reflection of content*. Focusing only on the verbal content of clients' messages is a first step in learning to respond to their combined voice, body, and verbal messages. When you reword, you may sometimes use the client's words, but sparingly. Try to stay close to the kind of language they use. Here are a few examples:

Patient: I'm finding it difficult to swallow.
Speech therapist: You're having trouble swallowing.

Parishioner: I'm delighted that you've come back to our church.
Priest: You're pleased to have me back in the parish.

Parent: I told my kids to go to hell.
Family counselor: You were real mad at them.

Employee: Some of the time I like my work here, but some of the time I'm less positive.
Manager: You have mixed feelings about what you do here.

A good rewording of verbal content can provide mirror reflections that are clearer and more succinct than original statements. Clients may show appreciation with comments such as "That's right" or "You've got me." A simple tip for rewording is to start your responses with the personal pronoun *you* to indicate that you reflect clients' internal viewpoints. Another tip is to slow your speech rate down to give you more time to think. You need a good memory and a good command of vocabulary to reword. To become confident, flexibile and fluent in the skill requires much practice.

Skill 7: Reflecting Feelings

Skilled helpers are very sharp at picking up clients' feelings. Reflecting feelings is both similar to, yet different from, rewording. Both reflecting feelings and rewording involve mirroring. Also, reflecting feelings usually involves rewording. However, the language of feelings is not words. Feelings are bodily sensations that may then have word labels attached to them. Consequently, rewording alone has distinct limitations. For example, clients may send voice and body messages that qualify—or negate—verbal messages. Gino says "I'm OK," yet speaks softly and has tearful eyes. A good reflection of feelings picks up these other messages as well. Reflecting feelings entails responding to clients' music and not just to their lyrics. To do this, helper responses incorporate appropriate voice and body messages.

Reflecting feelings may be viewed as *feeling with* a client's flow of emotions and experience and being able to communicate this back. Helping students often have trouble with the notion of reflecting feelings. They may just talk about feelings rather than offer an expressive emotional companionship. Inadequately distinguishing between thoughts and feelings can be another problem for both clients and helpers. For example, "I feel that equality between the sexes is essential" describes a thought rather than a feeling. On the other hand, "I feel angry when I see sex discrimination" labels a feeling. This distinction between thoughts and feelings is important both in reflecting feelings and when helping clients to influence how they feel by altering how they think. Constant reflective responding focused on feelings runs the risk of encouraging clients to wallow in feelings rather than to choose how to deal with them. Reflecting feelings involves both receiver and sender skills.

Receiver Skills

- Understanding clients' face and body messages
- Understanding clients' voice messages
- Understanding clients' verbal messages
- Tuning in to the flow of your own emotional reactions
- Taking into account the context of clients' messages
- Sensing the surface and underlying meanings of clients' messages

Sender Skills

- Responding in ways that pick up clients' feeling words and phrases
- Rewording feelings appropriately, using expressive rather than wooden language
- Using voice and body messages that neither add to nor detract from the emotions conveyed
- Checking out the accuracy of your understanding

Picking Up Feeling Words and Phrases

A good but not infallible way to find out what clients feel is to listen to their feeling words and phrases. Picking up feeling words and phrases is similar to rewording, but with a heightened focus on feelings rather than informational content. Sometimes helping students ask "Well, what did you feel?" after clients have just told them. They need to discipline their listening. Feeling phrases are colloquial expressions used to describe feelings words. For example, "I've got the blues" is a feeling phrase describing the word depressed. Following is a list of feeling words. Incidentally, it is cumbersome, when reflecting feelings, always to put "You feel" before feeling words; sometimes "You're" is sufficient (for example, "You're sad" instead of "You feel sad").

Feeling Words

accepted	confused	guilt-free	optimistic
adventurous	contented	guilty	outgoing
affectionate	cooperative	happy	pessimistic
aggressive	daring	humiliated	powerful
ambitious	decisive	hurt	powerless
angry	dependent	indecisive	rejected
anxious	depressed	independent	relaxed
apathetic	discontented	inferior	resentful
appreciated	embarrassed	insecure	responsible
assertive	energetic	interested	sad
attractive	envious	involved	secure
bored	excited	irresponsible	shy
carefree	fit	jealous	stressed
cautious	free	joyful	strong
cheerful	friendly	lonely	superior
competitive	frightened	loved	supported
confident	grieving	loving	suspicious

tense	unassertive	unfree	uptight
tired	unattractive	unfriendly	vulnerable
trusting	underconfident	unloved	wanted
unambitious	uneasy	unsupported	weak
unappreciated	unfit	unwanted	worried

The following are some dimensions of words and phrases that reflect feelings.

Intensity Try to mirror the intensity of clients' feeling words when you reword. For example, Imran has just had a negative experience about which he might feel either "devastated" (strong intensity), "upset" (moderate intensity), or "slightly upset" (weak intensity). Corresponding helper rewordings might be either "overwhelmed" (strong intensity), "distressed" (moderate intensity), or "a little distressed" (weak intensity). It is possible to either add or subtract intensity incorrectly.

Multiple and mixed feelings Sometimes clients use many words to describe their feelings. The words may form a cluster around the same theme, in which case you may choose only to reword the core of the feeling. Alternatively, clients may have varying degrees of mixed feelings ranging from simple opposites (for instance, happy/sad) to more complex combinations (for instance, hurt/angry). Good rewordings pick up all key elements of feelings messages. For instance:

Client: I'm sorry, but also relieved, not to get the promotion.
Helper: You're upset, but it's a weight off your shoulders.

Client: I like being with her, but I also like being on my own.
Helper: You appreciate her companionship, but enjoy your own too.

Assisting labeling of feelings Sometimes helpers assist clients in finding the right feeling words. Here reflecting feelings goes beyond rewording to helping choose words that seem right to them.

Client: I don't quite know how to express my reaction to losing my job. Possibly angry. Upset—no that's not quite it. Bewildered. . .
Helper: Hurt, anxious, confused—are any of these words appropriate?

Picking Up Voice and Body Messages

Much information about clients' feelings comes not from what they say but how they say it. Sometimes their verbal, voice, and body messages are congruent. In such instances, it is relatively easy to label feelings and intensity accurately. However, frequently clients' messages are heavily encoded. Clients may struggle to express what they *truly* feel in face of their conditioning about what they *should* feel. Also, it takes time for clients to trust helpers. Consequently, many emotional messages are indirect rather than loud and clear. Effective helpers are skilled at listening to clients' voice and body messages and to what is left unsaid or camouflaged. Also, helpers realize certain clients take time to develop skills of clearly identifying and articulating feelings. You need to be sensitive to the pace at which clients can work. Often they require patience rather than pressure.

Helpers unclear about clients' real or underlying feelings can check with them. For instance, you may make comments like "I think I hear you saying (state feelings tentatively). . . Am I right?" or "I would like to understand what you're feeling, but I'm still not altogether clear. Can you help me?" Another option is to say "I'm getting a mixed message from you. On the one hand you say you do not mind. On the other hand you seem tearful." After a pause, you might add "I'm wondering if you are putting on a brave face."

A further consideration in picking up feelings is to understand whether and to what extent clients possess insight into their feelings. For instance, as a helper you may infer that a parent is absolutely furious with a child. However, the parent may not be able to handle such an observation, since it clashes with the self-image of being a loving parent. Consequently, you may need to pick up three feelings: first, the parent's stated feeling of unconditional love for the child; second, the underlying anger with the child; and third, the feeling of threat if the parent's self-picture were challenged by your reflecting the anger you see.

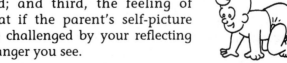

Sender Skills of Reflecting Feelings

When reflecting feelings, you may wonder how best to respond to the numerous verbal, voice, and body messages you have received. There are no simple answers. What you try to do is (1) decode the overall message accurately, and (2) formulate an emotionally expressive reflective response that communicates back the crux of the client's feelings. Here are a few guidelines for sending reflecting feelings messages.

1. *Send back the crux of the client's message.* Where possible, show that you have understood the client's main message or messages. Whatever else you do, communicate back the core feeling.

> **Client:** We just argue and argue and don't seem to get anywhere. I don't know what to do. It's so frustrating. I wish I knew the answer. I don't seem to be able to handle our relationship.
> **Helper:** You're extremely frustrated with constant unproductive arguments and not knowing how to improve matters.

2. *Be sensitive to clients' underlying feelings and agendas.* Sometimes there are no hidden agendas in what clients communicate. On other occasions, you may help them to articulate underlying feelings. However, sometimes you might intentionally not respond to underlying feelings and agendas. For example, clients may require more time to acknowledge the feelings on their own. Alternatively, they may not be ready for a deeper reflection. Also, when making deeper reflections, you run a greater risk of being wrong than when making surface reflections.

3. *Keep your response appropriately simple.* Use simple, clear language. Avoid unnecessary words and qualifications. However, be prepared to state different parts of multiple and mixed messages.

4. *Use voice and body messages to add expressiveness to your verbal messages.* You are not just talking about feelings, you are *reflecting* feelings. For instance, if a hypothetical suicide-prone client says "I feel terrible," you can adjust your voice and facial expression to mirror, to some extent, a sense of desperation. Congruence among your verbal, voice, and body messages is important. If you send mixed messages you may be perceived as insincere.

5. *State the client's main feeling at the front of your response.* Even though the clients may not start with their main feeling, they may feel better understood by you if you reflect their main feeling at the front of your response than if you reflect information first.

> **Client:** I've failed my statistics exam and have to repeat it. I'm so disappointed.
> **Helper:** You're bitterly disappointed at failing.

In this example, the helper has tuned in to feelings immediately. Imagine that the helper had replied "You failed your stats test and are bitterly disappointed." The helper has responded first to the client's head. By the time the helper reflects the feeling of disappointment, it may be too late for the client to experience being emotionally understood.

6. *Check out your understanding.* You respond to client statements with different degrees of tentativeness depending on how clearly they have communicated and how confident you are about receiving their messages accurately. However, all reflective responses should contain an element of checking whether you accurately understand your clients' internal viewpoints. Sometimes checking out may be achieved by slight voice inflections. On other occasions, you may check more explicitly.

Skill 8: Reflecting Feelings and Reasons

A useful variation of reflective responding is to reflect both feelings and the reasons for them. Reflecting reasons does not mean that you interpret or explain from your external viewpoint. Instead, where clients have already provided reasons for a feeling, you reflect these feelings back in a "You feel. . . because. . ." statement that mirrors the other's internal viewpoint. Here is an example:

Todd: I've struggled so hard to get to the end of the course and now I'm afraid I'm going to fail the last semester.
Helper: You're worried because you might fail after all that effort.
Todd: Yes. I get anxious just thinking of all the time I may have wasted.

Here the helper's "You feel. . . because. . ." response showed more understanding of Todd's predicament than if the response had stopped after "You're worried." Todd was able to emphasize that the meaning of passing was not only to get through the course, but also to avoid wasting so much time and effort. Put another way, the "because" part of the helper's response identified the thinking that contributed to Todd's feeling. Thus, "You feel. . . because. . ." reflections are useful, not only for helping clients tell their stories, but also for assessing how clients' thinking contributes to unwanted feelings.

Skill 9: Avoid Unrewarding Don'ts

If clients are going to self-disclose, explore problems and problematic skills, and experience their feelings more fully, they require psychological safety and space. Don't spoil your listening by sending clumsy verbal messages. Psychological safety and space are both quantitative and qualitative. If you are rarely accessible in person, or if, when present, you monopolize or keep interrupting, you are not giving clients the quantity of psychological safety and space they need. However, helpers can also deprive clients of the quality of safety and space they need by responding in ways that show lack of respect for their internal viewpoints. Showing such lack of respect not only makes it more difficult for clients to talk to you, but it also interferes with their inner listening. Clients may both block material from awareness and be more inclined to edit what they disclose for fear of disapproval.

Following are some ways that helpers communicate to clients that they are not totally safe and free to talk. I don't mean to imply you should never use any of them. You simply need be aware of their possible negative consequences before choosing to use them.

- *Directing and leading:* Taking control of what the client can talk about (for example, "I would like you to start with what happened to you when you were a child").
- *Judging and evaluating:* Making evaluative statements, especially ones implying that the client does not live up to your own standards (for example, "You are overpossessive of your children").
- *Blaming:* Assigning responsibility for what happens to clients in a finger-pointing way (for example, "It's all your fault").
- *Moralizing, preaching, and patronizing:* Telling clients how they should be leading their lives (for example, "People who help others are usually happier than those who live for themselves").
- *Labeling and diagnosing:* Placing superficial diagnostic categories on clients and their behavior (for example, "You're paranoid" or "You have an inferiority complex").
- *Reassuring and humoring:* Trying to make clients feel better, yet not acknowledging their true feelings (for example, "You'll be all right. Don't worry").
- *Not accepting clients' feelings:* Telling clients that their positive or negative feelings should be different from what they are (for example, "You've got no reason to be so depressed").
- *Advising and teaching:* Not giving clients the space to arrive at their own solutions (for example, "Why don't you go around to see her and try to make things up?").
- *Interrogating:* Using questions in ways that threaten clients with unwanted probing (for example, "Tell me about your weaknesses? Be specific").

- *Overinterpreting*: Offering explanations that come from your internal viewpoint and that bear little similarity to what clients might have thought (for example, "Your indecision about choosing a career is related to your fear of failing to live up to your father's perfectionist standards").
- *Inappropriately self-disclosing:* Talking about yourself in ways that interfere with clients' disclosures (for example, "You have troubles. Let me tell you mine").
- *Putting on a professional facade:* Trying to make yourself seem an expert and thereby communicating in a defensive or otherwise inauthentic way (for example, "I've had a lot of training and experience with problems such as yours").
- *Faking attention:* Insincerely pretending to be more interested and involved in what is being said than you are (for example, "That's so interesting").
- *Placing time pressures:* Letting clients know that your availability for listening is limited (for example, "You had better be brief").

A major don't not listed is breaking confidences. Quite apart from damaging specific helping relationships, breaking confidences represents a serious breach of ethics. All the above don'ts focus on verbal responses, but, as mentioned earlier, helpers' voice and body messages can also create a lack of psychological safety.

Skill 10: Avoid Poor Thinking Skills

You bring your thinking skills strengths and weaknesses to listening. All of the verbal dont's just mentioned that restrict clients' psychological space and freedom reflect poor thinking skills. You may talk to yourself in ways that create anxiety or calm you down. You may possess helpful or harmful rules about yourself, others, and the helping process. You may attribute responsibility for what happens in helping in ways that strengthen or weaken clients' capacities to develop self-helping skills. You may possess ways of perceiving clients and their reactions to your responses that make for accuracy or inaccuracy. The need for effective thinking skills on the part of both helpers and clients pervades this book. Despite its importance, the topic is only mentioned in passing here.

CONCLUDING COMMENT

Rewarding listening is the fundamental skill of supportive helping relationships. Without this basic skill of getting inside clients' internal viewpoints and showing that you understand and care about what they say, you severely (if not fatally) limit your capacity to help. Furthermore, you may add to clients' pain and distress by sending negative messages. In lifeskills helping, rewarding listening is central to assisting clients in managing problems and overcoming problematic skills patterns. Beginning students need to practice in order to develop the sensitive fluency of skilled helpers. Also, experienced helpers should pay close attention to whether they maintain high listening standards or let bad habits interfere. In most instances, rewarding listening needs be accompanied by other helper skills. We now turn to these additional skills.

 ## CHAPTER HIGHLIGHTS

- Lifeskills helping heavily emphasizes the importance of the helper-client relationship.
- Five ways that helpers and clients send and receive messages are: verbal, voice, body, touch, and action.
- Rewarding listening is the central skill in supportive helping relationships.
- Functions of rewarding listening include: establishing and maintaining rapport, helping clients disclose, helping clients experience and express feelings, creating a knowledge base, creating an influence base, and helping clients assume responsibility.
- Reflective responding entails tuning in to and mirroring with your verbal, voice, and body messages the crux of the meaning contained in your clients' verbal, voice, and body messages.
- Helpers always need to be aware of whether they respond inside or outside their clients' internal viewpoints.
- Barriers to possessing an attitude of respect and acceptance include: anxiety-evoking feelings, clients, and situations; trigger words, phrases, and attitudes; being prejudiced; unfinished business; needing to present a professional facade; emotional exhaustion and burnout; insufficient administrative support; and physical barriers.
- Helper body messages are important for: demonstrating interest and attention, showing responsiveness as clients talk, and framing verbal messages.
- Five dimensions of sending good voice messages are: Volume, Articulation, Pitch, Emphasis, and Rate (VAPER).

- Openers are permissions for clients to talk. Small rewards are brief verbal and nonverbal expressions of interest that help clients keep talking. Open-ended questions and cues help clients elaborate on their internal viewpoints.
- Rewording involves paraphrasing clients' key words. Good rewordings can be clearer and more succinct than clients' original statements.
- The language of feelings is not verbal. Consequently good reflections of feelings both pick up and communicate back nonverbal as well as verbal messages. Helpers require good skills at picking up feelings messages, including evaluating their intensity and whether they are multiple or mixed feelings. Sometimes helpers assist clients in labeling feelings.
- A variant of reflective responding is to reflect back feelings and the reasons for them. Reflecting feelings and reasons helps identify the thoughts that contributed to the feelings.
- You create unsafe emotional climates for clients by sending clumsy verbal messages. Don'ts to avoid include: directing and leading, judging and evaluating, blaming, moralizing, preaching and patronizing, labeling and diagnosing, reassuring and humoring, not accepting clients' feelings, advising and teaching, interrogating, overinterpreting, inappropriately self-disclosing, putting on a professional facade, faking attention, and putting unnecessary time pressures on clients.
- Poor helper thinking skills can impede rewarding listening (for example, anxiety-engendering self-talk, unrealistic helping rules, and inaccurately perceiving what clients say and do).
- For most clients, rewarding listening needs to be accompanied by other helper skills focused on managing problems and developing lifeskills.

CHAPTER FIVE

HOW TO IDENTIFY AND CLARIFY PROBLEMS

A matter that becomes clear ceases to
concern us.

—Friedrich Nietzsche

CHAPTER QUESTIONS

❀ *What are some of the main objectives of
initial helping sessions?*

❀ *What is the nature of the helper-client
relationship?*

❀ *What action skills are important for
identifying and clarifying problems?*

❀ *What thinking skills are important for
identifying and clarifying problems?*

INTRODUCTION

Here are some concerns that people might bring to helpers:

"I'm feeling depressed and apathetic."
"I wish I could relate better and have more social life."
"Our marriage is heading for the rocks."
"I feel stressed all the time."
"I've had a heart attack and want to look after my health better from now on."
"I'm having hassles with my boss and don't know what to do."
"I'm unemployed and want to rejoin the work force."
"I can't concentrate on my studies."
"I carry my parents around in my head all the time and can't decide what I want to do."

Clients bringing such problems to helpers want to move beyond being stuck, but are unclear how to proceed. In stage 1 of the lifeskills model, helpers go beyond developing the relationship to identify and clarify clients' problems. The previous chapter on rewarding listening skills heavily emphasized staying within clients' internal viewpoints. This chapter emphasizes using a range of skills to elaborate and clarify clients' internal viewpoints. In reality, the identifying and clarifying work of stage 1 often overlaps the assessing and redefining problems work of stage 2. Also, helpers use many identifying and clarifying skills, both when intervening and when ending and consolidating clients' self-helping skills (stages 4 and 5 of the model).

OBJECTIVES FOR INITIAL SESSIONS

This section restates the first three stages of the lifeskills helping model in terms of four main objectives for the initial helping session. These objectives apply to clients as well as to helpers.

1. Develop a supportive working relationship. Both helpers and clients need to feel that they can work together. Clients wish to be understood by helpers and to have some expectation of benefit from helping contacts. Though limited by ethical and professional considerations, a personal bond can develop between helpers and clients (Bordin, 1979; Kokotovic & Tracey,

1990). Helpers and clients are partners in developing the clients' skills resources. From the start, helpers convey understanding and support as a basis for developing clients' skills. The relationship in lifeskills helping is rarely an end in itself; rather, it is a vehicle for assisting clients to work on problems and problematic skills. There may be some healthy dependency on helpers. However, this dependency is transitional as clients develop self-helping skills.

2. Develop a working model.   Clients tend to be stuck at present levels of understanding. Both helpers and clients collaborate to develop working models. A working model consists of a set of hypotheses about how clients function in problem areas. Working models are statements of how individual clients feel, think, and act.

There are many advantages when helpers and clients work together in the detective work of developing working models. First, clients can provide valuable insights if allowed to do much of the work themselves; their contributions are greater when treated as active rather than passive partners. Second, clients as well as helpers are hypothesis makers and testers. Collaborating improves both helper and client skills as practitioner-researchers. Third, clients are more likely to own responsibility for possessing and altering skills weaknesses that they have played some part in discovering. Fourth, collaborating to understand clients' problems can develop the helping relationship more than rewarding listening alone. Helpers may be perceived as more empathic when active than when passive.

3. Develop a working definition.   Helpers assist clients to identify not only problems, but also their component parts. For example, a hypothetical client who starts by saying "I am depressed; help me" may then reveal contributing problems in the areas of relating poorly to spouse, having a difficult parent, being short of friends, not having adequate recreational outlets, and getting little satisfaction from work. The plot thickens. However, it is insufficient to leave clients hanging. Helpers need to assist clients to redefine their problems in skills terms so that they then have "handles" for working on them. Here the earlier distinction between *descriptive* and *skills* definitions of problems becomes important. Descriptive definitions clarify problems, but do not move much outside clients' existing concepts and internal viewpoints. Skills definitions identify the specific action and thinking skills weaknesses that sustain problems. Where possible, helpers should reach agreement with clients on skills definitions.

4. Develop working goals and interventions. By the end of the initial session (or, if necessary, initial sessions), helpers and clients should agree on preliminary statements of working goals to guide future work. Furthermore, helpers need to indicate how goals might be attained. As part of this process, they may discuss the appropriateness of different interventions. Bordin (1979) has suggested that there are three main elements that determine the quality and strength of the helper-client working alliance. In addition to the development of a personal bond (relationship), helpers and clients require agreement on treatment goals (goals) and on the tasks to achieve these goals (tasks). Helpers and clients who achieve each of these three elements in the initial session or sessions have a strong foundation for continuing to develop the working alliance. A final word: Sometimes it is appropriate to start implementing interventions during, as well as at the end of, initial sessions. Helpers make such decisions in light of progress made in sessions and individual clients' needs.

SKILLS FOR IDENTIFYING AND CLARIFYING PROBLEMS

In addition to rewarding listening skills, effective helpers use all the skills discussed in this chapter. Identifying and clarifying problems skills contain elements of stepping outside or going beyond clients' internal viewpoints. Nevertheless, these skills help clients elaborate and therefore more fully understand their internal viewpoints. Put another way, rewarding listening focuses on helping clients share their internal viewpoints with relatively little input from helpers' external viewpoints. The skills covered in this chapter focus on helping clients expand their internal viewpoints by means of greater input from the helper.

Structuring Skills

Objectives of Structuring

Structuring is a term used to describe the behaviors by which helpers let their clients know their respective roles at various stages of the helping process. Cormier and Cormier (1985) state: "*Structuring* refers to an interactional process between counselors and clients in which they arrive at similar perceptions of the role of the counselor, an understanding of what occurs in counseling, and an agreement on which outcome goals will be achieved"

(p. 53). Structuring occurs throughout helping, and even prior to helping (for example, through the publicity, image, and reputations of helpers and helping agencies). Here the focus is on structuring skills for initial sessions.

Effective structuring both leads to positive outcomes and prevents or minimizes the chance of negative outcomes. The functions of structuring in initial sessions include: establishing expectancies conducive to clients' working on rather than just talking about problems; outlining the initial session; providing an introductory rationale for working within the lifeskills helping framework; establishing the expectancy that change may be possible; and, if necessary, communicating limitations concerning the helping relationship (for instance, restrictions on confidentiality).

Too Much and Too Little Structure

Helpers may provide both too much and too little structure (Osipow, Walsh, & Tosi, 1984). If you provide too much structuring, clients may feel stifled by your agendas and reluctant or unable to reveal their own. You may establish a "teacher knows best" emotional climate that is conducive to dependency and resistance. Clients may perceive you as determined to fit them into your way of working whether it suits them or not. Furthermore, if you talk too much at the beginning, not only do you make it difficult for clients to talk, but also you may structure the helping process in too intellectual a way. Too little structuring also has dangers. Clients may feel anxious and confused. You too may be anxious and confused. In addition, clients may perceive that you have nothing of value to offer.

Helpers' voice and body messages may enhance or impede structuring. Again, negative outcomes may arise if helpers come on either too strong or too weak. For instance, clients may feel overwhelmed and put off by helpers who structure in loud voices and gesticulate too much. On the other hand, helpers who structure in diffident voices, with minimal use of gesture and eye contact, may convey insufficient commitment.

Some Structuring Skills

The objective of initial structuring is to begin the process of client self-helping. You attempt to establish working alliances in which you collaborate with clients as partners in developing their skills rather than doing things either to or for them. In a medical model of helping, physicians might say: "What can I do to cure my patients?" In the lifeskills model, helpers say, "How can I best collaborate with clients to develop their self-helping skills?"

Verbal message skills   At the start, helpers face the decision as to how much to structure. Already I've mentioned that lifeskills helping always starts with checking out where the client is. You may perform initial session structuring with at least two statements. The first statement gets the session started and allows clients to introduce their stories. The second statement establishes the agenda for the session's remainder. Here is an example of a possible opening statement to provide structure for a session's start.

> **Helper:** Hello, Jeff, my name is Debbie Roberts and I'm one of the student counselors here. We have about 40 minutes and everything you say is confidential. Would you please tell me why you're here?

After clients have had a chance to state why they came for helping, the following statement might establish structure for the session's remainder.

> **Helper:** You've given me some idea why you've come. What I'd like to do is to ask some more questions to help us understand your problems more fully (specify). Then, depending on what we find, I will review with you some skills to help you cope better. Once we agree on what skills might be useful, then we can look at ways to develop them. Does this way of proceeding sound all right?

One reason for not amalgamating both parts of the structuring in your opening statement is that the second part may be inappropriate for certain clients (for example, those requiring either information or referral). Furthermore, lengthy opening statements may show lack of empathy to clients' need to say at once why they have come. Some clients may seek emotional release and feel blocked by your talking too much too soon. Sometimes when sessions start you may notice from body language that clients are experiencing strong emotions (for instance, distress or anxiety). You can reflect such feelings and give clients permission to discuss them.

When structuring, helpers can incorporate statements that present a rationale for the lifeskills approach. The following are examples.

"It can be useful to think of problems in terms of the skills you need to cope better. This way you get some 'handles' or leverage to work for change."

"In the past you have probably learned some ineffective, along with some effective, ways of thinking and acting. My approach aims to improve how you think and act so that you can manage your problems (specify) better."

"The approach I take assumes that most of people's behavior is learned. Ineffective skills of thinking and acting can be unlearned and effective skills can be learned."

"My approach heavily emphasizes the development of self-helping skills. You will probably need to work hard to acquire and maintain them. It may speed matters up if you listen to a cassette recording of each session before you come to the next one. What do you think about this?"

The following are some guidelines for initial session structuring.

- Be flexible. Considerations include: your clients' expectations and problems, their emotional state, their age and intelligence level, at what stage of the initial session you are, how much time you have, and the helping context in which you work.
- Consider breaking your structuring down into more than one statement.
- Pay attention to timing.
- Use simple language.
- Use skills language.
- Be clear and relatively brief.
- Be consistent. Your remarks should be consistent with a lifeskills helping theoretical position.
- Emphasize helper-client collaboration.
- Emphasize work. Helping is not magic. Clients need to work to acquire and maintain skills.
- Check for questions and reservations. Do not assume that what you say is understood and agreed upon by clients.

Voice and body messages How you send voice and body messages is important when you structure. Your voice messages should indicate your commitment to what you do. Good voice message skills include: easy audibility, comfortable speech rate, firm voice, clear articulation, and appropriate variations in emphasis. Your body messages should support your verbal and voice messages (for example, by appropriate gaze, eye contact, and use of gestures). A theme throughout this book is the importance of helpers' paying great attention to their voice and body messages. Structuring is a clear instance where ineffective voice and body messages can countermand verbal messages.

Questioning Skills

Objectives of Questioning

Viktor Frankl tells the following psychiatrist joke:

> "Are you a psychiatrist?"
> "Why do you ask?"
> "You're a psychiatrist." (Frankl, 1975, p. 94)

Here, instead of unmasking, the psychiatrist has been unmasked. Often, as in this instance, helpers ask questions inappropriately. A major reservation about using questions is that they take clients out of their internal viewpoints. Some questions are asked more to make helpers feel secure than to help clients. However, judicious questioning can help clients better explore, clarify, and understand their internal viewpoints. Furthermore, questions assist helpers to identify what clients' problems are and to break them down into component parts. When this is done, you both possess more information for developing hypotheses about how problems are sustained. In this section the primary focus is on the use of questions to identify, clarify, and break down problems into their component parts.

The iceberg provides a good analogy for understanding the role of questioning in lifeskills helping. Much relevant information lies below the surface. In general, clients responding to permission to tell their stories reveal useful information. Area A in Figure 5.1 depicts this information. However, effective helper questioning enables clients to provide much additional information for identifying, clarifying, and breaking down problems; Area B depicts this. In addition, there may be additional information that clients may be either unaware of or unwilling to disclose, and helper questions may not tap this information. Area C depicts this highly private or unconscious information.

Another analogy for the role of questioning in initial sessions of lifeskills helping is that of plants and their root system. Helpers use questions to identify the various roots of problems. For example, a hypothetical client came to helping saying "I am depressed. Help me." This request represents the part of the plant that is above ground. However, by listening and effective questioning, the helper starts identifying roots of the client's problem in five different areas (see Figure 5.2). Helpers may

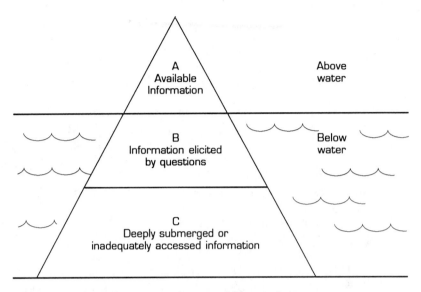

Figure 5.1 The information-about-problems iceberg

then ask further questions to clarify each root area and its relative importance.

In the case of this depressed client, the roots of the problem are located in the present rather than in the past. Questions concerning clients' childhoods may illustrate origins of problems and help them work through and understand painful events. Nevertheless, the major focus of questioning in lifeskills helping is not on how clients arrived at their present problems, but on how they are sustaining them now and may continue to do so in the future.

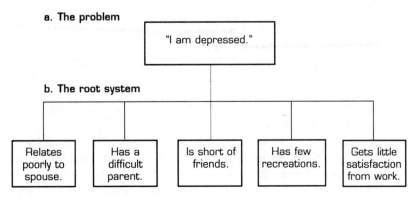

Figure 5.2 Identifying the roots of a problem

Strategies for Questioning

Spitzer and Williams (1984) classify clinical interviewing approaches into three types: smorgasbord, checklist, and canine. In the *smorgasbord* approach, helpers sample whatever seems interesting. In the *checklist* approach, helpers ask a series of closed-ended questions about particular symptoms "without giving the patient an opportunity to describe spontaneously the symptoms that are being talked about" (Spitzer & Williams, 1984, p. 6). In the *canine* approach, the helper is like a dog sniffing around for a buried bone. The helper continues to sniff around until the goal of that portion of the interview is reached and then moves on in search of another "bone."

In lifeskills helping, initial-session questioning takes the *detective* approach. Helpers collaborate with clients, first asking questions that describe, clarify, and break down their problems and then asking further questions that assist in redefining problems in skills terms. Hutchins and Cole (1986) use the term *systematic inquiry* for collecting information in a logical and orderly fashion about a specific topic. The detective approach contains elements of both systematic inquiry and canine "sniffing." Helpers encourage clients to offer information spontaneously—not just when questioned.

Choices When Questioning

Helpers have numerous choices when questioning, including the following:

1. *Purpose of questions.* Effective helpers ask questions that contribute to enlarging their own and their clients' understanding of problems and problematic skills patterns. They do not just ask questions for questioning's sake.
2. *Present versus past focus.* Lifeskills helping tends to focus more on clients' present than past.
3. *Amount of topics covered.* An issue is that of whether just to ask questions in the area of the presenting problems or conduct a broader reconnaissance (Sullivan, 1954). Practical considerations (for instance, what the client wants from helping), often influence how many topics you cover.
4. *Degree of detail.* How detailed should inquiries into each topic area be? When should helpers move on? Partly by intuition, effective helpers assess when areas may continue to yield valuable information and when to move on.

5. *Intimacy level.* Helpers need to be sensitive to the intimacy and threat levels of questions. They may still—tactfully—ask intimate questions if appropriate.
6. *Timing.* Helpers require caution regarding the timing and ordering of questions. They may defer some intimate or probing questions pending the establishment of greater trust.
7. *Number of questions.* Egan (1990) admonishes "Do not assault clients with volleys of questions" (p. 142). Helpers should avoid conducting interrogations that may lead to defensiveness or dependence, or both.
8. *Confirmatory questions.* Helpers may ask questions designed to elicit responses that fit pet theories. Sometimes they decide prematurely what clients' problems and skills weaknesses are, and then only ask questions to confirm their judgments.

Types of Questions

Helpers also need to choose among different types of questions, including the following:

Open-ended versus closed-ended questions Open-ended questions give clients considerable choice in how to respond, whereas closed-ended questions restrict choice. When working with new clients, many helpers use open-ended questions before asking more focused questions.

- *Open-ended question*: "What do you think of your previous experience in counseling?"
- *Closed-ended question*: "Was your previous counselor good or bad?"

How, what, when, where, and why questions Another way of categorizing questions relates to how, what, when, where, and why.

- *How questions* include: "How do you think, feel, or act (or a combination of these)?" "How did they think, feel, or act (or a combination of these)?" "How often does it happen?" and "How have you attempted to cope in the past?" How questions are particularly useful for eliciting details of how clients behave.
- *What questions* include: "What happened?" "What do you perceive as the problem?" "What preceded your thoughts, feelings, or actions?" "What is the meaning of that for you?" "What other ways are there of viewing it?" "What are you

afraid of?" and "What are the likely consequences of doing that?"
- *When questions* include: "When did it start?" and "When do you think it might happen again?"
- *Where questions* include: "Where does it happen?" and "Where is the evidence for that perception?"
- *Why questions* include: "Why did you behave that way?" "Why do you think they feel that way?" and "Why is it so important for you?" A risk of some why questions is that they may take clients into their heads rather than help them to focus on specific problematic thoughts, feelings, and behaviors.

Clarification questions Clarification questions seek information about, and clarify your perception of, clients' words and phrases. Examples include: "When you say _____, what do you mean?" and "Sounds to me like you're saying _____?"

Elaboration questions Elaboration questions are open questions that give clients the opportunity to expand on what they have already started taking about. Examples include: "Would you care to elaborate?" and "Is there anything more you wish to add?"

Challenging questions Challenging questions confront clients with the need to produce evidence for their perceptions. Examples include: "Where is the evidence for _____?" "What makes you think that?" and "Are there other ways of viewing the situation?"

Specific detail questions Specific detail questions aim to collect concrete information about clients' problems and problematic skills patterns. Examples include: "How frequent is it?" "How do you actually behave?" "How have you attempted to cope with it?" "What brings it on?" "What feelings are associated with it?" "What thoughts are associated with it?" "When did it start?" and "Where does it happen?"

Request for example questions Request for example questions ask clients to illustrate what they talk about. Examples include: "Can you tell me a specific instance?" and "Can you give me an example?"

"Show me" questions "Show me" questions ask clients to show the helper how they behaved. Sometimes the helper will impersonate the other person for the client in a role-play. Examples include: "Show me how you actually spoke to _____?" or "Imagine I am your _____, show me how you behaved?"

Eliciting personal meaning questions   The information clients provide often has personal or symbolic meaning for them. For example, whenever a husband would come home late without having called her, his wife would think he did not care about her (Beck, 1988). Eliciting personal meanings questions should be open and tentative since the client should, but won't always, know the answer better than anyone else. Illustrative questions include: "I'm wondering what the meaning of _____ is for you?" "What do you make of that?" and "Why is it so important for you?"

Work in Partnership with Clients

In lifeskills helping, questions are designed to provide information as much for clients as helpers. Helpers try to avoid questioning in ways that create dependency, passivity, and resistance. Following are some skills for collaborating with clients when asking questions.

Ask establishing agenda and transition questions.   Establishing agenda and transition questions have the advantage of getting clients involved in the detective work of identifying and clarifying problems. Clients are invited to participate in working on areas important for them. Questions might include: "You've mentioned three areas (specify)—which one would you like to focus on first?" or "Is there anything you would like to add before we move on?"

Intersperse reflective responding with questions.   Clients feel interrogated when helpers ask a series of questions in quick succession. Helpers can greatly soften their questioning if they pause to see if clients wish to continue responding and then reflect each response. Interspersing reflective responding has the added advantage of ensuring that helpers check the accuracy of their understanding. The following excerpt shows what you should avoid.

> **Client:** I'm getting very anxious over my upcoming test.
> **Helper:** What makes you so anxious?
> **Client:** The fact that I may fail.
> **Helper:** Why are you so afraid of failing?
> **Client:** Because then it will be harder to get a job.
> **Helper:** What sort of job do you want?

Below is a gentler approach to the same initial statement.

> **Client:** I'm getting very anxious over my upcoming test.
> **Helper:** You're very worried about your test. Would you say more about this?
> **Client:** Yes. It's in three weeks and I feel overwhelmed.
> **Helper:** So you experience this vital test as overpowering.
> **Client:** My whole future depends on it.
> **Helper:** You think it is make-or-break. Can you explain this further?

Though these are only short excerpts, the first helper controls and dominates the client, whereas the second facilitates the client's description of an internal viewpoint. The emotional climate in the first excerpt is in the head. The second excerpt encourages expressing feelings as well as thoughts.

Ask follow-up questions. Avoid jackrabbiting, in which you hop quickly from one topic to another (Hutchins & Cole, 1986). Always listen carefully and respect what clients have just said. Frequently, your next question can follow in such a way that it encourages clients to build upon their last response.
Questioning that is logically linked to clients' responses creates a feeling of working together rather than of being directed by you.

Encourage clients to do their own work. Often clients can both ask and answer their own questions. Interspersing reflective responding with questions provides clients with psychological space to do their own work. If helpers establish good relationships, clients will tell them a lot without being asked. Helpers may also use silences to encourage clients to engage in self-exploration and move beyond superficial answers. Furthermore, helpers can ask questions that encourage clients to think and feel for themselves. Illustrative questions are: "What information is important for helping understand your problem?" or "Just stay with the problem and try to get in touch with what you truly think and feel about it?"

Carefully observe how questions are answered. An art of questioning lies in decoding clients' answers. Much information is conveyed by what is left unsaid or only partly said, and by voice and body messages. Effective helpers are finely tuned to subtle client messages. They use tact both in asking questions and in responding to clients' answers. Clients whose anxieties, confusions, and vulnerabilities are sensitively picked up by helpers are more likely to answer questions honestly.

Use good voice and body messages. How you question is as important as what you say. For example, clients may feel overwhelmed if your voice is loud or harsh. If you use little eye contact and have a stiff body posture, they may feel less inclined to answer your questions. Helpers need to send questioning messages using good volume, articulation, pitch, emphasis, and speech rate. Furthermore, attending and responsive body messages need to be conducive to clients' feeling that helpers are interested in their answers.

Example of Questioning to Identify and Clarify Problems

Below is an excerpt from the start of an initial session between a student counselor and a client. Introductions have taken place in the waiting area. Counselor and client are now seated in the counselor's office.

> **Counselor:** We have about 45 minutes together. Please tell me why you've come? (open-ended opening question)
> **Client:** I'm getting very anxious about my upcoming test.
> **Counselor:** You're very worried about your test. Would you like to say more about this? (open-ended elaboration question)
> **Client:** Yes. It's in 3 weeks and I feel overwhelmed.
> **Counselor:** So you experience this vital test as overpowering.
> **Client:** My whole future depends on it.
> **Counselor:** You think of it as make-or-break. Can you explain this further? (eliciting personal meaning question)
> **Client:** If I fail the test it will show on my record and make it harder for me to get a good job.
> **Counselor:** So failure will jeopardize your prospects of good employment.
> **Client:** Yes. Is there anything you can do to help me?
> **Counselor:** I appreciate your worry. However, before answering that question, I would like to become clearer regarding your problem. Perhaps we can explore it further. Then I should be in a better position to suggest some skills that you might develop to cope better.
> **Client:** Where do we start?
> **Counselor:** Well, perhaps you can give me some basic information about what you're majoring in and what subject or subjects you are afraid of failing? (specific detail question)

Client: I'm in the final year of a business studies course and I'm afraid of flunking Accounting 2.

Counselor: What bothers you specifically about Accounting 2? (specific details question)

Client: I got very nervous about my Accounting 1 test and nearly failed the subject. My other grades are generally above average, but I just scraped through accounting. If it hadn't been for the marks on my homework assignments I would have failed.

Counselor: You're wondering whether history may repeat itself and you will do badly on your Accounting 2 test. How much of the grade does the test account for? (specific detail question)

Client: Fifty percent. I think I'm doing OK on my homework assignments. I just don't want to screw up the test.

Counselor: You're worried about messing up the test. I'm wondering, are you more concerned with how well you actually take the test—your test-taking skills—or how well you prepare for it—your revision skills—or both? (establishing agenda question)

Client: What I'm most afraid of is that I will go to pieces during the test.

Counselor: So you're worried about falling apart during the test. What precisely are you afraid you might do during the test? (specific detail question)

Client: Well, in my last accounting test I could scarcely hold my pen. My hand was shaking and my heart was pounding. At times I felt faint, as though I might blank out.

Counselor: The last time you had numerous distressing physical symptoms—hand shaking, difficulty holding your pen, heart pounding, feeling faint. In what ways did these feelings affect how you actually behaved during the test? (specific detail question)

Client: I couldn't think clearly and I didn't leave enough time to answer all the questions.

Counselor: When you say you couldn't think clearly, what do you mean? (clarification question)

Client: At times my head felt like cotton. I had to struggle to concentrate. These feelings of panic kept coming. I can't work with numbers under pressure.

In this brief excerpt, the counselor has identified that a major concern of the client relates to not being able to handle the Accounting 2 test-taking situation. The counselor is still in the early stages of discovering both the dimensions of the client's accounting test-taking difficulties and whether there are other roots to the problem that are outside the test-taking situation. The counselor uses questions, not only to discover the client's surface feelings and behaviors, but also to probe for the roots of the problem. Sometimes, when questioning, counselors store away information for future use without responding to it directly. For example, counselors might note that the client perceived the whole future as resting on this test, which is an example of black-and-white (polarized) thinking (Beck, 1988). This observation might form the basis for questions in stage 2 of the lifeskills model, as the counselor gathers more information to redefine the problem in skills terms.

Summarizing Skills

Purposes of Summaries

Summaries are brief statements of longer excerpts from helping sessions. Summaries can pull together various parts of extended communications and may take place at any stage of the helping process. Much of the time helpers summarize what clients communicate. However, since lifeskills helping has didactic as well as relationship emphases, some helper summaries relate to previously communicated educational content. Clients also use summaries, sometimes of their own accord and sometimes at the request of helpers. For example, clients can be asked to summarize the main points in a skills sequence they have learned.

Here the focus is on helper summaries in initial sessions. Such summaries serve numerous purposes. If clients have had a lengthy period of talking, helpers summarize to establish their presence and make the interaction two-way. Furthermore, if clients are telling their stories very rapidly, helpers may deliver summaries at a measured speech rate to calm them down. Where possible, helper summaries serve to move the session forward. Such summaries may clarify what clients have communicated, identify themes and problem areas, and form the basis for establishing session agendas.

Types of Summaries

Following are various types of summaries, many of them interrelated.

Basic reflective summary Basic reflective summaries can take place at any stage of helping. They are short summaries that helpers make after clients have spoken for more than a few sentences. Such summaries pull together the main feelings and content of what clients say. Basic reflective summaries serve a bridging function for clients, enabling them to continue with the same topic or move on to another. Other functions include: making sure helpers listen actively, rewarding clients for talking, showing understanding, checking your own understanding, and possibly clarifying clients' understanding. Sometimes summaries highlight each of the feelings, thoughts, and actions.

> **Helper:** You feel very unhappy with your boss. You think he doesn't appreciate you and manipulates people all the time to get his way. Your relationship has got to the point where you only speak to each other when absolutely necessary.

Reflecting feelings and reasons summary   Clients may convey one or more central feelings. At the same time they may either directly or indirectly suggest reasons for their feelings. Clients do not always speak in tidy and logically sequenced sentences. You may be faced with making order out of client statements that have varied in length and coherence. A summary reflecting feelings and reasons can usefully link emotions with their perceived sources.

> **Helper:** You feel tense and anxious all the time because you have your divorce coming up in 3 weeks and there still is considerable acrimony between you and Lorenzo in many areas: child custody, division of property, and even who gets the dog.

Clarification summary   In clarification summaries, helpers seek to ensure that they understand clients' internal viewpoints correctly. Clarification summaries are stated tentatively and allow clients to correct or add to what helpers say.

> **Helper:** May I run what you have been telling me back to check that I understand you correctly? You have a drinking problem, but much of the time find it hard to admit. Your wife has told you that if you keep up your present level of drinking she will leave you. You feel guilty about sometimes coming home drunk and abusing her. You find her both emotionally and sexually unresponsive. You're unsure of whether you want to stay in the marriage. Is that about right?

Theme summary   Theme summaries are reflections in which helpers fit together pieces of what clients communicate in order to identify themes. You may note recurring patterns of thoughts, feelings, and behaviors (for instance, fear of intimacy, preoccupation with homosexuality, avoidance of decisions, or need for approval). A theme summary puts together the different pieces of information that constitute a theme.

> **Helper:** As you've been talking, I've noticed a number of occasions where you have emphasized how important it is to you that others like you. At times it comes over so strongly that it is almost as though your psychological survival depends on it. You've mentioned how vital it is for you to be popular with the other girls at school, how upset you were when you thought your history teacher was not interested in you, and how you always make a big effort to please your parents and be nice to their friends.

Identification of problem areas summary Imagine that a client comes to helping and starts describing a number of problems. Summaries that overview or identify the problem areas mentioned can provide clients with clearer statements than they managed on their own. Furthermore such summaries may provide a basis for asking clients to prioritize which problems are most important or which ones they want to work on first.

> **Helper:** You started by talking about your problems with your housemate over keeping the place tidy. Then you moved on to discuss your problems with your mother, whom you perceive as excessively controlling and interfering even though you have moved away from home. You then talked about your mixed feelings about whether to stay in your relationship with Scott. You also expressed some dissatisfaction with your nursing studies and wondered if it is the right career for you. Which of these areas would you like to focus on first?

Details of problem summary In the initial session many questions seek to "flesh out" details of clients' problems. For instance, a client who reports difficulty sleeping may have difficulty first going to sleep, spend the night tossing and turning, or wake up early and not be able to get back to sleep—or a mixture of these. This pattern may happen every night or less frequently. Numerous possibilities require checking to arrive at an accurate descriptive definition. The same holds true for most other problems (for instance, marital conflict, job indecision, test anxiety, and specific phobias such as spiders). Helpers may take notes to assist their memories. Furthermore, helpers may collect further descriptive information later. The following illustrates a detail of problem summary.

> **Helper:** We've now spent some time exploring your sleep problem and these seem to be some of its main characteristics. Your problems with sleep started 3 months ago when you moved away from home and into an apartment at the time you accepted your first social-work position. You have difficulty getting to sleep practically every night. You like to get 8 hours of sleep a night, but currently get about 6 hours. When you can't get to sleep your brain becomes very active. You start worrying about everything that has happened during the day. You also worry about not being in top form the next day. You lie there feeling uncomfortable, angry with yourself, and somewhat depressed, until exhaustion takes over. A consequence of not sleeping properly is that you feel tired the next day. Most late afternoons when you get home you lie down for about an hour. Is there anything important that I've left out?

Other types of summaries   Other types of summaries include the following.

- *End of session summary:* Some helpers favor end of session review summaries along the lines of "Let's take a look at what we've accomplished in this interview. How does it appear to you?" (Brammer, 1985, p. 75). Such summaries can include an overview of homework.
- *Beginning of next session summary:* Helpers may summarize the previous session at the start of the next one. These summaries provide continuity. However, helpers need to be careful to allow space for clients to mention current concerns.
- *Problems redefined in skills terms summary:* As shown in the next chapter, redefining problems in terms of the thinking and action skills weaknesses that sustain them entails clearly and concisely summarizing diverse information.
- *Educational content summary:* Even in initial sessions, helpers may start teaching skills. Summaries consolidate the main points. Furthermore, helpers may request clients to summarize and, if necessary, correct their misunderstandings.

Focusing Skills

Ivey (1988) states: "Focusing is a skill that enables you to direct the client conversational flow into areas you want" (p. 203). Helpers need to be conscious of when, why, and how they choose to influence the helping process. Focused responding, focusing clients on themselves, and initiating focused exploration are three important skills.

Focused Responding

Client statements often have many parts to them. Consequently, you can choose where to focus. Ivey, in particular, has drawn attention to this skill (Ivey, 1988; Ivey, Ivey, & Simek-Downing, 1987). Take the following statement:

> **Cheryl:** I've just had the most terrible fight with my mother-in-law. I can't seem to control my temper. OK, there are many problems between the kids and me, but why does she have to interfere? Right now I feel as though I could kill her.

This statement provides a challenge for a helper who may be trying to reflect all of it accurately. Depending upon what you wish to achieve in your interviewing, you may choose a focus from many options.

1. *Focus on the feeling.* "You feel like murdering your mother-in-law."
2. *Focus on the feeling and the thinking behind it.* "You feel like murdering your mother-in-law because . . ."
3. *Focus on one or more of the problems.* For instance, focus on controlling anger, coping with interference, or dealing better with the kids. You could also choose to focus on problematic skills.
4. *Focus on the other person or persons.* For instance, focus on the mother-in-law or the kids.
5. *Focus on the helper.* The helper might share a reaction to Cheryl's statement (for instance, "What do you want from me?").
6. *Focus on the environmental context.* There may be broader social, cultural, racial, sex-role, and economic issues that would provide an insight into the problem (Ivey, 1988).

You need to approach focused responding with caution. You may block clients from exploring and experiencing material that is important for them (rather than for you). Also you may get in the way of clients doing their own work. For instance, an excessive focus on Cheryl's mother-in-law's behavior might block Cheryl from looking at her own behavior. (However, Cheryl might better examine her own behavior if assisted to focus on her mother-in-law's perspective.) A further danger is that helpers focus on areas of special interest to them (for example, paying excessive attention to sexual material). A reverse problem is that helpers may not focus sufficiently on some topic areas.

Focusing Clients on Themselves

Frequently clients require help in speaking for themselves. By failing to send "I" messages, clients may distance themselves from their feelings, thoughts, and actions (Gordon, 1970). "I" messages involve the use of the first person singular. Clients avoid speaking for themselves when they start with words like "you," "people," "we," and "it." Also, sometimes clients avoid sending "I" messages by asking questions in the hope that they can agree with the answer.

Here are examples of messages transposed into "I" messages.

Owning a Feeling

> Client's non "I" message: "He is impossible when he behaves like that."
> Client's "I" message: "I feel hurt and frustrated at his behavior."

Owning a Thought

> Client's non "I" message: "What do you think about women serving in combat roles?"
> Client's "I" message: "I think women should serve in combat roles."

Owning an Action

> Client's non "I" message: "The car crashed into the garage door."
> Client's "I" message: "I crashed the car into the garage door."

Helpers need to develop skill in assisting clients to focus on and speak for themselves. The following are three ways to encourage your clients to send "I" messages.

1. *Respond as though clients send "I" messages.* You can respond to clients in ways that use the word "you" as though they had sent an "I" message, even when they have not. For instance, to a client who says "He is impossible when he behaves like that," you might respond "You feel hurt and

frustrated at his behavior." Your response implicitly encourages the client to express feelings directly.

2. *Request the use of the first person singular.* If clients repeatedly fail to send "I" messages, you might consider openly drawing this to their attention. However, you have to judge whether this intervention will be threatening to the client. Also, you may have the further decision of how to handle clients' behavior if they revert to their old ways.

3. *Model sending "I" messages.* If you are open in your own behavior and use "I" messages to own your feelings, thoughts, and actions, your example may help clients to do likewise.

Initiating Focused Exploration

One way to establish focus is to ask clients to prioritize areas for exploration. However, you may wish to initiate explorations of specific areas yourself. Furthermore, you may wish to focus (define) further when exploring specific areas. For example, in attempting to clarify Ron's stress difficulties, the helper may initiate focused exploration of related areas such as Ron's recreational activities and attention to keeping fit. Within the area of recreational activities, the helper may explore why Ron no longer participates in a specific activity, say bike riding, that previously he enjoyed. Helpers use their focusing skills to collect information on parts of problems not mentioned by clients. Helpers also need to know when they reach diminishing returns. Furthermore, they need to be able to shift the focus from one topic to another.

Confronting Skills

The word *confrontation* may conjure up images of clients sitting on hot seats while helpers attack them psychologically and strip them of their defenses. I do not advocate such hot-seat confrontation. I use confrontations to expand clients' awareness of thoughts, feelings, and actions. Confrontations may stimulate clients to provide additional information about problems and problematic skills.

Challenging is an alternative word for "confronting." The skill is that of challenging clients' existing perceptions so that together you can work with more and better information. Sometimes a challenge or confrontation from the helper's external viewpoint can broaden and deepen clients' perceptions by reframing the picture. Egan observes: "If challenge is successful, clients are helped to replace blind spots with new perspectives"

(Egan, 1990, p. 186). Helpers can also use confronting skills to challenge inconsistencies, possible distortions of reality, and inadequately acknowledging choice.

Confronting Inconsistencies

You may experience inconsistencies in messages your clients send, that are similar to the following:

- *Inconsistency between verbal, voice, and body messages:* "On the one hand you say that you are nervous, but you smile."
- *Inconsistency within verbal messages:* "You say you are doing poorly, but report being in the top 10 percent of your class."
- *Inconsistency between words and actions:* "You say you love your children from your former marriage, but you are behind on your support payments."
- *Inconsistency between past and present statements:* "You now say you hate her, but about 10 minutes ago you were saying how much you love her."

How you confront involves verbal, voice, and body messages. A common helper response when confronting inconsistencies is "On the one hand you say . . . , but on the other hand, . . . " (for example, "On the one hand you say you are fine, but on the other hand I catch a note of pain in your voice"). This way of confronting is often shortened to "You say . . . , but . . . " (for example, "You say you are fine, but I catch a note of pain in your voice").

Confronting Possible Distortions of Reality

When clients talk to helpers they may make statements like the following.

> "They are all out to get me."
> "I have no friends."
> "I'm a terrible mother."
> "I'm no good with women (or men)."
> "She (or he) doesn't love me any more."

All of these may be examples of unrealistic perceptions that harm rather than help clients. Clients' perceptions are of varying degrees of accuracy. Sometimes helpers need to challenge perceptions directly or else assist clients to test their own reality (Beck, 1976, 1988; Beck & Weishaar, 1989). Clients often jump to conclusions on insufficient evidence ("I have no friends"), and use polarized thinking ("Either I'm perfect or no good at all").

They may also fail to own responsibility for their thoughts, feelings, and actions ("They made me do it"). You need to judge whether to continue listening within their internal viewpoints or to confront possible distortions of reality.

A good form for confronting possible distortions of reality is "You say . . . , but where's the evidence?" (for example, "You say you have no friends, but where's the evidence?"). Such a response reflects the client's internal viewpoint and then invites him or her to produce evidence to support it. The client may then make a remark like "Well, Roberta never calls me any more." Then the helper may confront the client again with a question like "Is there any other way of looking at that?" With the questions "Where's the evidence?" and "Is there any other way of looking at that?" you invite speakers to produce their own evidence or provide different perceptions to confirm or disconfirm their version of reality. On other occasions you may suggest some evidence from your external viewpoint.

Confronting, Not Acknowledging, Choice

Lifeskills helping heavily emphasizes personal responsibility. You can confront clients with their role as choosers in their lives. One way to do this is to highlight their choice processes. For example, clients who say "I must send my children to private schools" might be confronted with the fact that they have some choice in the matter. Another example is that of Serena, aged 37, who says of her father, "I resent having to visit him every weekend." Here the helper responds by both reflecting her resentment and confronting her seeming failure to assume responsibility for being a chooser: "You feel resentful, but I wonder whether you sufficiently acknowledge that you *choose* to visit him every weekend." Such a confrontation might open the way to exploring both how Serena thinks (for instance, not always acknowledging that she has choices), and how she acts (possibly not asserting herself enough with her father). Yet another way of confronting clients with their choices is to focus on the verbs they use. For example, if a client says "I *can't* do that," the helper may ask "Can you say 'I *won't* do that'?"

Confronting by Reframing

Helpers may also challenge clients' existing perceptions by offering new perspectives. Geldard (1989) observes: "Sometimes a skillful counselor can change the way a client perceives events or situations by 'reframing' the picture which the client has described" (p. 58). Though the facts remain the same, the picture may look different in a new frame. Beck observes of relationships going downhill that partners begin to see each other through negative frames (for instance, "He's mean and manipulative" or "She's irresponsible"). He states: "Reframing consists of seeing these negative qualities in a different light" (Beck, 1988, p. 267).

Here is an example of a helper confronting a client with a reframe.

Tim, 16, perceived his mother as disliking him because she was always nagging him about doing household chores. The helper acknowledged his anger, but offered the reframe that his mother was a single parent who had to go to work to support the family and got very tired because she had more on her plate than she could handle. When she felt exhausted, she became irritable.

In this example, "the nagging mother who dislikes me" gets reframed as "the over-tired and overwhelmed single parent." Reframing is integral to the lifeskills helping model. Most clients do not perceive their thinking and behavior in skills terms. Stage 2 of the model, in which problems are redefined in skills terms, reframes the pictures provided by clients' problems by stating them in skills, rather than descriptive, language.

How to Confront

The following are some guidelines on how to confront.

1. *Start with reflective responding.* Always start your response by showing that you have heard and understood clients' messages. Then build on this understanding with your confronting response. This way you are more likely to keep clients' ears open to your viewpoint.
2. *Where possible, help clients to confront themselves.* By reflecting inconsistency, you allow clients to choose their own conclusions about it. Similarly, by asking clients to search for evidence to back their statements, you help them to confront themselves. Assisting clients in self-confrontation often leads to less resistance than directly confronting them from your own external viewpoint.
3. *Do not talk down.* Keep your confrontations at a democratic level. They are invitations for exploration. Avoid "you" messages. A major risk in confronting clients is that they perceive what you say as put-downs.
4. *Use a minimum amount of "muscle."* Only confront as strongly as your goal requires. Strong confrontations can create resis-

tances. Although sometimes necessary, such confrontations are generally best avoided—especially in initial sessions where trust is not yet established.

5. *Avoid threatening voice and body messages.* Try to avoid threatening voice and body messages like raising your voice and pointing your finger.

6. *Leave the ultimate responsibility with clients.* Allow clients to decide whether your confrontations actually help them to move forward in their explorations. Many of your confrontations will involve slight challenges. If well timed and tactfully worded, such challenges are unlikely to elicit a high degree of defensiveness.

7. *Do not overdo it.* Nobody likes being persistently challenged. With constant confrontations you create an unsafe emotional climate. You can help clients move forward with skilled confronting responses; however, you can block them and harm your relationship if you confront too often or too clumsily.

Self-Disclosing Skills

Helper self-disclosure relates to the ways in which you let yourself be known to clients. Usually the term refers to intentional verbal disclosure. However, there are numerous other ways in which helpers send messages—including voice and body messages, availability, office decor, written communications, and size of fees! Though the following discussion focuses mainly on intentional verbal disclosure in initial sessions, it has relevance to later sessions as well.

A useful distinction exists between self-involving responses and self-disclosing responses. McCarthy (1982) observes: "Self-disclosure responses are statements referring to the past history or personal experiences of the counselor, and self-involving responses are direct present expressions of a counselor's feelings about or reactions to client statements and/or behaviors" (p. 125). Another way of stating this is that there are at least two major dimensions of helper self-disclosure: showing involvement and disclosing personal information.

Showing Involvement

Appropriate helper disclosures that show involvement assist in forming a working alliance. In particular, positive self-involving statements expressing positive rather than negative feelings about clients draw favorable reactions (Watkins, 1990). Self-involving disclosures can personalize the helping process, so that clients feel they relate to real people. Even negative reactions can be used constructively as invitations for exploration. There is a here-and-now quality about reacting to clients. The following are three areas for self-involving statements:

- *Responding to specific disclosures.* Such comments include: "I'm delighted," "That's great," and "That's terrible."
- *Responding to clients as people.* Positive comments are: "I admire your courage," "I appreciate your honesty," and "I like your sense of humor."
- *Responding to the helping relationship.* Illustrative comments are: "I'm uneasy because I sense you want to put me on a pedestal," "I find my attention wavering and wonder why," and "I'm pleased at your willingness to cooperate and work hard."

Disclosing Personal Information

Research has yet to offer any definite conclusions on helpers' sharing personal information (Watkins, 1990). Disclosing personal information and experiences may help clients feel that you understand what they go through. For instance, unemployed clients may not only feel more positive when helpers share past unemployment experiences, but they may also talk more readily. In some types of helping, disclosure of shared experiences forms part of the helping process (for instance, disclosure of experiences by recovering alcoholics and addicts in Alcoholics Anonymous and certain drug-treatment programs).

Helpers have many choices in disclosing personal information: first, whether to mention it; second, how honest to be; third, whether to go beyond disclosing facts to disclosing feelings (for instance, not only having been unemployed but also having to struggle against depression and feelings of uselessness); fourth, how you coped with your experience; fifth, how you feel about it now.

Here are some tentative guidelines for appropriate disclosure of personal information and experiences.

1. *Be self-referent.* Do not disclose third-parties' experiences.
2. *Be to the point.* Do not slow down or defocus the interview through irrelevance or talking too much.
3. *Use good voice and body messages.* Be congruent. Your voice and body messages should match what you say.
4. *Be sensitive to clients.* Have sufficient sensitivity to realize when your disclosures may help clients and when they may be unwelcome or a burden. For instance, if you are currently

emotionally involved in getting divorced, you must judge whether you have sufficient detachment to disclose the experience constructively. Also, be sensitive to how clients receive your disclosures and decide accordingly whether to continue.

5. *Be sensitive to helper-client differences.* Expectations for helpers differ across cultures, social class, race, and gender, and so do expectations regarding appropriateness of helper self-disclosure.

6. *Do not do it too often.* Helpers who keep talking about themselves risk switching the focus of their work from their clients to themselves.

7. *Beware of countertransference. Countertransference* refers to both negative and positive feelings towards clients based on unresolved areas in helpers' lives. Intentionally or unintentionally, some helpers may use both involving and information self-disclosures to manipulate clients to meet their own needs for approval, intimacy, and sex. This highlights the importance of being aware of your motivation and also of behaving ethically.

Understanding Context Skills

Viewing Problems in Context

Helpers require skills of eliciting information about and understanding the contexts of problems. Problems and problematic skills do not exist in a vacuum. Rather they exist in networks of contextual variables whose relevance differs in each instance. Following are just some of the possible contexts pertinent to clarifying and understanding clients' problems (see Figure 5.3). These contexts are also relevant to negotiating areas of difference between helpers and clients.

1. *Cultural context:* The values and communication patterns of clients' cultures. Exposure of clients to mainstream culture and desires for assimilation. Issues of culture shock, alienation, mistrust, and loneliness. (Cultural issues can be relevant to native-born, migrant, and overseas-visitor clients.)

2. *Racial context:* The extent of clients' racial identity and pride. Exposure to racial discrimination and skills at handling it. Values, communication patterns, and family structures that differ from the culture of the racial majority.

3. *Social class context:* Rules for behavior differ widely among social classes. Helpers need to understand many client behaviors

(for instance, manners, dress, and language) in the context of their social classes.

4. *Family of origin context:* Here *family of origin* refers to parents and stepparents. The family of origin context may be direct or indirect. Take the example of Julio and Nancy, a couple in their twenties who have a distressed marriage. Up to four natural parents, and possibly some stepparents too, may directly tell them how to behave. They may also receive advice from relatives. In addition, families of origin indirectly influence Julio and Nancy's relationship through parental "voices in the head," many of which go unrecognized. In multicultural societies, such as the United States and Australia, cultural and family of origin contexts intermingle. In the extreme, all four of a couple's natural parents may be culturally different.

5. *Work/study context:* The work/study context can be relevant both to work-related problems and nonwork problems. For instance, workers whose companies have just been taken over may experience additional work stress. This stress may then manifest itself in increased irritability at home, creating problems there too.

6. *Health/medical context:* Clients' states of physical health can, in varying degrees, contribute to psychological problems (for example, glandular problems causing apathy). Furthermore, clients may behave differently when on medication than when not. Frequently helpers need to explore the past and current medical contexts of clients' problems. Opinions from medical practitioners are often essential. A related area meriting exploration is that of clients' prior experiences of seeking and receiving psychiatric and psychological help.

7. *Gender context:* Feminist helpers and gender-aware helpers (Good, Gilbert, & Scher, 1990) consider that most, if not all, problems need to be understood within gender perspectives. Helpers require sensitivity to differences in biological functioning and experiencing (for instance, in regard to menstruation and menopause). However, the main area of gender sensitivity relates to learned sex-role behavior and expectations (for instance, on relationships and career choice). Furthermore, gender-aware helpers frequently emphasize understanding the historical, social, and political contexts of gender learning and discrimination.

8. *Sexual preference context:* Homosexual clients may or may not live within the context of the rules and values of the gay and lesbian communities. The attitude of mainstream (straight) cul-

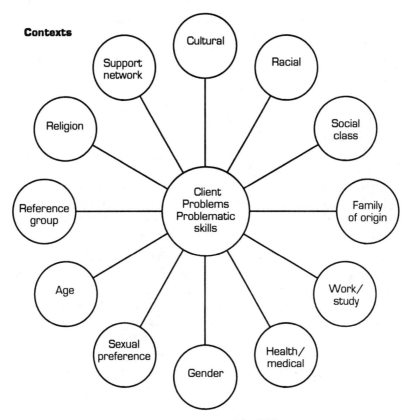

Figure 5.3 Some potentially relevant contexts for identifying and clarifying clients' problems and problematic skills

ture toward homosexual or bisexual preference provides a further context for understanding certain clients' problems. In addition, changing attitudes toward homosexuality within the helping professions, whereby the stigma of mental illness is no longer attached to it, provide still another context.

9. *Age context:* The physical process of aging may contribute to some clients' problems. Others may face deprivations (for instance, companionship and employment) on account of age. In addition, the respect accorded to age differs greatly across cultures. *Ageism,* discrimination on the basis of age, may be more a feature of Western than of Asian cultures.

10. *Reference group context:* Humans are social animals who tend to associate in groups. Frequently, valuable understandings about clients' behaviors may be gained by placing them in the

context of group norms. For example, a different understanding of a problem may stem from the helper's discovering that a teenager stole a car in response to a peer group dare rather than on his own.

11. *Religious context:* Clients' religious faith can be a source of strength. Furthermore, sharing the same religious beliefs and ethics can strengthen the working alliance. However, religious faiths (albeit sometimes misunderstood) can be sources of self-oppression. In addition, some skills weaknesses may be sustained on religious grounds (for example, confusing lack of assertion with humility). Since religion is a central part of many clients' lives, helpers need to be sensitive to the religious context and its influence. Also, some helpers require awareness of their limitations in understanding religiously motivated people.

12. *Support network context:* A valuable insight into clients' problems may come from exploring their support networks. Murgatroyd (1985) observes: "When a person seeks help from a stranger it is often a sign that their own helping networks are inadequate" (p. 151). Support networks can consist of spouse, family, friends, colleagues, ministers, and helping professionals, to mention but a few. How isolated are clients? Who is available to offer support and how useful might their support be? What are the clients' skills of accessing and using a support network?

Possessing Understanding Context Skills

Clients vary in the number of contextual considerations relevant to identifying and clarifying their problems. Helpers also vary in the range of clients they see. Most helpers require a range of understanding context skills, some of which are presented here.

Possess contextual knowledge. If helpers work with specific groups (for instance, immigrants from a certain country, or gay and lesbian clients), they should be familiar with the assumptions, values, and shared experiences of these groups. Even those possessing a good understanding of specific cultures and minority groups need to update their knowledge continually. For example, helpers working with homosexual groups need up-to-date information about legislation concerning homosexual behavior and about the transmission and treatment of AIDS.

Demonstrate contextual empathy. Helpers can show contextual empathy with their voice, body, verbal, and action messages. We can look at demonstrating cultural empathy as an example.

British people tend to speak more softly than North Americans. Japanese do not use eye contact as much as people from Western cultures (Pease, 1981). In the Arctic, "it may be best to sit side by side rather than opposing with a forward trunk lean" (Ivey, 1987, p.169). Helpers dealing with people from different cultures need to take into account both the different ways their voice and body messages will be perceived and the way they perceive clients' voice and body messages. You cannot assume that good intentions lead to good cross-cultural results. Furthermore, in responding to verbal messages, helpers need to be sensitive to topics that may have particular meaning for people from different cultures. For instance, a desire for harmonious family relationships contains a much stronger cultural message when expressed by Asians than Anglo-Saxons. Sometimes high levels of empathy can only be offered by people who speak clients' primary language.

Give permission to discuss helper-client differences.   Helpers and clients come from different contexts. Helpers may quickly become aware that they differ from clients on significant characteristics. One possibility is to acknowledge the difference (for instance, racial or cultural) and ask what clients think and feel about it. A possible advantage of being direct is that it provides clients with opportunities to air and work through mistrust. A risk is that such questions may reflect more helpers' than clients' concerns, and hence defocus clients.

Give permission to discuss problems in terms of their broader contexts.   Often a high degree of helper-client matching on significant contextual characteristics is not possible. Nevertheless helpers can show sensitivity to contextual issues in clients' problems. One way to do this is to acknowledge a possible deficiency in understanding the context of clients' problems and to ask them to fill in gaps (Poon, Nelson-Jones, & Caputi, 1991). The following is a simplified illustration.

> **Asian student**: My father wants me to go into the family building business and I feel under a lot of pressure to continue on my building course to please him.
> **Helper**: It sounds as though you have mixed feelings. You have reservations about continuing your building course, yet don't want to go against your father's wishes. Cultural considerations are often important in understanding such problems and if you feel they are relevant to your case, please feel free to share them.

Focus questions on broader contexts. As part of their attempts
elicit relevant information, helpers may use questions focusing
on the broader contexts of clients' problems. Depending on what
seems potentially relevant to clients' problems, helpers might
ask questions focused on one or more of the contexts depicted in
Figure 5.3: cultural, racial, social class, family of origin, work/
study, health/medical, gender, sexual preference, age, reference
group, religion, and support network. This list is far from exhaustive. The earlier presentation of these broader contexts provides an indication of topics within each context for focused
questioning.

Managing Initial Resistances Skills

What Are Resistances?

Resistance may be broadly defined as anything that gets in the
way of helping. Clients can both bring resistances to helping
and have them activated during it. Resistances can be present at
any stage of the helping process. At best most clients are ambivalent when they come to helping. At the same time as they
want change, they may have anxieties both about changing
and about the helping process (for instance, the need to disclose
weaknesses). Some clients may come reluctantly (for example,
"problem" children sent to school counselors for disrupting
class).

Sullivan (1954) observed that there were cultural handicaps to
the work of the psychiatrist. These "antipsychiatric" elements in
the culture can also lead to resistances in nonmedical helping.
Such culturally handicapping norms include: people ought not
to need help; people should know themselves; and people
"should have 'good natural instincts' and 'good intuition' which
ought to govern them in choosing the 'right' way to act and
think" (p.37). Other cultural thinking errors contributing to resistances are that people who need helping are "sick" and that
people should be able to solve all problems by "common sense."

Helpers may wrongly attribute the sources of clients' resistances and blame them for lack of cooperation and progress.
Clients' resistances may be the consequence of poor helping skills
(for instance, unrewarding listening). Furthermore, some helping
models—especially if incompetently applied—may engender resistances (for instance, the lack of structure of the person-centered approach or the didactic nature of the rational-emotive
approach). Helpers may also bring resistances to their work (for
example, fatigue, burnout, and prejudices). Yalom (1989) mentions his difficulty, when faced with an overweight female client,

in overcoming his resistances to obesity. Also, helper resistances may interact with client resistances to slow down or stop progress.

Dealing with Initial Resistances

Following are skills for dealing with initial resistances. Since there are so many variations and reasons for resistances, it is impossible to cover all contingencies.

Use rewarding listening skills. Beginning helpers, and even those more experienced, may both sustain and create clients' resistances through poor skills. Resistances are a normal part of initial sessions. If you listen rewardingly, you do much to build trust for lowering resistances. Some clients' resistances manifest themselves in aggression. Rather than justify yourself or allow yourself to be sucked into a competitive contest, one approach to handling such aggression is to reflect it back. Locate the feelings clearly in the client, but indicate that you have picked it up loud and clear. Where clients provide reasons for their hostility, you can reflect these too. Just showing clients that you understand their internal viewpoint, especially if you do it consistently, may diminish resistances.

Join with clients. Sometimes helpers can lower clients' resistances by helping them feel that they have a "friend at court." For instance, helpers can initially listen and offer support to children expressing resentment about parents.

> **Client:** I think coming here is a waste of time. My parents keep picking on me and they are the ones who need help.
> **Helper:** You feel angry about coming here because your parents are the people with problems.

In the above instance you could focus on parental deficiencies before focusing back on the client. You use your client's need to talk about parental injustices as a means of building a working relationship. Another example is that of a pupil referred to the school counselor by the principal. Here the helper responds more to voice and body than to verbal messages.

> **Pupil:** (looks down and sighs)
> **Counselor:** I sense that you are uncomfortable about being here (if no response after a pause). Would you care to tell me your side of the story?

Give permission to discuss reluctance and fears. If you receive overt or subtle messages from clients that they have reservations about being in helping, you can bring the agenda out into the open and give clients permission to elaborate. In the following example, a parole officer responds to a juvenile delinquent's seeming reluctance to disclose anything significant.

> **Parole officer:** I think maybe you don't want to talk to me because I'm your parole officer. I'm wondering what exactly are your reservations?

In the previous section, I mentioned giving permission to discuss differences in helper-client characteristics (for instance, culture and race) that may create reluctance to participate in helping.

Invite collaboration. The collaborative nature of the working relationship in the lifeskills helping approach both prevents and overcomes many client resistances. Initial structuring by the helper aims to create the idea of a partnership, a shared endeavor in which clients and helpers perform the detective work of finding out how clients can better attain goals.

Enlist client self-interest. Help clients identify reasons for participating in the helping process. For instance, Troy, a male client who perceives his parents as picking on him, might be helped to see he could be happier with better skills for coping with parents. Questions that challenge clients regarding the adequacy of their own behavior may also enlist self-interest. Such questions include "Where is your current behavior getting you?" and "How is that behavior helping you?" Questions that encourage clients to think about goals are also useful (for example, "What are your goals in the situation?" and "Wouldn't you like to be more in control of your life?").

Reward silent clients for talking. Some clients find it difficult to talk, whether in or out of helping. Others may find it particularly difficult to talk to helpers. Without overpowering, helpers may have to respond to these clients more frequently and more obviously. For example, helpers may use more small rewards when clients talk. Also, helpers may encourage clients by reflectively responding to most statements. Helpers may also reflectively respond to the difficulty certain clients have in talking, even though the client may not have said this.

The preceding are just some ways of working with resistances and reluctance. Helpers need be sensitive to the pace at which different clients work. Clients who feel pressured by helpers may become even more resistant. Furthermore, if attacked prematurely and clumsily, clients may reinforce their defenses. When dealing with client resistances, helpers require sensitivity, realism, flexibility, and tact.

Thinking Skills

I deal briefly here with the important topic of helper thinking skills for stage 1. (I will discuss assessing clients' thinking skills in the next chapter and interventions focused on clients' thinking in Chapter 10.) Following are areas of helper thinking skills relevant to stage 1 of the lifeskills model (and frequently to later stages as well).

Own responsibility for choosing. Helpers need always to be conscious that they are choosers (Nelson-Jones, 1987). They make choices in regard to their verbal, voice, body, touch, and action messages. They choose how they think and how they feel. Throughout helping they continually make decisions about how to respond to clients' communications. In addition, in initial sessions there is a heavy emphasis on choosing how best to identify, clarify, and break down problems. Helpers should not only own responsibility for choosing, but also for the consequences of choices. Helping choices are best viewed as hypotheses modifiable in light of feedback.

Use self-talk. In initial sessions, helpers can use self-talk in ways that create anxiety in themselves and their clients. Trish is a beginning helper. After a semester-long skills practicum, she is about to see her first client and record the session for her supervisor. Trish is highly nervous and worsens matters with the following self-talk.

> **Trish:** Help. I've got this important interview coming up. I wonder whether I'm going to do all right. I'm scared the client will notice that I'm anxious and lacking in skills. What if the client has a problem that is out of my depth? How will I manage then? Also, my supervisor will listen and hear all my mistakes.

A more constructive way for Trish to approach her first real session would be to use coping self-talk. Coping self-talk consists of calming and coaching self-statements: calming statements to relax herself and coaching statements to stay focused on how best to proceed. Trish could use the following coping self-talk.

Trish: Help. I'm feeling anxious because this is my first time with a real client. Now calm down and take a few deep breaths. I'm pretty certain I can cope with the situation. I've done a lot of practicing and received good feedback. My supervisor just wants me to do the best I can and does not expect me to be perfect. I can start the interview with a good opening statement and speak calmly and clearly. Then I can use my rewarding listening skills. I do not have to control everything that happens. Already, I'm starting to feel better by using my coping self-talk skills.

Helpers can also use coping self-talk during and after their sessions. For instance, they can calm themselves and think how best to act if clients get hostile during sessions. They can talk to themselves constructively after sessions (for instance, by acknowledging what went right and not just focusing on what went wrong).

Choose realistic personal rules. Helpers can place unnecessary pressures on themselves by their unrealistic personal rules (Nelson-Jones, 1990a), irrational beliefs or "mustabations" (Ellis, 1962, 1989). The coined term "mustabation" refers to rules containing words like "must," "ought," or "should." Helpers can place demands on themselves ("I *must* be perfect"), their clients ("My clients *must* always appreciate me"), the helping process ("Helping *must* always go smoothly"), and the environment ("Other people *must* always understand and support my helping endeavors").

Helpers need to identify unrealistic personal rules and reformulate them into more realistic or rational rules.

Unrealistic rule: "I must be perfect."
Realistic rule: "I would like to perform as competently as I can."

Unrealistic rule: "My clients must always appreciate me."
Realistic rule: "Though it is pleasant to have clients' approval, my main focus is on helping them to the best of my ability."

Unrealistic rule: "Helping must always go smoothly."
Realistic rule: "Helping is somewhat unpredictable and I can tolerate mistakes and setbacks."

Unrealistic rule: "Other people must always support and understand my endeavors."
Realistic rule: "I can try my best to explain what I do as a helper, but ultimately I can only influence other people and not control what they think."

Choose to perceive accurately. Helpers perceive themselves, others, their clients, and events with varying degrees of accuracy. It is important not to jump to conclusions when attempting to identify and clarify problems. Rather you need to carefully sift fact from inference and, if appropriate, accumulate more information to build and test your inferences. Below are some specific perceptual errors to avoid (Beck 1976, 1988; Beck & Weishaar, 1989).

- *Tunnel vision:* Focusing on only a portion of the available information regarding a problem rather than taking into account all significant data.
- *Magnifying and minimizing:* Magnifying or exaggerating the qualities and significance of other people and events or minimizing them.
- *Negativeness:* Overemphasizing negative aspects of clients and yourself and minimizing positive aspects. Always searching for weaknesses rather than for strengths. Applying negative labels to yourself and others (for example, "I'm a loser" or "That client is impossible").
- *Selective inattention:* Overlooking or being inattentive to material that may cause you anxiety (Sullivan, 1954). Denying and distorting information through defensive thinking.
- *Overgeneralizing:* Making sweeping generalizations unsupported by evidence: "All my initial sessions go well," "My clients never stick to the point," or "She failed in one relationship, therefore she failed in all her previous relationships."
- *Catastrophizing:* Making highly negative predictions unsupported by evidence: "My first session this afternoon did not go well, so all my other sessions will go badly too."
- *Polarized thinking:* Perceiving in either/or and black-and-white terms: "Either clients are very cooperative or very uncooperative," and "Clients either continue having problems or are cured."
- *Self-rating:* Going beyond functional ratings of specific characteristics to devaluing yourself as a whole person: "I'm having difficulty learning helping skills, therefore I am a rotten person."
- *Mind reading:* Helpers may believe they can tell what clients think. However they may neither have collected adequate evidence nor checked out their conclusions.

Attribute cause and responsibility accurately. Helpers may err either in the direction of attributing too much or too little cause and responsibility to themselves. Here are helpers' statements attributing *too much* responsibility to themselves.

"I'm responsible for everything that happens in my helping sessions."

"I'm solely responsible for the outcomes of helping."

"Everything that goes wrong in helping is my fault."

Here are helper statements attributing *too little* responsibility to themselves.

"Jennie is not saying much because she is a shy person." (Jennie may be shy, but the helper also has poor rewarding listening skills.)

"Boris has a lot of resistances to being helped." (The helper may have contributed to these resistances.)

        CHAPTER HIGHLIGHTS

- Four objectives of initial helping sessions are to develop a supportive working relationship, a working model, a working definition, and working goals and interventions.
- Structuring describes the behaviors by which helpers let clients know their respective roles at various stages of the helping process.
- Structuring statements in initial sessions may be made more than once; voice and body as well as verbal messages are important.
- Questions can help identify and clarify the roots of problems.
- Helper choices when questioning include purpose, past or present focus, amount of topics covered, degree of detail, intimacy level, and timing.
- Types of questions include: open-ended versus closed-ended; how, what, when, where, and why; clarification; elaboration; challenging; specific detail; request for example; "show me"; and eliciting personal meaning.
- Questioning skills for working in partnership with clients include: establishing agenda and transition questions; interspersing reflective responding; asking follow-on questions; and encouraging clients' work.
- Summarizing skills entail making brief statements of longer excerpts from helping sessions.
- The functions of summaries include clarifying, identifying themes, identifying problem areas, and feeding back details of problems.
- Focusing entails directing and influencing the helping conversation into specific areas.

- Focusing skills include focused responding to parts of clients' communications, focusing clients on themselves, and initiating focused exploration.
- Confrontations are challenges that expand clients' existing perceptions so that together you can work with new and better information.
- Helpers use confronting skills for challenging inconsistencies, possible distortions of reality, and not acknowledging choice. Also, confronting skills include reframing problems by offering new perspectives.
- Showing involvement and disclosing personal information are two important areas of helper self-disclosure.
- Self-involving disclosures can be in response to specific disclosures, clients as people, and the helping relationship.
- Often helpers need to clarify and understand the contexts of clients' problems. Relevant contexts for problems include cultural, racial, social class, family of origin, work/study, health/medical, gender, sexual preference, age, reference group, religious, and support network.
- Understanding context skills include obtaining knowledge, demonstrating contextual empathy, giving permission to discuss helper-client differences, giving permission to discuss problems in terms of broader contexts.
- Skills for managing initial session resistances include rewarding listening, joining, inviting collaboration, and enlisting client self-interest.
- Thinking skills for identifying and clarifying problems include owning responsibility for choosing, coping self-talk, realistic personal rules, perceiving accurately, and accurately attributing cause and responsibility.

STAGE

2

ASSESS PROBLEMS AND
REDEFINE IN SKILLS TERMS

Chapter 6 presents helper skills for assessing clients' feelings, thoughts, and actions. The chapter ends by reviewing skills for redefining clients' problems in skills terms.

CHAPTER SIX

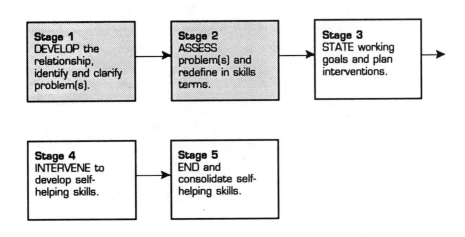

HOW TO ASSESS PROBLEMS AND REDEFINE IN SKILLS TERMS

We remain shackled to a scientifically
outmoded conceptual framework and its
terminology.

—Thomas Szasz

CHAPTER QUESTIONS

❀ *What is the role of assessment in lifeskills helping?*

❀ *How can helpers and clients assess feelings?*

❀ *How can helpers and clients assess thinking skills?*

❀ *How can helpers and clients assess action skills?*

❀ *What are helper skills for redefining clients' problems in skills terms?*

ROLE OF ASSESSMENT

Assessment in lifeskills helping is performed both with and for clients. Also, assessment aims to develop clients' self-assessment skills for the future. During stage 1, you develop working models of clients' problems and problematic skills. Clients come to helping with hypotheses, albeit inadequate, of what their problems are and how they are sustained. During the identifying and clarifying problems process, clients may start revising their models. Often the process of systematically eliciting descriptive information about clients' problems loosens their existing conceptualizations.

Stage 2 continues loosening clients' existing conceptualizations of problems. However, the process does not stop there. The desired outcome of stage 2 is to reconceptualize problems so that clients now have "handles" for change; what Egan (1990) calls *leverage*. Helpers use their skills not only to elicit basic descriptive information but also to explore the adequacy of hypotheses about problematic skills that are sustaining problems. Helpers work with clients to assess information, both volunteered and elicited. Together helpers and clients move from descriptive definitions of problems into skills redefinitions.

The Helper's Role

Helpers should always offer supportive relationships when assessing and redefining clients' problems in skills terms. Rewarding listening skills are fundamental. Furthermore, many skills used for identifying and clarifying problems (for instance focusing and summarizing) are relevant for assessing and redefining problems. In stage 2, you move beyond offering accurate *responsive* empathy based on understanding clients' internal viewpoints to offering accurate *active* empathy in which you expand clients' internal viewpoints to provide a fuller understanding of problems and problematic skills.

Helpers are practitioner-researchers who formulate hypotheses about how clients sustain problems. Sources of such hypotheses are descriptive information provided by clients, information elicited as helpers try on initial hypotheses, helping theory, knowledge of relevant research, and previous experience of clients. Where possible, you attempt to work openly with clients. You treat clients as intelligent people who, despite defenses and anxieties, wish to help themselves through greater self-understanding. You assist clients to do much of their own assessing rather than doing all of it for them. You never lose sight of the fact that helping is temporary. Especially where client contact extends over a number of sessions, helpers teach clients how to redefine problems in skills terms.

Can assessment be overdone? The answer is a resounding yes. You need to be sensitive to the amount of information required for assessing problems. Furthermore, you need to take into account clients' perceptions of when "enough is enough." Ideally, you need both to collect information and also to redefine problems in skills terms as frugally as possible.

The Client's Role

Like helpers, clients are also hypothesis makers and testers. To date, their hypotheses about how to solve their problems are inadequate. Frequently they are stuck in faulty definitions of problems. Clients can actively collaborate with helpers to generate hypotheses, provide information for assessing hypotheses, and evaluate conceptualizations of problems. They can participate in various attempts to assess their feelings, thoughts, and actions. For example, they can strive for honesty in experiencing and expressing feelings. They can be open about how they think, even if it be in socially undesirable ways. They can assist in exploring and evaluating hypotheses about how they think. In addition, they can share specific details of how they have acted in the past, monitor their current actions, and participate in role-plays.

Assessment is for clients' even more than for helpers' benefits. Clients can engage in testing the adequacy of original conceptions of problems and make corrections. They can provide confirmatory, corrective, or negative feedback about helpers' hypotheses. Clients can cooperate with helpers to develop more accurate and economical skills redefinitions of problems. Often, if active in assessing and redefining problems, clients acquire good motivation for change. Furthermore, active participation in assessing and redefining problems fosters acquisition of these skills for later self-helping.

ASSESS FEELINGS

Why Assess Feelings?

The following are examples of clients' feelings statements.

"I get panic attacks."
"I have suicidal thoughts."
"I have high blood pressure."
"I can't control my temper."

"I never know what I want."
"I lack energy."
"I'm sexually unresponsive."

Helpers assess feelings for numerous reasons, some of which are mentioned below.

Protect clients.   Helpers have an ethical duty to protect clients. At the back of most helpers' minds when meeting new clients is the question "Is this client a suicide risk?" Helpers also seek to understand the intensity and nature of clients' pain. Such understanding is partly to protect clients, but also to make appropriate skills definitions of problems.

Evaluate emotional responsiveness.   Helpers always need to be mindful of clients' ability to experience feelings. Feelings may be viewed as the core of human personhood and identity. Helpers seek to assess how responsive clients are, both to themselves and others. To what extent are clients in touch with their valuing process? Are clients in touch with significant feelings or do they deny and distort such feelings? To what extent are clients in touch with wants and wishes?

Clarify real agendas.   Paying close attention to feelings may assist helpers to clarify what clients' real agendas are. Sometimes clients give feelings clues that more substantial problems underlie their "calling-card" explanations for coming. For example, by voice and body messages, a woman who presents wanting to discuss a problem child may indicate her real agenda is marital dissatisfaction. Also, sometimes helpers need to allow clients space to clarify feelings before they know which problem to work on in skills terms.

Dave, 50, had been divorced for five years and had custody of three children—Beth, 17, Jan, 15, and Marty, 13. For the last year, Dave had been seeing Maria, 45, a divorcee who also had three children with ages ranging from 6 to 17. Dave came to helping confused about whether or not he wanted to develop his relationship with Maria further or get out of it. Dave's helper, Mel, spent much of the initial session assisting Dave to get in touch with and explore his feelings concerning: his past, present, and possible future with Maria; his fears of commitment after the pain of his divorce; his anxieties about how good he was at communicating in close relationships; his needs for companionship; and his fears of being lonely for the remainder of this life. As the session progressed, Dave became clearer regarding his wish to work on his skills at relating to Maria.

Obtain leads about thinking and action skills weaknesses.   Another reason for assessing feelings is to assist clients in regulating unwanted feelings and in expressing appropriate feelings. Since feelings reflect our animal nature, they are not in themselves skills. Nevertheless, assessing feelings accurately can be a major route to identifying thinking and action skills weaknesses. For example, clients admitting their anger, hurt, and guilt have better starting points for developing the thinking and action skills to manage these feelings than clients who deny or distort them. You also need to assess clients' skills at expressing feelings. For example, Betsy knows what she feels about her boyfriend Chico, but is too inhibited to reveal it.

Be aware of medical and psychiatric considerations.   A simple mind-body split is erroneous. Nevertheless, you need to be aware that medical considerations can influence how clients feel. Non-medically trained helpers should acknowledge their limitations and seek appropriate medical or psychiatric advice. Occasions where you need to take medical and psychiatric considerations into account include clients who are on medication (Burns, 1989; Ponterotto, 1985); have a physical illness (for instance, cancer), that affects how they feel; show psychophysiologic symptoms (for instance, peptic ulcers and migraine headaches); exhibit the effects of substance abuse; or suffer from schizophrenia, delusional disorders, and mood disorders (American Psychiatric Association, 1987).

Develop clients' self-assessment skills.   Helpers work together with clients to assess feelings. In their pasts, many clients have had their feelings invalidated. Skilled assessment can both affirm the importance of awareness of feelings and help clients to experience, identify, and explore significant feelings. Clients' feelings may take time to emerge and be shared with you. Revealing and assessing feelings occurs throughout helping. Also, where possible, you can assist clients to develop skills at assessing feelings for after helping.

Dimensions of Feelings

In the section on reflecting feelings (Chapter 4), I discussed some ways of identifying feelings by picking up feeling words and by attending to voice and body messages. Now I review dimensions of feelings more from the viewpoint of assessing problems than making rewarding listening responses.

Capacity to feel Helpers need to be aware of clients' abilities to experience feelings (Rogers, 1951, 1959, 1961, 1975). Some clients lack emotional responsiveness across a wide range of feelings. Other clients may have difficulty experiencing specific feelings (for example, sexuality or anger). Clients' difficulties in experiencing feelings can be at different levels. An extensive and longstanding incapacity to experience feelings may have different implications for how helping might proceed than a more focused and less severe problem of experiencing feelings. One of the outcomes of any extended helping contact is that clients should become better at experiencing and expressing feelings.

Energy level Related to clients' ability to experience feelings is their energy level. How much mental and physical energy do they have? To what degree do they possess vitality or seem apathetic? If clients' energy levels are very low, helpers should ask them to check with their doctors whether there are medical explanations.

Self-esteem Helpers need to be aware of clients' confidence levels. Clients with very low self-esteem are potential suicide risks. Clients with reasonable self-esteem possess a useful asset for working on problems and problematic skills. Words to describe low self-esteem include worthlessness, hopelessness, helplessness (Seligman, 1975), and despair. Self-statements indicating lack of self-esteem include "I'm no good," "I never do anything right," and "I can't cope." Adjectives to describe high self-esteem include confident, strong, self-accepting, worthwhile, and emotionally resilient.

Anxiety and defensiveness Helpers need to assess how anxious clients are and in what areas of their life anxiety occurs. Is their anxiety a pervasive trait, or is it a state attached to specific situations? Helpers also need to assess how clients show anxiety, both in obvious ways and also in terms of their less obvious defensive processes or security operations (Clark, 1991; Sullivan, 1953, 1954). Pay attention to ways in which clients' anxieties—and yours too—can distort the helping process.

Mood A mood is a state of mind or feeling. The American Psychiatric Association's *Diagnostic and Statistical Manual of Mental Disorders (DSM-111-R)* defines mood as "prolonged emotion that colors the whole psychic life; it generally involves either depression or elation" (American Psychiatric Association, 1987, p. 213). However, moods are often relatively transient in duration, lasting only a few moments, a day, or a week (McNair, Lorr, & Droppleman, 1981). Helpers can assess severity, direction, duration, and fluctuations in clients' moods.

Psychological pain   Effective helpers are skilled at locating areas of psychological pain and assessing their severity. Sometimes, during helping, clients acknowledge major areas of psychological pain that they have hitherto either repressed or suppressed. Helpers also need to be conscious of the pain that clients may experience when discussing certain material (for instance, rape or sexual abuse).

Physical reactions   Physical reactions both represent and accompany feelings. For example, physical reactions associated with shyness include: dry mouth, blushing, nausea, feeling faint, perspiring, knotted stomach, pounding heart, shaking, mind going blank, and shallow, rapid breathing. Sometimes clients react to their physical reactions. For example, in anxiety and panic attacks, clients may experience feeling tense and anxious and then become even more tense and anxious because of this. Helpers need to develop skills at empathically describing physical reactions with appropriate words.

Psychophysiologic disorders   Psychophysiologic or psychosomatic disorders are caused and maintained primarily by psychological and emotional, rather than physical or organic, factors. Psychophysiologic disorders can affect the skin (for instance, acne), and the body's musculoskeletal, respiratory, cardiovascular, blood and lymphatic, gastrointestinal, and endocrine systems. The more common psychophysiologic disorders include peptic ulcers, migraine headaches, asthma, and high blood pressure. Psychophysiologic disorders may be distinguished from *somatoform disorders* (phony or imitative, rather than actual, physical disorders).

Predominant feelings   Sometimes clients present with a specific feeling that they wish to handle better (for example, anxiety in test taking or public speaking situations). In other instances, a predominant feeling may emerge as helping progresses (for instance, self-pity, resentment, anger, or wariness). Teyber (1989) uses the term *characterological feeling* to describe these central feelings that clients experience as their fate because they have "always been there and it seems like they always will be" (p. 84). Helpers need to keep an eye or ear out for repetitive and central feelings that clients handle with difficulty. Before, and even during helping, clients may find it hard to acknowledge such feelings.

Complex and conflicted feelings   Clients' feelings are frequently complex. Helpers require skills at eliciting, clarifying, and articulating the different elements of what may be multiple and mixed feelings. Also, clients may need to learn to avoid thinking about their feelings in static, rigid, and simplistic terms. Feelings often come in twos and threes. For example, anger may be accompanied by hurt and guilt or depression by anxiety and sadness. Though not always with the same intensity, feelings are frequently accompanied by their opposites. Ambivalent feelings include: happy–sad, love–hate, pleased–displeased, and approach–avoidance. Sometimes clients experience ambivalent feelings simultaneously and sometimes sequentially.

Antecedents and consequences of feelings   When assessing feelings, helpers may assess their antecedents and consequences. The antecedents of feelings can stretch back into clients' childhoods. For example, the pain of a present loss may reactivate the pain of an earlier loss. Anger may be hard to express now, because such feelings were suppressed in clients' families of origins. Frequently helpers explore current antecedents and consequences of feelings (for example, thoughts prior to experiencing feelings, and positive and negative consequences after expressing feelings).

Strength and persistence of feelings   Often feeling intensity is described by words like *mild, moderate,* or *severe.* For example, clients may be mildly depressed, moderately depressed, or severely depressed. There can be different perceptions of what is mild, moderate, or severe both among helpers and between helpers and clients. Persistence of feelings may be described by words like chronic and acute. *Chronic* implies persistent whereas *acute* implies sharp and short. In addition, disorders like schizophrenia may be in partial remission or full remission (American Psychiatric Association, 1987), meaning that the absence of symptoms is either partial or complete.

Appropriateness of feelings   Often helpers and clients attempt to assess appropriateness of feelings. Did the client experience an appropriate quantity of an appropriate feeling, and was this appropriately expressed? Helpers and clients assessing the appropriateness of feelings must take into account clients' unique styles of expressing feelings and numerous situational, contextual, and cultural considerations. One way of assessing appropriateness of feelings is to assess what their consequences were for clients and others. To what extent and in what ways were there positive or negative emotional and behavioral consequences (Ellis, 1962, 1989)? Another way is to assess certain feelings in terms of psychiatric classification.

Unclear feelings   Clients may either be unclear about feelings or communicate feelings unclearly, or both. Sometimes feelings are masked (for instance, depression may mask anger). On other occasions feelings are displaced: anger at failing a test may be taken out on a roommate, spouse, or parent. Sometimes the real agenda is unclear. For instance, married couples may argue over little things and avoid confronting more serious differences and relationship fears. Frequently expression of feelings is inhibited or diluted. Some clients obscure feelings by going to the other extreme: They dramatize and magnify feelings. Social desirability considerations pervade the early stages of helping. Clients may play out social roles to please helpers. Clients may also have acquired poor skills at using feeling words and framing their verbal feeling messages with appropriate voice and body messages. Many feelings take time to emerge. Helpers require sensitivity to the pace at which clients both can and wish to reveal their emotional selves.

Feelings about helping and helpers   Clients invariably have feelings about both helping and helpers. Clients may resist or cooperate in the helping process. They may feel pleased or frustrated with their progress. In addition, clients may have a range of feelings about helpers: on dimensions such as like–dislike, trust–mistrust, competent–incompetent, and dependent–independent. Sometimes clients express feelings that helpers find difficult to handle (for example, liking, sexual attraction, anger, and sadness). Often there is a reciprocity of feeling between helpers and clients (for example, mutual like or dislike).

Skills for Eliciting and Assessing Feelings

Helpers need to realize the importance of feelings both for human functioning and for helping clients change. Many skills for assessing feelings involve enlisting clients' cooperation in sharing feelings. Following are some skills useful for eliciting and assessing feelings.

Be a rewarding listener. In supportive and trusting relationships, clients assist helpers to understand how they feel. Rewarding listening provides a safe emotional climate for clients to experience and share feelings. Helpers sensitive to clients' feelings and feeling nuances legitimize the importance of experiencing and discussing feelings. You require good skills at picking up and reflecting back feelings messages. Receiver skills include paying attention to feelings words; observing voice and body messages; and being keenly attuned to any mismatch between voice, body, and verbal messages. Sometimes you can infer feelings from what is left unsaid or partially said. Sender skills that you can use to help clients share feelings include showing attention with voice and body messages, reflecting feelings, reflecting reasons, and offering companionship as clients explore new and sometimes unexpected feelings.

Helpers need to be sensitive when clients encounter feelings difficult either to experience or share. You must always be aware of the pace at which clients wish to reveal feelings. Often a box of tissue helps! You can make the following remarks to encourage but not pressure clients to share feelings.

"I realize that this may be a painful area for you to discuss."
"You seem upset. Just take your time in sharing what you feel."

Observe body messages and listen for voice messages. Probably clients' voice and body messages provide the most valid source of information about how they feel. From the moment of first contact, skilled helpers closely watch out for body messages and listen for voice messages. Clients differ in how clearly they send messages. However, both consciously and intuitively, skilled helpers listen "with the third ear" and observe "with the third eye" for deviations, omissions, and discrepancies in communications. They look out for feeling fragments or glimpses that are clues to more substantial and as yet unshared feelings. Skilled helpers have highly developed capacities for sensing out what seems false. Their ability to tune in to their own feelings, as well as experience with numerous previous clients, provides a base for formulating feelings hypotheses.

Use advanced reflection of feelings. As a result of observing and listening, you may sense what clients "only half see and hint at" (Egan, 1990, p. 214). Frequently clients repress, suppress, or otherwise inhibit feelings. Advanced reflection of feelings entails making exploratory responses that help clients articulate more personally relevant, emotionally tinged, and threatening areas of their experiencing. You require sensitivity to reflect partially hidden agendas. Sometimes you may choose not to mention such agendas to avoid upsetting clients. Advanced reflections of feelings check out your hunches or feelings hypotheses. Such responses generally require humility and tentativeness. Inaccurate, clumsily worded, and badly timed responses can do more harm than good.

Example A: The helper gets the impression that the client talks around the area of lesbian feelings.

> **Helper:** You've mentioned a couple of people you know who do not find lesbian life easy. I'm wondering whether lesbianism may be an issue for you too?

Example B: The helper senses that the client is very taken with a woman he has recently met, yet he keeps expressing reservations about her.

> **Helper:** You seem to be stating numerous reasons why you should be careful about starting a relationship with Brenda. However, the overriding feeling I get is that you're swept off your feet by her and can't get her out of your mind. Nor do you want to.

Example C: The helper has a hunch that a client who recently had a big fight with her mother either is, or soon will be, feeling guilty about how she behaved.

> **Helper:** On the one hand you have a sense of triumph at giving Mom a piece of your mind, but I catch an undercurrent of guilt and sorrow at how you behaved. Am I correct?

Use focusing on feelings questions. Questions can assist clients in being specific about feelings and physical reactions. Frequently, since you cannot assume common meaning, you need to clarify labels clients attach to feelings. For instance, follow-up questions to a client who says "I am very depressed" might be "When you say you are very depressed, what exactly do you mean?" or "When you say you are very depressed what are your specific feelings and physical reactions?" or "You feel very depressed. Tell me more about that feeling." Then you assist the client in pinpointing feelings and physical reactions. Sometimes helpers check out feelings or physical reactions (for instance, "Do you feel suicidal sometimes?" or "How is your appetite?").

However, most often questions elicit rather than suggest feelings and physical reactions.

Helpers assist clients to distinguish between feelings and thoughts. If clients respond to feelings questions with how they think, you may choose to keep them focused on feelings.

> **Client:** I feel very depressed.
> **Helper:** When you say you feel very depressed, what exactly do you mean?
> **Client:** I am having problems in my job and in my marriage.
> **Helper:** You're having problems at work and at home. These are thoughts or reasons why you may be very depressed. However, could you tell me more about the actual depressed feelings you experience?

Helpers may need to assist clients in expanding and elaborating their feelings (Teyber, 1989). Open-ended feelings questions and cues can be helpful ("Describe the feeling more fully"). Further questions and cues that helpers may use to elicit and clarify feelings include the following.

> "Tell me more about the feeling."
> "Describe how your body experiences the feeling."
> "In which part of your body do you experience the feeling?"
> "Do you have any visual images that capture the feeling?"
> "Are there any metaphors that illustrate the feeling?"
> "How has your mood been and how is it today?"
> "How confident a person are you?"
> "Are there any other feelings that accompany that feeling?"
> "How do you feel here and now?"

Helpers may need to ask follow-up questions that encourage clients to expand on their feelings. For example, "You say you experience tension in your stomach. Can you describe the experience more fully?" Depending on how clients respond to such open-ended questions, helpers may then ask specific questions (for example, "How persistent?" and "How intense?").

Use emotion-eliciting techniques. Sometimes helpers consciously attempt to induce feelings so that both they and clients can acknowledge and assess them.

> *Live observation:* Helpers can take clients into difficult situations, observe their reactions, and listen to what they say about how they feel.

Visualizing: Clients can be asked to shut their eyes and visualize how they saw and experienced the emotions attached to a particular scene.

Role-play: Helpers may role-play scenes with clients (for example, an argument with a parent). The helper may then process the emotions elicited by the role-play.

Task assignment: Helpers and clients may agree on between-session tasks for clients. Clients are asked to monitor and record feelings before, during, and after these tasks.

Encourage clients to monitor feelings.   Without setting specific tasks, helpers can encourage clients to monitor their feelings and physical reactions. Such monitoring can raise self-awareness, as well as help clients to learn a valuable skill: namely, listening closely to their feelings.

Daily rating forms: Clients can be asked to rate themselves daily on feelings such as mood (very happy to very depressed), anxiety level (not anxious at all to very anxious), feelings of stress (very relaxed to very stressed), and so on. Ratings may be on scales ranging from 1 to 3, 5, 7, 9, or 10. For instance, clients could be asked to give themselves a mood score for each day using the following scale.

Very happy   1   2   3   4   5   6   7   Very depressed

Specific incident logs: Clients can keep logs of how they feel in relation to specific difficulties they experience. For example, shy clients can keep logs that record their feelings before, during, and after being in company. Below is a possible format for such a log.

Date and time	What happened	My feelings and physical reactions

Consider using questionnaires.   Though it is not advocated for most clients, helpers can use questionnaires to assess feelings. Some questionnaires focus exclusively on assessing feelings: for example the Beck Depression Inventory (Beck, 1978; Kendall, Hollon, Beck, Hammen & Ingram, 1987); the State-Trait Anxiety Inventory (Spielberger, 1983); and the Profile of Mood States (POMS) (McNair, Lorr & Droppleman, 1981). POMS asks subjects how they have been feeling during the past week, including today, and provides scores on six identifiable mood states: tension-anxiety, depression-dejection, anger-hostility, vigor-activity, fatigue-inertia, and confusion-bewilderment. Other questionnaires have sections on feelings. One of these is Lazarus's Multimodal Life History Questionnaire (Lazarus, 1981). Questionnaires may also focus on the stimuli that elicit feelings. For example, Wolpe's Fear Inventory asks respondents to indicate how disturbed they are by each of a range of "things and experiences that may cause fear or other unpleasant feelings" (Wolpe, 1973, p. 283). Helpers may also devise their own questionnaires focused on feelings.

Be sensitive to cultural differences.   Cultures differ greatly in the ways in which they express emotions. In addition, somatic symptoms associated with distress differ across cultures. Helpers working with people from different cultures should approach their task with "open-mindedness to the presence of distinctive cultural patterns and sensitivity to the possibility of unintended bias because of such differences" (American Psychiatric Association, 1987, p. xxvi). Western helpers should be particularly careful in assessing feelings of people from non-Western cultures. In addition to cultural considerations, helpers need to take sex-role and social class considerations into account. You should also be aware that clients' perceptions of you as dissimilar on cultural, racial, gender, and social class variables may also influence whether and how they reveal feelings.

Be prepared to wait and see.   Even with skilled helpers, clients' feelings may take time to unfold. Clients brought up to deny feelings may change slowly. Helpers require sensitivity to the pace at which clients are comfortable with experiencing and sharing feelings. Invariably initial-session assessments of feelings require updating. Sometimes such assessments require substantial modification as you get to know more about clients, and clients learn more about themselves.

Form feelings hypotheses.   When assessing feelings, helpers form hypotheses both to guide collection of information and also to state conclusions. Feelings hypotheses are open to modification as helping progresses. Following is a case study of a company executive who saw a helper after being fired. Initially, this case study illustrates forming feelings hypotheses. Later I use the same case study to illustrate forming thinking skills hypotheses, forming action skills hypotheses, and redefining problems in skills terms.

Case study: Jim Blake
Part 1: Introduction

Jim Blake, 45, was a divisional controller of a large conglomerate before being fired a week ago when his division was closed down. Jim is married with two teenage children, both at private school. He was earning a package of over $100,000 and has a substantial mortgage. Jim's wife Lyn is not in the workforce. Jim had 20 years of service with the company and has received a 6-month severance package to tide him over while he finds another job. In addition, Jim's company has arranged for him to have the services of an external outplacement specialist, Sam Rushton.

The initial helping session is held on company premises immediately after Jim receives the news of his severance, which is effective immediately. Jim expresses shock, disbelief, and anger at being fired. He is also highly anxious about his future prospects, dreads a long period of unemployment, and is worried that his family's standard of living may be drastically curtailed. Sam allows Jim to share these feelings, discusses strategies for breaking the news to his family, and makes an appointment for him to meet the next day in Sam's external office.

In this second session, Jim reports that he spent a night sleepless with worry and feels very depressed. He feels in crisis and is overwhelmed at his misfortune. He still feels extremely bitter at his rejection after so many years of loyal service and fantasizes giving those responsible for his firing a sharp piece of his mind. Sam accepts Jim's feelings and then assists him in identifying and clarifying the main areas of his problem. To some extent, the financial area is dealt with by Jim's own expertise. However, Jim still has catastrophic predictions of financial disaster and inability to cope.

Regarding getting another job, Jim swears he never wants to go through the experience of being fired again. He thinks of setting up his own business, though he is vague about this. Jim admits to great indecision regarding what he wants to do for the rest of his life. He feels that all his life he has been doing the "right" thing, first for his parents and later as a male "wage slave" for his wife and family. Having worked for the same company for 20 years, he has little idea of how to get another job. Part of him wants to rush back into the workforce to ease the anxiety of unemployment. Jim wonders how good he will be at presenting himself in interviews. Also, he worries about what kind of references his former employers will give him.

Jim's work difficulties emerge during the session. Jim sees himself as better with figures than with people. He finds it difficult to tell people working under him what to do and even more difficult to confront them with their mistakes. Frequently, because of his financial knowledge and analytical skills, he would have good ideas for direc-

tions the company might take. However, either he inhibited sharing his ideas or they were discounted because of his poor presentation skills and inadequate persuasive powers.

Jim acknowledges family difficulties and fears that these will worsen with his unemployment especially if, as probable, his job search lasts for more than three months. His wife Lyn has very mixed feelings about him. On the one hand she respects his reliability, industry, and obvious concern for the children. On the other hand, she feels that he is emotionally inexpressive, avoids rather than confronts marital issues, and is no longer fun to be around. Apparently there are no third parties in the relationship. Jim cares for Lyn, but does not find her nearly as supportive as before. At times he thinks that, after the children, Lyn cares for her horses more than him, and that she stays with him partly as a means of maintaining her lifestyle. Jim said he loves his children Chris, 14, and Mark, 17, but that they see him as too ready to pick on wrongdoings rather than prize them for themselves. Jim also mentions that he is the only son of an elderly widowed mother who lives nearby. He visits her regularly and feels responsible for her well-being.

Jim's health and stress difficulties are uncovered when identifying and clarifying problems. Jim is a compulsive worker, often staying late at the office and working weekends. He suffers from tension headaches when overworked. A recent medical examination showed that his blood pressure was too high. Jim mentions that he was becoming increasingly aware how stressed his body feels much of the time. He finds it hard to switch off and relax. Jim used to enjoy tennis and golf, but gave up golf as too time-consuming and tennis as too much effort. Jim has few recreational outlets, though he enjoys music and gardening. He feels he was reasonably sociable at the time of his marriage, but became less so after the children were born. Now he sees himself in company as the strong, silent type. Jim observes that, without a job, he will not know what to do with his time.

Jim has never seen a counselor before. Though desperate, he sees receiving help as a sign of weakness. He wants to stand on his own two feet as soon as possible. Sam detects Jim's resistance in talking about himself and gathers that he does not disclose much in personal and work dealings. Jim is not on medication, nor does he want to be.

Case study: Jim Blake
Part 2: Form feelings hypotheses

During the two initial sessions the counselor, Sam Rushton, formed a series of feelings hypotheses about Jim. Sam had the advantage of observing Jim's voice and body messages. Sam's feelings hypotheses are presented systematically here. In real life, helpers may not take these items into account in such an ordered way.

Capacity to feel: *Jim is somewhat out of touch with his capacity to feel. He does not know his desires regarding employment and has difficulty expressing emotions at home. Jim might require long-term help to develop good skills at experiencing and listening to his feelings.*

Energy level: *Jim's energy level seems lower than usual. Even before he was fired, Jim diverted too much energy into worrying. Effective helping should be able to raise both his short-term and long-term energy level, and zest for life.*

Self-esteem: *Prior to being fired, Jim's self-esteem was only moderate. Though he derived some self-esteem from family, much came from work. Jim's fragile self-esteem has taken a major knock and his confidence is very low.*

Anxiety and defensiveness: *Even before being fired, Jim was an anxious person, especially with people. He dealt with many anxiety-evoking problems by denial and avoidance. Now Jim admits to being highly anxious, though his anxiety may lessen as he comes to terms with his changed circumstances.*

Mood: *Immediately after being fired, Jim masked the full extent of his depression. By the second session, Jim felt very depressed. However, in neither session did Jim appear a suicide risk.*

Psychological pain: *Jim is in considerable psychological pain as his work world falls apart. Other areas of psychological pain include relationship difficulties at home and work. Jim may also experience pain as he becomes aware how much of his life has been spent living other people's shoulds, oughts, and musts.*

Physical reactions: *Jim reports spending a sleepless night. Undoubtedly he experiences other physical reactions not mentioned in the case study.*

Psychophysiologic disorders: *Jim suffers from tension headaches and high blood pressure. Further questioning is required to establish their severity and health risk.*

Predominant feeling: *In the first session, Jim's predominant feelings were shock and anger; in the second session, depression and anger. In both sessions he was very anxious.*

Complex and conflicted feelings: *Jim's feelings toward his future career are complex and conflicted. Jim also appears to have very mixed feelings about his marriage. The full complexity of his feelings in both career and marital areas has yet to emerge.*

Antecedents and consequences of feelings: *As illustrated later, how Jim thinks contributes to the negativeness of his feelings. A possible consequence of Jim's anger toward his former company is that he may behave in self-defeating ways (for instance, harming his reputation with them).*

Strength and persistence of feelings: *Jim's anger toward his company is strong and his depression moderately severe. Though it was not fully revealed in the initial sessions, Jim may also be very angry with Lyn. Persistence of feelings remains to be seen.*

Appropriateness of feelings: *Jim's strong initial feelings of anger, anxiety, and depression at being fired may be appropriate. In fact, Sam would worry more if Jim covered up his feelings. However, if such strong feelings persist, they may be disproportionate and unhelpful to Jim.*

Unclear feelings: *Sometimes Jim communicates feelings poorly (for instance, voice and body messages are not sufficiently congruent with verbal messages). Furthermore, Jim needs more time and psychological space to become clearer about underlying feelings.*

Feelings about helping and helpers: *Jim is highly ambivalent about receiving help, seeing his wish for support as a sign of weakness. Also, Jim finds it difficult to talk about himself. Jim respects Sam's competence and sincere wish to help him. By the end of the second session Jim and Sam have established some emotional bonding.*

ASSESS THINKING SKILLS

Assessing clients' thinking skills and helping clients think about how they think is central to the lifeskills helping approach. Feelings differ from thoughts. In the previous section, feelings were not referred to in skills terms. Clients' feelings reflect their animal nature. Clients can think about how they think, feel, and act, but they can feel only how they feel. If clients wish to change how they experience, express, and handle feelings, they need to focus on the thinking and action skills choices influencing them.

Thinking Skills Areas

Helpers always need to be conscious not just of what clients' think, but how they think. Lifeskills helpers help clients think about how they think, alter thinking skills weaknesses, and develop self-helping skills for working independently on their thinking. Few beginning helpers think of their own thinking in skills terms. Consequently, you may require a new way of viewing yourself as well as your clients. Assessing and working with your own thinking skills is one of the best ways to learn to work effectively with clients' thinking skills. The following is an overview of some thinking skills areas that you can assess and subsequently work on with clients. In all thinking skills areas, people can make choices about how and what they think. Later in this chapter each thinking skills area is illustrated with reference to Jim Blake's thinking difficulties.

Owning responsibility for choosing   In their waking hours, clients are always choosers. Clients can make choices in relation to themselves, others, and the environment. Within limits they can choose how they think, feel, and act. Clients can be the authors or architects of their lives (May & Yalom, 1989; Yalom, 1980). However, often clients are unaware of the full extent of their existential responsibility to create their own lives. Also, they may knowingly or unknowingly relinquish some of this responsibility. Many clients deceive themselves into thinking they own more responsibility for their choosing than is the case. They may possess an illusion of autonomy that masks a constricted approach to life.

Being in touch with feelings   Being in touch with feelings is important, since feelings are often the parents of thoughts. Furthermore, clients out of touch with their valuing process lack a firm base for assessing inner and outer information. Clients may experience difficulty sorting out their real feelings, as contrasted  with what they have been taught to feel and think. Furthermore, clients may acknowledge specific feelings, but dilute or distort their strength. Clients badly out of touch with feelings lack a firm sense of their own identity. They may experience themselves as leaves in the breeze, waiting to be blown about by what others think. Also, they may be indecisive, since they lack a clear inner referent for assessing decision options.

Using self-talk constructively   Here self-talk refers to how people talk to themselves before, during, and after difficult situations (Meichenbaum, 1977, 1983, 1985, 1986; Meichenbaum & Deffenbacher, 1988). Clients can talk to themselves in ways that engender or worsen negative emotions and lead to self-defeating actions. The following are characteristics of self-talk likely to engender negative emotions.

- *Emphasizing mastery rather than coping:* Clients setting unrealistically high standards are prone to worry about whether and how they can attain them.
- *Catastrophizing:* Clients can convince themselves that the worst will happen.

- *Adversely reacting to physical symptoms:* Clients can worsen their feelings of anxiety, even to the extent of full-blown panic attacks, by negatively talking to themselves about bodily sensations such as tension, nausea, breathlessness, palpitations, choking, hot-and-cold flushes, and sweating.
- *Being overly self-conscious about what others think:* Clients can freeze up with anxiety by talking to themselves as though they are the center of other people's attention.
- *Putting oneself down:* Clients can erode their confidence with statements like "You fool" or "I can't do anything right."
- *Focusing on past setbacks rather than successes:* Clients can tell themselves what went wrong and ignore what went right.

Often self-talk that heightens anxiety, lowers performance. In addition, clients may have poor skills at coaching themselves through difficult tasks. For instance, they may not set themselves clear goals, break tasks down, or concentrate on the task at hand.

Possessing realistic personal rules Personal rules provide the standards by which clients judge themselves and others. Ellis (1980, 1989) coined the term *mustabation* to refer to rigid personal rules characterized by musts, oughts, and shoulds. He identifies three major clusters of irrational beliefs that create inappropriate feeling and action consequences.

1. I *must* do well and win approval for all my performances . . . (p. 5).
2. Others *must* treat me considerately and kindly . . . (p. 6).
3. Conditions under which I live *must* be arranged so that I get practically everything I want comfortably, quickly, and easily . . . (p. 7).

Some of the main characteristics of unrealistic or self-oppressing personal rules include:

- *Demandingness:* Clients think of wants and wishes as demands rather than preferences.
- *Perfectionism:* Clients put pressure on themselves and others to be perfect. Nobody's perfect.
- *Self-rating:* Clients rate themselves on their total worth as persons, rather than on how functional are specific characteristics for achieving goals.
- *Awfulizing:* Clients think it is absolutely awful if they, others, or the environment are not as they should be.

Choosing to perceive accurately   Clients, like most humans, are prone to misperceive themselves and others (Beck, 1976, 1988; Beck & Weishaar, 1989). Negative self-labels are unrealistically negative perceptions either of clients' specific characteristics or of themselves as persons. More clients seem to make unrealistically negative than positive inferences about themselves. They are much better at listing what is wrong than what is right. This perceptual habit of ignoring assets and focusing on deficits perpetuates feelings such as anxiety, depression, and diminished confidence and vitality.

Clients may also allow feelings to influence how they perceive others, including helpers. They make judgments without adequately taking into account available facts. Central to all marital counseling is assisting partners to perceive each other more accurately (and usually much less negatively). In the preceding chapter I listed some perceptual errors for helpers to avoid. These are also perceptual errors for clients to avoid (for instance, tunnel vision, magnifying and minimizing, negativeness, selective inattention, overgeneralizing, and polarized thinking).

Attributing cause accurately   Clients can stay stuck in problems through wholly or partly misattributing their causes. Possible misattributions for the causes of problems include: "It's my genes," "It's my mental illness," It's my unfortunate past," "It's my bad luck," "It's my poor environment," "It's all their fault," or "It's all my fault." Clients commonly succumb to the temptation to externalize problems: it's someone else who is responsible. They attribute cause from outside to inside. However change requires attribution of cause from inside to outside. Furthermore, clients can adversely affect their confidence and mood by misattributing causes of positive and negative events. For instance, depressed people may overestimate their responsibility for negative events in their own and others' lives (Beck, Rush, Shaw, & Emery, 1979). In addition, clients can influence their motivation to achieve by how they attribute cause for their successes and failures. For instance, they may rightly or wrongly assign the causes for their academic successes and failures to such factors as ability, effort, anxiety, task difficulty, staff competence, or luck.

Predicting realistically   In a sense, all client problems contain disorders of prediction. Many clients predict risk inaccurately by overestimating bad consequences. They may fear change, failure, or even success. However, some clients underestimate the risk of bad consequences (for instance, in excessive gambling or grandiose business ventures). Clients can also predict reward inaccurately by either overestimating or underestimating good consequences. Two trends are common in underestimating reward. First, clients may be poor at perceiving the potential rewards of proposed courses of action. Second, even when rewards are identified, they may not give them the weight they deserve. Predicting realistically entails thinking accurately about future consequences. Independent of notions of risk and reward, some clients are poor at consequential thinking (for instance, they may remain unaware of, and fail to predict, how their behavior affects others).

Clarifying values Clients may require assistance in clarifying their values. Values are the underlying principles and priorities that guide people's lives. Another way of viewing clients' values is that they represent their philosophy of life. When clients become clearer as to their values, they tend to find it easier to set goals. Illustrative values are love, friendship, religion, materialism, aesthetics, intellect, hedonism, social consciousness, and self-actualization. It is important for clients to have reasonable similarity of values when entering long-term relationships, be they personal or work.

Setting realistic goals Some clients have difficulty articulating goals and consequently relinquish much opportunity to create their futures. Goals can be short-term, medium-term, or long-term and in various areas (for instance, relationships, study, work, recreation, health, and finances). When in close relationships, clients' goals may need to be negotiated so that they become shared goals. Apart from not possessing goals, errors in goal setting include not reflecting values, insufficient realism, inadequate specificity, and unclear time frames. Clients' goals in relation to problem areas may suffer from not being expressed in skills language. Also, clients may not focus on how to think as well as on how to act.

Visualizing skills Lazarus (1989) observes ". . . when a person's most highly valued representational system is visual, he or she is inclined to respond to the world and organize it in terms of mental images" (p. 514). Clients may use mental images or pictorial thinking to support or to oppress themselves. Negative images can influence feelings towards self and others. For instance, in one research study, some 90 percent of anxious patients reported visual images prior to and concurrent with their anxiety attacks (Beck, Laude, & Bohnert, 1974). Absence of the capacity to visualize calming images can contribute to tension and anger. Clients who visualize themselves as socially incompetent may feel shy.

How clients visualize others influences their feelings towards them. For instance, angry clients may be poor at using visualizing to understand others' positions and take a balanced view of them. In addition, some clients are poor at communicating visual images (for instance, sharing sexual fantasies). Frequently clients' negative visual images impede their performance (for example, imagining acting incompetently in either social or academic situations can lead to self-fulfilling prophecies). Clients may also be poor at visualizing positive and negative consequences of their behavior. For instance, clients engaged in job searches may be poor at visualizing what it is actually like to work for specific employers.

Realistic decision making   Clients may possess decision-making styles that lessen their effectiveness. For instance, they may be hypervigilant and try too hard to take every consideration into account. Conversely, they may be impulsive and rush into major and minor decisions. Some clients do their best to avoid decisions altogether. Sometimes decisions are best made in collaboration with others. In such instances, decision errors include being overly competitive or compliant. Rational decision making can be viewed as taking place in two main stages: (1) confronting and making decisions, and (2) implementing and evaluating them. Clients may have weaknesses in either or both stages. An illustrative weakness when making decisions is failure to generate sufficient decision options. An illustrative weakness when implementing decisions is poor planning.

Preventing and managing problems   Frequently clients seek help because of poor skills at preventing and managing problems. Skills weaknesses may be in such areas as confronting problems, assessing and redefining problems in skills terms, setting goals, planning, implementing plans, and evaluating consequences. Where possible, clients should develop skills both for preventing problems and for catching them early (for instance, not allowing stress to endanger health).

Skills for Eliciting and Assessing Thinking

When assessing thinking, helpers and clients work together to establish clients' thinking skills strengths and weaknesses. It is important to help clients become more aware of their thought processes (Beck & Emery, 1985). With increased self-awareness, clients may start correcting their own thinking errors. Furthermore, they are better accomplices in the detective work of uncovering faulty thinking. You aim to train clients in how to think about how they think. The following are some skills for eliciting and assessing thinking.

Build a knowledge base. It is essential that helpers wishing to work with clients' thinking skills develop their knowledge of how people think. You cannot help clients if you do not know what to look for. In addition, you may limit your effectiveness if you only focus on one or two thinking skills. How can you develop your knowledge base? First, you can read the works of cognitive therapists such as Ellis (1962, 1980, 1989), Beck (1976, 1988; Beck & Weishaar, 1989), and other therapists who  work with clients' thinking—for instance, Frankl (1959, 1967, 1969), Glasser (1965, 1984), Lazarus (1981, 1989), Meichenbaum (1977, 1983, 1985, 1986), and Yalom (1980; May & Yalom, 1989). Second, you may read secondary sources such as *Thinking Skills: Managing and Preventing Personal Problems* (Nelson-Jones, 1990a). Third, you can work on your own thinking skills, either independently or with helpers or in training groups. Fourth, you can work with clients, preferably under supervision at first.

Think in skills terms. Important cognitive theorists like Beck, Ellis, and Meichenbaum do not use skills language when thinking about how clients think. However, you are encouraged to do so. Failure to think in skills terms may cause you to focus on only one or two, rather than on many, potential thinking skills weaknesses. In addition, stage 2 requires you to redefine clients' problems in skills terms. You will find it difficult to do this if you aren't already assessing clients' skills. However, when eliciting and assessing thinking, you may choose not to use skills language openly with clients, but leave this until your redefining statement.

Collect information. Rewarding listening skills are always important when collecting information about how clients think. Other ways of eliciting and collecting information about clients' thinking include the following.

> *Client self-report:* Clients may have insight into their own thought processes (for example, tendencies to rigid personal rules or negative self-labeling) without knowing what to do about them.

Think aloud: Thinking aloud involves encouraging clients to speak aloud their thought processes in relation to specific situations (Blackwell, Galassi, Galassi, & Watson, 1985). For instance, clients can be asked to take helpers in slow motion through their thoughts and feelings in relation to specific anxiety-evoking experiences. Additionally, clients can use think aloud when confronted with real or simulated situations.

Thought listing: Clients can be asked to list, and possibly rank in terms of importance, thoughts about specific problems. Clients can list thoughts within the ABC framework, where A equals the activating event; B, the client's thoughts about the activating event; and C, the feelings and action consequences of the client's thoughts (Ellis, 1962, 1989). At B, Ellis asks clients to distinguish between rational and irrational thoughts.

Thought charting: Thought charting entails clients' keeping a record of the thoughts associated with specific situations involving negative feelings. Beck and Emery (1985) observe: "The most common method by which a patient can become aware of his thinking between sessions is the thought record" (pp. 194–95). At it simplest, thought charting involves the double-column technique: recording situations in one column and thoughts and feelings in the other column. Thought charts may also use the ABC framework: a column each for (A) activating events, (B) thoughts, and (C) feelings and actions consequences. Thought charting encourages clients to see links between how they think, feel, and act.

Counting: Helpers can ask clients to count the frequency of specific types of thoughts (for instance, negative self-labels). Clients may use index cards to make frequency records. Counting may help clients become aware of the repetitive nature of their thinking.

Focusing on thinking questions: Clients can be asked what they think about themselves, their behavior, others, and specific situations. Then helpers can ask follow-up questions that encourage clients to elaborate, specify, and reveal personal meanings. Before leaving an area, you may ask the open-ended question "Can you think of anything else that might be relevant?" Such a question may elicit further information that might have been lost had you moved on prematurely. Intersperse reflective responding with focusing on thinking questions. Also, remember that sometimes focusing on feelings questions open up the way for focusing on thinking questions.

Helper: And how did you feel when that happened?
Client: I felt mad as hell.
Helper: You felt really mad? Why do you think that was?

Helpers can also use questions that challenge clients' thinking (for example, "Where's the evidence?" Resist the temptation to answer your own questions. Also, you may need to rephrase questions that clients do not appear to understand.

Thought eliciting techniques: Thought-eliciting techniques are similar to feelings-eliciting techniques; the same techniques may be used to elicit thoughts and feelings.

Live observation: Helpers can accompany clients into situations that cause them difficulty (for instance, returning something to a store or driving a car after an accident) and ask them to recount their thoughts.

Visualizing: Clients can be asked to conjure up images that elicit feelings and to identify the accompanying thoughts. They can visualize past, present, or future scenes and get in touch with harmful and helpful thoughts.

Role-play: Helpers can conduct role-plays with clients (for instance, telephoning someone for a date) and then explore their thoughts and feelings.

Task assignment: Helpers can encourage clients to perform feared tasks and afterwards record their thoughts and feelings. Clients can view such tasks as personal experiments to collect evidence about themselves.

Questionnaires: There are numerous self-report measures to assess thinking—for example, the Anxious Self-Statements Questionnaire (Kendall & Hollon, 1989), the Attributional Style Questionnaire (Petersen et al., 1982; Petersen & Villanova, 1988), and the Fear of Negative Evaluation Scale (Watson & Friend, 1969). In addition, helpers can develop their own measures of thinking.

Use a whiteboard. A whiteboard is an important tool for working with client thinking. It has many uses. First, you can use the whiteboard to help elicit thoughts. Frequently clients find that the visual display of their thoughts stimulates them to generate more thoughts. However, you may need to probe to elicit their less-obvious thoughts. Second, the whiteboard enables thoughts to be visually stored so that clients can see linkages between them. Third, the whiteboard is useful for tracing

links between stimulus or activating events (A), intervening thinking (B), and feelings and action consequences (C). Fourth, the whiteboard is useful for showing redefinitions of clients' problems in skills terms. Fifth, correct use of the whiteboard encourages a cooperative working alliance between helpers and clients. Clients can observe their contributions being written onto the whiteboard and feel that they are valued. A whiteboard is also valuable later on when intervening to develop clients' thinking skills.

Make inferences.   Helpers make inferences both about clients' areas of difficulty and pain and about possible thinking skills weaknesses. Inferences about thinking may stem from clients' words, feelings, and actions. You can obtain clues from how clients use language. For example, use of words like should, ought, or must may indicate unrealistically rigid personal rules. Use of expressions like "I can't" and "I had no choice" may indicate insufficient ownership of responsibility for choosing. Self-talk like "What will people think of me?" and "I wonder if I look as stupid as I feel" is not only negative but also indicates an unrealistic rule about needing others' approval.

Both helpers and clients require skills at making linkages between feelings and underlying thoughts (Beck, 1988). Often strong, persistent negative feelings indicate thinking difficulties. You require sensitivity to more subtle clues that come from voice messages, body messages, or what is left unsaid. You and your clients should also make linkages between self-defeating actions and thinking. Clients need to develop skills at doing this for themselves.

Form hypotheses.   Helpers identify and collect evidence that helps them form hypotheses about clients' thinking skills weaknesses. Helpers may generate many more hypotheses than they eventually share with clients when redefining problems in skills terms. As part of the process of assessing thinking, you may collect further information that either supports or negates your hypotheses. Conversely, you may choose not to collect further information about some hypotheses.

Case study: Jim Blake
Part 3: Form thinking skills hypotheses

This is a continuation of the Jim Blake case study, this time focusing on forming thinking skills hypotheses. As helper Sam Rushton listens and probes, he develops hypotheses concerning how Jim's thinking skills weaknesses may sustain his problems. Here I list hypotheses by thinking skills rather than by problem areas (for instance, being fired, finances, getting another job, work difficulties, family difficulties, and health and stress difficulties). However, when interviewing, Sam might have explored thinking skills hypotheses in relation to specific problem areas. Later, when offering a redefinition of Jim's problems in skills terms, he might link the main themes of Jim's thinking skills weaknesses across different problem areas.

Owning responsibility for choosing *The following items might illustrate that Jim is not fully owning responsibility for being a chooser in his life.*

Getting fired: *Jim may have allowed himself to stay in a rut. Conceivably he might have initiated a move out of the company before being fired.*

Getting another job: *Jim appears not to have realized that now he has a positive opportunity to make choices, despite the pain of being fired. Jim has yet to choose to accept responsibility for developing job search skills.*

Family difficulties: *Jim appears to have been relating to his family on the basis of repetitive habits, some of which do not work. He can choose to think, feel, and act differently.*

Health and stress difficulties: *Jim appears to have given up much of his capacity for choice in his leisure and recreational life. This in turn negatively impacts his health, and his family and work lives.*

Being in touch with feelings *The following are some items illustrative of a possible skills weakness in acknowledging feelings.*

Getting another job: *Jim appears out of touch with his wants and wishes after years of doing the right thing by others. He may not be fully in touch with his strengths.*

Family difficulties: *Jim may be emotionally inexpressive. He may not be fully in touch with his negative feelings about his wife or his positive feelings toward wife and children.*

Health and stress: *Jim seems not to listen sufficiently to his body. Also, he is out of touch with his need for recreation and fun.*

Using self-talk constructively *Jim may both use negative self-talk and fail to use coping self-talk.*

Being fired: *Jim appears not to be coping by using self-talk to manage his anger; rather, his negative self-talk may fan his anger.*

Getting another job: *Jim may need to develop self-talk skills for calming himself down and coaching himself through interviews.*
Work difficulties: *Jim may have engaged in negative self-talk that contributed to his avoiding confrontations with subordinates.*
Family difficulties: *Jim may need to develop appropriate self-talk to make it easier for him to become more assertive and emotionally expressive.*

Possessing realistic personal rules   *Jim may have some unrealistic personal rules contributing to self-defeating feelings and actions.*

Being fired: *"Life must always be fair," "People who are fired must be failures"—these rules contribute to feelings like anger, anxiety, and depression.*
Finances: *"I must maintain my present living standard or else I am a failure as a person"—such a rule puts considerable pressure on Jim, who now equates his worth as a person with his earning capacity.*
Getting another job: *"I must be seen by others as successful"—this rule overemphasizes others' approval as contrasted with self-approval.*
Family: *"It is not manly to show emotions," "Family conflict must be avoided where possible"—the first rule is a sex-role stereotype and the second ignores possibilities for constructive conflict.*

Choosing to perceive accurately   *Jim may need to learn to discipline how he perceives himself and others.*

Being fired: *Jim's perceptions of his former employer may be negatively colored by his emotions. If he does not keep his paranoia and anger in check, he may damage himself by losing existing goodwill.*
Getting another job: *Jim may attach all sorts of negative self-labels to himself ("I'm no good," "I'm a failure," and so on). He needs to engage in a search of his strengths. Also, Jim must realistically appraise his abilities, interests, skills, and experience.*
Family: *Jim's perceptions of his wife and children may be inaccurate (for instance, he may overemphasize weaknesses). His perceptions of how he behaves in the family may also be inaccurate: he may be less sensitive and open to feedback than he thinks.*

Attributing cause accurately   *Items that indicate Jim may have difficulties in this area include the following.*

Getting fired: *Jim may unrealistically blame his company colleagues for their decision.*

Getting another job: *Jim may be passive and wait for others to help him rather than committing himself fully to managing his career transition.*

Work difficulties: *Jim may wrongly attribute some of his people skills weaknesses to "That's just the way I am" rather than seeing them in terms of learned behavior that, with appropriate assistance, he can alter.*

Family difficulties: *Jim may externalize the cause of any problems with Lyn and the children: "It's their fault." Alternatively he may blame himself, yet do nothing about it because "That's the way I am."*

Health and stress: *Jim may have blamed the company for his overwork rather than to have asserted himself and set limits on his workload.*

Predicting realistically *Items illustrative of possible problems here include the following.*

Finances: *Jim's catastrophic predictions of financial disaster are probably unrealistic, especially in light of his financial expertise.*

Getting another job: *Jim may have unrealistic expectations of what is involved in getting another job and how long this might take.*

Work difficulties: *Jim may unrealistically predict negative consequences of raising issues with subordinates and insufficiently focus on gains.*

Family: *Jim may overemphasize the negative consequences of being more emotionally expressive and attempting to work through issues. Consequently, he remains stuck in his present behavior.*

Health and stress: *Jim has been underestimating the negative consequences of overwork and underrecreation. His body gives him clear warning signals.*

Clarifying values *Jim seemingly needs to get much more in touch with what his true values are, to provide a firmer basis for seeking meaning in the remainder of his life. The need to clarify values permeates all areas of his functioning including work, health, and family.*

Setting realistic goals *Though Jim may have been proficient at articulating goals for his company, this proficiency may not carry over into setting realistic goals for himself.*

Getting fired: *Jim appears not to have set clear goals for any future contact he may have with his previous employer.*

Getting another job: *Jim has now to articulate career goals and goals for planning and implementing either his job search or the establishment of a business.*

Work difficulties: *Jim might consider establishing goals for developing skills to handle his work difficulties (for instance, assertion and public-speaking skills).*

Family difficulties: *In conjunction with Lyn, Jim might develop goals for working on his family problems. Even if Lyn does not cooperate initially, Jim can still develop goals for changing his behavior.*

Health and stress: *Jim clearly needs to develop goals to protect his health and ease his stress. Also, he might set himself goals for developing his leisure interests.*

Visualizing skills   *Indications that Jim may have inadequate visualizing skills include the following.*

Finances: *Jim may not only verbalize the worst but also have negative graphic images.*

Getting another job: *Jim may have poor skills at visualizing life in different environments, visualizing life's changing for the better, and using visualizing to rehearse interview skills.*

Family difficulties: *Jim may unnecessarily be feeding himself negative images about himself, his family, and their future.*

Health and stress: *Jim may need to develop a clearer visual picture of what may happen to him unless he learns to manage his stress better.*

Realistic decision making   *Jim may not always use realistic decision-making skills.*

Getting fired: *Jim may have diluted or denied the evidence that his job was at risk as a way of avoiding making the difficult decision to move on.*

Getting another job: *Jim may be at risk of making an impulsive decision to ease his anxiety about being unemployed. Other ways he might handle his anxiety include either avoiding decisions or being hypervigilant about every detail to the point of indecision.*

Family difficulties: *Jim may lack skills of making decisions in family matters collaboratively with Lyn. Many of their tensions may stem from lack of clarity over who makes which decisions and how.*

Preventing and managing problems   *Jim clearly has a number of problem areas in his life that he either avoids or deals with inadequately.*

Work difficulties: *Over a period of years he appears not to have solved his lack of assertion problems.*

Family difficulties: *At no stage does Jim appear to have attempted a systematic approach to breaking down and tackling his family difficulties.*

Health and stress difficulties: *Jim has shown insufficient skills for preventing and managing his health and stress problems.*

Jim has many problem areas. His thinking skills weaknesses are extensive. Both Jim and his counselor may wish to narrow down both which problems they work on and what are the most important thinking skills to focus on. However, the preceding analysis illustrates that the same thinking skills difficulties often occur in more than one problem area. Consequently, developing better thinking skills in one problem area can carry over into other s.

ASSESS ACTION SKILLS

Action skills are observable behaviors. Helpers need to pay close attention to assessing action skills, because if clients are to manage most problems better, they must act better. Action skills interact with thinking and feeling. Improved thinking needs to be followed by effective action. Furthermore, if clients are to feel better, they frequently need to take action to achieve feelings goals (for example, clients wishing to be less lonely need to use developing friendship skills).

Generally, beginning helpers find it easier to think in terms of action skills than thinking skills. However, a common mistake is to focus only on verbal skills. Action skills involve five main message categories: verbal, voice, body, touch, and action. The first four message categories usually assume face-to-face contact. The fifth category, action messages, does not require direct contact (for instance, sending flowers to someone you love).

Skills for Eliciting, Observing, and Assessing Action Skills

When helpers assess action skills they seek both to identify which skills are important and to evaluate current performance. Following are some helper skills for assessing clients' actions and for helping clients observe themselves.

Build a knowledge base. As with thinking, when assessing actions, helpers need to think in skills terms. In addition, helpers require a knowledge base of action skills for client populations they service. If you do not know what constitutes skilled behavior in an area, you cannot assess it properly. For example, helpers working with aggressive children require knowledge of action skills for managing aggression and behaving assertively. Helpers working with the unemployed require knowledge of action skills such as making resumes, seeking employment information, and handling interviews. Helpers working with sexual-problem clients require knowledge of action skills for managing sexual dysfunctions. Finally, helpers working with school and university students' study and test-taking problems require knowledge of how to study and take tests effectively.

Collect information in interviews.   Helpers can collect information about observable actions either inside or outside interviews. Here are some ways you can collect information in interviews.

   Client self-report: Clients can tell you how they behave outside helping. Limitations of client self-report include your not observing the behaviors and thus being reliant on their versions of events. Clients may edit what they say to protect their self-pictures.
   Observing clients: Depending on the areas of clients' problems, you may learn much from observing their verbal, voice, and action messages as they relate to you. For example, shy clients may perform their shyness behaviors right in front of you.
   Focusing on actions questions: Focusing on actions questions aim to elicit specific details of actions. "How" questions are useful (for example, "How did you behave?" and "When you did that (specify), how did he/she react?"). You may need to direct clients to provide details of voice and body, as well as of action, messages. Furthermore, you may need to assert yourself to ensure that clients provide you with specific behavioral information. How questions go beyond "What actually happened?" to identify participants' specific skills strengths and weaknesses. How questions include probing how clients avoid carrying out desired behaviors (for instance, "When you wish to study but are unable to, how do you behave?").
      Frequency is a dimension of focusing on action questions (for example, "How many . . . ?" or "How many times did you . . . ?"). Duration is another dimension (for example, "Over what period were you . . . ?" or "How long does it take you to . . . ?" or "How many minutes do you . . . each

day?"). Kazdin (1989) observes: "In most behavior modification programs, the goal is to increase the frequency of a response rather than its duration. There are notable exceptions, of course" (p. 65).

Role-play: A further focusing on action cue is "Show me." Clients can be invited to illustrate the verbal, voice, and body messages they used in an interaction either on their own or in a role-play with you playing the other party. For instance, parents having difficulty disciplining children can show you how they attempt this. Role-play allows the possibility of an interaction that goes beyond an initial "show me" demonstration lasting for one parental statement. You can video role-plays and play them back to clients to illustrate points and develop clients' self-observing skills.

Collect information in natural settings. Helpers may wish to supplement interview information with that collected in clients' natural or home environments.

Helpers as observers: You can go with clients into situations in which they experience difficulty and observe how they behave (for instance, requesting a drink in a bar or relating to children at home).

Clients as observers: Always encourage clients to become more aware of how they behave in problem areas. More formally, clients can use behavior monitoring worksheets and thinking, feeling, and action logs. Furthermore, you can set clients tasks (for instance, telephoning to ask a girl out) and get them to record how they behave.

Third parties as observers: With permission, you may also collect information about how clients act from third parties (for instance, spouses, parents, siblings, peers, or supervisors). Note, and possibly explore, differences between third parties' and clients' observations. You may need to train third parties in what to look for and in how to observe systematically.

Explore the antecedents and consequences of actions. Helpers can encourage clients to understand inner and outer events that preceded actions. For instance, how did they think and feel before they acted? What events in their outer environment influenced their actions? You can also assist clients to become much more aware that their actions always have consequences—and also of what they are. Furthermore, you can assist clients to see the extent to which consequences of actions influence subsequent behaviors.

Form action skills hypotheses.   As helpers listen to clients and collect information, they form action skills hypotheses. You may feel confident about some hypotheses at the end of an initial session. You may make other hypotheses more tentatively. Still other hypotheses emerge as helping progresses. Clients may also share ideas about unhelpful actions. Such observations always merit attention, not least because clients show some responsibility for their problems and problematic skills.

Helpers may formulate many hypotheses concerning broad areas in which clients may need to develop skills. Often helpers leave detailed assessment of specific skills weaknesses until subsequent sessions when there is more time to do the job thoroughly. Also, by then, helper and client may have prioritized the skills that require detailed attention.

Case study: Jim Blake
Part 4: Form action skills hypotheses

The counselor, Sam Rushton, formed the following hypotheses concerning Jim Blake's possible action skills weaknesses. He listed these by each of Jim's problem areas.

Getting fired   *Reestablishing limited contact with former employer (for instance, regarding references).*

Getting another job   *In conjunction with the thinking skills entailed in rigorous career decision making, Jim appears to have weaknesses in the following action skills:*

> *Making a resume*
> *Information-seeking about advertised job opportunities*
> *Creating and using an informal contact network to find out about*
>   *unadvertised job opportunities*
> *Creating and implementing a job marketing plan*
> *Interview skills*
> *Gathering information to assess job offers*
> *Establishing his own business (if he decides on this option)*

In addition, Jim seems to have skills weaknesses regarding finding meaning in activity despite being unemployed. Specific action skills weaknesses include:

Managing time that has previously been highly structured
Finding and engaging in meaningful activities, both work-related
and recreational

Finances Given Jim's financial background, this area may be adequately covered. Nevertheless Jim possesses an action skills weakness in not discussing his affairs with another knowledgeable and trusted financial expert.

Work difficulties Though Jim's action skills weaknesses appeared in his previous job, they may hold him back in a new job. Also, Jim's perception that he lacks people skills may create a reluctance to go for jobs he might handle well once he develops his people skills. Possible action skills Jim needs to develop include the following:

Giving instructions assertively
Giving feedback assertively
Disclosing more of himself so he appears more human
Rewarding listening skills
Public speaking skills
Group discussion skills

Family difficulties In the family, Jim appears to have action skills weaknesses across a range of relationship skills, including the following:

Rewarding listening
Expressing feelings
Expressing affection
Giving balanced feedback
Asserting himself
Acknowledging and managing anger
Managing conflict
Engaging in joint decision making
Engaging in shared pleasant activities
Improving social conversation skills

Health and stress Jim's action skills weaknesses include the following:

Inadequate muscular and mental relaxation skills
Inadequate time spent on recreational activities, such as music,
gardening, sports, and socializing. (Jim may have to develop
skills in specific recreational areas to gain the most from them.)
When employed, inadequate assertion skills to set limits on his
workload

REDEFINE PROBLEMS IN SKILLS TERMS

The desired outcome of stage 2 of the lifeskills helping model is a clear initial statement of the skills weaknesses on which helpers and clients need to work if clients are to manage present and future problems better. Helpers and clients should arrive at mutually agreed-upon conceptualizations of problems. Put another way, clients make poor choices that sustain problems. Good redefinitions of problems in skills terms break them down and identify specific skills areas in which clients can make better choices. During later working sessions, problems may be still further broken down into their component skills. However, such detail may be inappropriate for initial sessions. Initial skills definitions pinpoint or flag areas for later work.

Skills definitions are sets of hypotheses about skills weaknesses sustaining clients' problems. Though forming the basis for goal setting and intervening, they should be open to modification in light of feedback and new information. In short, initial redefinitions of problems in skills terms are subject to continual testing and also to major or minor reformulations as helping progresses.

Some Skills for Redefining Problems

Below are some helper skills for redefining clients' problems in skills terms.

Present a rationale   In earlier structuring statements helpers may have presented rationales to clients that their problems might be broken down and translated into thinking and action skills terms. In any event, it is probably worth reemphasizing why problems are redefined in skills terms. Below is a possible transition statement a helper might make when starting to offer a skills redefinition.

> **Helper:** Well, Jan, for the past 30 minutes or so we've been exploring in some detail the problems in your relationship with your daughter Pammie. I'm now about to test a way of viewing your problems in skills terms. I will try to identify and put on the whiteboard some of the main ways your thinking and behavior may create difficulties for you both. I present these as thinking and action skills because that allows us to work in specific areas rather than go around in circles using vague generalities. If possible, we need to agree

on the main skills areas in which you experience difficulty. Your feedback is vital since you are unlikely to work on skills where you do not see the point.

Given good rationales, most clients accept a skills focus. However, some clients may express reservations about redefining problems in skills terms. They may be unused to viewing their behavior in such terms and take time to adjust. They may view skills redefinitions as mechanistic and be afraid that they will be treated as objects rather than people. Also, certain clients may be ready to own neither their problems nor their roles in sustaining them. Agreeing to skills redefinitions assumes a degree of personal responsibility for having and sustaining problems.

Make clear and concise redefinitions. Helpers need to be mindful that redefinitions of problems in skills terms are for clients' benefits. Unless clients understand them, redefinitions are pointless. Always use simple and clear language. Aim to summarize key thinking and action skills weaknesses in areas of immediate concern to clients. Furthermore, be sensitive to the amount of material clients can absorb. It is much preferable that clients be comfortable with a small amount of material than confused about a lot. In later sessions, you can further redefine problems in skills terms.

Besides clarity and brevity, the following are some other characteristics of good redefinition statements.

- They bear a clear relationship to information clients provide.
- They are formulated in conjunction with clients.
- They relate to a problem or problems of high priority to clients.
- They are stated as hypotheses.
- Clients are likely to perceive them as relevant and own them as a basis for working on their problems.
- They lend themselves to setting helpful and realistic working goals.

Use a whiteboard. When redefining problems in skills terms, using a whiteboard has many advantages. The discipline of writing up your T redefinition—a column each for thinking and action skills weaknesses—imposes a degree of clarity on you. The visual image may increase clients' understanding and retention of what you communicate. Furthermore, having a written definition before their eyes makes it easier for clients to provide feedback. If necessary, you can openly work together on the whiteboard to formulate more mutually agreeable redefinitions of problems.

Use checking skills.   Valid working definitions of clients' problems in skills terms are both formulated in collaboration with clients and then further checked out with them to see if they fit. If clients have reservations about your working definitions, explore them further. Assuming the reservations are not misunderstandings, you may then choose either to elaborate how you arrived at your definitions or to modify them in light of discussion.

Attend to feelings.   Always, when redefining problems, helpers need to attend to clients' feelings. Formulating working definitions focused on thinking and action skills is not an arid intellectual exercise. The following are among the areas in which you require sensitivity to clients' feelings. First, you should look out for any client reservations regarding taking a skills approach to their problems. If possible, work through these reservations together. Second, be aware that often you deal with highly sensitive material and that you always require tact. Often clients find it difficult to accept responsibility for their problems and not externalize them; do not make it harder for them by being clumsy. Third, your redefinitions in thinking and action skills terms may focus on changing clients' feelings (for instance, anger or shyness). Fourth, good redefinitions deepen not just clients' thoughts, but their feelings of being understood by you. A myth of Rogers' person-centered approach is that clients feel more understood by helpers who stay within their internal viewpoint rather than actively expanding their self-understanding. Fifth, good redefinitions can improve clients' morale and motivation. Whereas previously they may have been stuck, now they have "handles" with which to work. A glimmer of light appears. Problems formerly experienced as insurmountable may now seem manageable.

Encourage between-session learning.   From the start of lifeskills helping, you can encourage clients to take an active role in learning. Already I have mentioned working closely with clients during sessions, including using a whiteboard. You can use between-session time to build their self-assessing skills. For example, you may record sessions and ask clients to play them back before subsequent sessions. Many clients find this useful for further exploring and assessing problems and problematic skills.

They find that there is too much material to remember and absorb the first time around without listening again to sessions. In addition, you may request that clients keep records of how they think, feel, and behave in targeted skills areas. Clients can keep folders of their helping work. Items to go in folders include redefinitions of problems, behavior monitoring records, main learnings from individual sessions, and homework worksheets and exercises. It may be more important for clients than for helpers to keep records.

Case study: Jim Blake
Part 5: Redefine problems in skills terms

The first time the counselor, Sam Rushton, saw Jim Blake was on company premises immediately after he was fired. In this highly charged emotional atmosphere, no attempt was made to identify, clarify, assess, or redefine Jim's problems in skills terms.

Towards the end of the second session, held off company premises, Sam and Jim agreed that the two areas in which Jim needed to work immediately were handling his emotions about being fired and getting another job. Using a two-column T format on a whiteboard (one column each for thinking and action skills), Sam redefined each of these problems. Sam observed that some clients preferred the terminology of inner- and outer-game skills to thinking and action skills. Sam worked first with handling being fired because it was an immediate and less-complex problem than getting another job. Sam wrote the skills definition in the first-person singular to help Jim identify with it, and checked out Jim's reactions. Sam mentioned that the skills redefinition would form the basis for a statement of working goals.

Handling being fired
Thinking skills weakness hypotheses
Perceiving my former company inaccurately
Using self-talk to heighten my anger
Possessing unrealistic personal rules concerning being fired

Action skills weakness hypothesis
Avoiding contact with my former employer (for instance, regarding references)

After checking the accuracy and comprehensibility of this skills redefinition with Jim, Sam reformed it into a statement of working goals (see Chapter 7). Again using the T format on the whiteboard, Sam and Jim formed the following redefinition of Jim's getting another job problem.

Getting another job
Thinking skills weakness hypotheses

Insufficiently owning responsibility for my choices in life

Insufficiently being in touch with my wants and wishes

Negative self-talk (for instance, when faced with interviews)

Possessing unrealistic personal rules (for instance, regarding achievement)

Perceiving myself inaccurately (for instance, possessing negative self-labels)

Making unrealistic predictions about the possible length of my job search

Insufficient clarity regarding my values

Poor goal-setting skills, both in regard to career goals and job search goals

Insufficiently realistic and rigorous career decision making skills

Action skills weakness hypotheses

Inadequate skills at making a resume

Inadequate information seeking about advertised job opportunities

Poor skills at creating and using an informal contact network to find out about unadvertised job opportunities

Poor skills at creating and implementing a marketing plan

Poor interview skills

While unemployed, poor skills at managing time and engaging in meaningful activities

Sam and Jim discussed this redefinition in skills terms of Jim's problem of getting another job. Once satisfied that he and Jim agreed on a common conceptualization of the problem and problematic skills, Sam reformed them into a statement of working goals (see Chapter 7). Sam told Jim that, if he wanted, either Sam might work with him on his other problems (for example, family difficulties), or he could refer him to another helper. Jim said he would like to think about this, but might take Sam's offer. He mentioned that breaking down his problems into their component skills made him feel more able to cope with them. Sam replied that Jim's other problems too could be broken down into thinking and action skill components.

 CHAPTER HIGHLIGHTS

- Assessment in lifeskills helping is performed *with* clients and *for* clients. Helpers and clients are hypothesis makers and testers.

- Helpers should always offer supportive relationships when assessing and redefining clients' problems in skills terms.
- Reasons for assessing feelings include: protecting clients, evaluating emotional responsiveness, clarifying real agendas, obtaining leads about thinking and action skills weaknesses, noting medical and psychiatric considerations, and developing clients' self-assessment skills.
- Dimensions of feelings that helpers and clients assess include: capacity to feel, energy level, self-esteem, anxiety and defensiveness, mood, psychological pain, physical reactions, and psychophysiologic disorders.
- Among helper skills for eliciting and assessing feelings are: rewarding listening, advanced reflection of feelings, focusing on feelings questions, and emotion-eliciting techniques such as visualizing and role-play.
- Helpers and clients can assess the following thinking skills: owning responsibility for choosing, being in touch with feelings, using self-talk constructively, possessing realistic personal rules, choosing to perceive accurately, attributing cause accurately, predicting realistically, clarifying values, setting realistic goals, visualizing skills, realistic decision making, and preventing and managing problems skills.
- Skills for eliciting and assessing thinking include building a knowledge base and thinking in skills terms.
- Helpers and clients can collect information about thinking skills from: client self-report, thinking aloud, thought listing, thought charting, counting, focusing on feelings questions, questionnaires, and thought-eliciting techniques such as live observation, visualizing, role-play, and task assignment.
- Helpers make inferences and form hypotheses about clients' thinking skills strengths and weaknesses.
- Helpers and clients can collect information about action skills in interviews (for instance, from client self-report, observing clients, focusing on actions questions, and role-plays).
- Helpers and clients can also collect action skills information from clients' natural or home settings.
- Helpers use information collected when identifying, clarifying, and assessing problems to redefine them in skills terms. Redefinitions are statements about thinking and action skills weaknesses that are sustaining problems.
- Some skills for redefining problems include: presenting a rationale, clarity and efficiency, using a whiteboard, checking clients' reactions, and attending to feelings. Helpers can also encourage clients to observe and assess problematic skills between sessions.

STAGE

3

STATE WORKING GOALS AND
PLAN INTERVENTIONS

Chapter 7 reviews how helpers and clients translate redefinitions of problems in skills terms into statements of working goals. Chapter 8 reviews skills of choosing and planning interventions to develop clients' self-helping skills.

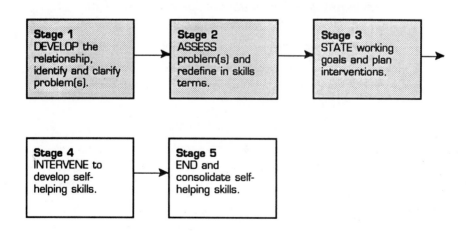

Stage 1
DEVELOP the relationship, identify and clarify problem(s).

Stage 2
ASSESS problem(s) and redefine in skills terms.

Stage 3
STATE working goals and plan interventions.

Stage 4
INTERVENE to develop self-helping skills.

Stage 5
END and consolidate self-helping skills.

 CHAPTER SEVEN

HOW TO STATE WORKING GOALS

It is not enough to take steps which may
some day lead to a goal; each step must be
itself a goal and a step likewise.

—von Goethe

CHAPTER QUESTIONS

❀ *What differences are there between
stating goals for problem management
and for altering problematic skills?*

❀ *What are some advantages and risks of
stating working goals?*

❀ *What are some considerations in goals
decisions?*

❀ *How do helper thinking skills influence
working goals?*

❀ *What are some helper action skills for
stating working goals?*

PROBLEM MANAGEMENT AND
PROBLEMATIC SKILLS GOALS

Though overlapping, a distinction exists between problem management and problematic skills goals. Short-term problems dominate much of helping. Clients want help to cope with immediate problems or crises—be they getting a job, dealing with a disruptive child, sleeping better, giving up excessive drinking, passing a test, or feeling less anxious. Statements of problem management goals can be general or specific. Often clients' *general* problem goals are obvious from their presenting concerns (for instance, feeling less depressed or sleeping better). On other occasions, helpers may need to probe and spend time with clients to discover their real agendas or underlying problems. *Specific* problem management goals entail stating the outcomes by which helpers and clients can evaluate whether clients are adequately managing problems. Frequently, helpers need to work with clients in shaping general statements of outcome goals into more specific statements. For instance, "I want to lose weight" needs to be translated into weight-loss objectives stated in terms of pounds or kilograms. Effective helpers would also specify a period for maintaining weight loss.

Where possible, lifeskills helping goes beyond stating problem management goals to stating problematic skills goals. If clients are to attain problem management goals, they require assistance in developing skills strengths. In Chapter 2, I mentioned that clients' problems often extend both *horizontally*, or to other current similar situations, and *vertically*, or to future similar situations. Problematic skills goals stem from redefinitions of clients' problems in skills terms. Such goals can encompass thinking and action skills for managing a specific current problem, other similar current problems, and similar future problems. Ideally lifeskills are for life, not just for managing immediate problems.

Helpers and clients can have both problem management goals and problematic skills goals. From Chapter 6, let's use the example of Jim Blake to illustrate similarities and differences between problem management goals and problematic skills goals. Getting another job is one of Jim Blake's problem areas. Jim's problem management goal of getting another job could be further specified in terms of what kind of job and by when. The various problem management steps in obtaining a job could be stated as sub-goals, each with a time frame. For instance, making a resume, information seeking about advertised job opportunities, creating and using an informal contact network, creating and implementing a job marketing plan, and developing interview skills are each sub-goals with target dates. However, only the sub-goal of developing interview skills is stated in skills language. The other sub-goals are stated as tasks. For instance, while Jim needs to make a resume, he also needs to develop skills of making and updating his resume. The risk of stating only sub-goals as tasks is that it increases the likelihood of inadequately specifying and instructing the requisite sub-skills. This shortcoming may not only lead to inefficiencies in managing the current problem, but also contribute to less transfer of learning for handling future job-getting situations.

Helpers should state problematic skills goals or sub-goals in terms not only of action skills but also of thinking skills. For instance, Jim may set himself the task sub-goal of making a career decision. He may even decide on a time frame for this. However, there is a huge difference between the task sub-goal of making a single career decision and that of developing skills for making effective career decisions, not only for now but in the future. If career decision making is viewed as a single task rather than as a set of skills, helpers may play down or ignore some other thinking skills that Jim requires beyond straightforward decision-making skills. For instance, Jim may also need to work on possessing realistic personal rules about achievement.

ADVANTAGES AND RISKS OF WORKING GOALS

Establishing working goals has both advantages and risks. The following are some advantages of collaborating with clients to state working goals.

- *Helping clients become authors of their lives:* Stating working goals helps clients assume rather than avoid personal responsibility for managing problems and problematic skills. Goals negotiated with clients enable them to become authors of their lives, rather than to drift aimlessly or live out other people's goals as if they were their own.
- *A bridge to working:* A great risk in helping is that helpers and clients talk rather than work. Helping may become directionless without working goals (Cormier & Cormier, 1985). Stating working goals clearly establishes an expectancy that helpers and clients expend effort to attain them.
- *Clarity of focus:* Well-stated working goals clearly identify the problematic skills on which clients need to work. Where con-

fusion and aimlessness may have reigned before, now clients have reasonably clear objectives toward which to strive. Working goals focus on what is important and thus econo- mize client effort by excluding or deemphasizing peripheral activities.

- *Increased motivation:* Working goals can increase clients' moti- vation and persistence, because they provide clients with something tangible to attain. Also, working goals may in- crease helpers' motivation because they too have objectives to attain.
- *A basis for planning interventions:* If working goals are stated clearly, helpers and clients have an adequate base for select- ing strategies and planning interventions.
- *A basis for evaluation:* Despite working goals' differing in how easy they are to measure, statements of goals provide a basis for clients and helpers to evaluate progress and success. Cli- ents can monitor and evaluate targeted skills at the start of, during, at the end of, and after helping.
- *An impetus for self-helping:* Statements of working goals iden- tify skills strengths that clients require both now and in the future. After helping, clients are more likely to remember clear statements of skills strengths than if no such statements exist. They can use this knowledge to consolidate targeted skills.

There are also risks to stating goals. Such risks usually happen if goals are set and stated the wrong way or prematurely. Most risks are not inherent in setting goals.

- *Insufficient emphasis on feelings:* Some clients require time, space, and support to get in touch with their capacity to feel and their wants and wishes. A risk of stating goals is that clients are insufficiently helped to experience themselves as feeling persons. There can be an overemphasis on thinking and doing, at the expense of experiencing feelings.
- *Premature restriction of focus:* Goals stated too rigidly at the outset interfere with helpers' and clients' dealing with emerg- ing problems and problematic skills. The die has been cast too soon. Furthermore, some problems are so complex that simple statements of goals in initial sessions do not do them justice.
- *Inaccuracy and superficiality:* Helpers may wrongly assess prob- lems and problematic skills, and this inaccuracy is reflected in statements of working goals. Furthermore, helpers may only focus on parts of problems and on less, rather than more, important problematic skills.
- *Eliciting resistances and rejection:* Statements of goals may elicit resistances, "yes . . . but" responses, and even open defiance.

Working goals that may seem intellectually tidy to helpers may be emotionally untidy for clients who ultimately have to implement them. Clients' resistances and reservations must be openly aired or later they may manifest in lack of commitment.

- *Controlling and pressuring clients:* Helpers may state goals more to meet their own needs for certainty and achievement than to help clients. They may have their own agendas and pet theories that they work into goal statements. In addition, helpers may state goals in ways that pressure clients (for instance, unrealistically high goals, or stating them in a demanding manner).

CONSIDERATIONS IN GOALS DECISIONS

Besides the distinction between problem management goals and problematic skills goals, there are many other considerations when deciding on goals.

Superordinate goals In lifeskills helping, there are two main categories of higher (superordinate) goals. In Chapter 1, I distinguished between the ultimate goal of lifeskills helping (personal excellence) and mediating goals (specific lifeskills). Another category of superordinate goals is that of learning to apply the lifeskills helping model as a self-helping skill for managing problems and altering problematic skills. Instead of helpers' using the model to assist clients in identifying and working on problematic skills, clients learn to do much of this work on their own. The lifeskills helping model aims to assist clients in using targeted skills in future similar situations. However, if the model itself is taught as a set of skills, clients can apply it on their own to problems and problematic skills different from those for which they originally requested help. Though my lifeskills model and Egan's (1990) problem management model differ, Egan too regards his problem management model not just as a helper tool, but also as a client self-helping tool.

Goals as hypotheses Helpers and clients are both practitioner-researchers: helpers in how best to help, clients in how best to live. Helpers need to view problematic skills goals scientifically. They are really a series of "If . . . then . . ." hypotheses. For instance, "*If* I develop my career decision-making skills, *then* I will make better career decisions both now and in the future." Career decision-making skills might then be broken down into a series of sub-hypotheses contributing to the main hypothesis. Another example is that of a shy teenager wishing to be more outgoing: "If I possess a more realistic personal rule concerning others' approval, then I am likely to become more outgoing." Though not always using the language of research, helpers and clients hypothesize which problematic skills contribute to sustaining problems. They then state as working goals developing strengths in targeted skills. As hypotheses, such goals are open to modification in light of feedback and changing circumstances. For instance, clients and helpers may find that another problematic skill is more important to achieving desired outcomes than one initially agreed upon.

Initial and emergent goals In initial sessions, helpers can identify, clarify, and redefine some problems in skills terms and then negotiate goals that stand throughout helping. Goals are more likely to be stable where problems are relatively focused and have brief time frames (for instance, passing an upcoming driving test). However, on other occasions helpers take into account emergent goals in addition to, as modifications of, or even instead of, initial goals. Situations where helpers need to pay attention to emerging goals include the following. First, some clients may be highly anxious and badly out of touch with their valuing process. Highly vulnerable clients may require nurturing relationships to lower their defenses to the point where they are prepared to accept some responsibility for working on their problems. Until they have had more time to share feelings and trust helpers, it may be premature to negotiate thinking and action skills goals. Second, some problems (for example, marital problems) may be so complex that helpers are either unwilling or unable to state a full range of goals at the end of an initial assessment. Too full a statement of problematic skills goals may only confuse clients, and it risks turning helping into an arid intellectual exercise. Also, too rigid an early skills definition of clients' problems may exclude much valuable information that will emerge during helping. Third, both for focused and for more complex problems and problematic skills, helpers need always to be prepared to alter and fine-tune goals in light of feedback and changed client circumstances.

Imposed or negotiated goals A basic question is "Whose goals are these?" Goals can be helper-centered or client-centered. Ideally, goals are both. Helpers and clients collaborate to identify, clarify, assess, and redefine problems in skills terms. When helpers sensitively and thoroughly conduct stages 1 and 2 of the lifeskills helping model, statements of working goals in stage 3 should seem the logical outcome of this earlier work. The negotiations involved in arriving at common conceptualizations of clients' problems and problematic skills essentially mean that working goals based on these conceptualizations have been negotiated too. Because the ground has been prepared, both helpers and clients subscribe to the same goals.

The risk of helpers' imposing their own agendas as goals is ever present. Sometimes helpers are insufficiently thorough in redefining problems in skills terms and rush into goal statements to meet their own needs for certainty and achievement. Beginning helpers may be especially prone to this. Some helpers may work within a narrow range of thinking and action skills, and so suggest a more restricted or lopsided range of goals than desirable. Helpers may present skills redefinitions and goals to clients in ways that leave little room for discussion. In addition, clients may be prone to say yes to working goals when they mean no or maybe. Helpers may fail to recognize cues that further negotiation and explanation are necessary.

Commitment to goals   Clients can have varying degrees of commitment to goals (Janis & Mann, 1977; Watson & Tharp, 1989). Sometimes clients openly express doubts about their commitment. On other occasions clients may talk about commitment, but later fail to act on it. It is one thing for helpers to state goals, another for clients to agree to them, and still another for clients to work to implement them both in the present and in the future. Client ambivalence is almost always a feature of commitment to working goals. On the one hand, they wish to be problem-free, yet on the other hand, they resist fully admitting personal responsibility for changing problematic skills. In varying degrees, they still believe in magical solutions. Fear of change, fear of failure, and fear of success can each interfere with commitment (Nelson-Jones, 1992). Commitment to working goals may entail giving up the payoffs and secondary gains of previous patterns of behavior (for instance, blaming others, or substance abuse). In addition, clients may go back to environments that reward skills weaknesses rather than help build targeted skills strengths.

Helpers need to pay close attention to clients' degrees of commitment to goals. Clients may be more likely to commit themselves to goals that are negotiated rather than imposed. Goals expressed in skills terms may require further explanation and clarification, both initially and later. It is difficult for clients to be committed to working goals that they do not fully understand. You may need to work with the client in exploring the rewards for change, as well as the losses in not changing. You need to acknowledge that there may be heavy costs to clients in giving up long-established habits of self-defeating thinking and acting. You can identify and discuss with clients potential difficulties and potential setbacks that may lower confidence. In addition, when planning interventions, if possible you need to build in rewards. For instance, early alleviation of psychological pain or early success in achieving a sub-task may strengthen commitment to goals. Also, supportive helping relationships reward clients.

Defining goals   One way of defining goals is in terms of progress in altering problematic skills rather than in coping with a specific problem. However, even when focusing on problematic skills, helpers and clients need to consider criteria for progress and goal attainment. In reality, since clients have to maintain skills strengths throughout their lives, problematic skills weaknesses are never cured. Nevertheless, helpers can think in terms of how best to observe and measure changes in problematic thinking and action skills, even if they are somewhat imprecise. For instance, the overall goal of a stop-smoking program is in its title. However, helpers also need to think of how to measure the

component skills of quitting smoking and maintaining this change. For instance, a smoker may have a thinking skills predicting weakness that "lung cancer cannot happen to me." For a given period, clients might keep a log of how many times this thought occurred, and also whether they disputed it and then made a more realistic predictive self-statement. The problematic skills goal might be, by the end of the period, either to eliminate the false prediction completely or, if it occurs, always to dispute and replace it.

HELPER THINKING SKILLS

How helpers think influences how they set goals. The following are some thinking skills relevant to setting and stating goals.

Use the lifeskills conceptual framework and language.   Helpers stating goals in the lifeskills model need to assess and conceptualize problems within it. Helpers think not just about problems, but about identifying problematic skills that sustain problems. In stage 2 (assess problems and redefine them in skills terms), lifeskills helpers almost invariably break problems down into their thinking and action skills components. Helpers state both overall goals and problematic skills sub-goals necessary to attain and maintain the overall goals.

Attribute accurately. "Who owns the working goals?" and "Who owns the responsibility for attaining working goals?" If helpers and clients collaborate well in the detective work of stages 1 and 2 of the lifeskills model, then redefinitions of their problems in skills terms should be reasonably clear to clients. Statements of working goals follow easily from mutually agreed-upon conceptualizations of problems and problematic skills. Helpers have fulfilled their responsibilities in assisting clients to understand their problems in ways that they can work on them. The working goals can be owned by both clients and helpers, though in different ways. Clients own the goals for themselves, whereas helpers own the goals as guides for how to help. Both helpers and clients also own responsibility for attaining working goals: the helper's being a professional responsibility, the client's being a personal responsibility.

Helpers need to beware of attributing too much responsibility for forming working goals to themselves. Clients are more likely to feel responsible for attaining goals if they have contributed to shaping them. Goals need to be realistic for clients, perceived as important for managing their problems, consistent with their values, and comprehensible. Forming and stating working goals is a shared responsibility between helpers and clients.

Possess realistic personal and helping rules. Unrealistic personal and helping rules may negatively influence how helpers set goals. Here are some unrealistic helper rules that may contribute to faulty statements of working goals.

"I must get quick results."
"I must always help clients set high goals."
"I must be the person in control."
"I must always state working goals comprehensively."
"Clients must always be treated as though they are highly vulnerable."
"I must always state working goals before the end of the initial session."
"I must never revise initial statements of working goals."
"All helping must be short-term."
"All helping must be long-term."

"I must always be liked by my clients."
"I must never make mistakes when stating working goals."

Helpers may need to identify, dispute, and reformulate unrealistic personal rules that place unnecessary demands on themselves and clients. Unrealistic rules can rigidify the helping process, as well as pressure or infantilize clients. Furthermore, helpers may be excessively vulnerable to client feedback and "things needing to go right." Ideally, helpers formulate and state working goals, not on the basis of their own irrational thinking, but solely in clients' best interests.

Perceive accurately. In many ways, how accurately you perceive may influence how you state working goals. First, you may have ignored or misperceived significant information when identifying, clarifying, and assessing clients' problems. For instance, your perceptions of your clients' problems may be colored by your own past struggles and present circumstances. Hence your skills redefinitions may have suffered and, in turn, your statements of working goals. Second, you may misperceive how realistic your goals are for clients. Third, you may misperceive how well your clients comprehend your statement of working goals, even though you may have checked this with them. Fourth, you may misperceive cues of resistance and lack of commitment and thus not address them. Perceiving your clients accurately is always difficult, since helpers bring so much of their own "stuff" into helping. Nevertheless, you need to be aware that you are always at risk of distorting clients. Try to identify and correct the specific ways in which you do this.

Predict realistically. Statements of working goals assume the prediction that if clients achieve some or all of the targeted skills they will have made progress in managing problems. Helpers may overpredict or underpredict clients' capacities to develop skills strengths. They may set working goals that are unrealistically high or low. Furthermore, helpers may inaccurately predict the rewards and costs of clients' efforts to change their behaviors. In predicting reward inaccurately, helpers may overestimate or underestimate good consequences. Similarly, in predicting cost inaccurately, helpers may underestimate or overestimate bad consequences (Nelson-Jones, 1990a). Predicting reward and cost accurately is relevant to predicting clients' persistence in working toward targeted goals. To counteract tendencies to inaccurate predictions when setting goals, helpers can review probability more stringently and reassess clients' coping capacities. Also, helpers can plan interventions to assist clients in handling difficulties and setbacks.

HELPER ACTION SKILLS

Statements of working goals are the "flip side" of redefinitions of clients' problems in skills terms. Helpers take the redefinitions expressed in terms of thinking skills and action skills weakness hypotheses and turn them into statements of positive helping and self-helping objectives. Much overlap exists between the skills for redefining problems in skills terms and stating working goals.

Present a rationale. Toward the end of stage 2, the helper presented a rationale for redefining problems in skills terms. Once helper and client have arrived at a mutually agreed-upon conceptualization of a problem area in skills terms, the helper can make a transition statement that introduces the idea of working goals.

> **Helper:** Jan, we have now identified and agreed upon some possible thinking and action skills weaknesses by which you may contribute to your poor relationship with Pammie. Your overall goal is to have a good mother-daughter relationship with her. By reversing your possible skills weaknesses into positive objectives, you can more easily see where you might work to develop skills strengths. I would hope that possessing a positive statement of goals will motivate you to persist in working on them both now and in the future. Also, such a statement of goals gives us a focus for discussing how best to attain them However, if new or different goals emerge, we can update or change our statement of goals.

Use a whiteboard. A great advantage of using a whiteboard is the ease with which two-column T redefinitions of thinking and action skills weaknesses can be edited into statements of desired skills strengths. In addition, the board makes it easier for clients to discuss goals. A further advantage of a board is that both the clients and you can copy the same statement of thinking and action skills goals for each problem.

Use checking skills. Even though you have checked your redefinition with your clients and, if necessary, modified it, you should still check their reactions to seeing their problematic skills weaknesses expressed as positive working goals. Clients may require further clarification regarding some of the skills. Though you may try to clarify skills goals, you may have to defer detailed explanations to subsequent sessions. Furthermore, clients may not fully grasp the meaning of certain skills, especially thinking skills, until they have become proficient in using them.

Attend to feelings.   Some clients feel very positive about statements of working goals and see them as highly motivating. However, statements of working goals may threaten others. Goals connote the need for effort and change. A degree of ambivalence is inevitable in regard to working goals. Pay attention to resistances and reservations. Helpers require sensitivity to voice and body cues to detect inadequate commitment. Even though clients may verbalize commitment and confidence, their nonverbal messages may indicate otherwise. If possible work through with clients their reservations and commitment difficulties. Some clients feel more comfortable about goals when they become clearer about how to attain them.

Be flexible.   Many reasons exist why you need to be flexible in stating working goals. You always take client and problem considerations into account. Some clients may only come for one session (for instance, in regard to asking for a promised pay raise), and seek a strategy for handling their problem rather than a skills analysis. Children may require brief and simple statements of working goals focused more on action skills than on thinking skills, though the latter may be relevant. With clients having complex problems, you might state working goals for the problem area of most priority to your client. You could then indicate that other problem areas will be dealt with in similar fashion or mention one or two illustrative working goals for each problem area. If a specific problematic skill crops up in many different problem areas (for instance, unrealistic personal rules), you may state developing realistic personal rules as a broad working goal. Another occasion for flexibility is that people in crisis may require goals and a plan to deal with their immediate predicament. Helping these clients think about problems in skills terms and stating working goals may come later, if at all.

Examples of Stating Working Goals

Following are some examples of stating working goals. The first example consists of statements of working goals, one brief and the other fairly detailed, for two of Jim Blake's work-related problems. The second example is a statement of working goals for a shy college student, Anita Walton.

Example 1
Case study: Jim Blake
Part 6: State working goals

Having agreed on a two-column T redefinition of Jim's problem of being fired (see Chapter 6), counselor Sam Rushton told Jim that he would edit it on the whiteboard so that it became a statement of the skills strengths needed to manage the problem better.

Handling being fired
Thinking skills goals
   Perceive my former company accurately
   Use self-talk to cope with my anger
   Possess realistic personal rules concerning being fired

Action skills goal
   Make limited contact with my former employer (for instance, regarding references)

Sam checked Jim's reactions to this statement of working goals. Then he and Jim wrote down the working goals to help remember them. Sam and Jim then moved on to a common conceptualization in skills terms of Jim's getting-another-job problem. Again, Sam used the whiteboard. Once he and Jim were satisfied with the two-column T redefinition (see Chapter 6), Sam edited it to make it a statement of working goals.

Getting another job
Thinking skills goals
   Own more responsibility for my choices in life
   Become more in touch with my wants and wishes
   Use coping self-talk (for instance, when faced with interviews)
   Possess more realistic personal rules (for instance, regarding achievement)
   Perceive myself more accurately (for instance, work on lessening my negative self-labels)
   Make realistic predictions about the possible length of my job search
   Clarify my values
   Develop goal-setting skills, both career goals and job search goals
   Develop more realistic and rigorous career decision-making skills

Action skills goals
   Develop professional resume-making skills
   Develop skills at creating and using an informal network to find out
      about unadvertised job opportunities
   Develop my skills at creating and implementing a marketing plan
   Improve my interview skills
   Develop my skills at managing time and engaging in meaningful
      activities independent of full-time employment

Sam checked Jim's reactions to the preceding list of goals. Sam mentioned that when Jim next came, they would discuss a plan to help Jim attain his working goals.

Example 2
Case study: Anita Walton

Anita Walton, a 19-year-old college student, came to see a helper, Maureen Perrone, because she thought she was too shy. During stages 1 and 2 of the lifeskills helping model, Maureen formulated many thinking and action skills weakness hypotheses. However, Maureen only used some of the main hypotheses in her skills redefinition of Anita's shyness problem. After some discussion and minor changes, Anita agreed to Maureen's conceptualization of her problem.
   Anita's thinking skills weaknesses included:

1. Possessing an unrealistic personal rule regarding her absolute need for others' approval
2. Misperceiving social situations by jumping to negative conclusions about others' reactions to her
3. Misattributing responsibility by thinking others should always make the first move to initiate contact
4. Using negative self-talk before, during, and after social exchanges

Anita's action skills weaknesses included:

1. Speaking with a very quiet and diffident voice
2. Possessing poor initiating contact skills
3. Possessing poor self-disclosure skills
4. Possessing poor telephone skills

Using the two-column T format, one column for thinking skills weaknesses and the other column for action skills weaknesses, Maureen wrote her redefinition of Anita's problem on the whiteboard. Maureen then edited what she had written into the following statement of *working goals. Maureen then checked Anita's reactions. Afterwards both helper and client recorded it. Maureen said that she would define these skills goals more fully in subsequent sessions.*

Anita's overall goal: *To feel, think, and act more confidently with people my age, especially males*

Anita's working goals

Thinking Skills Goals	Action Skills Goals
Possess a realistic personal rule about approval	Speak with a louder, more confident voice
Perceive others' reactions to me accurately	Develop my initiating more contact skills
Attribute responsibility for initiating better	Develop my self-disclosure skills
Use coping self-talk	Develop my telephone skills

 CHAPTER HIGHLIGHTS

- Though overlapping, a distinction exists between problem management and problematic skills goals.
- Problem management goals can focus on both general and specific desired outcomes.
- Problematic skills goals entail targeting for development the thinking and action skills that sustain problems.
- Statements of working goals are redefinitions of clients' problems in skills terms stated as goals to be worked toward both now and in the future.
- Advantages of stating working goals include: helping clients become authors of their lives, building a bridge to working, clarity of focus, increased motivation, providing a basis for evaluation, providing a basis for planning interventions, and being an impetus for self-helping.
- Risks in stating working goals include: insufficient emphasis on feelings, premature restriction of focus, inaccuracy and superficiality, eliciting resistances and rejection, and controlling and pressuring clients.
- Considerations in goal decisions include: superordinate or higher goals, goals as hypotheses, initial and emergent goals, imposed or negotiated goals, commitment to goals, and how to define goals.

- Helper thinking skills for setting and stating goals include: using the lifeskills conceptual framework and language, attributing accurately, possessing realistic personal and helping rules, perceiving accurately, and predicting realistically.
- Helper action skills for stating goals include: presenting a rationale, using a whiteboard, using checking skills, attending to feelings, and being flexible.

CHAPTER EIGHT

HOW TO PLAN INTERVENTIONS

Little by little does the trick.

—Aesop

CHAPTER QUESTIONS

❀ *What do the terms* interventions *and* plans *mean?*

❀ *What are some criteria for choosing interventions?*

❀ *What are different kinds of plans?*

❀ *What are some considerations in developing plans?*

❀ *What are skills for working with clients when choosing and planning interventions?*

Statements of working goals provide the bridge to choosing interventions. Helpers, as practitioner-researchers, hypothesize not only about goals, but also about ways to attain them. This chapter focuses on some of the many issues and skills in choosing and planning interventions. Though we are concentrating on initial sessions, helpers also choose and plan interventions for working goals that emerge during helping.

Some readers might consider that this chapter on choosing and planning interventions could be better placed after the chapters on the various interventions, but I have started with planning interventions for two reasons. First, in helping, choosing and planning interventions naturally comes before intervening. Second, readers may find it easier to understand the five stages of the DASIE lifeskills model if they are presented in the order in which they occur, rather than having to jump back and forth. You can still choose either to read or reread this chapter after reading the subsequent chapters on interventions.

INTERVENTIONS AND PLANS

Helpers make choices, both concerning specific interventions and about interventions in combination. An important distinction exists between interventions and plans.

Interventions In lifeskills helping, interventions are intentional behaviors designed to help clients attain problem management and problematic skills goals. In the context of this and subsequent chapters, interventions are "helping strategies" (Cormier & Cormier, 1985), "effective procedures" (Hutchins & Cole, 1986), or "therapy techniques" (Goldfried & Davison, 1976).

Interventions, or strategies for change, can be either helper-centered or client-centered. Put simply, with helper-centered interventions helpers do something to or for clients (for instance, helpers may give clients advice on how to behave). With client-centered interventions, helpers develop clients' capacities to intervene in their own problem and problematic skills areas (for instance, helpers may assist clients in how to monitor their thinking). Both helpers and clients can be the intervening agents. In lifeskills helping, the object of all helper interventions should be to strengthen clients' own interventions: "I (as a helper) am of most use to you (as a client) if I help you to intervene, at first with my assistance but later on your own, to develop and maintain *your* skills to manage *your* problems."

Helpers require a repertoire of interventions or intervention skills to cover a range of clients' lifeskills weaknesses. You may need to specialize in the most useful interventions for the client populations with which you deal because the range of clients' problems and skills weaknesses is so vast.

Plans   Plans are overall statements of how to combine and sequence interventions for managing problems and attaining working goals. They are the outlines, maps, or diagrams that enable helpers and clients to get from where they are to where they want to be. The term *treatment plan* is sometimes used (for instance, Cormier & Cormier, 1985). A possible risk in using the term is that it may connote helper-centeredness rather than helpers' developing clients' skills to help themselves. The term *working plan* may be more appropriate, since plans provide frameworks within which both helpers and clients work. Plans imply arranging interventions beforehand. However, as the Roman writer Publius Styrius observed in the first century B.C.: "It is a bad plan that admits of no modification."

CHOOSING INTERVENTIONS

Many beginning helpers, after stating working goals, experience a sense of emptiness about their ability to do anything useful to help clients attain these goals. Going beyond assessment to choosing and planning interventions creates added pressures for them to "deliver the goods." It takes time for helpers to build a repertoire of interventions and confidence about their effectiveness. Frequently even experienced helpers find that decisions about interventions are not clear-cut and involve trade-offs between conflicting considerations. Beginning helpers' anxieties about choosing interventions are not in themselves detrimental—how you handle your anxieties determines this.

Criteria for Choosing Interventions

This section focuses more on *how to choose* interventions than on *choosing how* to implement interventions. Once you have statements of working goals, your next step is to choose appropriate interventions. You are not starting from scratch. Even as you clarified, assessed, and redefined clients' problems in skills terms, you were probably making intervention hypotheses. Now is the time to refine these hypotheses. Below are some criteria to include in your decision making about interventions.

Importance of maintaining a supportive relationship Whatever other interventions you choose, always offer them within the context of supportive helping relationships. A risk for some helpers when breaking down problems, setting working goals, and specifying interventions is that they become too technique oriented. The person-emphasis of supportive relationships may be the major intervention for some vulnerable clients until they gain more confidence and insight. For all clients, supportive relationships can contribute to the quality of the working alliance (Kokotovic & Tracey, 1990) and facilitate clients' motivation. Furthermore, supportive relationships can assist more task-oriented interventions (for instance, by providing a better emotional climate for role-plays and coached performance of skills).

Emphasis of interventions on managing problems or altering problematic skills You and your client may choose to focus more on managing an immediate problem than on altering problematic skills. How you intervene will be heavily influenced by such a decision. Situations where there may be more emphasis on problem management than on problematic skills interventions include the following. First, clients may be in crisis. They may feel overwhelmed by the intensity of their emotions and be in shock, disoriented, highly anxious, extremely depressed, very angry, contemplating suicide, and fearing insanity or nervous breakdown. The objectives of helper interventions in crises include protecting clients, calming them down, and assisting them in here-and-now problem-solving and planning so that they regain a sense of control over their lives. A clear focus on problematic skills is deferred until later, if at all. Second, clients may need to cope with immediate problems (for instance, upcoming tests, public-speaking engagements, or confrontations with difficult people). Together, helpers and clients develop game plans for dealing with immediate situations rather than emphasizing self-helping skills for afterwards. Third, clients may have limited goals. Dealing with an immediate problem may be all that they have time or inclination for. Fourth, your own schedule as helpers may be so busy that all you can offer is Band-Aid problem management assistance.

Relevance of interventions for attaining working goals Lifeskills helping heavily emphasizes both thinking and action working goals rather than either on its own. Having taken the trouble to assess clients and negotiate working definitions, helpers have laid the basis for selecting interventions. For instance, with shy Anita (see end of Chapter 7), who has a thinking skills goal of possessing a realistic personal rule about approval, the helper might consider a range of interventions focused on developing this personal-rule skill (for instance, providing a rationale for the intervention, identifying existing unrealistic rules both inside and outside helping sessions, demonstrating disputing and reformulating rules, rehearsing and coaching the client, and setting appropriate homework). For Anita's action skills goal of speaking in a louder more confident voice, the helper might consider a range of interventions (for instance, asking Anita to get feedback from significant others on how they find her voice, encouraging Anita to speak up during helping, exploring how Anita thinks and feels when she speaks quietly or loudly, setting Anita systematic tasks that require speaking more loudly both inside and outside helping, and possibly getting Anita to see a speech therapist). Your choice of working goals provides a good framework for your choice of interventions, with each intervention having many sub-choices as to how you actually apply it.

Helper competence to administer interventions   Cormier and Cormier (1985) observe that "if your only tool is a hammer, you will probably treat everything as if it were a nail" (p. 297). Wise helpers know the limitations of their tools. You need to acknowledge the range of interventions within which you can work effectively. Initially, beginning helpers might focus on building a repertoire of central helping interventions. For example, the intervention of helping clients to build the thinking skill of identifying, disputing, and reformulating unrealistic personal rules is pertinent to numerous client problem areas (Ellis, 1980, 1989). Similarly, the intervention of helping clients learn skills of delivering assertive verbal, voice, and body messages has widespread relevance (Alberti & Emmons, 1990). Another criterion for developing your repertoire of interventions is to focus on those of most use to client populations with which you work or are likely to work. As time goes by, most helpers acquire a fund of practical knowledge concerning what working goals and interventions are helpful for which kinds of problems and problematic skills weaknesses.

Beginning helpers cannot expect to perform interventions competently without adequate training, practice, and supervision. A small number of interventions performed thoroughly will generally help clients much more than a greater number performed superficially. Also, you put much less pressure on yourself if you are aiming to achieve limited agendas rather than attempting too much. Though some beginning helpers are overambitious, many underestimate their helping potential. This underestimation may lead beginning helpers either to not suggest interventions or not implement them confidently. Self-consciousness and a degree of discomfort are inevitable when learning new interventions. If underconfident, you require good training and supervision coupled with realistic self-appraisal. Also, you need to be open to client feedback about how well you implement interventions. Experienced helpers too may doubt themselves as they take risks to develop their repertoire of interventions. Nevertheless, it is important that they continue to build their skills.

Theoretical and research support for interventions Skilled helpers operate within theoretical frameworks. The interventions you offer should be based on psychological principles of learning, maintaining, and changing behavior. The lifeskills framework presented in Chapter 1 provides an introductory theoretical statement for assessing interventions. You should aim to know and keep abreast of the practitioner and research literature in the areas in which you help or intend helping. This way you can find out about both existing and new interventions. Also, you can assess their empirical support. Sometimes you may come across findings in the literature that indicate interventions used in combination are more effective than interventions used in isolation. For instance, in marital work, focusing on increasing the exchange of rewarding behaviors between partners is more helpful in combination with communication training (Jacobson et al., 1985). On other occasions, you may find that different interventions proved effective in achieving similar outcomes. For instance, Moon and Eisler (1983) conducted a study on anger control with undergraduate subjects randomly assigned to cognitive stress inoculation, problem-solving, social-skills, or minimal-attention groups. At post-treatment, all treatment groups reported significantly fewer anger-provoking incidents and had significantly lower scores on an anger inventory than the control group. However, there were also between-group differences: the problem-solving and social-skills groups displayed more socially skilled assertive behavior in the presence of anger-provoking stimuli than the cognitive stress inoculation group. Reasons that different interventions may lead to similar outcomes include the common contribution of the helping relationship across each intervention and the increases in clients' self-efficacy beliefs (beliefs in their ability to cope with their environments) brought about by different interventions. When reading research studies, pay particular attention to the maintenance of treatment gains. Also, always read the research literature critically.

Client considerations   Numerous client considerations influence both choosing and implementing interventions. Client considerations include the following.

1. *Anxiety level and sense of worth:* Helpers always need to take into account how psychologically vulnerable clients are and how badly their anxieties interfere with how they feel, think, and act. For example, marital conflict communication interventions assume clients' abilities to accept some responsibility for contributing to marital distress. Specific interventions for building career decision-making skills may be premature for clients badly out of touch with their valuing process. Action skills interventions to assist highly anxious clients to initiate friendships may need to await their obtaining sufficient sense of self-worth to implement them.

2. *Motivation and resistances:* With its emphasis on developing clients' self-helping skills, motivation is a critical issue in lifeskills helping. As with goals, clients can say yes to interventions when they mean no or maybe. Helpers need to assess clients' motivation for implementing interventions and explore potential difficulties and resistances. Clients need to own interventions both intellectually and emotionally to exhibit commitment to attaining them. Interventions that bring early rewards, including relief of psychological distress, enhance motivation.

3. *Expectations and priorities:* Related to motivation is the degree to which interventions are geared to outcomes that clients want and expect from helping. You always need to take clients' priorities into account. For instance, clients who enter helping wanting to manage an immediate problem may not want interventions focused on longer-term skills building. Also, clients seeing career issues as the main focus for helping may resist interventions focused on their personal lives.

4. *Age and maturity:* Helpers need to adjust interventions to the age of clients. For example, though friendship skills for adults and preteen children have similarities, children and adults require somewhat different skills for relating to peer and friendship groups. You must also take into account how much both children and adults know about relationships. In addition, you need to deliver interventions according to the age and maturity of clients (for instance, by varying use of language).

5. *Intelligence level and ability to comprehend interventions:* Depending on their intelligence level, some clients may find difficulty comprehending certain interventions (for instance, the thinking

skill of identifying possible misperceptions, generating alternatives, and choosing best-fit perceptions). Helpers need to work
with interventions that clients can comprehend. Ultimately clients have to understand the choices involved so that they can
implement lifeskills on their own.

6. *Culture:* Helpers need to take into account clients' cultures
when choosing and implementing interventions. For instance,
the rules for work and personal relationships differ greatly across
cultures (Argyle, 1986). Consequently, relationship skills interventions must take into account relevant cultural rules.

7. *Sex and gender:* Depending on their biological sex, clients may
have learned different skills strengths and weaknesses. Helpers
need to be careful to avoid fitting clients into masculine and
feminine stereotypes. Nevertheless, they can still assess where
inappropriate sex-role conditioning interferes with the development of clients' lifeskills and choose interventions accordingly.

8. *Support factors:* Families, peer groups, friendship groups, and
work colleagues can support or interfere with skills acquisition.
Sometimes clients can be trained to identify and use environmental supports better. As part of this process, they may also
learn skills of being more supporting to others. On other occasions interventions may focus on helping clients develop skills to
protect themselves from environmental pressures.

9. *Practical considerations:* Practical considerations may influence
your choice of interventions (for instance, pressing current difficulties, threatening upcoming tasks, unexpected challenges and
stresses, time available for helping, whether or not the client
lives locally, financial circumstances, and so on).

Development of self-helping skills Where possible, select and
implement interventions that develop clients' self-helping skills.
Some interventions may directly address issues of clients' maintaining skills (for instance, helping clients develop realistic expectations and attributions about the difficulty of acquiring and
maintaining skills). Helpers may also choose to implement interventions in ways that emphasize self-helping (for instance, by
ensuring that clients understand and can verbalize the sequence
of choices involved in specific skills—as one example, self-administered relaxation as contrasted with helper-administered relaxation).

Appropriateness of group interventions Helpers need to consider
whether clients might best attain some or all of their working

goals by attending one or more lifeskills training groups (Nelson-Jones, 1992). Other clients might benefit from joining longer-term interactional groups, if possible incorporating a skills focus (Corey, 1990; Gazda 1989; Yalom, 1985). Considerations relevant to selecting group interventions include the nature of the clients' problems, the availability of appropriate groups, and clients' willingness to participate in group work instead of, concurrently, or after individual work.

Appropriateness of interventions involving third parties   Sometimes you may choose to work with clients' environments. For instance, with depressed or acting-out pupils, school counselors may choose to work with clients' parents or families as well. You can also involve third parties as helper's aides. For instance, you can enlist parents, teachers, or peers to help shy clients develop confidence and skills. In a work setting, you can enlist the help of supervisors and managers (for example, in developing employees' public speaking skills).

Appropriateness of referral   Making referrals generally implies your assessment that other helpers can deal with clients' problems and problematic skills better than you can. You may start making referral hypotheses early in stage 1 of the lifeskills model. Whether you implement them, then or later, depends on whether and when you become sufficiently clear that referral is in your clients' best interests. If problems and problematic skills emerge that would be better dealt with by others, you may make referrals at later stages of helping.

Many considerations influence decisions as to whether referral is the best intervention. Ideally, helpers build up referral networks that enable them, where appropriate, to suggest suitable alternative helpers. You may neither have such a network nor be able to locate suitable alternative helpers. Your continuing to work with clients may be better than nothing. Often beginning helpers are acutely aware of their lack of experience. Your perception that clients require referral may be heavily colored by your doubts and anxieties. Another option is to continue working with clients, but obtain suitable supervision and support. On some occasions, you may rightly decide that others can work better with clients. Considerations influencing decisions about referring clients to other helpers include training, skills, values, time, cost, convenience, and availability ((Shaffer, 1976).

Sometimes you can make referrals and still work with clients. For instance, you may refer clients with little energy to a physician as part of your assessment of their problems and problematic skills. Also, you can make referrals as part of overall treatment plans. For instance, when working with unemployed clients, you can refer them to workshops on job-seeking skills.

PLANNING INTERVENTIONS

Almost invariably helpers use interventions in combination rather than in isolation. Consequently, in addition to developing hypotheses about interventions, helpers develop hypotheses about how interventions might best be combined. In short, they develop working plans of varying degrees of structure to attain working goals.

Kinds of Plans

Clients come to helping with a wide variety of problems, expectations, motivations, priorities, time constraints, and lifeskills strengths and weaknesses. In lifeskills helping, helpers tailor interventions and plans to individual clients. The following are included among the kinds of working plans that lifeskills helpers might consider.

Problem management plans Problem management plans are outlines of interventions and steps required to assist clients to manage specific problematic situations. Often, in short-term helping, plans emphasize managing problems rather than altering problematic skills. Helpers wishing to focus on problematic skills may make treatment compromises in the interests of practicality. All clients may have time or motivation for is to manage immediate situations (for instance, a request for a pay raise, an imminent public-speaking engagement, a statistics test, or a visit from the in-laws). Even in longer-term helping, helpers and clients can develop plans to deal with specific situations. However, in longer-term helping, planning for specific situations is more likely to take place within the framework of altering problematic skills weaknesses in the direction of strengths. Below are two examples of problem management planning.

Example A: Short-Term Helping

Emelio was a part-time student majoring in medical radiation. He was referred to the student counseling service by a faculty member after failing a mid-term exam in pathology, a subject he was already repeating. During the initial assessment, the counselor assessed

*Emelio as having limited motivation both for study and for counsel-
ing. However, Emelio was interested in obtaining his medical radia-
tions qualification. He needed to pass the pathology course to do this.
Emelio and the counselor agreed that the best way to spend the
remainder of the first session was to develop a plan (or "survival kit")
that would assist him to pass pathology. Here, as is often the case in
brief helping, the statement of working goals merged into planning
interventions to attain them. Using the whiteboard, the counselor and
Emelio outlined the following problem management plan.*

1. *Obtain accurate and specific feedback on my strengths and weaknesses in the pathology mid-term exam I failed (within the next
   week)*
2. *Do weekly essays on major topics and get teaching assistant's
   feedback (for remainder of semester)*
3. *Attend all pathology lectures (for remainder of semester)*
4. *Attend all pathology tutorials (for remainder of semester)*
5. *Define the pathology syllabus more precisely (within the next
   week)*
6. *Review possible final-test questions (within the next three weeks)*
7. *Take properly structured notes (starting immediately)*
8. *Keep in contact with full-time classmates, so as not to miss tips
   about important areas for study and revision (starting immediately)*
9. *Organize study time systematically (prioritizing and time charting
   to be done as homework assignment)*

*At the end of the session, Emelio wrote down this plan. A month later,
Emelio returned for a follow-up session. He reported he had made
progress in items 1–8 of his plan. Much of the second session was
spent developing Emelio's skills of systematic time charting.*

Example B: Extended Helping

*Katy came for counseling with numerous presenting concerns includ-
ing depression, low self-esteem, difficulty holding down relationships,
and anxieties about being a female engineer. Katy's working goals
included thinking and action skills for being more assertive. During
her fifth weekly session, Katy and her counselor planned how best to
manage a specific current problem in Katy's life. Katy's first job after
graduation was with a leading construction engineering company.
When hired, she was promised a salary review after her first year's
service. The company had not conducted this review 3 months into
her second year. Katy and her counselor formulated her overall problem management goal, which was, before the end of 2 weeks, to ask*

her boss for a salary review. They then stated thinking and action skills working goals. For instance, an illustrative thinking skills goal was to develop a more realistic personal rule about discussing money. Illustrative action skills goals focused on verbal, voice, and body messages for raising the issue of her salary review and requesting that it be conducted. Katy and her counselor then developed a plan for how to make a salary review request when face to face with her boss. This plan included strategies for handling possible countermoves by her boss. The counselor demonstrated, coached, and rehearsed Katy in the component skills of the plan.

Problematic skills: structured plans   Helpers and clients may consider a highly structured approach the best way to obtain some working goals. Structured plans or programs are step-by-step training and learning outlines of interventions for attaining specific goals. Structured plans are commonly used in lifeskills training groups such as in assertion or stress management groups (Hopson & Scally, 1981; Gazda, 1989; Nelson-Jones, 1992). Structured plans may also be used to train individual clients in skills where working goals are clear and specific. Three variations of structured plans are predetermined programs, tailor-made programs, and partially structured programs.

1. *Predetermined programs:* Helpers may work with clients using existing, or modifications of existing, packages or programs to develop skills. Such skills development programs may be in areas like parenting, career decision making, and weight control. Below are examples of helpers and clients using predetermined programs.

Herb suffered from hypertension. A central working goal was to develop his relaxation skills, both physical and mental. Herb's helper decided that the best way to develop the relaxation skills was to use a program based on Bernstein and Borkovec's (1973) Progressive Relaxation Training: A Manual for the Helping Professions.

Lucy suffered from agoraphobia. Working goals included developing Lucy's self-talk skills for coping with feelings of panic and being able to leave home and perform feared tasks, such as going on buses and into stores. Lucy's helper negotiated with her that treatment interventions would be based on Mathews, Gelder, and Johnston's (1981) Programmed Practice for Agoraphobia: Clients' Manual.

2. *Tailor made programs:* Programs of interventions can be tailor-made to specific problems or to specific persons. When tailor-

made to specific problems, they resemble predetermined packages. For instance, when Jim Blake saw the outplacement counselor Sam Rushton about getting another job, Sam could either fit Jim into an existing program for unemployed executives, or design a program specifically geared to Jim's skills weaknesses and needs, or combine the two approaches. In the tailor-made approach, Sam develops a step-by-step outline to attain the working goals. Here Jim can be part of the planning process, with his specific goals, wishes, and circumstances taken into account. The structured plan is suggested rather than prescribed.

3. *Partially structured programs:* Helpers and clients can design programs to attain working goals that have elements of structure, yet fall short of step-by-step structured programs. For instance, in the case of the unemployed executive Jim Blake, another option for his counselor was to set aside certain sessions for testing to assess interests and aptitudes, and others for developing specific action skills such as resume writing and interview skills. The agendas for the remaining sessions would be open for negotiation at the start of each session. Following is another example of a partially structured program—a continuation of the Anita Walton case study from the end of Chapter 7.

Anita Walton's main presenting concern was shyness. Her helper, Maureen Perrone, worked with Anita to set the following working goals. Anita's thinking skills goals were to: possess a realistic personal rule about approval; perceive others' reactions to me more accurately; attribute responsibility for initiating better; and use coping self-talk. Anita's action skills goals were to: speak with a louder, more confident voice; develop my initiating contact skills; develop my self-disclosure skills; and develop my telephone skills. Maureen Perrone had an extremely heavy client load that rarely allowed her to do long-term helping. She assessed Anita as not being seriously underconfident and suggested that they work for 3 further sessions at 2-week intervals. Maureen's aim was to give Anita maximal self-helping skills within a limited time. Maureen suggested the following program to Anita. The first session had already been spent on assessment and stating working goals; the second session would mainly focus on interventions for Anita's thinking skills; the third session would mainly focus on interventions for Anita's action skills; the fourth session would be spent filling learning gaps and consolidating trained skills as self-helping skills. During the fourth session, Maureen and Anita would review the advisability of holding a follow-up session, say 3 months later. Anita agreed to the program, which allowed for flexibility within sessions but ensured that attention was clearly paid to both thinking and action skills, rather than to one set of skills at the expense of the other.

Problematic skills: Open plans Open plans allow helpers and clients without predetermined structure to choose which interventions to use to attain which working goals, and when. Many considerations influence decisions to adopt open plans. Some clients may require nurturing relationships to help them get more in touch with their feelings and reduce their anxieties. They may not be able to work effectively on thinking and action skills weaknesses until feeling less vulnerable. Also, some cases are complex and difficult to understand. Helpers risk prematurely deciding on interventions if they opt for too much structure too soon. Open plans allow helpers and clients to collaborate in setting session agendas. Such session agendas can emphasize material and the skills on which clients and helpers currently want to work. Open plans have the great advantage of flexibility. Clients may be more motivated to work on skills and material that have relevance at any given time than being run through existing programs independent of current considerations. I revert to the example of Rob, used in Chapter 2, to illustrate a helper's use of an open plan.

Rob's overall goal was to improve his relationship with one of his teenage daughters, Ruth, and to improve his marriage. Sue Clark, Rob's counselor, negotiated the following statement of working goals. Rob's thinking skills goals were: (1) to acknowledge that I am a chooser and responsible for my thoughts, feelings, and actions; (2) to use coping self-talk when faced with provocations; and (3) to develop realistic personal rules concerning standards of family behavior. Rob's action skills goals included: (1) developing good listening skills; (2) developing assertion skills, specifically about how I state my wishes about my daughter's behavior; and (3) developing conflict negotiation skills. Sue Clark realized that Rob's objective was to develop some skills as quickly as possible rather than have a long-term helping relationship. She suggested to Rob that, instead of developing a formal plan to attain his working goals, the best way to proceed was to use appropriate interventions to develop his thinking and action skills in relation to material brought in to each session. This would allow both of them flexibility on what they covered in each session, yet not preclude spending additional time on training specific skills if necessary. Sue was confident about her repertoire of interventions for working on Rob's thinking and action skills. Sue also required Rob to do homework, including listening to recordings of each helping session.

Considerations in Planning

Some helpers are good at designing and executing group lifeskills programs, but poor at planning educational or training interventions for individual clients. They find it advantageous to combine interventions sequentially and systematically for groups, but for various reasons become less disciplined with individuals. Even when adopting open plans, some effective lifeskills group leaders still fail to use their training skills adequately. In the preceding section I emphasized varying degrees of structure for plans. Here I focus on plans for clients who are likely to develop skills from structured learning sequences. Most considerations mentioned are also relevant to plans for managing specific problem situations.

Preparation time   If you decide to design treatment plans for individual clients, when do you do it? Though you may discuss with clients possible interventions for attaining working goals, you may find it difficult to develop systematic plans during the same sessions. Instead, you may need to take time to do this before the next session. Some helpers do not develop systematic plans because they are unwilling to spend out-of-session time doing this task.

Involvement of clients and others   Helpers need to consider at what stage and how much to involve clients in planning. Helpers' prior discussions about working goals provide some protection against making unacceptable plans. In addition, you always need to check that clients understand and are comfortable with proposed plans. If necessary, you can modify plans in light of client feedback. Sometimes you may consider it helpful to involve clients early in the planning process. Advantages of such involvement include taking clients' wishes and priorities into account and clients' being more likely to implement plans that they have had some say in making. With clients' permission, you may sometimes involve significant others when planning (for instance, partners, care-givers, or parents).

Sequencing of interventions   What is the best way to sequence activities so as to attain working goals? Sometimes the logic in sequencing interventions is clear. For instance, with most unemployed executives, there are three logically sequenced steps in assisting them to become reemployed: (1) evaluation and career planning, (2) developing a job marketing plan, and (3) implementing a job marketing plan (Davidson, 1988). Also, within an individual intervention like perceiving more realistically, the sequence of sub-interventions is clear: namely, identifying unrealistic perceptions, generating and evaluating alternative perceptions, and choosing the best-fit perception. Here the learning tasks are cumulative. In action skills interventions, helpers often use step-by-step tasks to develop clients' skills and confidence.

Time frame for plan Helpers, clients, and the learning process all influence time allocated for carrying out plans. For instance, helpers may have restricted amounts of time to work with clients. In addition, you may want clients to participate in learning activities offered by others (for instance, workshops that are only available on specific dates). Client considerations include varying degrees of urgency in acquiring skills and different abilities to pay, if fees are involved. Learning process considerations include the degree to which sessions and planned activities should be intensive rather than spaced out, or a combination of the two. Also, should you plan for one or more follow-up or booster sessions?

Management of learning considerations Helpers need to consider what is the best way to present interventions. For each intervention, when should helpers use the following training and learning methods: assessment and facilitating client self-assessment, facilitation, verbal presentation, demonstration, in-session rehearsal, coaching, and homework assignments? Also, helpers need to make decisions concerning the overall balance between facilitation and didactic (teaching) input. Other considerations include availability of written training materials, such as training manuals and handouts, and of audiovisual materials and equipment. A further set of learning considerations includes sensitivity to the costs and rewards for clients of carrying out plans. How difficult are the plans' various elements? Where are clients' support factors, including how supportive their helpers are? When do clients obtain rewards from implementing planned activities?

Emphasis on maintenance and development of skills Always, when initially planning interventions, consider how to help clients maintain trained skills as self-help skills for afterwards. Both structured and open plans should emphasize clients' learning to use skills on their own. You can emphasize client thinking skills relevant to maintenance. As mentioned, examples of pertinent client thinking skills are possessing realistic expectations about the difficulty of maintaining change and understanding the sequences of choices in targeted skills well enough to instruct themselves and, if necessary, make corrections. You can also plan interventions in ways that help clients maintain action skills. Ways of doing this include emphasizing overlearning, practice in real-life settings, and anticipating and working through difficulties in applying skills.

Helpers may defer developing more formal maintenance plans to stage 5 of the lifeskills model (ending and consolidating trained skills as self-help skills). At that stage you can take clients' end-of-helping skills levels into account, as well as their current estimations of obstacles to maintaining skills. In short-term helping, planning interventions, intervening, and ending and consolidating self-helping skills may become compressed into one another. In such circumstances, helpers and clients have to plan for maintenance as best they can.

Evaluation of outcomes of plan   In Chapter 6, I discussed ways of assessing feelings, thoughts, and actions. When making plans, keep in mind the importance of clients' developing self-assessment skills and monitoring their own progress. By stating working goals in skills terms, you have defined the areas in which it is important to observe change. Plans are successful to the extent that they efficiently help clients develop and maintain self-helping skills. If plans do not produce desired results, examine the reasons closely and, if necessary, modify plans. Be prepared to modify plans in light of important information emerging during helping.

Outlining Plans

Especially where plans involve some detail, consider writing outlines of plans. Such outlines may guide both yours and your clients' work. Below is an outline of a structured plan by the counselor Sam Rushton for his client Jim Blake, the recently fired executive, to develop Jim's getting-another-job skills.

Case Study: Jim Blake
Part 7: Outline Intervention Plans

Sam has already seen Jim twice, the first time on company premises immediately after Jim was fired and the second time in Sam's office a few days later. In this second session, Sam and Jim agreed on a statement of working goals (see Chapter 7). Sam said that at the start of their next session he would present a plan to help Jim to attain these goals. Sam mentioned that this plan would have three elements: counseling sessions; planned activities both to assess Jim's aptitudes and interests and to develop specific skills; and homework. Sam and

Jim agreed that, though the job search might well take longer, a month should be the time frame for developing basic, effective job search skills.

Draft of plan to assist Jim Blake to develop getting-another-job skills

Session	Working goals	Illustrative content
Week 1 Session 3: Counseling	Greater realism about job search Own more responsibility for choices Become more in touch with wants and wishes Clarify values Possess more realistic achievement rules	Present and discuss plan in context of realities of job searching Check out current state Facilitate self-exploring Further discuss and challenge unrealistic achievement rules **Homework** Conduct positive asset search Read about career planning Write own occupational history focusing on choices
Planned activity: Testing	Perceive self more accurately Collect data relevant to job search goals	Complete interest, aptitude, and occupational self-evaluation measures
Week 2 Session 4: Counseling	Perceive self more accurately Get in touch with wants and wishes Further work on job search goals Possess more realistic achievement rules	Review current state and homework Discuss test results and feedback Facilitate self-exploring **Homework** Thinksheet on rules Career planning exercise
Planned activity: All-day workshop	Create a job-marketing plan Utilize informal networks Develop resume skills	Presentation, demonstration, coaching, and practice in each skills area **Homework** Further develop job marketing plan and work on resume

(continued on next page)

**Draft of plan to assist Jim Blake to develop
getting-another-job skills** *(continued)*

Session	Working goals	Illustrative content
Week 3 Session 5: Counseling	Develop goal-setting skills Develop skills at creating job marketing plan Own more responsibility for choices Be more in touch with wants and wishes Manage time when unemployed	Review current state and homework Develop job plan Facilitate self-exploring Assess thinking and action skills for managing nonwork time and set goals Work on thinking skills as needed **Homework** Refine job plan Collect information for job plan Do exercise on using nonwork time
Planned activity: All-day workshop	Use coping self-talk Improve interview skills Improve skills at using informal network	Perform presentation, demonstration, coaching, and practice in thinking and action skills for interviews and networking **Homework** Continue data collection Imagine rehearsal of job interviews using coping self-talk
Week 4 Session 6: Counseling	Develop thinking and action interview skills Develop other thinking and action skills as needed	Review current state and homework Coach and rehearse interview skills as needed Anticipate difficulties and setbacks in implementing job plan **Homework** Implement job plan Exercise: Anticipating difficulties

(continued on next page)

**Draft of plan to assist Jim Blake to develop
getting-another-job skills** *(continued)*

Session	Working goals	Illustrative content
Session 7: Counseling	Adapt thinking skills for maintaining behavior Maintain action skills	Review current state and homework Facilitate self-exploring Develop thinking and action skills strategies for maintaining and consolidating self-helping skills **Homework** Implement job plan Monitor progress in using skills and make corrections as needed

Follow-up sessions and telephone support as needed.

SKILLS FOR WORKING WITH CLIENTS

So far this chapter has mainly explored how helpers think when making intervention and planning hypotheses. Where detailed plans are not involved, helpers tend to discuss plans for how to attain working goals immediately after agreeing on goals. Following are some skills for working with clients.

Make transition statements. You may have signalled moving on to discussing interventions as part of your rationale for presenting working goals (for instance, with a sentence like "Also, such a statement of goals gives us a focus for discussing how best to attain them"). The following are examples of possible transition statements after you have finished presenting and checking your client's agreement to working goals.

> "Now that we have agreed on working goals, let's spend some time discussing how best to attain them."
> "I would like to move on now to discuss ways in which we might work to build your skills."
> "Having agreed on working goals, we now need to plan how best to attain them."

Enlist collaboration and commitment. Since the purpose of any intervention or combination of interventions is to develop client self-helping skills, it is crucial that you encourage their collaboration. One way of encouraging collaboration is to involve clients from the start in the process of choosing interventions and planning their sequencing. You may jointly develop a plan using a whiteboard. On occasions when you present plans, you can do so in ways that imply that plans are series of suggestions for discussion that, if necessary, can be modified or fine-tuned. Check your clients' comprehension and feelings about proposed plans. Explore reservations and, if necessary, negotiate changes in plans. Explore with clients the payoffs and rewards, as well as the costs, of implementing plans.

Give simple explanations and answers. Without insulting your clients' intelligence, offer clear and simple explanations for suggested interventions and plans. You can give clients too much information, so that they feel confused rather than motivated to work. Be prepared to answer questions, but keep your answers simple and to-the-point. In initial sessions, the purposes of discussing interventions and plans are as much emotional and motivational as instructional. Clients feel better if they perceive their helpers know ways that they can work on problems and problematic skills. Often it's best to defer describing the detail of interventions until later, when clients require information for working on specific skills.

Discuss expectations and contract. You and your clients can discuss your expectations of yourselves and each other in implementing plans. For instance, you may indicate that you expect regular attendance over a specified number of sessions, with possibly a joint review of progress at the end of this period. You may stress the necessity of diligently carrying out homework assignments. Sometimes helpers give clients written plans. These plans can assume the status of contracts of varying degrees of formality.

Start implementing plans. After helpers state working goals and discuss plans, they can then assign homework. One type of homework assignment is for clients to observe and monitor feelings, thoughts, and actions in targeted skills areas. Sometimes clients can be instructed to start developing specific skills (for instance, speaking louder or taking a few gentle risks in disclosing more information about themselves). Getting clients started on implementing plans right away has many advantages. First, it reinforces the idea of working rather than talking relationships. Second, clients may feel better as a result of working on problems and problematic skills that have worried them for some time. Third, implementing plans may lead to short-term rewards that build motivation and commitment. Fourth, getting started enables profitable use of the time between first and second sessions. Ultimately this may mean one or more fewer sessions.

 ## CHAPTER HIGHLIGHTS

- A useful distinction exists between interventions (helping strategies) and plans (how to use interventions in combination).
- Criteria for choosing interventions include: importance of maintaining supportive relationships; emphasis of interventions on managing problems or altering problematic skills; relevance for attaining working goals; helper competence; theoretical and research support; client considerations (for example, anxiety level); development of self-helping skills; and appropriateness of group interventions involving third parties; and referral.
- Three categories of plans are: problem management plans; structured plans for problematic skills; and open plans for problematic skills.
- Considerations in planning include: preparation time; involvement of client and others; sequencing of interventions; time frame for plan; how to manage learning; emphasizing maintenance and development of skills; and evaluation.
- Helpers may need to outline plans for their own and clients' benefits.
- Skills for working with clients when choosing and planning interventions include: making transition statements; enlisting collaboration and commitment; giving simple explanations and answers; discussing expectations and contract; and starting implementing plans.

STAGE

4

INTERVENE TO DEVELOP
SELF-HELPING SKILLS

After helpers redefine clients' problems in skills terms, state working goals, and plan how to attain them, they provide interventions or strategies to build clients' self-helping skills. Chapter 9 focuses on some central training skills for most interventions. Chapters 10, 11, and 12 focus on interventions for thinking skills, action skills, and feelings.

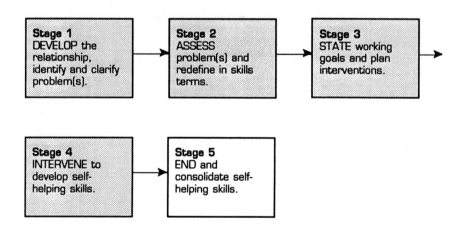

Stage 1
DEVELOP the relationship, identify and clarify problem(s).

Stage 2
ASSESS problem(s) and redefine in skills terms.

Stage 3
STATE working goals and plan interventions.

Stage 4
INTERVENE to develop self-helping skills.

Stage 5
END and consolidate self-helping skills.

CHAPTER NINE

HOW TO USE TRAINING SKILLS
TO DELIVER INTERVENTIONS

The proverb warns that "You should not bite the hand that feeds you." But maybe you should, if it prevents you from feeding yourself.

—Thomas Szasz

CHAPTER QUESTIONS

❀ *What are training skills?*

❀ *Why should helpers possess training as well as helping relationship skills?*

❀ *What are speaking skills for presenting interventions?*

❀ *What are demonstrating skills?*

❀ *What are coaching skills?*

❀ *What are assigning homework skills?*

THE HELPER AS TRAINER

In much of helper training, the emphasis is on receiver (listening) skills rather than on sender (training) skills. Helpers, as lifeskills educators, also require educational or training skills. Helping is an educational process in which helpers flexibly use both relationship and training skills to assist clients to attain learning goals for now and later. This approach is consistent with Krumboltz's definition of counseling as a learning process designed to help people learn more effective ways of coping with their emotional, social, and career problems (Krumboltz, 1988; Sampson & Krumboltz, 1991). Lifeskills helping encourages clients to learn for themselves and to understand, retain, and use what they have learned.

What Are Training Skills?

A broad definition of training skills includes how to facilitate, assess, and design programs, as well as how to intervene (Nelson-Jones, 1992). Here I focus on the skills of delivering interventions, especially when first introducing clients to them. Clients, as learners, require helpers as trainers to guide learning. Helpers, as trainers, require not only knowledge of what interventions to provide, but also skills of how to intervene. The *what* of intervening needs to be supplemented by the *how* of intervening. The following examples show helpers sabotaging their effectiveness through poor training skills.

Maritza is a rehabilitation-counselor trainee on placement. She attempts to explain the thinking skill of identifying, disputing, and reformulating unrealistic personal rules to a client, Roberto, who devalues himself because of the aftereffects of an industrial accident. Maritza's presentation is muddled and she answers Roberto's questions poorly. She also speaks in a monotone and keeps tugging at her hair. Roberto is little the wiser about the skill Maritza tries to communicate, and feels frustrated both with himself and her.

Lee is an Asian-American helper who tries to teach Tuan, a refugee from Vietnam, assertion skills. Lee spends a lot of time discussing with Tuan what he might say when he faces racial discrimination. However, at no stage does Lee demonstrate the voice and body messages that might accompany Tuan's assertive verbal messages. Consequently, Tuan does not really know how to be assertive.

Jason is a career counselor who thinks that Tracey requires better interview skills to increase her employability. He talks about interview

*skills and demonstrates some of them. However, Jason never encour-
ages and helps Tracey to rehearse interview skills. Tracey tells her
friends that she still goes to pieces in job interviews and devalues
herself for not using the skills Jason has shown her. Furthermore, at
no stage has Jason suggested to Tracey that she do specific homework
assignments to build skills.*

Helpers, as trainers, regard good skills in three broad areas as
central to most interventions; namely, speaking, demonstrating,
and coaching (*tell, show,* and *do*). In Chapter 2, I mentioned that
the corresponding learning modes were hearing, observing, and
doing. In the preceding examples, Maritza exhibited skills weaknesses in the area of tell, or helping Roberto learn from hearing;
Lee, in the area of show, or helping Tuan learn from observing;
and Jason, in the area of do, or helping Tracey learn from doing.
You are more likely to impart lifeskills and clients are more
likely to learn them if you use all three modes. When initially
presenting a lifeskill, "tell" may be accompanied by "show" and
then "do." On many occasions all three modes interact. For example, when clients rehearse skills, "do" may be interspersed
with "show" and "tell." Figure 9.1 shows the interrelationships
between learning from hearing, observing, and doing.

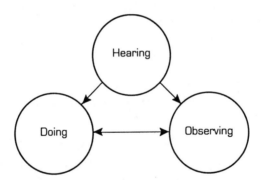

Figure 9.1 Representation of interrelationships of learning from
hearing, observing, and doing

Helping Relationship and Training Skills

Effective helpers require both good facilitative or relationship
skills and good training skills. Helpers who only possess good
relationship skills are unable to impart specific skills clearly and
efficiently. They operate on the assumption that all clients have

lifeskills strengths latent in their repertoires that will be unblocked by empathic helping relationships (Rogers, 1951, 1959, 1961, 1980). While such an assumption may be appropriate for some clients, it is not true for most. Imagine trying to learn how to drive a car with an instructor who only provided you with an empathic relationship? The relationship might support your learning, but in most instances would be insufficient to help you learn the required skills, let alone learn them efficiently. Most clients do not have sufficient skills strengths latent in their repertoires that you and they can rely on the quality of the helping relationship alone.

The majority of clients are stuck and require more active help to develop skills to move forward. Nevertheless, the helping relationship is central to this learning process in many ways. Such ways include strengthening the working alliance, helping assessment and client self-assessment, assisting client self-exploration and experiencing of feelings, providing the emotional climate for clients to take risks and to look more closely at the consequences of their behaviors, and allowing clients to be open about difficulties in implementing skills. Nevertheless, central as supportive relationships may be, they are insufficient. Clients are likely to gain most from helpers who offer good supportive relationships and also impart skills effectively. The helping relationship supports an active approach to training and learning.

SPEAKING SKILLS

Reasons for Speaking Skills

Whether you facilitate or train, you require effective speaking skills. For instance, after listening, you require speaking skills to communicate your reflective responses and summaries. Also, you require speaking skills when stating working definitions and goals and when negotiating plans. Here I emphasize using speaking skills when you first intervene to train clients in specific lifeskills. Following are some occasions when you might require speaking skills.

- When offering reasons for developing skills
- When initially describing component parts of skills
- When providing commentaries for skills demonstrations
- When coaching clients as they rehearse skills
- When answering client questions about skills
- When negotiating homework

Speaking skills for training are somewhat different from those for facilitating. Some beginning helpers find it difficult to make the switch from reflecting their clients' thoughts and feelings to imparting skills information. The latter requires you to be more active. You cannot feed off your clients' most recent utterances. Without overwhelming clients, communicate information as clearly and as interestingly as possible. Always be conscious that the best learning requires clients' developing their own self-talk about how to implement skills.

Manage Speech Anxiety

Presenting lifeskills information to individual clients, couples, or even families may not be as anxiety-evoking as presenting the same information to training groups. Because numbers are smaller, helpers are at less risk of suffering a bad attack of MATO (my anxiety takes over). A certain amount of anxiety facilitates rather than debilitates performance (Alpert & Haber, 1960). Whether presenting to individuals or groups, beginning helpers may suffer from debilitating speech anxiety for three reasons. First, as a beginner you still require time to become comfortable in your knowledge of the skill. Second, your outer-game skills may be poor (for instance, you may possess poor delivery skills). Third, you may have inner-game or thinking skills weaknesses that interfere with the relaxed concentration required to present lifeskills well.

Speech anxiety has many dimensions. Feelings that may be associated with speech anxiety include tension, insecurity, vulnerability, embarrassment, and confusion. Physical reactions include nausea, a dry mouth, butterflies in your stomach, and your mind going blank. Verbal messages include using confused and rambling sentences. Your vocal messages may convey anxiety (for instance, too many "ums" and "ers," and speaking too quickly or softly). Your body messages may be inappropriate (for instance, hair tugging, scratching, or excessive smiling).

Following are some illustrative thinking skills weaknesses associated with speech anxiety even in individual helping.

1. *Own responsibility for being a chooser.* You may inadequately own responsibility for working on presentation skills. You may be paying considerable attention to developing helping relationship skills without realizing the need to develop training skills. Consequently (albeit unwittingly) you choose to ignore an important area of your development as a helper.

2. *Be in touch with your underlying feelings.* You may deny or dilute your feelings of anxiety about the training aspect of helping. This tuning out may impede your working on the problem. In addition, when it comes to the more didactic aspects of helping, you may feel vulnerable and insufficiently acknowledge any feelings of strength and competence.

3. *Use self-talk constructively.* You may either use negative self-talk or fail to use coping self-talk, or both. Negative self-talk statements include "I can't cope," "I can't do anything right," and "I feel totally confused" (Kendall & Hollon, 1989). You may fail to recognize the coaching and calming dimensions of coping self-talk (Nelson-Jones, 1990a).

4. *Choose realistic helping rules.* You may place unrealistic musts, oughts, and shoulds on yourself and clients (for instance, "I must be an excellent presenter of skills immediately" or "Clients must always understand me").

5. *Perceive yourself and others accurately.* You may over-emphasize your skills weaknesses in presenting skills and fail to take your skills strengths into account. You may be hypersensitive to any cues of negative feedback from clients.

6. *Accurately attribute cause.* You may assume too much responsibility for clients' learning. You may also attribute the causes of your speech anxiety wrongly (for instance, to your genes or to your unfortunate previous attempts to present skills to clients). For some helpers, insufficient preparation creates anxiety.

7. *Make realistic predictions.* Beginning helpers may be beset by either undue pessimism or undue optimism, or oscillate between the two regarding their abilities to present skills well.

8. *Have goals that you articulate clearly.* If you suffer from anxiety when presenting skills to clients, make overcoming such anxiety a goal. Some helpers increase their anxiety by having unrealistic goals about what is attainable, both in individual presentations and also in helping.

9. *Use visualizing to best effect.* You may be visualizing the worst when you describe skills to clients. Your negative and catastrophic imaginings may interfere with competent performance. Much better is to use your imagination to rehearse and practice behaving competently (Lazarus, 1977).

The skills you require to manage anxious thinking about speech are the same skills clients require to manage their thinking skills weaknesses. In Chapter 10, I describe ways in which you and your clients can work to develop your thinking skills.

Outline Presentation

Prepare Clear Content

Clients cannot be expected to comprehend poorly presented skills, let alone know them well enough to instruct themselves once helping ends. Many beginning helpers experience difficulty in explaining skills clearly. Some are aware of this, others less so. In some cases, anxiety is a factor. All too often neophyte helpers do not properly understand skills they present. Consequently their explanations are either muddled or clearly inaccurate. On other occasions, beginning helpers may understand the skills, but not communicate their understanding clearly.

When leading training groups, helpers may give mini-lectures of 5 or 10 minutes. Individual helping lends itself to a more informal and interactive approach than is sometimes possible in training groups. Nevertheless, helpers still require the skills of introducing and describing the key points of any lifeskills they impart. Systematic preparation is desirable, especially for beginners. Such preparation should not lead to rigid presentations. When clear in their own minds, helpers better address individual clients' needs and learning rates.

Following are some helper skills of preparing clear content.

Know your material. Do not overlook this seemingly obvious guideline. Most classroom teachers realize that being required to present material to others forces them to understand it more thoroughly than when they were students. It is unethical not to have a reasonable knowledge of any skill you impart. Once you have stated working goals, if you require more knowledge of a skill, try to obtain it prior to the next session. You will lose credibility with clients if they suspect you are poorly informed.

Outline your presentation. Though you may initially describe a skill in the first session, usually you do not present it systematically until subsequent sessions. This interval gives you time to prepare thoroughly. Especially if you have not helped clients acquire a specific skill before, consider preparing a systematic outline of how you might communicate the skill's component parts. Such an outline does not mean that you have to communicate all the skill at once. In individual helping you can adjust the pace of training to the pace of clients' learning. Following is an outline of what could become a series of brief presentations on identifying, disputing, and reformulating personal rules for Margaretha, a married client with two children, who comes to you saying she wants to learn to control her anger.

**Outline of Presentations to Develop
Realistic Personal Rules Skills**

Rationale for skill:
    Interaction of thinking, feeling, and actions
    ABC framework
    Choosing what you say to yourself at B
    Example of a client's unrealistic rules

Identifying anger-engendering rules:
    Inappropriate feelings
    Self-defeating actions
    Characteristics of mustabatory rules (for instance,
        demandingness)

Disputing unrealistic rules:
    Searching for evidence
    Looking for double standards
    Examining realism of predictions
    Questioning put-downs of self

Reformulating unrealistic into realistic rules:
    Characteristics of realistic rules
    Example of a realistic rule
    Reformulate Margaretha's unrealistic rules

Changing actions along with rules:
    "Stop, think, act"
    Alternative ways of acting
    Practice, practice, practice

Use appropriate language. Following are four dimensions of using appropriate language.

1. *Use skills language.* Your brief presentations should clearly identify the skill or sub-skill you wish to describe. During your presentations, without overdoing it, help clients to think of targeted behaviors in skills terms. Emphasize the importance of viewing trained skills as self-helping skills.
2. *Use clear language.* Take the intelligence level and sociocultural background of clients into account. Use straightforward and unambiguous language (for instance, *active listening* or *listening and showing understanding* may be better terms than *empathic listening* or *reflective responding*). Be concise and specific. Aim to describe skills as simply as possible so that clients can easily describe the skills to themselves. Avoid long sentences—the language of speech uses shorter sentences than written language (Bernstein, 1988). Also, the longer

your sentences, the fewer the clients who comprehend them (Goddard, 1989).

3. *Use practical language.* Helper presentations of lifeskills focus on the mechanics of how to perform a skill or sub-skill. They are not academic discourses. To enlist motivation and interest, relate your presentations to clients' own material and experiences.

4. *Use humor.* The language of lifeskills helping is not the language of boredom. Rightly used, humor can illustrate points and make learning fun. Furthermore, humor can relax clients and lower defensiveness and resistances. However, if wrongly used, humor can divert both clients and helpers from goals.

Consider using audiovisual aids.   Audiovisual aids may help you present information more clearly. You need to think carefully about how to integrate audiovisual aids into your skills presentations so they are not disruptive. Following are some audiovisual aid possibilities.

1. *Whiteboard:* The structure of your presentation will be clearer if written on the board than if you just speak it.

2. *Flipcharts:* Especially if you have already prepared material for use with more than one client, you can integrate flipcharts into your presentation. An advantage of chart material is that it is reusable.

3. *Training manuals and handouts:* You can help clients consolidate learnings either by referral to the relevant sections in training manuals or by handouts.

4. *Audiocassettes and videotapes:* You can use recorded audiocassette or videotape presentations either within sessions or for homework assignments. In addition, you may ask clients to play back a recording of your last session before coming again.

Develop Delivery Skills

If you prepare clear content, you are only part way to introducing and describing skills effectively. You still need to put your message across. In Chapter 4, I emphasized sending good voice and body messages when you listen. Here I focus on sending good voice and body messages when you present material to clients. You want to avoid client MEGO ("my eyes glaze over") when you describe skills (Valenti, 1982). Presenting information to individuals or couples does not require the theatrical performance skills of presenting information to larger numbers. Nevertheless, even in individual helping, your voice and body are delivery tools for holding interest, emphasizing points, and enlisting motivation.

Send Effective Voice Messages

Perhaps even more when you send messages than when you receive them, you need to develop an awareness of your voice as a delivery tool. For better or worse, your voice messages frame your verbal messages. Let's take the VAPER acronym (Nelson-Jones, 1992) and suggest how you can use volume, articulation, pitch, emphasis, and rate when you deliver content.

Volume When presenting skills, you are under less obligation to adjust your volume to reflect that of clients than when responding as a listener. Without overwhelming clients, you need to speak reasonably loud, possibly louder than when you respond. Some helpers may be better at being gentle listeners than outgoing talkers. If this is true of you, you may need to project your voice more when presenting skills.

Articulation Clear articulation may be more important when you present than when you respond. If you enunciate poorly when sending listening responses, clients at least are able to put what you say in the context of their previous utterances. They do not have this opportunity when you present information for the first time. Instead, they may be struggling to understand both delivery and content. Also, the longer speakers talk, the more poor enunciation distracts.

Pitch Any pitch errors you possess (for instance, uncomfortable highness, lowness, or narrowness of range) may be more pronounced when you present information than when you respond. One reason is that, when responding, you will tend to modify your pitch to match your client's. Another reason is that, when presenting information, you may be less conscious of pitch because you are thinking of what to say. Furthermore, you have more scope for pitch errors, since you are likely to speak longer when presenting material than when responding.

Emphasis When, as a listener, you use reflective responses, you will emphasize the same words and phrases that clients emphasize. As a presenter of information, you emphasize words and phrases to highlight your main points. Your use of emphasis should convey interest and commitment.

Rate As with responding, when describing skills, speak fairly slowly. A slow but comfortable speech rate gives you time to think and gives clients time to comprehend. Effective use of pauses can both clarify and emphasize what you say, and also allows clients to ask questions. Pause errors include: too many, too few, too long, too short, and making extraneous sounds such as "ums" and "ers."

Send Effective Body Messages

Sending effective body messages when describing a lifeskill is partly a matter of avoiding interfering messages and partly of sending good messages. Unlike presenting skills in training groups, in individual helping you are likely to be seated. Many body messages for attending to clients when listening are still appropriate when delivering content (for instance, relaxed body posture, physical openness, sensitivity to physical proximity and height, appropriate clothing and grooming, and appropriate facial expressions). Following are some additional suggestions for using effective body messages when you present.

Gestures Use gestures economically to help explain what is being said. Fischer (1972) states there are three main types of gestures: *emphatic* gestures, such as pointing a finger, designed to make it clear that what is being said is important; *descriptive* gestures (for instance, stretching your arms out when you say that marital partners are poles apart), designed to help illustrate your points; and *symbolic* gestures, to which a commonly understood meaning has been ascribed (for instance, shaking your head to say no). Another broad category of gestures is that of *distracting* gestures: touching your head, scratching your nose, pulling lint off your cuff, waving your arms around, tugging your hair, and so on. Learn to use gestures to work for rather than against your training messages.

Gaze and eye contact Talkers tend to use much less gaze and eye contact than listeners (Argyle, 1983). Nevertheless, when presenting, you require an adequate gaze level to read clients' reactions. Present lifeskills as though you are conversing with clients rather than talking at them. Your use of gaze and eye contact may be the most important way of relating directly to clients. Gaze and eye contact errors include: looking down too much, including reading from training manuals; looking at the ceiling or out of the window; looking through clients; and keeping turned away as you write on the whiteboard rather than checking client reactions.

Put Content and Delivery Together

In the preceding discussion, I focused on managing speech anxiety, preparing clear content, and using good voice and body message delivery skills. You may have practiced long and hard to develop your responsive skills of good listening, so that clients want to talk to you. Show the same conscientiousness in developing sender skills to impart information, so that clients want to hear you. An analogy may be made with effective parenting: Parents not only need to listen so that their kids will talk, they also need to talk so that their kids will listen (Gordon, 1970). You may need to rehearse to gain fluency in describing different lifeskills to clients. Furthermore, effective helpers combine talking and listening skills in such a way that clients feel part of the training process and not just receptacles of others' knowledge—the so-called *jug-and-mug* approach! Such helpers develop emotional climates where clients are motivated to learn, ask questions, and take risks.

At risk of repetition, use speaking skills to help clients develop self-instruction skills. Ideally, when learning new skills, clients start by being receptive to your voice in their heads. However, they then need to replace your voice with their own voice. Your public speech becomes their private speech.

DEMONSTRATING SKILLS

By demonstrating skills, effective helpers add "show" to "tell." One of the main ways in which people learn is from observation or from models (Bandura, 1969, 1977, 1986). Perry and Furukawa (1986) define modeling as "the process of observational learning in which the behavior of an individual or group—the model—acts as a stimulus for similar thoughts, attitudes, or behaviors on the part of an individual who observes the model's performance" (p. 66). In real life, much modeling is unintentional. However, helpers can consciously promote observational learning of desired skills and sub-skills. The everyday word *demonstrating* is used here in preference to modeling. Both *model* and *demonstrator* describe the person demonstrating.

Goals for Demonstrating

Demonstrating may be used to initiate new skills strengths, develop existing skills strengths, release existing skills strengths, and inhibit and weaken existing skills weaknesses. Goals for demonstrating and observational learning can be viewed in the following categories.

Thinking skills   Thinking skills include possessing realistic rules, using coping self-talk, and perceiving accurately. I briefly reviewed thinking skills in the previous section on speaking skills.

Aretha, a helper, works with Vince on his public-speaking skills. As part of her plan, she aims to train Vince to use coping rather than negative self-talk before, during, and after speaking situations. Aretha demonstrates coping self-talk by verbally giving examples of appropriate coping self-talk statements and also by giving Vince a handout with examples of public-speaking coping self-talk statements.

Action skills   Action skills demonstrations focus on observable behaviors. In action skills demonstrations, helpers need to pay attention to voice and body as well as to verbal messages.

Aretha and Vince have working sub-goals to develop Vince's public-speaking delivery skills by (a) speaking at a comfortable rather than a rapid rate, (b) being easy to hear rather than too quiet, (c) making good gaze and eye contact with his audience, and (d) using gestures to emphasize points. Aretha demonstrates one skill at a time, then coaches and rehearses Vince in it before moving on to the next skill. Ultimately Aretha demonstrates and coaches Vince in all four skills together. Aretha also encourages Vince either to record or, if possible, videotape his own competent performance of the skills so he can use himself as a model in future. In addition, she encourages Vince to observe good public speakers and assess how they use the targeted skills.

Action skills with accompanying self-talk   Here the demonstrator focuses both on action skills and on accompanying self-instructions.

To speak effectively in public, Vince needs to combine both thinking action skills. Aretha demonstrates to Vince in slow motion how he can use calming and coaching self-instructions when speaking. Aretha's demonstration intersperses "think aloud" self-instructions with demonstrating action skills.

Who Demonstrates?

Demonstrations can take place both inside and outside helping sessions. Following are options that may be used singly or in combination for whoever demonstrates.

1. *Helpers:* Helpers may demonstrate skills, both initially and when coaching and rehearsing clients.
2. *Clients:* Clients can be asked to demonstrate skills for themselves. For instance, helpers may start by audiocassette recording demonstrations of thinking skills, but then assist clients to make recordings using their own voices and material. Self-demonstrations of action skills may be in clients' imaginations (Kazdin, 1976) or by "self-as-model" edited videotapes of their own performances (Cormier & Cormier, 1985; Hosford, Moss, & Morrell, 1976; Hosford & Johnson, 1983).
3. *Third parties:* When recorded material is used, third parties may demonstrate skills.
4. *Puppets and cartoon characters:* Puppets may be used as demonstrators, especially with children (Peterson & Ridley-Johnson, 1980). Cartoon characters can also be used to present lifeskills. For instance, comic-strip characters with dialogue balloons can be used to demonstrate thinking skills.

Methods of Demonstration

Helpers have many options when presenting demonstrations. These options, which are not mutually exclusive, are summarized in Table 9.1.

Table 9.1 Methods of demonstrating lifeskills

Methods of Demonstrating Lifeskills	Skills Areas		
	Thinking Skills	Action Skills	Action Skills Plus Self-Talk
Written demonstration	✓	Difficult	Difficult
Live demonstration	✓	✓	✓
Recorded demonstration	✓	✓	✓
Visualized demonstration	Less suitable	✓	✓

Written

Helpers can demonstrate lifeskills through the written page—either handouts or passages in books and training manuals. Thinking skills in particular lend themselves to written demonstration. Written demonstrations can be supplemented by visual images such as cartoons. Written demonstrations can be easily stored and retrieved by helpers and clients. Furthermore, written examples can introduce subsequent written or live exercises.

Helpers need not restrict themselves to others' material; instead they can develop their own material. Such material is especially useful where many clients have similar problems. Following is an example of a written demonstration for shy students of the skill of generating and evaluating different perceptions and choosing the "best-fit" perception rather than jumping to negative conclusions. Here is an example of how shy people can perceive more accurately.

Handout: How Shy People Can Perceive More Accurately

1. *Targeted skill:* The skill demonstrated in this example is that of generating and evaluating different perceptions and choosing the best-fit perception.
2. *Reason for skill:* Many shy people jump to negative conclusions about others' reactions without thinking realistically about the available information. They fail adequately to distinguish between fact, what actually happens, and inference, what they think about what happens. Thus they sustain their shyness by inferring negatively rather than attempting to make their inferences match the facts as closely as possible.

Here is an example of jumping to a negative conclusion.

Shirley sits with a group of her classmates in the cafeteria and observes two of them, Ben and Lynette, talking intently to each other. Shirley thinks, "Ben and Lynette must think I'm a boring person." The consequence of this thought is that she feels less motivated to participate in the group than before.

Here is an example of generating and evaluating different perceptions.

Alternatively, Shirley could have said to herself, "I feel uneasy because Ben and Lynette are talking to each other. Let's stop and think what is the best way to perceive this. One possibility is that they are bored with me—however I have no evidence for this. Another possibility is that they are saying nice things about me. I also have no evidence for this. A third possibility is that they often ignore other people and just talk to each other. Again, there is no evidence that this happens all the time. A fourth possibility is that they have found something of interest that they want to share and that this does not reflect negatively on me. This seems to be the best way to perceive the situation ("best-fit" perception). Recently, both Ben and Lynette have been friendly to me. Also, they ignore the other people at the table and not just me."

Live

Possibly most individual helping demonstrations are live. Helpers demonstrate live when initially presenting skills, when coaching clients afterwards, and when working with current material that clients bring into later sessions. Live demonstrations have the advantage of here-and-now communication. Clients can receive verbal, voice, and body messages as they occur. Also, you can interact with clients and, if appropriate, show different or simpler ways to enact skills.

Live demonstrations have limitations as well as advantages. Unless demonstrations are recorded, clients have no copies to review on their own. Though it is more appropriate for thinking than for action skills, getting clients to listen to recordings of all or part of helping sessions is one approach to this problem. In live demonstrations it may be difficult to portray scenes involving more than one person. However, helpers can conduct role-plays with clients to overcome this limitation. Here, a potential disadvantage is that clients may be so absorbed in playing roles that they insufficiently attend to what helpers demonstrate.

A variation of live demonstration is Bandura's *participant modeling* intervention. This intervention has been used particularly to train those suffering from phobias (Bandura, 1976; Jeffrey, 1976). For example, clients may watch helpers performing progressively more threatening tasks in relation to feared objects such as snakes. After each demonstration, clients are given both guidance and ample opportunities to perform demonstrated behaviors under favorable conditions. Examples of favorable conditions include both joint performance of sub-tasks with helpers and also performing sub-tasks under protective conditions (for instance, touching snakes while wearing gloves).

Another variation of live demonstration is to encourage clients to observe good and poor demonstrators of targeted skills in their everyday lives. For instance, clients with public-speaking problems can monitor the skills of good and poor public speakers. Clients with difficulty initiating contact with others can observe how socially skilled people do this. Clients with poor parenting skills can be asked to observe parents they admire.

Recorded

Recorded demonstrations can be on film, audiotape, and videotape. Helpers rarely if ever use films outside of group work. Disadvantages include darkened rooms, the need to purchase films, and the costs of projection equipment and, sometimes, a projectionist. Audiocassettes and videotapes can be either integral parts of initial skills demonstrations or used for homework assignments. Advantages of audiocassette and videotape demonstrations include that they can be reproduced, can be loaned to clients, lend themselves to repeated viewing, can either be placed on pause or switched on and off, and can be used with different clients.

Audiocassette demonstration   Audiocassettes are particularly useful for demonstrating thinking skills. With audiocassettes, as contrasted to videotapes, clients can be taken through the sequences of choices entailed in targeted skills without visual distractions. Initial audiocassette demonstrations of thinking skills are best done by helpers. It is unreasonable to expect clients to demonstrate skills that they do not properly understand. However, later in the learning process, helpers can assist clients to make up their own demonstration cassettes. If clients switch to using themselves as demonstrators during helping, they may be more likely to maintain skills afterwards. Clients will probably require repeated listening to their demonstrations for the thinking skills to become part of their everyday repertoires (Ellis, 1987). Disadvantages of audiocassette demonstrations are that they are not as spontaneous as live demonstration and that they may be insufficiently geared to individual clients' needs. Often a combination of audiocassette, written, and live demonstration is the most effective way to impart thinking skills.

Apart from recording helping sessions, the following are different ways to approach audiocassette demonstrations. First, you can make up a demonstration cassette targeted at a particular skill or sub-skill required by an individual client. Second, you can make up audiocassette demonstrations relevant to common client problems. For instance, you could record the earlier example of a written demonstration for shy students of the skill of generating and evaluating perceptions with different voices for the commentator, Shirley, Lynette, and Ben. You can build up a library of skills audiocassettes relevant to your client population. Some recordings may demonstrate action skills (for instance, the verbal and voice message dimensions of being assertive). Other recordings may demonstrate instructions for action skills (such as progressive muscular relaxation) (Jacobson, 1938). Third, you can use commercial self-help audiocassette demonstrations of targeted skills (Yamauchi, 1987). Fourth, you can assist clients to make their own demonstration cassettes.

If possible, use highly sensitive recording equipment and encourage clients to do the same. Clients resist listening to poor-quality cassettes. There are cassette recorders on the market that eliminate virtually all motor noise and background hiss. Be prepared to rehearse and rerecord your efforts if they are inadequate. Michael Jackson and Whitney Houston do this, and so can you!

Videotape demonstration A major advantage of video over audio demonstration is that clients can observe body messages. Many lifeskills training videotapes are already on the market. However, commercial videotapes may not suit your needs. If you make your own demonstration videos, you have the choice of whether or not to bring in outside resources. Here I assume you make your own videotapes.

When making demonstration videotapes, specify body message sub-goals as well as verbal and voice sub-goals. For instance, if you were to make a video demonstrating how a teenager, Chrissie, might return a compact disc to a store, you could tape her demonstrating the body message skills of adequate eye contact, erect posture, and good use of gesture. You require many of the skills of film directors when making demonstration videotapes. For instance, you may need to coach demonstrators in acting. Rehearsing and shooting scenes, you may decide to rewrite parts of the script. Much trial and error goes into making polished demonstration videotapes.

During sessions, you can use videos to demonstrate skills (for instance, excerpts of how to make an assertive request for a behavior change, demonstrate attention and interest when listening, or answer questions at a job interview). Clients may also view demonstration videotapes without helpers present. Webster-Stratton (1988) and her colleagues assigned parents of problem children to either an individually administered videotape modeling treatment, a therapist-led group-discussion videotape modeling treatment, a group-discussion treatment without watching videotapes, or a waiting list control group (Webster-Stratton, Kolpacoff, & Hollinsworth, 1988). Both of the videotape modeling conditions involved parents meeting for 10–12 weekly sessions and watching over 200 vignettes of parent-child interactions. One-year follow-up findings showed very few differences between the three treatment conditions. The results "suggested the potential power of parents to learn how to change their own behaviors, as well as their children's behaviors, from self-administered videotape programs" (Webster-Stratton, Hollinsworth, & Kolpacoff, 1989, p. 550).

You may want to make video demonstrations of action skills with accompanying self-talk. Ultimately clients have to instruct themselves through action skills sequences of choices. Following are some ways to incorporate self-talk.

1. *Think aloud:* Here demonstrators pause every now and then to verbalize relevant self-instructions out loud.
2. *Voice overs:* Voice overs of the demonstrator's self-instructions may be edited into demonstration videotapes. Voice overs are less disruptive to demonstrations than think aloud. However, a major disadvantage is that voice overs are beyond most helpers' technical resources.
3. *Subtitles:* Frequently, subtitles translate the spoken word. For demonstrations of action skills plus self-talk, subtitles can demonstrate relevant inner, rather than outer, talk. Advantages of subtitles over voice overs are that they do not provide added (and possibly distracting) sound, and they can be left on the screen longer.
4. *"Think" balloons:* "Think" balloons containing relevant self-talk can float above demonstrators' heads in videos. However, the technical competence required to superimpose "think" balloons onto moving images is well beyond the scope and budgets of most helpers.

Visualized Demonstration

Visualized demonstration is sometimes called covert modeling (Cautela, 1976; Cormier & Cormier, 1985; Kazdin, 1976). Helpers ask clients to visualize (imagine) the demonstration scenes that they describe. Depending on the instructions, clients visualize either themselves or third parties demonstrating targeted action skills. Visualized demonstration has the advantage of flexibility. Different situations can be readily presented to clients' imaginations, depending on their needs and how fast they learn. Clients can follow up in helping sessions after visualized demonstration and rehearsal at home.

Visualized demonstration has potential disadvantages. It is only appropriate for clients who can visualize scenes adequately. Also, clients never actually see skills demonstrated. Consequently, even when instructions are well given, there may be important gaps between what you describe and what clients visualize.

In general, clients visualize best when relaxed (Kazdin, 1976). Helpers may start by asking clients to visualize neutral scenes to check their visualizing capacities. For example, a client could be asked to visualize a recent conversation with a friend. Following are three guidelines for visualized demonstrations.

1. *Set the scene.* Describe the situation in which targeted lifeskills are enacted in sufficient detail that clients can easily visualize it.
2. *Describe the targeted skill(s).* Describe clearly what the targeted skills are and how they are used. Remember to describe voice and body, as well as verbal, components of skills.
3. *Depict favorable consequences.* Where appropriate, get clients to visualize demonstrator use of targeted skills receiving rewards.

Helpers can develop different visualized demonstrations around targeted skills. For instance, visualizations may be graduated by threat or difficulty. In addition, clients can visualize themselves coping with different consequences when using targeted skills.

Demonstrator Skills

The following are some demonstrator skills that go beyond speaking well.

Prepare adequately. Even live demonstrations require adequate preparation. You must know your material thoroughly to integrate good demonstrations into skills presentations. Making recorded demonstrations takes time and effort. Pay attention to demonstrator characteristics. For example, generally the greater the similarity between demonstrators and observers, the greater the effect of demonstration on subsequent behaviors (Perry & Furukawa, 1986). Rather than being perfectly competent, Kazdin (1976) suggests the advantage of demonstrators' showing behaviors similar to observers', but then overcoming problems. Also, it is important that demonstrators be attractive to clients (Bandura, 1977).

Pay attention to characteristics of the demonstration and not just of the demonstrator. One issue is whether to demonstrate incorrect as well as correct behaviors. You may plan to demonstrate negative behaviors briefly as a way of highlighting positive ones. However, make sure not to confuse clients, and always have the major emphasis on correct rather than incorrect skills. Another consideration is that some skills may be so complex or difficult that you need to plan a series of demonstrations. For instance, a late-adolescent girl having difficulty standing up to her mother may observe her helper demonstrate how to handle a low-level confrontation before observing more difficult confrontations. When clients should perform the demonstrated skills is a further consideration. Client performance of demonstrated skills can be simultaneous (Klingman, Melamed, Cuthbert, & Hermecz, 1984), interspersed between demonstrations (Bandura, 1976), following demonstrations, or not happen at all.

Provide an introduction.   Take care how you introduce demonstrations. Your initial demonstration of a skill is likely to be part of a tell, show, and do sequence. Explain to clients the importance of learning from demonstration (Sarason, 1976). You may increase clients' attention by telling them what to look for and informing them that afterwards they will perform demonstrated behaviors (Perry & Furukawa, 1986).

Provide instructions and a summary.   During live and recorded presentations, you can intersperse breaks with instructions on what to watch for. At the end of a demonstration, you can summarize the main learning points and, possibly, give participants a handout listing them.

Check clients' learning.   During, and at the end, you may ask clients whether they understand the points you demonstrate. Also, clients can summarize the main points of demonstrations. Research suggests that observers actively summarizing the main points of demonstrations are better able to learn and retain this information (Bandura, Grusec, & Menlove, 1966; Perry & Furukawa, 1986). Probably the best way to check clients' learning is to observe and coach them as they perform demonstrated behaviors.

Extend demonstration into homework.   Demonstrations can be integrated into homework. Clients can listen to recordings of all or parts of sessions in which you demonstrate skills live. Furthermore, they can listen to and watch recorded audiocassettes and videotapes. In addition, you can instruct clients to observe people in their daily lives as they demonstrate targeted skills.

COACHING SKILLS

Here I focus on coaching clients to perform skills after initial presentations. Learning from hearing and observing must be translated into learning from doing. I have listened to the supervision tapes of many beginning helpers who describe and demonstrate skills, but then omit coaching clients in how to perform them. Following are some helper skills for coaching clients in lifeskills.

Balance didactic and facilitative coaching. In *didactic* coaching, helpers give a series of explicit instructions to clients on how to perform skills. The helper's comments take the form "First you do this, then you do that" and so on. The helper is the expert, taking clients through sequences of performance choices.

In *facilitative* coaching, helpers have two important objectives: first, to draw out and build upon clients' existing knowledge and skills; and, second, to help them acquire the skills of self-coaching. Helpers' initial comments may include "Now that you have listened to and observed the initial presentation and demonstration of _____ skill (specify skill), what have you learned about how to do it?" "How do you feel about using the skill just presented?" or "Can you describe to me the self-talk you require to use the skill?"

When coaching, helpers require both facilitative and didactic skills. For example, helpers might start by building on the existing knowledge and skills of learners, but then intersperse didactic instructions when clients go badly wrong. Didactic coaching alone can produce resistances. Also, coaching without using facilitative skills lessens the likelihood of targeted skills being owned and integrated into clients' daily routines.

Give clear instructions. Include clear instructions for coached performance in your initial presentations and demonstrations of skills. Helper or client summaries at the end of demonstrations can be ways of ensuring that instructions for performing skills are clear. When coaching, you may need to give specific instructions, tips, and prompts that build targeted skills (Karoly & Harris, 1986). Coaching should always emphasize ways in which clients can help themselves (for instance, by translating clear instructions into clear self-instructions).

Break tasks down and consider number of trials. When initially getting clients to perform them, you may decide to break down skills and sub-skills. Consider how much clients can assimilate in each learning trial. For example, with a teenager wishing to return a defective compact disc to a shop, one trial might focus on verbal messages, another on voice messages, another on body messages, and another on putting it all together. Another way of breaking down learning trials is to include graded steps. Here you coach clients in using targeted skills in progressively more difficult situations. With or without graded steps, clients may require many coached attempts before performing skills competently within, let alone outside, helping sessions.

Use behavior rehearsal and role-play. By definition, when you coach you also rehearse clients in targeted skills. Behavior rehearsal and role-play are not always the same. Clients can rehearse action skills on their own without role-plays (for instance, rehearsing relaxation skills). Also, they can mentally rehearse thinking skills and visually rehearse action skills plus accompanying self-talk. Role-plays are especially useful for rehearsing action skills. Behavior rehearsal and role-play skills are covered in more detail in Chapter 12.

Use feedback skills. When coaching, helpers are managers of feedback. Following are some feedback dimensions to bear in mind (Egan, 1990; Gazda, 1989; Gilbert, 1978; Hopson & Scally, 1981; National Training Laboratory, 1967; Osipow, Walsh, & Tosi, 1984).

1. *Client self-feedback or helper feedback:* Throughout, encourage clients to develop skills of monitoring and assessing their behavior and its consequences for self and others. As a guideline, after each behavior rehearsal, clients should be the first to comment on their learnings and reactions to their performance. Nevertheless, your feedback remains essential because of your special knowledge of targeted skills.
2. *"I" or "you" message feedback:* Take responsibility for your feedback and send, or at least imply, "I" messages. For example, "Tim, I think Sally would appreciate your request for a date more if your voice were louder" is different from "Your voice should have been louder when asking Sally for a date." However, Tim might still have received the latter statement as an "I" message if you had already established the ground rule that your feedback always represents perception rather than fact and is open for discussion.
3. *Specific or nonspecific feedback:* Feedback should always be specific and concentrate on targeted behaviors. For instance,

in the previous example, suggesting to Tim that his voice might be louder is far preferable to telling him his voice quality is poor.

4. *Verbal or demonstrated feedback:* Feedback may be given largely through words. Often, however, you communicate feedback even more clearly if you accompany verbal description with demonstration. For instance, in the Tim-and-Sally example, you could demonstrate Tim's present voice loudness and then demonstrate a more appropriate loudness.

5. *Confirmatory or corrective feedback:* Feedback can be confirmatory or corrective. Confirmatory feedback reinforces correct behaviors, whereas corrective feedback lets clients know which specific behaviors require altering and in what ways. Much feedback is both confirmatory and corrective—for example, "Tim, when you asked Sally to go out I thought that you gave a good verbal 'I' message (confirmatory), but that your voice was too quiet" (corrective). Persistent corrective feedback, without some confirmatory feedback, can weaken clients' motivation to work and change.

6. *Audiovisual feedback:* Cassette feedback may be especially useful when helpers coach verbal messages, voice messages, and thinking skills. Putting clients' thoughts on the whiteboard provides useful visual feedback. Video feedback is especially beneficial when helpers coach body messages. Audiovisual feedback lends itself to client self-assessment. Furthermore, it provides a factual basis for helper-client discussions.

7. *Feedback or reward:* You may provide feedback in the form of reward. You can say "good" or "well done" in response to specific behaviors that clients implement well. Also, you can use nonverbal forms of reward such as nods and smiles. However, beware of clients' performing targeted behaviors only under conditions of external reward rather than self-reward.

8. *Verbal or nonverbal feedback:* Much feedback, for good or ill, is nonverbal. Disinterested looks and voice messages can greatly interfere with good verbal coaching messages. Conversely, good voice and body messages when giving feedback increase the likelihood of clients' receiving the verbal messages positively. Whether or not you speak, show interest when clients perform demonstrated skills.

9. *Cultural feedback considerations:* Helpers coming from different cultural backgrounds than clients require sensitivity to differences in cultural rules concerning giving and receiving feedback. Give clients permission to relate how feedback is handled in their cultures.

ASSIGNING HOMEWORK SKILLS

After presenting, demonstrating, and coaching clients in new skills, helpers can assign relevant between-session homework. Many reasons exist for setting homework (Cormier & Cormier, 1985; Egan, 1990; Hutchins & Cole, 1986). These reasons include: speeding up the learning process; encouraging clients to monitor, rehearse and practice skills; helping the transfer of trained skills to outside life; finding out about difficulties in using skills in real life; and increasing the client's sense of self-control and of personal responsibility for developing targeted skills. Following are some central skills for assigning homework.

Offer reasons for homework.   Helpers can often enhance clients' motivation for completing homework assignments if they explain its importance. You can introduce the idea of homework at the start of tell, show, and do sequences.

Now, Gill, first I am going to describe _____ (specify which) skill, then I am going to demonstrate it for you, then I am going to coach you in it, and then we will discuss some homework to develop your skill in real life.

Following is an example of a statement that a helper might make at the conclusion of a speaking, demonstrating, and coaching sequence. In this example, the helper attempts both to elicit reservations and also to gain a commitment to the idea of doing homework.

Gill, we have now been through a tell, show, and do sequence in relation to _____ (specify which) skill. However, learning any new skill can require much work and practice until you are comfortable using it in real life. Throughout helping, I am likely to negotiate homework assignments with you so that we can use the time between sessions to best effect. I would now like to discuss activities for you to do before our next session. Do you have any problems with the idea of doing between-session homework?

Negotiate realistic homework.   I use the word *negotiate* to highlight the importance of client participation in homework decisions. I assume that clients are more likely to comply with homework assignments that they have had a say in designing. Following are three aspects of realistic homework.

1. *Consolidates earlier learning:* The homework is a logical extension of the speaking, demonstrating, and coaching sequence that has just taken place. Do not introduce new skills and ideas that clients have had insufficient time to assimilate before the session ends.
2. *Considers appropriate difficulty level:* The tasks take into account clients' understanding of and readiness to perform targeted skills. Where appropriate, suggest graded steps.
3. *Assigns realistic amount:* Work out with clients what constitutes a realistic amount of homework. It is preferable for clients to make a definite commitment to a small amount of homework than to make a vague commitment to a larger amount. Encourage clients to view homework in terms of learning contracts, not just with you but, more importantly, with themselves (Wehrenberg, 1988).

Give clear instructions in take-home form. How can clients know precisely what homework you expect? What, when, how often, and how recorded are the pertinent questions. Sometimes clients have already received handouts summarizing the main learning points of a skill. Where possible, give homework instructions in take-home form. At the very least, you can use a standard instructional form (Figure 9.2). Either fill out the form yourself or supervise clients as they do this.

If you require clients to fill out forms such as monitoring logs, specific worksheets and thinksheets, and homework record logs, provide these forms yourself. This practice ensures clear instructions and saves clients' writing out homework forms before filling them in.

Anticipate difficulties and setbacks. Explore with clients their motivation for completing homework tasks. Where possible, identify and help clients work through resistances. Also, identify rewards for completing homework. If you have negotiated realistic amounts, clients will be more likely to complete homework. Sometimes implementing a skill requires asking clients to give up long-established habits; here it can be especially important not to assign too difficult a homework load too soon. Also, some clients will be returning to unsupportive, if not downright hostile, environments. You may need to prepare these clients more thoroughly before suggesting they implement targeted skills in real-life settings. Such preparation is likely to include devising strategies for coping with negative feedback. In Chapter 13, I discuss more thoroughly how to prevent client relapses.

Homework Assignment Instructions

For_____(client's name)

During the period_____

Targeted skill(s)

1. _____

2. _____

3. _____

4. _____

5. _____

Instructions

_____

_____

_____

_____

_____

_____

_____

_____

_____

_____

_____

Figure 9.2 Homework assignment instructions form

Signal a joint progress review Let clients know that at, or around, the start of the next session, you will together review their homework progress. Your declared interest should motivate them to do homework.

CONCLUDING COMMENT

This chapter focused on basic training skills, somewhat in isolation from each other. When intervening, you put helping relationship, speaking, demonstrating, coaching, and setting homework skills together. You start from where clients are and use training skills to help them get to where they want to be. Always remember that, after helping, clients need to retain and develop trained skills as self-helping skills. Beginning helpers need to rehearse and practice hard to develop good training as well as good helping relationship skills. Obtain training, and train yourself, in training skills.

 ## CHAPTER HIGHLIGHTS

- Helpers require training skills in three broad areas central to delivering most interventions: speaking, demonstrating, and coaching (or tell, show, and do).
- Speaking skills include: managing speech anxiety; preparing clear content; and the delivery skills of sending good voice and body messages.
- Observational learning is extremely important for acquiring and developing applied lifeskills.
- Demonstrations can focus on thinking skills, action skills, and action skills with accompanying self-talk.
- Methods of demonstration include: written, live, recorded (for instance, audiocassettes or videotapes), and visualized.
- Demonstrator skills include: preparing adequately, providing an introduction, providing instructions and a summary, checking clients' learning, and (where appropriate) including demonstrations in homework assignments.
- Learning from hearing and observing must be translated into learning from doing.
- Assist clients to become their own coaches for acquiring, maintaining, and developing targeted skills.
- Coaching skills include: balancing didactic and facilitative coaching, giving clear instructions, breaking tasks down and

paying attention to the number of learning trials, using behavior rehearsal and role-play, and using feedback skills.
- Consolidate initial learning from hearing, observing, and doing by assigning relevant homework.
- Assigning homework skills include: offering reasons for homework, negotiating realistic homework, giving clear instructions
in take-home form, anticipating difficulties and setbacks, and
signaling a joint progress review.
- Beginning helpers need to rehearse and practice hard to develop good training as well as good helping relationship skills.

❀ ❀ ❀   **CHAPTER TEN**   ❀ ❀ ❀

HOW TO FOCUS ON THINKING SKILLS

There is nothing either good or bad, but thinking makes it so.

—William Shakespeare

CHAPTER QUESTIONS

❀ *Why is it important that clients think about how they think?*

❀ *How are thinking skills related to feelings and actions?*

❀ *Why is it important that helpers attend to feelings when focusing on thinking?*

❀ *What are the PTC and STC frameworks?*

❀ *What reasons can helpers offer for working with clients' thinking?*

❀ *What is a desirable helping relationship when focusing on thinking skills?*

❀ *What are helper interventions for 10 different thinking skills?*

Focusing on how both helpers and their clients think is a major theme of this book. In Chapter 2, I used the analogy of the inner game (how you think) and the outer game (how you act). Most often people feel and think before they act. Then their subsequent actions influence how they think and feel. Look again at Chapter 6 for details on how to assess thinking skills in initial sessions. Problems redefined in skills terms almost invariably include one or more thinking skills weaknesses, which, in turn, become working goals.

This chapter looks at skills for working with clients' thinking. Most of the skills are relevant to working with your own thinking too. Unless you develop skills at understanding and working with how you think, you risk ineffectiveness when focusing on how clients' think. Paraphrasing Luke 4:23 ("Physician, heal thyself"): "Helper, learn thinking skills by working with your own as well as clients' material."

THINKING ABOUT THINKING

Both helpers and clients are hypothesis makers and testers who have the reflective capacity to think about how they think. Why do both helpers and clients need to develop such skills? Unless clients can think about how they think, they risk condemning themselves to repetitive patterns of thinking skills weaknesses. They do not have the tools to take responsibility for how they think. Unless they develop a language categorizing different thinking skills, they cannot target specific skills for development. Furthermore, helpers and clients capable of thinking about how they think are better able to define themselves and create their own lives. For example, those capable of understanding how their thinking has been affected by parental and cultural rules are in a stronger position to free themselves from unwanted "voices in the head" than those unable to analyze how they think. Also, helpers and clients can use skills of thinking about how they think to increase their sense of self-efficacy, or belief in their capabilities to exercise control over events that affect their lives (Bandura, 1977, 1986, 1989). In addition, those able to think about how they think are capable of learning and instructing themselves in how to think more effectively. Ideally, what Martin (1987) terms "cognitive instructional counseling" leads to cognitive instructional self-helping.

How helpers and clients think about how they think gives them the capacity to influence how they feel and act. For example, good use of thinking skills can help you and your clients get in touch with your feelings, wants, valuing process, and sexuality. Effective thinking skills contribute to releasing desirable feelings and regulating debilitating feelings. Thoughts and feelings tend to be the precursors of action. Developing the capacity for thinking about thinking can help remove blocks and inhibitions to action. Without losing spontaneity, effective thinking skills can help people think before they act—including their identifying action skills for managing specific situations.

Attend to Feelings

Working with clients' thinking skills is not an arid intellectual exercise. Always, you require sensitivity to their feelings and your own. Following are some reasons why, when focusing on thinking, it is important to attend to feelings.

1. *Assess readiness and motivation.* Helpers need to take into account client readiness to work on thinking skills. For instance, vulnerable clients may wish to use the early phases of helping to discharge and discuss feelings of hurt and pain. Some clients may be so anxious and may distort information so badly that they have insufficient insight to explore thinking difficulties until they are less anxious. Clients take differing lengths of time to trust helpers. Until trust is established, they may be neither willing nor able to deal with their faulty thinking choices.

2. *Elicit thoughts and feelings.* Working with clients' thinking can be a delicate process in which helpers create the emotional climate for clients' thoughts and feelings to emerge. Helpers and clients collaborate in unearthing both dysfunctional feelings and the thoughts and thinking skills weaknesses that sustain them. Helpers' lack of empathy blocks clients' experiencing, identifying, and exploring feelings and associated thoughts.

3. *Distinguish clients' own thoughts.* Helpers need to attend closely to feelings in order to help clients distinguish what they think from what they have been taught to think. You may need to give clients permission to articulate their thoughts and support them through the pain and guilt of going against significant others' ways of thinking.

4. *Acknowledge defenses and resistances.* Helpers require awareness of barriers and resistances to acknowledging and working with specific thoughts and thinking skills weaknesses. Frequently, clients do not bare their souls. You require sensitivity to the degree of threat the client feels in focusing on certain areas of life. You have various options (for example,

helping clients acknowledge and work through resistances, or backing off temporarily or permanently).

5. *Check emotional validity of thinking skills hypotheses.* Hypotheses about clients' dysfunctional thoughts and thinking skills weaknesses must have emotional validity if they are to work for change. It is possible, while overtly agreeing with helper-offered thinking skills hypotheses, for clients to disagree covertly. You require skills at checking the emotional validity for clients of how they think about their thinking. Furthermore, you require skills of helping clients do their own work. Conclusions that clients reach for themselves about their thinking are more likely to feel right for them.

6. *Offer support during learning, rehearsal, and practice.* Helpers need to pay attention to clients' feelings as they train clients in thinking skills. Feelings requiring attention include: confusion about understanding a skill properly; insecurity about being asked to demonstrate it in a helping session; and disappointment when unsuccessfully practicing the skill outside helping.

Rewarding listening skills are central when working to develop clients' thinking skills. The desirable helper-client relationship is one of mutual collaboration in pursuit of working goals. Helpers support clients in many ways: emotionally, by facilitating exploration of thoughts and feelings, helping clients check out and analyze the information they generate, and encouraging clients as they learn. At all times, helpers attempt to listen to the information from their own feelings as well as to show sensitivity to the feelings and personal meanings of clients.

The PTC and STC Frameworks

As noted in Chapter 6, Ellis (1962, 1980, 1989) developed a simple ABC framework for thinking about thinking: A represents the activating event; B, a person's rational or irrational beliefs about the activating event; and C, the emotional and behavioral consequences of both A and B. Ellis reckons that much of the time people are aware only of what happens at points A and C. However, what happens at point C is mediated by beliefs at point B.

The PTC and STC frameworks extend Ellis' ABC framework by (a) distinguishing between problems and specific problematic situations, (b) allowing more room for other thoughts and beliefs (for instance, attributions and perceptions), and (c) incorporating skills language.

The PTC framework applies to overall problems:

P   Your overall problem
T   Your thoughts and thinking skills relating to the overall problem
C   Your feelings and actions that are the consequences of P and T

The STC framework applies to specific situations within overall problems:

S   The situation
T   Your thoughts and thinking skills relating to the situation
C   Your feelings and actions that are the consequences of S and T

When helpers redefine problems into their thinking and action skills components, the thinking part represents an analysis within the PTC framework. Sometimes, where problems are specific, the PTC and STC frameworks overlap. However, on other occasions, helpers may focus on how clients think in relation to a specific situation within an overall problem area. For instance, Jason is the manager of a building supplies sales yard. His overall problem area is managing anger at work and at home. A specific situation he wants to work on is managing his anger toward one good but difficult customer.

Offer a Rationale

Before the intervention stage, helpers may present rationales for focusing on thinking skills. For example, you might state such a rationale when redefining problems. You may also offer reasons when you intervene. You can use the PTC or STC frameworks to highlight the importance of how clients think in relation to managing either overall problems or specific situations. Some clients react favorably to analogies (for example, the inner-game and outer-game analogy). Also, you could use humor (for example, encouraging clients to avoid "stinkin' thinkin"). Some clients may find the distinction between "thinking smart" and "thinking dumb" useful. Another way of emphasizing the importance of effective thinking is to make the distinction between self-support and self-oppression (Nelson-Jones, 1990a). When offering reasons for focusing on thinking, incorporate clients' own material to heighten interest. Following is an example of a brief rationale given to a shy male college student for developing the skill of coping self-talk when asking girls out.

> **Helper:** Tony, we agreed to spend part of this session looking at how you can use self-talk to feel more confident and skilled when asking girls out. Let's look at what happens in a simple STC framework, where S is a situation in which you want to ask a girl for a date, T represents what you think or how you talk to yourself about asking a girl out, and C represents how you feel and act (the consequences of the situation). At the moment, it seems as if you are talking to yourself in ways that increase your anxiety and lower your performance. To attain your working goal of developing coping self-talk, you need to become more aware of your negative self-talk at T (for instance, "I'm going to screw up"), and develop the skills of substituting self-talk that calms you down and focuses on how you can best achieve your task. Does this make sense to you?

THINKING-FOCUSED INTERVENTIONS

In the balance of this chapter, I describe interventions for 10 thinking skills. These interventions are in addition to offering a supportive relationship, presenting skills clearly, demonstrating, coaching, and assigning homework. This listing of thinking skills is not exhaustive. Some of the skills overlap and are interrelated. The numbering of the skills does not reflect any order of importance. Which skills you and clients focus on depends upon your working definition and goals. At all times, remember that you are imparting self-helping skills. Clients need to understand the thinking skills well enough to instruct themselves outside of helping. Interventions are suggested for the following thinking skills.

Skill 1: Own responsibility for choosing.
Skill 2: Use coping self-talk.
Skill 3: Choose realistic personal rules.
Skill 4: Choose how you perceive.
Skill 5: Attribute cause accurately.
Skill 6: Predict realistically.
Skill 7: Set realistic goals.
Skill 8: Use visualizing skills.

Skill 9: Make decisions rationally.
Skill 10: Prevent and manage problems and alter problematic skills.

Skill 1: Own Responsibility for Choosing

How can helpers assist clients to attain the working goal of owning more responsibility for being choosers in their lives? Four dimensions of owning responsibility for choosing are choice awareness, responsibility awareness, existential awareness, and feelings awareness (Nelson-Jones, 1990a). Choice awareness consists of awareness of the fact that people are always choosers in their lives, even in relation to suffering and genuinely adverse external circumstances—for instance, poverty, racial discrimination, or even concentration-camp internment (Frankl, 1959). Responsibility awareness means that people recognize that they are responsible for creating their lives through their own choices. Thus clients may need to become more effective authors or architects of their lives (May & Yalom, 1989). Existential awareness consists of awareness of the existential parameters in which all humans lead their lives (for example, death, fate, and isolation). Feelings awareness entails the capacity to listen to your bodily sensations and to your inner valuing process.

Assisting clients to make better choices permeates helping. Clients may resist owning responsibility for choosing. Sometimes these resistances are very deep-rooted. Below are some suggestions for helping clients become more responsible for their choices.

Raise consciousness. Some clients may need to be told in simple language that they are responsible for their choices. They may require help in seeing that they can choose, not only how they act, but also how they think and feel. In the past, they may have taken a passive stance to life and waited for things to happen to them. You can encourage them to see that they can be active agents in shaping their lives.

Encourage choice language. Helpers can assist clients to become more aware of how their use of language restricts their choices. You can encourage: using "I" statements; using verbs that acknowledge choice (for example, "I won't" rather than "I can't"); and avoiding static self-labeling (for example, "I am a poor correspondent" rather than "I choose to be a poor correspondent").

Facilitate exploring choices. Skilled helpers assist clients in exploring choices and their consequences. Clients are always choosers. Spending time exploring choices is valuable to developing their skills of owning responsibility for their choices. You do not make clients' choices for them, but assist them in learning to choose for themselves.

Explore opposites. You may help some clients become more aware of their capacity for choice by getting them to explore opposite ways of thinking and behaving. For example, "Think of someone who makes you feel angry. Now imagine yourself going out of your way to do something to make that person happy. How might he or she react?" Often clients can gain insight into their choices in sustaining problems by exploring opposite ways of viewing them.

Confront not acknowledging choice. Sometimes clients insufficiently acknowledge choices. Here you may need to strengthen their perceptions and will to be choosers (for instance, in regard to resisting peer group pressure). Clients may make statements like "I had no choice but to. . . ." You can either challenge such statements or help clients challenge themselves. You can not only confront clients with how they restrict choice, but also help them explore the consequences for themselves and others of this behavior.

Confront externalizing. All clients and helpers, in varying degrees, externalize thoughts, feelings, actions, and responsibility for problems onto others. Looking at others' shortcomings is easier than looking at our own. Skilled helpers resist colluding with clients who consistently see themselves as the victims of others' persecution. You require both confronting and facilitative skills in assisting clients to look at their own behavior and choices.

Explore defenses. Helpers can assist clients to acknowledge and become aware of the impact of any characteristic "security operations" or "defensive processes" they possess (Arlow, 1989; Clark, 1991; Freud, 1936; Sullivan, 1953). Defensive processes diminish choice awareness in the interest of making life more psychologically comfortable in the short term. Illustrative defensive processes include denying or distorting information, rationalizing or making excuses, and projecting unwanted aspects of oneself onto others. You need to assist exploration of defenses with skill and caution. Clients' defenses alleviate their anxiety and may protect highly sensitive areas.

Raise consciousness concerning death, dying, and finiteness. Helpers may assist some clients by increasing their death awareness (Feifel, 1990; Yalom, 1980). Relevant interventions include: (1) assisting clients in imagining the process of dying and their own deaths; (2) encouraging clients to write their own obituaries; (3) facilitating clients in reminiscing about their contacts with dying people and with death; and (4) encouraging clients to make contact with dying people (for instance, by visiting hospices).

Skill 2: Use Coping Self-Talk

Meichenbaum and others have trained many different clienteles in coping self-talk. Targeted problems include managing anger, managing stress, being creative, curbing impulsiveness, managing pain, and controlling weight (Meichenbaum 1977, 1983, 1985; Meichenbaum & Deffenbacher, 1988). One way to help clients understand that they engage in self-talk is to ask them to close their eyes for 30 seconds and think of nothing. Most become highly aware that they cannot rid themselves of self-talk.

Emphasize Value of Coping Self-Talk

Coping self-talk is a useful thinking skill for managing feelings. Its goals are to calm anxieties and help clients deal effectively with the task at hand. Thus, coping self-talk is about coping (doing as well as I can) rather than about mastery (being perfect and having no anxiety). Coping is a much more realistic goal than mastery.

Coping self-talk involves replacing negative self-talk statements with helpful ones. Let's take the example of Anne and Mary at a party. Note how Anne's self-talk oppresses her, while Mary's self-talk supports her.

> **Anne:** I know that I am going to find this party difficult. Everybody is looking at me. I feel unattractive. I don't want to make a mistake. I'm feeling tense and, when this happens, I know it will only get worse.
> **Mary:** I enjoy parties and meeting new people. Although I get a little anxious with strangers, I know I can overcome it. I have developed some good party skills and these usually work. All I have to do is my best.

Distinguish Calming and Coaching Dimensions

Coping self-talk contains two major elements: calming and coaching. Calming and coaching statements tend to be inter-spersed in coping self-talk. Two important aspects of *calming* self-talk are as follows.

- *Tell yourself to stay calm.* Simple self-statements include "keep calm," "relax," and "take it easy." In addition, you can in-struct yourself to "take a deep breath" or "breathe slowly and regularly."
- *Tell yourself you can cope.* Sample self-statements include "I can handle this situation" or "My anxiety is a signal for me to use my coping skills."

Coaching self-talk can help you to cope with shyness in the fol-lowing ways.

- *Specify your goals.* An example could be "I will go up and talk to a minimum of three new people at the party."
- *Break tasks down.* Think through the steps needed to attain your goal.
- *Concentrate on the task at hand.* Instruct yourself in the specific elements of competent behavior.

You can use coping self-talk before, during, and after stressful social situations (for example, going to a party full of strangers, or going out with a new date). Examples of possible coping self-talk statements *before* stressful social situations include:

"This anxiety is a sign for me to use my coping skills."
"Calm down. Develop a plan to manage the situation."
"I know if I use my coping skills I can manage."

Examples of possible coping self-talk statements *during* stressful social situations include:

"Take my time. Breathe slowly and regularly."
"Relax. I can manage if I just take one step at a time."
"I don't have to be liked by everyone. All I can do is the best I can."

Examples of possible coping self-talk statements *after* stressful social situations include:

"Each time I cope it seems to get easier."

"I'm proud of the way I'm learning to manage my fears."
"I've shown myself I can do it now."

As you instruct clients in the calming and coaching dimensions of coping self-talk, remember to provide opportunity for comments, feedback, checking understanding, and relating the content of the presentation to the client's own material.

Relate Coping Self-Talk to Action

. Both helpers and clients should use coping self-talk *along with* taking appropriate action. For instance, a shy person requires not only the thinking skill of coping self-talk, but also the action skills of performing competently in social situations. Consequently, in the same session you are likely to work with both thinking and action skills. You can encourage clients to write their coping self-talk statements on cue cards for rehearsing before difficult situations.

Skill 3: Choose Realistic Personal Rules

Albert Ellis has been particularly prominent in highlighting the importance of realistic personal rules, or what he terms "rational" as contrasted with "irrational" beliefs (Ellis, 1962, 1980, 1989). Personal rules represent a form of self-talk, much of which goes on below conscious awareness. Personal rules provide standards for judging our own and others' behavior. Many clients possess rules representing the internalization of others' standards rather than rules thought through by themselves. Such rules can be benign and realistic so long as they help clients meet their needs. However, unrealistic rules can cause clients to be tyrannized by their shoulds. Such unrealistic rules contribute to negative emotions (for instance, anger and anxiety) and self-defeating actions (for instance, withdrawal and temper tantrums).

Assist Clients to Identify Unrealistic Personal Rules

Helpers can assist clients to develop skills of recognizing that they may possess one or more unrealistic personal rules. Clients should watch for danger signals such as the following.

1. *Inappropriate feelings:* Persistent inappropriate feelings are one signal alerting clients to unrealistic personal rules. Clients can ask themselves questions like "Is this feeling appropriate for the situation?" and "To what extent does this feeling have unnecessary negative consequences for me?"

2. *Inappropriate actions:* Inappropriate feelings and actions are interrelated. Clients can ask themselves questions like "Are my actions helping or harming me and others?," "Am I over-reacting?," and "Is my behavior self-defeating?"
3. *Inappropriate language:* Ellis (1980), as noted earlier, coined the term *mustabation* to refer to rigid personal rules characterized by musts, oughts, shoulds, and have-tos. Such language may signal irrational beliefs or rules.
4. *Linkages between stressors:* You can assist clients in the skills of identifying which rules are most important. For example, it may be more important for clients, whose anger at home is related to self-induced stress at work, to focus on stress rules than anger rules.

Help Clients Put Unrealistic Rules into the STC Framework

Assuming adequate initial explanation, helpers should encourage clients to do their own work rather than spoonfeed them. Below are two examples of clients' rules put into the S (situation), T (thoughts), and C (feelings and action consequences) framework. The first example focuses on an unrealistic *personal* rule and the second example on an unrealistic *relationship* rule.

Jeff is a family man with two children.
S   His children do not overtly show appreciation for how hard he works to support them.
T   "I must always have my kids' approval or else I am less of a person."
C   Hurt, self-pity, and anger. Curtness with children that creates emotional distance.

Jodie and Wally are a newly married couple.
S   Jodie and Wally disagree over how much time to spend with the in-laws.
T   "We must never have conflict in our marriage."
C   Both Jodie's and Wally's negative feelings persist. The in-law issue in their relationship is not openly worked through.

Assist Clients to Dispute Unrealistic Rules

Ellis (1980) considers disputing to be the most typical and often-used method of his rational-emotive therapy (RET). *Disputing* means challenging unrealistic rules. An issue for helpers is whether to dispute clients' rules or to assist clients in doing their own disputing. One approach is to demonstrate the skill first, then coach clients in developing disputing skills. Take the earlier example of Jeff, whose personal rule was "I must always have my kids' approval or else I am less of a person." Following are questions that Jeff might ask himself (or be asked).

> "What evidence exists that I cannot survive without my kids' approval?"
>
> "Does the fact that my kids do not overtly show approval for what I do mean that they do not notice it?"
>
> "Is it realistic to expect children to be aware of what their father does for them outside the home, let alone always appreciate it?"
>
> "Would I expect the children of my friends to show approval in the same way that I expect my kids to, or do I have a double standard?"
>
> "Did I always show appreciation for what my parents did for me?"
>
> "What is it about me that may make me vulnerable to not receiving overt appreciation from my kids?"
>
> "How exactly does not having constant appreciation from my kids make me less of a person?"

Clients must become aware that they may need to dispute the same unrealistic rule again and again. They may possess well-established habits of re-indoctrinating and re-contaminating themselves.

Assist Clients to Reformulate Unrealistic Rules

Reformulating means substituting realistic for unrealistic characteristics in specific personal or relationship rules. Assist clients in understanding some of the main characteristics of realistic personal rules.

- Expressing preferences rather than demands (for example, "I'd prefer to do very well but I don't have to") (Sichel & Ellis, 1984, p. 1).
- Emphasizing coping rather than mastery or being perfect.
- Basing rules on clients' own valuing process rather than rigid internalizations of others' rules.
- Showing flexibility or, where appropriate, being amenable to change and updating.
- Avoiding self-rating (for example, "I am a person who acted badly, not a bad person") (Sichel & Ellis, 1984, p. 1).

Then, assist clients in reformulating unhelpful into helpful rules. Get them to do much of the work. Make sure the reformulations are in clients' own language, since they have to live with their new rules. I illustrate reformulating with the examples of Jeff's unrealistic *personal* rule and Jodie and Wally's unrealistic *relationship* rule.

Jeff

Unrealistic personal rule: "I must always have my kids' approval or else I am less of a person."

Realistic personal rule: "I would prefer to have my kids' approval much of the time. However, it is more important that I take responsibility for how well I behave toward them and to approve of what I do."

Jodie and Wally

Unrealistic relationship rule: "We must never have conflict in our marriage."

Realistic relationship rule: "We would prefer not to have serious conflicts in our marriage. However, differences and conflict are part of all close relationships. We need to develop skills of working through rather than avoiding conflicts."

It is important that clients take away, remember, and practice reformulated rules. Encourage either recording them or writing them down. Such records should be used for homework and reminder purposes—playing back the recording or posting the reformulated rules in an obvious place. Emphasize that maintaining reformulated rules requires practice, practice, practice!

Encourage Clients to Change Actions along with Reformulated Rules

Effective thinking should lead to effective action. Psychologists differ over whether practice is best approached gradually, from less to more difficult tasks, or "floodingly," going straight to a difficult assignment. With either approach, encourage clients to develop relevant action skills (for instance, unappreciated Jeff might need to improve his showing affection skills). Ellis (1980, 1989) asks clients to do practice assignments repetitively and floodingly. He believes that, by jumping in at the deep end over and over, clients find that their worst fears rarely materialize. Other psychologists advocate a more gradual approach. For instance, they would ask a woman afraid of saying no to people to say no to a less-threatening person before repeating the behavior with more-threatening ones. Often clients do not have much choice. A difficult encounter or an imminent exam is the reality they face.

Skill 4: Choose How You Perceive

Aaron Beck is a prime advocate of helping clients influence their feelings by choosing more realistic perceptions. In particular, he has focused on the thoughts that precede depression (Beck, 1976; Beck, Rush, Shaw, & Emery, 1979), anxieties and phobias (Beck & Emery, 1985), and anger in relationships (Beck, 1988). You can assist numerous clients with a wide range of problems to develop skills of challenging and altering their distorted perceptions and perceptual processes.

Help Clients Become Aware of the Influence of Perception on Feelings

You can let clients know that they may have tendencies to jump to unhelpful conclusions that contribute to negative feelings. You could illustrate this point through stories. For example, you can ask clients to imagine that someone has stepped on their toe. Realistically they might experience some pain. If they perceived the toe-treading as accidental, they might also feel mild irritation, but this should not persist. However, if they perceived the toe-treading as intentional, they might feel very angry. In each instance, how they perceive influences how they feel.

Clients can be encouraged to monitor upsetting perceptions. Ideally, they should monitor them as they happen. Clients need to develop the skill of becoming aware of the thinking that accompanies inappropriate feelings. Get clients to set aside some time each day to monitor and record upsetting perceptions. They can fill in a thinksheet with the following three column headings.

A. The Situation (inc. date and time)	B. My Feelings	C. My Thoughts (perceptions)

Help Clients Learn the Difference between Fact and Inference

Clients' perceptions of themselves, others, and the world are their subjective "facts." Often, however, they fail to realize these perceptions may be based on inference rather than fact. A favorite illustration of this point by one of my Stanford University professors was: "All Indians walk in single file. At least the one I saw did." That one Indian was seen is a fact; that they all walk in single file is inference. Facts are the true data of experience; inferences are deductions and conclusions drawn from the data. Inferences are both necessary and useful, so long as their assumptions are both recognized and accurately evaluated. All too often, however, clients treat their inferences as facts. This deprives them of accurate information on which to base further thoughts, feelings, and actions. Here is an example:

> *Fact:* Husband comes home very late from work three nights in a row.
> *Wife's inference:* "He does not love me any more. He has a girlfriend."

Assuming the husband had legitimate reasons for staying out late, which he may even have explained to her, the wife was making an erroneous inference that could have serious repercussions for their relationship. However, we don't know the husband's track record. It may have supported his wife's inference!

Help Clients Identify Characteristic Perceptual Distortions

Helpers can assist clients to become aware of characteristic ways in which they distort how they perceive. Regarding distressed couples, Beck (1988) observes: "These cognitive distortions occur automatically, often in a fraction of a second, and the number of distortions that can take place in that short period is considerable" (p. 159). Especially under stress, clients are likely to activate their perceptual "fault lines." Awareness of characteristic distortions provides clients with information with which to check specific perceptions. They have a start in knowing where to look and what to avoid.

Using the STC framework, following are some perceptual distortions that clients may have at T that lead to negative feelings and action consequences at C.

- *Tunnel vision:* Focusing on only a portion of the available information in a situation rather than taking into account all significant data.
- *Polarized thinking:* Perceiving in black-and-white terms. For example, "I am either a total success or a total failure."
- *Negative labeling:* Attaching negative and critical labels to yourself and others. Overemphasizing the negative at the expense of the positive or neutral. Going beyond a functional rating of a specific characteristic to devalue your whole personhood.

- *Personalizing*: Perceiving yourself as the center of attention more than is warranted. For instance, "Everybody in the office is aware of how poorly I perform."
- *Overgeneralizing*: Making global comments that are probably untenable if the evidence is checked. For example, "My daughter *never* does anything for me" and "I *always* try to understand my employees' viewpoints."
- *Misattributing*: Failing to assign cause and responsibility accurately for your own and others' behavior. Giving biased explanations of others' behavior and intentions (for instance, "He is not good at showing affection because he has a poor personality").

Help Clients to Stop, Think, Generate, Evaluate, and Choose the Best-Fit Perception

Helpers can assist clients to realize that they have choices in how they perceive. Help clients to check the accuracy of their information base when they become aware that they either feel and act, or are at risk of feeling and acting, in inappropriate ways. Clients can ask themselves the following kinds of questions.

"Stop . . . think. . . . Am I jumping to conclusions in how I perceive?"
"Are my perceptions based on fact or inference?"
"If based on inference, are there other ways of perceiving the situation more closely related to the facts?"
"What further information might I need to collect?"
"Does my way of perceiving this situation reflect any of my characteristic perceptual distortions?"
"What perception can I choose that best fits the available facts?"

Generate different perceptions. Clients are often very poor at generating alternative ways of viewing people and situations. Here is an example in the STC framework.

S Gary has cooked a nice dinner for his girlfriend Wendy, who is 30 minutes late.
T Gary thinks, "Wendy is very inconsiderate of my feelings."
C When Wendy finally arrives, Gary verbally attacks her and they have a fight.

You need to tactfully inform Gary that he requires the skill of perceiving accurately rather than jumping to conclusions. One element of this skill is acknowledging that you have choices in how you perceive and in looking for alternative explanations. You could help him generate alternative perceptions at T. For example: "Wendy may have had a flat tire"; "Wendy may have been forced to stay late at work"; "Wendy may have stopped off to buy me a present."; and "Wendy and I may not have made our arrangement clear enough."

Evaluate different perceptions.   Another element of the skill of perceiving accurately is evaluating different perceptions and choosing the best-fit perception. For instance, you might assist Gary in evaluating the perception that "Wendy is very inconsiderate of my feelings." How closely does the inference fit the facts? Then you encourage Gary to evaluate the other perceptions generated. Gary decides that the best-fit perception in this case is "Wendy and I may not have made our arrangements clear enough." The feelings consequence of this perception is that Gary is not angry with Wendy. The action consequence is that Gary welcomes Wendy and they calmly talk over what went wrong.

Help Clients Develop Reframing Skills

Reframing is a variation of the skill of generating and evaluating different perceptions and choosing the best-fit perception. Either the helper or the client places a situation, feeling, or behavior within a different frame. Reframes should not be rationalizations. Often reframing focuses on one alternative perception rather than generating and evaluating a series of different perceptions. Helper-offered reframes confront clients with new ways of perceiving events. However, clients can also develop skills of generating and evaluating their own reframes. Following is an example of a helper-offered reframe.

> **Client:** I feel guilty that, since returning to work after being off with stress problems, I'm not performing my supervising job to my full ability. I like to do as well as I can by the company.
> **Helper:** I get the impression that what you do is really important to your company and that, even though you don't feel 100 percent, your being back at work has saved them from a lot of problems.

How can helpers assist clients to develop reframing skills? First identify reframing as a useful self-helping skill. The concept of reframing may be easier for certain clients to grasp than that of generating and evaluating different perceptions. Second, as in the above example, use the client's material to demonstrate how to reframe. Third, where appropriate, encourage clients to suggest their own reframes (for instance, by questions such as "Can you think of a way to reframe that?"). Fourth, encourage clients to practice the skill of reframing in their daily lives. Fifth, assist clients to assess, not only the consequences of individual reframes on how they feel and act, but also the longer-term consequences for developing reframing as a self-helping skill.

Skill 5: Attribute Cause Accurately

Earlier I mentioned the skill of owning responsibility for choosing. Here I elaborate on how to assist clients' motivation by working with them on how they attribute cause for what happens in their lives. Attributions are the explanations, interpretations, or reasons that clients give themselves for what happens. They influence how clients think about the future, as well as how they feel and act. Frequently, clients make attributional errors that interfere with their motivation and effectiveness. Let's take the example of the women's movement. When women attributed their lack of status to male dominance, they were relatively powerless. However, when women also attributed their lack of status to insufficient assertion, they empowered themselves.

Help Clients Become Aware of Inaccurate Attributions

Frequently clients' attributions of cause are partly rather than totally inaccurate—a partial truth gets converted into a whole truth. For instance, a partial cause of Rosemary's difficulties may be that she was rejected by her father when she was growing up. However, Rosemary can immobilize herself from working for change if she attributes the whole cause of her difficulties to her father's past behavior. Following are some attributional errors for different areas.

Causes of problems Many misattributions can cause clients to remain unnecessarily stuck with problems. Here are some examples.

1. *"It's my genes."* Though genetic endowment does limit capacities, clients also limit themselves. For instance, clients who say that they are "naturally" lazy obscure their own roles in sustaining their laziness.
2. *"It's my mental illness."* The medical profession has done psychology a huge disservice by fostering the concept of

mental illness. For most psychological problems, the attribution of mental illness overemphasizes the role of heredity and physical factors and underemphasizes the role of learning and choice.

3. *"It's my unfortunate past."* As shown in the example of Rosemary, an unfortunate past may contribute to problems and skills weaknesses. However, clients are unlikely to change unless they assume responsibility for how they sustain their problems.

4. *"It's my poor environment."* Adverse social, economic, and psychological environments may make it more difficult for clients to fulfill themselves. However, even in Nazi concentration camps people could change and grow (Frankl, 1959).

Feelings of depression Clients' attributions of cause for positive and negative events in their lives affect their self-esteem. Following are some inaccurate attributions that may contribute to depression.

1. *"I am the cause of all negative events."* Clients can overemphasize their role in negative events in their own and others' lives (Beck, Rush, Shaw, & Emery, 1979).

2. *"I am never the cause of positive events."* Clients can deny and distort their roles in positive events in their own and others' lives.

3. *"I am unable to act on my environment in such a way as to produce desired results."* Frequently, depressed people think of themselves as powerless or helpless to influence their environments (Schulman, Seligman, & Amsterdam, 1987; Seligman, Abramson, Semmel, & von Baeyer, 1979).

Relationship conflicts Often clients require help in acknowledging their contributions to sustaining problems. Following are some common attributional errors.

1. *"It's all your fault."* Instead of looking at conflicts from inside to outside, clients view them from the outside to inside. Disliking what they see outside provides a convenient excuse for not looking at their own behavior.

2. *"You must change first."* Here clients allow their feeling, thinking, and actions to be dependent on their partner's behavior. Unwittingly, clients give up some control over their lives.

Becoming and staying unemployed Depending on clients' specific situations, the following attributions may be inaccurate.

1. *"It was my fault."* Numerous external reasons contribute to unemployment (for instance, recessions, company takeovers, and technological changes). Clients may genuinely not be responsible for their job loss.
2. *"It was their fault."* Some clients may fail to acknowledge that they have personal and work-related skills weaknesses that increase the chances of their being fired.
3. *"The state should provide for me."* Whatever clients' political persuasions, the reality is that they are likely to receive only limited help from the government.
4. *"My work skills are adequate."* Clients may need to review the accuracy of this assumption. For example, their work skills may be in demand, but they perform them poorly. Alternatively, their work skills may be obsolete.

Academic successes and failures Helpers may assist both underachieving and overstriving students to be more realistic about the attributions they make for their academic successes and failures. Following are some causes to which students may attribute academic success and failure (Nelson-Jones, 1990a; Weiner & Kukla, 1970). Needless to say, there is a subjective element in what students perceive as success or failure.

1. *Aptitude:* Aptitude is an internal and stable attribute.
2. *Effort:* Effort is an internal attribute largely within a client's control.
3. *Task difficulty:* Task difficulty is composed of the task's realistic level of difficulty and any of the client's perceptual distortions that magnify or minimize it.
4. *Luck:* Academic results due to chance are outside clients' control.
5. *Anxiety:* Anxiety can both help and hinder academic performance (Alpert & Haber, 1960). The effects of debilitating anxiety may be inadequately recognized.
6. *Staff competence:* Good or poor teaching may help or hinder achievement.
7. *Socioeconomic considerations:* Some students need to take outside work to support themselves, some live in inadequate housing, and so on.
8. *Peer group pressure:* The peer group either values or does not value academic success.

Alter Inaccurate Attributions

Helpers can use some of the skills already described for helping clients alter unrealistic attributions. For example, you can encourage clients to examine the evidence for their attributions and see how closely they fit the facts. Then clients can generate and evaluate alternative attributions. In addition, clients can dispute attributions and reformulate them into more realistic attributions. For example, the attribution in a relationship conflict that "It's all my partner's fault" can be reformulated to "Even though I may not like how my partner behaves, I need to look at how I behave toward my partner and, where possible, change my behavior to achieve both our goals and my own." You can also assist clients to conduct behavioral experiments in which they act on altered attributions. For example, a husband's "It's all my partner's fault" attribution is disproved if he acts differently toward his wife, who in turn acts better towards him.

Helpers can both provide new information and encourage clients to collect additional information that checks existing attributions. For instance, you can inform clients who wrongly diagnose themselves as schizophrenic that they do not possess any of its key symptoms. Also, you can encourage clients attributing their math problems to insufficient aptitude to collect additional information by taking a math-aptitude test.

Skill 6: Predict Realistically

Clients lead their lives into the future rather than into the past. Predictions are thoughts and images that forecast the future. George Kelly (1955) took a rational approach to prediction when he wrote: "The two factors from which predictions are made are the number of replications already observed and the amount of similarity which can be abstracted among the replications" (p. 53). Invariably clients experience disorders of prediction that are of varying degrees of intensity. Anxiety is a disorder of prediction (Beck & Emery, 1985). Also, distorted predictions play a large part in depression—for instance, hopelessness (Beck, Riskind, Brown, & Steer, 1988), helplessness (Abramson, Seligman, & Teasdale, 1978), and perceived self-inefficacy (Bandura, 1989).

Help Clients Become Aware of Their Predictive Style

Helpers can assist clients to become more aware of their predictive styles and their consequences, both in general and in relation to specific problems. Moreover, clients can become more aware of where specific skills weaknesses lie. Predicting risks and rewards are interrelated. Following are the main options.

Predict risk inaccurately

1. *Underestimate bad consequences.* For example, some research into health issues indicates that people tend to underestimate their own, relative to others', risk for various illnesses and negative life events (Weinstein, 1980, 1984). Compulsive gamblers and stock-market speculators have a similar tendency.
2. *Overestimate bad consequences.* Fear of change, failure, or success can be powerful motivators for clients to overestimate negative consequences of actions. Many clients engage in catastrophic predictions.

Predict reward inaccurately

1. *Overestimate good consequences.* Overestimating good consequences frequently accompanies underestimating bad consequences (for instance, in compulsive gambling).
2. *Underestimate good consequences.* Many helping clients underestimate good consequences. They have a predictive style that focuses far more on risk than reward. Two trends are common in underestimating reward. First, clients are poor at identifying rewards. Second, even when clients identify rewards, they minimize their significance.

Help Clients Become Aware of Current Predictions and Their Consequences

A simple two-column technique can be useful for eliciting clients' assessments of risks and rewards in specific situations. For example, using the STC framework, the S (situation) is that Sean is a shy 30-year-old bachelor wondering whether to ask Suzanne for a date. Sean's helper places the following two-column headings on the board to elicit Sean's thoughts or predictions at T.

Risks (minuses)	Rewards (plusses)

Then the helper assists Sean in articulating his fears about asking Suzanne out (for instance, "This might contribute to keeping me depressed" and "I could get hurt"). At this stage, Sean has difficulty predicting that there will be rewards from his actions.

Helpers can go beyond pinpointing predictions to exploring their consequences at C. Exploration can focus on consequences for clients (for instance, Sean's overemphasis on the risks rather than the gains may lead to persistent loneliness). You can also assist clients to become better at predicting consequences for others (for instance, drug addict Jana may need to see more clearly the dangers for others of sharing her needles).

Help Clients Generate and Evaluate Additional Risks or Rewards

If clients' predictive errors lean toward underestimating risks, helpers may need to assist them in developing the skill of generating what other risks there may be. Most clients tend toward overestimating risks. Frequently, they need to develop skills of generating and evaluating potential rewards.

Sean started by mentioning items to go in the risks column when asking Suzanne for a date, but had difficulty generating items for the rewards column. Sean's helper worked with him to generate some potential rewards for asking Suzanne out, including the following: "I might have a chance of a strong relationship," "I might gain more experience in developing relationships," and "I might gain confidence and a more positive self-image." Working to generate rewards enabled Sean to obtain a more balanced picture about asking Suzanne out. Sean decided the rewards outweighed the risks, acted on his changed predictions, and Suzanne later became his first steady girlfriend.

Help Clients to Assess Probability

Helpers can assist clients to review their assumptions about the likelihood of risks or rewards actually occurring. Clients may wrongly assign high probability to low-probability events or low probability to high-probability events.

Fifteen years ago an assistant professor, Daniel, had an extremely painful nervous breakdown. Now Daniel is a full professor. Recently, on doctor's orders, Daniel took sick leave for a "vacation" because he had started experiencing his pre-breakdown symptoms of 15 years earlier. A few days before returning to his university, he experienced chronic anxiety. A major contributor to his anxiety was his prediction that he might have another breakdown. Daniel's helper assisted him to assess the evidence for his prediction. Once Daniel faced the facts, he realized that this time he had taken preventive action and had the skills to monitor his load and seek further assistance, if necessary. Consequently, Daniel recognized that the chances of having another full-blown breakdown were close to nil. This realization lowered his anxiety, thus further reducing the likelihood of another breakdown.

Questions that clients might ask themselves in assessing probability fall into two categories. First, what *rational* basis do I have for making a particular prediction? Here clients need to assess the connections between facts and inferences. Second, what *irrational* considerations might interfere with the accuracy of my prediction? The perceptual distortions mentioned earlier, clients' states of emotional arousal, and their physical condition might each interfere with their ability to predict.

Help Clients to Assess Their Coping Capacity and Support Factors

Clients may predict based on inaccurate assessments of their skills at coping with particular situations. They may engage in focusing on their weaknesses and need to counteract this by searching for and affirming their resources. Additionally, clients may possess many support factors that they inadequately acknowledge (for example, people who can help them prepare for upcoming tasks, friends and relatives who can provide emotional support, and opportunities to repeat failed tasks). Encourage clients to identify, acknowledge, use, and develop appropriate supports (Emery, 1982).

Encourage Clients to Reality-Test Predictions

The most conclusive way for clients to test the accuracy of their predictions is to reality-test them. Here are two examples of clients whom helpers might encourage to reality-test predictions.

Maureen, age 27, is afraid to tell her husband how she would like him to make love to her. She predicts, "If I tell him, he'll be furious."

Wayne, a widower, is reluctant to throw a party to mark his sixtieth birthday. He predicts, "No one will want to come."

In the above cases, each client needs to set a specific goal. For example, Maureen's might be to tell her husband how to pleasure her better within the next month. Wayne's goal might be to throw a moderate-sized party on, or within 2 weeks of, his sixtieth birthday. You may need to assist clients to think through and develop the action skills for attaining their goals. For example, Maureen requires verbal, voice, and body message action skills to make an assertive request for her husband to change his behavior.

Skill 7: Set Realistic Goals

Clients may bring to helping different errors in setting goals. Some clients may possess goals, but these goals may be unrealistically high or low. Furthermore, the goals may be based on what others think they should be, rather than on their own valuing process. Other clients lack clear goals. Still more require assistance in stating their goals clearly. Some of the rewards for clients of setting realistic goals include increased authorship of their lives, clarity of focus, finding increased meaning, and gaining increased motivation. Risks to clients who set unrealistic goals include: self-alienation, emphasizing doing over being, putting too much pressure on themselves, and compromising their health.

Assisting vulnerable clients to formulate clear goals may entail long-term helping. Such clients lack a sense of their identity. You may need to assist these clients in getting more in touch with their feelings and wishes. Furthermore, you may need to caution clients against making major decisions until they are less anxious.

Many other thinking skills are relevant to assisting clients in setting realistic goals. Clients' goals need to be based on realistic personal rules. Furthermore, where clients' goals involve others (for instance, getting engaged or married), they need to perceive them accurately. In addition, clients can use visualizing skills to formulate goals. Also, when setting goals, clients can engage in the steps of rational decision making.

Assist Clients to State Goals Clearly

Clients are more likely to attain goals that they have stated clearly. You can make them aware of the following criteria for effective goals.

- *Do your goals reflect your values?* Clients' goals should reflect what they consider to be worthwhile in life.
- *Are your goals realistic?* Clients' goals are realistic when they adequately acknowledge both external and personal constraints. Encourage clients to set goals reflecting potentially attainable standards.
- *Are your goals specific?* Assist clients in stating goals as specifically as possible. Ideally, clients' goals should be stated so that they can easily measure the success of attempts to attain them. For instance, "I will introduce myself to three new people in my ballroom dancing class" is much preferable to "I want to meet some new people."

- *Do your goals have a time frame?* Goals can be short-term, medium-term, or long-term. Vague intentions are insufficient. Assist clients in stating a realistic time frame for attaining goals (for instance, "By the end of this month, I will introduce myself to three new people in my ballroom dancing class").

Once goals are stated, you may need to work with clients to identify the thinking and action skills required to attain them. In the preceding example, you might assist the client in articulating the thinking and action skills helpful in meeting three new people in the ballroom dancing class. Sometimes you may need to assist clients in breaking tasks down into more easily attainable sub-goals (for example, an initial goal of meeting one new person, a second goal of meeting two new people, and a third goal of meeting three new people).

Skill 8: Use Visualizing Skills

Visual images play a large part in everyone's lives. Glasser (1984) asserts that 80 percent of the perceptions people store in their memory albums are visual. Visual images interact with feelings—for example, in one research study some 90 percent of anxious patients reported visual images prior to and concurrent with their anxiety attacks (Beck, Laude, & Bohnert, 1974). Lazarus observes that a tendency to react with visual images is particularly strong in certain clients. He writes, "When a person's most highly valued representational system is visual, he or she is inclined to respond to the world and organize it in terms of mental images " (Lazarus, 1989, p. 514).

Help Clients Develop an Awareness of Visualizing

Some clients may need to become more aware of the role of visual images in sustaining their problems. Following are a few ways that helpers can highlight the importance of visualizing.

Questions Helpers who ask questions about clients' visual imagery are more likely to assist clients to recognize its importance than helpers who avoid the area. Sample questions might be "Were you aware of any visual images that accompanied the anxiety attack?" and "To what extent do you use visual imagery to help cope with the situation?" As clients answer questions, helpers can assess their visualizing powers. Clients can also be asked to close their eyes and recount specific instances as though they were describing a slow motion replay of a movie. In general, the more clients can experience sensations and feelings attached to images, the greater is their potential for using visualizing as a self-helping skill.

Explanations   You can incorporate visual images into the PTC or STC frameworks used to explain problems or problematic situations. For instance, the STC framework requires elaboration to:

S   the situation
T   your thoughts and *visual images*
C   your feeling and action consequences

Exercises   You can use exercises to illustrate various aspects of visualizing. A simple exercise to highlight the presence of visualizing is to ask clients to think of someone they love. Almost invariably they will get a visual image. You can show the relationship between visualizing and feelings by getting clients first to visualize something that "makes" them feel happy and then something that "makes" them feel afraid.

Helpers can assist clients to develop visualizing skills for numerous purposes (Lazarus, 1977; Nelson-Jones, 1990a). Visualizing skills are most effective when used in conjunction with other thinking and action skills. Here I illustrate visualizing by focusing on three of its uses: namely, becoming more relaxed, performing better, and breaking bad habits.

Help Clients Use Visualizing to Relax

When clients visualize, it is best that they be relaxed. In addition, relaxation can be a useful skill for clients to develop if they suffer from such problems as tension headaches, hypertension, and feelings of excessive stress. Furthermore, relaxation is a useful skill for helping manage such feelings as anxiety (Deffenbacher & Suinn, 1988; Wolpe, 1973) and anger (Deffenbacher, Story, Brandon, Hogg, & Hazaleus, 1988). The most common helping approach to relaxation is probably the Jacobson progressive muscular relaxation technique (Jacobson, 1938), more fully described in Chapter 12. Visual imagery may be used independently of, as well as in conjunction with, muscular relaxation. You can assist clients in the following elements of visual relaxation.

Identifying relaxing scenes   Encourage clients to identify one or more favorite scenes conducive to their feeling relaxed (for instance, looking at a valley with lush green meadows or sitting in a comfortable chair at home).

Developing self-instructions Though helpers may initially relax clients, the idea is for clients to develop visual relaxation as a self-helping skill. First, you demonstrate how clients can instruct themselves in visual relaxation. Then you rehearse clients as they use their own instructions. Clients may wish to record their self-instructions for playback outside of helping sessions. Here is a brief example.

> **Client:** I'm lying on an uncrowded beach on a pleasant, sunny day, enjoying the sensations of warmth on my body. There is a gentle breeze. I can hear the peaceful noise of the sea steadily lapping against the nearby shore. I haven't a care in the world, and enjoy my feelings of peace, calm, relaxation, and well-being.

Using visual relaxation in daily life You can assist clients in identifying opportunities for taking time out in their daily lives to use visual relaxation. Encourage them to keep visual relaxation monitoring logs of their daily practice and use of the skill. Clients can also record the consequences of using visual relaxation skills.

Help Clients Use Visualizing to Perform Better

Visualized rehearsal and practice, and visualizing attaining goals, are two main ways in which clients can use visualizing to enhance how they perform tasks.

Visualized rehearsal and practice Clients may have limited opportunity to rehearse and practice skills in real life (for instance, going for a job interview or speaking in public). However, they have virtually unlimited opportunity to use visualized rehearsal and practice. While it is no substitute for the real thing, visualized rehearsal has many advantages. These advantages include assisting clients to: break tasks down and focus on the processes of skilled performance; identify potential setbacks and ways of coping with them; and rehearse and practice coping self-talk along with their visualizing skills.

Following are instances of clients' using visualized rehearsal and practice.

Wendy, 61, a recently retired widow, has a goal of asking her friend Louise if she can join her bridge group. Wendy visually rehearses the best way to do this, including how she might respond if Louise says no.

Bruce, 41, a car-factory foreman, visualizes different ways he can assertively tell workers when their work is not up to standard.

Duncan, 23, a police officer, visualizes how he can calmly yet firmly react to people who call him a pig when he is on crowd-control duty.

Visualizing attaining goals   Visualized rehearsal and practice focuses on the *processes* of skilled performance. However, clients may also enhance their performance if they visualize themselves being successful in attaining goals (Lazarus, 1977; Woolfolk, Parish, & Murphy, 1985). For example, if clients rehearse hard and then visualize that they are going to perform very competently when speaking in public, they are more likely to do so than if they visualize lack of success. Often clients are far too good at visualizing the worst. They need to be able to counteract this tendency by visualizing successful experiences. Also, helpers can encourage clients, even when imagining the worst possibility, to visualize how they can cope successfully in such adverse circumstances (Emery, 1982).

Help Clients Use Visualizing to Break Bad Habits

There is an Oscar Wilde aphorism: "I couldn't help it. I can resist everything except temptation." Visualizing can be a useful skill when trying to overcome bad habits. Clients with bad habits, instead of dwelling on negative consequences, often switch to dwelling on short-term rewards. If clients sincerely wish to bread bad habits, the time to reward themselves is when they have resisted temptation, not when they have given in to it. Visualizing realistic negative consequences and visualizing exaggerated negative consequences are two ways helpers can assist clients to bread bad habits.

Visualize realistic negative consequences.   How can you assist clients to visualize realistic negative consequences from such activities as smoking or engaging in unsafe sex? One way is to encourage clients to collect visual images of negative consequences (for instance, full-color photographs of the effects of smoking on lung tissue, or of AIDS-related symptoms like Kaposi's sarcoma and malignant lymphomas). In addition, clients can be encouraged to develop visualizations, possibly including photographic images, of the negative consequences of bad habits. Also, clients can develop the following self-helping skill: When tempted, they can instruct themselves to "Stop!" and then intensely visualize the negative consequences of giving in to the temptation. Clients may then engage in substitute rewarding activities involving little or no risk.

Visualize exaggerated negative consequences. Cautela (1967) developed what he termed a "covert sensitization" approach to undermining and resisting temptations. Clients are encouraged to visualize exaggerated negative consequences whenever an unwanted temptation is anticipated or experienced. For instance, if clients wish to break the habit of overeating, and they have targeted rich cakes as a food to avoid, they might practice visualizing the following sequence.

> **Client:** I am at home, sitting around the table at dinner, and a rich cake is being served. As I see it, I start getting nauseated. I accept a piece. As I take my first bite, I vomit all over the table and my clothes. I throw up all my dinner in a disgusting, smelly mess. Seeing and smelling my vomit makes me retch even more violently. I feel very weak and faint. Everybody is looking at me in disgust. As I get up from the table, having made up my mind to eat no more, I feel better. I wash, change, and feel great because I've stopped eating rich food.

I prefer encouraging clients to visualize realistic rather than exaggerated negative consequences. Realistic consequences can be horrific enough! However, some clients may find that exaggeration increases the power of their negative imagery, with a beneficial effect on their will power.

Skill 9: Make Decisions Rationally

Frequently clients are faced with decisions. Such decisions include making choices about jobs and career, determining major areas of study, choosing a college or graduate school, getting married or divorced, or giving up a bad habit. Decisions produce varying degrees of conflict and anxiety. Clients may fear the consequences of making the wrong decision. Additionally, they may be under stress at the time of making the decision (for instance, about quitting college). How can you assist clients to make better decisions and, even more important, to become better decision makers? The main thrust of all helping interventions is to assist clients to make better choices. Here I discuss two areas, decision-making styles and rational decision making, in which you specifically focus on clients' decision-making processes.

Help Clients Become Aware of Their Decision-Making Styles

Clients have styles of decision that may be helpful or harmful (Arroba, 1977). In reality, each client possesses a profile of decision-making styles. Furthermore, they may make different decisions in different ways. Also, their styles may alter when they make decisions in conjunction with other people.

You can assist clients to become more aware of their decision-making styles and their positive or negative consequences. Though far from an exhaustive listing, here are eight styles that describe how people make individual decisions.

- *Rational*: You dispassionately and logically appraise all important information and then select the best option in light of your criteria.
- *Feelings-based:* Though you may generate and appraise different options, the basis for choice is what intuitively feels right. This style emphasizes getting in touch with what you truly feel.
- *Impulsive:* You make decisions rapidly, based on sudden impulses. You act on initial and surface feelings rather than exploring and evaluating options.
- *Hypervigilant:* You try too hard. You become so anxious and aroused by the conflict and stress triggered by the decision that your decision-making efficiency decreases. You may become indecisive and fail to see the forest for the trees.
- *Avoidant:* You cope with decisions by refusing to confront them, hoping they will go away, and procrastinating over them.
- *Conformist:* You conform to what others expect of you. You allow your decisions to be heavily influenced, if not made, by others.
- *Rebellious:* You rebel against what others expect of you. Your decisions are dependent on what others think, though in an oppositional way.
- *Ethical:* The framework for your choice is a code of ethics, be it religious or secular.

Sometimes helpers need to assist clients to become more aware of their styles of joint decision making. Frequently, clients are in situations where they have differences or potential conflicts of interest with others (for instance, their partners). Following are three main styles of joint decision making.

- *Competitive:* You operate on an "I win, you lose" basis and view decisions as competition for scarce resources. You think and, very likely behave, aggressively.
- *Compliant:* You are nonassertive and go along with or give in to the other person. This can be an "I lose, you win" style.

- *Collaborative:* You search assertively for a solution that best meets each person's needs. You search for an "I win, you win too" solution. If necessary, you make rational compromises in the interest of the relationship.

You can assist clients in identifying their decision-making styles and exploring their strengths and weaknesses. Some clients may need to think through the consequences of their decision-making styles more thoroughly (for instance, impulsively choosing friends, or buying goods on credit). You require skills such as reflective listening and confrontation when clients explore decision-making styles and their consequences. You may need to challenge clients who distance themselves from responsibility for decisions and who do not perceive their consequences accurately.

Help Clients Develop Rational Decision-Making Skills

Some clients require assistance in learning to make decisions in a systematic fashion. Rational decision making can be viewed as taking place in two main stages: first, confronting and making the decision; second, implementing and evaluating it. Following is a seven-step framework for rational decision making within the context of the two main stages.

Stage 1: Confronting and Making the Decision

Step 1:   *Confront the decision.* Component skills include acknowledging the need for decisions and clearly stating the decision to be made.

Step 2:   *Generate options and gather information about them.* Some clients may be poor at generating options and thus restrict their decision effectiveness. Other skills weaknesses include inability to identify and gather relevant information.

Step 3:   *Assess the predicted consequences of options.* Clients need to perceive accurately and to evaluate positive and negative short-term and long-term consequences, both for themselves and others.

Step 4:   *Commit yourself to a decision.* Clients need to go beyond making rational decisions to committing themselves to implement them. Clients may have various barriers to commitment, including post-decisional anxieties and conflict (Janis & Mann, 1977).

Stage 2: Implementing and Evaluating the Decision

Step 5:   *Plan how to implement the decision.* Component skills of planning include: stating goals and sub-goals clearly; breaking down tasks; generating and assessing alternative courses of action; anticipating difficulties and setbacks; and identifying sources of support.

Step 6   *Implement the decision.* Clients need to consider when best to implement decisions and be open to feedback during implementation. Clients may require skills of rewarding themselves for performing targeted behaviors (for instance, by positive self-talk, or more tangible rewards such as a new item of clothing or special entertainment).

Step 7:   *Assess the actual consequences of implementation.* Rational decision making requires accurate perception of feedback and a willingness to act on it. Clients may stick with original decisions or modify or discard them.

Especially if you work in a decision-related area (for instance, as a career counselor), you can make clients more aware of the steps of rational decision making. One approach is to go through the steps, preferably using a whiteboard, and then giving clients a handout. In addition, you can ask clients to identify decision-making strengths and weaknesses. Take into account previous skills weaknesses when assisting clients to deal with current decisions. Clients can also work through current decisions in terms of the steps of rational decision making. Here, focus on developing clients' skills rather than doing the work for them. For example, rather than saying "Your options seem to be . . . ," you might ask "What are your options and what information do you require to assess them adequately?"

Skill 10: Prevent and Manage Problems and Alter Problematic Skills

Decision making and problem management overlap. The previous section focused on making decisions at major and minor turning points, where clients need to decide among options. Here the focus is helping clients use thinking skills to prevent or manage thoughts, feelings, and behaviors that are problematic for them.

Help Clients to Prevent Problems

Helpers can assist clients to recognize the preventive function of using good thinking skills in their daily lives. When thinking effectively, clients may be less disposed to a range of problems. Good thinking skills make them more confident persons, less prone to be threatened by imaginary (as opposed to real) difficulties. Clients can also acquire skills of anticipating problems and nipping them in the bud. For example, clients able to anticipate when they are at risk of excessive stress are in a better position to take preventive action than those less aware. Given awareness of the risk of allowing themselves to be excessively stressed, clients may still need to use a range of thinking skills to prevent them from giving in to bad habits (for instance, possessing realistic rules about achievement). Also, clients who have come to helping with stress-related problems are never totally cured. They still need to use their thinking skills to prevent recurrences.

Help Clients to Manage Problems and Alter Problematic Skills

Managing problems effectively requires clients to use many of the same skills as for making decisions. Nevertheless, there are important differences (for instance, in how problems are assessed and redefined). The lifeskills helping model is a self-helping model. Helpers train clients to use the model to manage future problems and problematic skills. The five-stage DASIE model can be modified to CASIE when used for client self-helping purposes.

C	Confront	Identify and clarify my problem.
A	Assess	Look at my problem and redefine it in skills terms.
S	State	Verbalize working goals and plan self-helping interventions.
I	Implement	Put my plan into action.
E	Evaluate	Check out the consequences of implementing my plan.

Because of limited exposure, clients in short-term helping are unlikely to learn how to apply the lifeskills helping model to future problems. Clients in longer-term helping will acquire some knowledge of the model as they and their helpers work with the problematic skills underlying their problems. Furthermore, helpers may identify characteristic thinking skills weaknesses. Consequently, longer-term clients have a start in knowing where to look when assessing future problems. In addition, helpers can systematically train clients in how to prevent and manage problems. Such training may form part of stage 5 of the DASIE helper-client model—end and consolidate self-helping skills. Here helpers may use clients' anticipated future problems as case material to develop preventing and managing problems skills. Helpers require both good relationship and good training skills to translate the DASIE model effectively into its CASIE (client self-helping) format.

 ## CHAPTER HIGHLIGHTS

- Developing your own thinking skills is a good way to learn how to work with clients' thinking skills.
- When focusing on how clients think, you always require sensitivity to how they feel.
- Helpers and clients can usefully view thinking skills within the PTC (problem, thinking, consequences) and STC (situation, thinking, consequences) frameworks.
- Clients may work better if helpers present them with easily comprehensible rationales for focusing on how they think.
- Interventions for helping clients to own their responsibility for choosing include: raising consciousness about being a chooser; encouraging choice language; facilitating exploring choices; exploring opposites; confronting *not* acknowledging choice and externalizing; exploring defenses; and raising consciousness concerning death, dying, and finiteness.
- Helpers can train clients in the calming and coaching dimensions of coping self-talk and help them to combine self-talk with action.
- Interventions for choosing realistic personal rules emphasize assisting clients to: identify unrealistic rules; put unrealistic rules into the STC framework; dispute unrealistic rules; reformulate unrealistic into realistic rules; and change actions along with reformulated rules.
- Interventions for helping clients choose how they perceive include assisting them to: become aware of the influence of perception on feelings; know the difference between fact and inference; identify their characteristic perceptual distortions; learn to stop, think, generate, evaluate, and choose the best-fit perception; and develop reframing skills.
- Helpers can assist clients to develop skills of identifying inaccurate attributions and altering them to more accurate attributions. The skills for perceiving accurately are relevant to attributing accurately.
- Clients may inaccurately predict risk, reward, or both. You can assist clients to: become aware of their predictive styles;

become aware of current predictions and their consequences; generate and evaluate additional risks or rewards; assess probability; assess their coping capacity and support factors; and reality-test predictions.

- Helpers can assist clients to develop goal setting skills. Criteria for effective goals include: reflecting values, being realistic, being specific, and having a time frame.
- Helpers may need to develop clients' awareness of visualizing. Areas in which clients can develop visualizing skills include: relaxing, performing better, and breaking bad habits.
- With assistance, clients can become more aware of their decision-making styles and their consequences. In addition, clients can learn to apply the steps of rational decision making.
- The five-stage DASIE lifeskills helping model can be modified to CASIE when used for client self-helping purposes. CASIE's five stages are: (1) confront, identify, and clarify my problem; (2) assess my problem and redefine it in skills terms; (3) state working goals and plan self-helping interventions; (4) implement my plan; and (5) evaluate the consequences of using my plan.

❀ ❀ ❀   **CHAPTER ELEVEN**   ❀ ❀ ❀
HOW TO FOCUS ON ACTION SKILLS

Activity is the only road to knowledge.
—George Bernard Shaw

CHAPTER QUESTIONS

❀ *Why is it always important to focus on action skills?*

❀ *Why do helpers need helping relationship skills when developing clients' action skills?*

❀ *What are some skills for handling resistances to focusing on action skills?*

❀ *How can helpers develop client self-monitoring skills?*

❀ *How can helpers assist clients to rehearse action skills?*

❀ *How can helpers and clients time-table desired activities?*

❀ *How can helpers and clients plan sub-goals and sequence graded tasks?*

❀ *How can helpers assist clients to generate and evaluate alternative actions and action skills?*

❀ *How can helpers and clients design action skills experiments?*

❀ *How can helpers and clients design and use exercises and games?*

❀ *How can helpers assist clients to use self-reward?*

❀ *How can helpers use aides?*

❀ *How can helpers assist clients to identify and use supports?*

However well clients feel and think, unless they act effectively they are unlikely to attain personal goals. Action skills provide the link from the inner to the outer world, from self to others and the environment. Helpers and clients cannot afford to ignore action skills. Whereas the last chapter focused on how to develop clients' thinking skills (their inner game), this chapter focuses on how to develop clients' action skills (their outer game). Action skills entail verbal, voice, body, and touch messages. They relate to how clients act on their own and when with others. Though they are interrelated, here I focus more on learning new action skills and on developing existing strengths rather than on lessening and extinguishing existing weaknesses.

Helpers who have inadequately assessed clients may fail to (or may inadequately) intervene on action skills. Following are two examples of inadequate assessment.

Lucia was a beginning helper who brought a cassette of an initial interview to a supervision session. Lucia's client was Katrina, who spent much of the session talking with great intensity about her relationship with Carl, a student in her home economics class. Lucia never asked questions that established how Lucia and Carl actually related. At the end of the session, it emerged that Katrina and Carl had never spent any time together outside class. The so-called relationship took place largely within Katrina's head. Lucia had failed to elicit relevant information about how Katrina behaved to enable her to set appropriate action skills goals for subsequent interventions.

Andrew was a beginning helper who brought a cassette of an initial interview with Georgia, age 17, to a supervision session. Andrew allowed Georgia to talk at great length about how angry she was with her parents' behavior toward her. Every now and then Georgia would make remarks about how she behaved toward her parents (for in-stance, spending most of her time in her room, and not making the effort to socialize with her parents' friends). By allowing Georgia's main focus to be on how her parents treated her and never focusing on how Georgia behaved toward her parents, Andrew lost the opportu-nity to assess Georgia's action skills properly. Indeed, he probably colluded in keeping Georgia stuck in her present pattern of unproduc-tive behavior.

WHEN TO INTERVENE ON ACTION SKILLS

There are three main options for intervening on clients' action skills: (1) action skills before thinking skills, (2) thinking skills before action skills, and (3) thinking and action skills together.

1. *Action skills before thinking skills*: Without necessarily using skills language, you may focus early on getting clients to change how they act. A reason for intervening on action skills first is that many clients understand the need to change how they act more easily than the need to change how they think. Through-out helping, some clients work better with an approach focused on overt actions rather than on covert thoughts. Furthermore, some helpers consider that "It is much easier to change concrete actions, or to introduce new ones, than it is to change patterns of thinking" (Beck, 1988, p. 208). In addition, early successes in changing actions can instill confidence. For example, when working with severely depressed patients, Beck initially attempts to restore their functioning to premorbid levels through interven-tions such as scheduling activities (Beck, Rush, Shaw, & Emery, 1979). Early changes in actions can also engender goodwill in others. For instance, distressed couples who see some immediate positive changes in each other's behavior may create a better emotional climate to work on deeper issues (Beck, 1988; Stuart, 1980).

2. *Thinking skills before action skills:* Sometimes both helpers and clients may wish to intervene on thinking skills before turning to action skills. For example, clients may have numerous fears about changing their outer behavior. Changing private thoughts may seem less risky than altering outer behavior, which is mostly public. You may have to work with clients' fears about performing skills adequately, coping with the consequences of failure, coping with the consequences of success, and reluctance to give up rewarding secondary gains. Often, in relationship

conflicts, clients may externalize their problems onto partners. You can assist them to see their need for change before working with relevant action skills.

3. *Thinking and action skills together:* Frequently you can intervene simultaneously on thinking and action skills. For example, with clients whose fears about change are not excessive, you can work to overcome such fears when they train relevant action skills. You can focus on thinking and action skills when targeting distressing feelings such as anxiety, anger, shyness, and stress. Sometimes a thinking skill contributes to learning an action skill (for example, using visualized rehearsal of assertion skills). Thinking skills invariably are part of maintaining action skills (for instance, having a realistic expectation about taking responsibility for maintaining and developing skills after helping). Also, clients need to develop the capacity for self-instruction through the sequences of choices entailed in implementing action skills. Then action skills more clearly become self-helping skills.

IMPORTANCE OF THE HELPING RELATIONSHIP AND SUPPORT

Helpers need to create safe and constructive emotional climates for clients to develop action skills. You require helping relationship skills to support client learning both within and outside helping sessions. Remember, when focusing on action skills, that helpers always require sensitivity to clients' feelings.

Support In-Session Learning

Why is it important that you remember to use helping relationship skills to develop clients' action skills? The temptation for some helpers is to emphasize the didactic mode at the expense of facilitation. Following are reasons why clients require emotional support as they develop action skills. First, you avoid creating resistances in clients who feel they are taking part in a mechanical, teacher-knows-best process. Second, if feeling supported and understood, clients are more likely to engage in honest initial assessments of their skills strengths and weaknesses. Third, clients can air and work through their reservations about change. Fourth, they may feel freer to take part in decisions about learning goals and processes. Fifth, clients are more likely to motivate themselves and take risks in various learning

activities (for instance, role-plays). Sixth, after structured learning experiences, clients require debriefing. If they feel supported
and understood, they may be freer to give you and themselves
honest feedback about progress. Furthermore, they may feel better able to make links between in-session learning and out-of-
session reality.

Support Out-of-Session Learning

You can also use helping relationship skills to support out-of-
session learning. For example, toward the end of each session,
you can discuss with clients the appropriate homework goals
and activities. If they are in a good helping relationship, clients
can be more honest about which activities appeal to them and
why. Also, clients may share fears and anxieties about carrying
out tasks and discuss ways of overcoming anticipated difficulties.
Helping relationship skills are also useful when you debrief clients about homework. You can help clients to be honest and
accurate in assessing how they acted and what the consequences
were.

Attempts to implement targeted skills in real life can generate
strong feelings. Clients may feel discouraged at real or imagined
setbacks or elated at real or imagined successes. Effective helpers
support clients in their sorrows and joys as they struggle to acquire and apply action skills in their daily lives. Often clients
both require and show considerable courage as they use skills
outside helping.

MANAGE RESISTANCES TO
WORKING ON ACTION SKILLS

Having thoroughly conducted the first three lifeskills helping
stages, you run less risk of eliciting client resistances in the fourth
stage, when intervening to develop action skills. By now clients
should have agreed to develop specific action skills. Nevertheless, they may still have resistances of varying degrees of strength
(for instance, residual resistances about change, resistances
about the learning process, and resistances to applying skills
outside helping).

In Chapter 5, I reviewed some helper skills for dealing with
initial resistances. These skills were: rewarding listening, joining
with clients, giving permission to discuss reluctance and fears,
inviting collaboration, enlisting client self-interest, and rewarding silent clients for talking. Most of these skills are relevant to

dealing with resistances in the intervention stage. Here I focus on some additional managing resistances skills.

Work through clients' thinking blocks. Go beyond allowing clients to discuss their reluctance and fears to pinpoint the specific thoughts contributing to resistances. You may need to use a mixture of assessment, rewarding listening, and questioning skills. Beck (1988) lists four main beliefs that interfere with partners in distressed relationships changing their behavior: defeatist beliefs, self-justifying beliefs, reciprocity arguments, and the-problem-is-my-partner. Helpers can assist clients to identify such beliefs, challenge the thinking skills weaknesses involved in them (for instance, unrealistic prediction and inaccurate attribution), and help them choose more realistic ways of thinking.

Be clear and specific when presenting skills. Sometimes clients resist learning action skills because they do not understand them properly. In order to minimize this possibility, develop good presentation and demonstration skills. Furthermore, check how well clients understand skills.

Use reward skills. Your genuine interest in helping clients achieve action skills goals should reward their efforts. In addition, you can send verbal and nonverbal positive feedback messages, such as "Well done," and a smile. Furthermore, you can encourage clients to give themselves positive feedback when they attain goals and sub-goals.

Arrange for early success. Where possible, build in an easily attainable goal or sub-goal to allow clients to experience early success. Such success should strengthen their motivation.

Understand and anticipate difficulties. Where clients resist using skills in outside settings, find out their reasons for this. Often clients feel that they cannot cope with real or imagined difficulties. Help clients be specific about what might go wrong. Once such fears are out in the open, helpers and clients can develop strategies to deal with them.

Use confronting skills. Reward skills are the carrot, confronting skills are the stick. You can confront clients who state action skills goals and then make little effort to attain them. A possible response to a discrepancy between goal and effort is: "On the one hand you agreed to _____ (specify) as an action skills goal, yet I experience little

enthusiasm or effort on your part to attain it. What do you think of this observation?" In addition, you can either confront clients or assist clients to confront themselves with the consequences for self and others of not working hard enough on action skills.

Encourage clients to view themselves as researchers.   Clients may be more willing to attempt to use action skills outside helping if they do not feel that their whole personhood is at stake. One way of lessening threat is to encourage them to view attempts to change behavior as personal experiments in which they try out different behaviors and evaluate what happens. An extreme example of such an approach is Kelly's fixed-role therapy, where clients adopt a changed role for a specified period of time to see how it suits them (Kelly, 1955).

DEVELOP CLIENT, SELF-MONITORING SKILLS
(you must have why to monitor)

Following are examples of clients engaging in systematic self-monitoring.

Juan, 17, is trying to stop smoking. As part of his program, he not only keeps a daily tally of how many cigarettes he smokes, but also keeps a log of the time, antecedents, and consequences of each time he smokes.

Joanna, 53, is receiving help for depression. Joanna has a goal of increasing the number of times she engages in pleasant activities. She keeps a daily chart of each time she engages in a number of specific pleasant activities (Lewinsohn, Munoz, Youngren, & Zeiss, 1986).

Seiji, 39, has had heart problems and is on a weight-loss program. He keeps a chart listing his daily weight. Also each time he eats between meals, he records the time, what happened immediately before, what he eats, and the consequences of his behavior.

Theo, 26, is an unemployed client searching for a job. Theo keeps a daily record of each time he engages in a range of specific job-search activities (for instance, making phone and written applications).

Systematic self-monitoring or self-observation enables clients to become more aware of their thoughts, feelings, and actions. Here the main focus is on self-monitoring of actions. Systematic self-monitoring can be important at the start of, during, and after interventions focused on developing specific action skills.

Initially, it establishes a baseline and increases awareness. During an intervention, it acts as a reminder, a motivator, and a check on progress. Afterwards, self-monitoring is relevant to maintaining gains, though information may not be collected as systematically as during helping. Self-monitoring is best thought of as an adjunct to other interventions. The effects of self-monitoring as a treatment intervention alone are often short-lived (Thoresen & Mahoney, 1974).

Methods of Self-Monitoring

Following are some methods of self-monitoring.

Diaries and journals Keeping a diary or journal is one way of monitoring action skills. Clients may pay special attention to writing up critical incidents where skills have been used well or poorly. Although diaries and journals may be useful, some clients find this approach too easy to ignore and too unsystematic.

Frequency charts Frequency charts focus on how many times clients enact a specific behavior in a given period of time—be it daily, weekly, or monthly. For example, clients may tally up how many cigarettes they smoke in a day and then transfer this information to a monthly chart broken down by days. Take the earlier example of unemployed Theo, who is recording his job-search behaviors. Theo's helper gives him a job-search activity self-monitoring chart and suggests that he fill it out for the next two weeks. The chart has activities on the horizontal axis and days on the vertical axis (see Table 11.1). Where clients are only monitoring single actions, they may use wrist counters or pocket counters (Thoresen & Mahoney, 1974). However, they still need to transfer information gathered by such methods to frequency charts.

Stimulus-response-consequences logs To become more aware of their behavior and its consequences, clients can fill in three-column stimulus-response-consequences logs.

Stimulus (What happened?)	Response (How did I act?)	Consequences (What resulted?)

For example, clients who work on anger management skills might record each time they feel angry in the stimulus column, what they did in the response column, and the consequences for themselves and others in the consequences column.

Table 11.1 Theo's self-monitoring chart for recording job-search activities

Activity	1 M	2 T	3 W	4 Th	5 F	6 Sa	7 Su	8 M	9 T	10 W	11 Th	12 F	13 Sa	14 Su	15 M
Written application															
Phone application															
Letter inquiry															
Phone inquiry															
Cold canvass															
Approach to contact															
Employment center visit															
Interview attended															

Situation-thoughts-consequences logs Filling in three-column situation-thoughts-consequences logs can help clients to see the connections between how they think and how they act.

Situation (What happened and when?)	Thoughts (What did I think?)	Consequences (How did I feel and act?)

Use of targeted skills logs Helpers and clients need to go beyond monitoring actions to monitoring action skills. During the intervention stage, clients can usefully monitor and evaluate their use of targeted skills. For instance, a helper works with a teenager, Lori, on how to make assertive requests to her parents. Together, helper and client agree on the following verbal, voice, and body message sub-skills for each time Lori makes such a request: verbal messages, make "I" statements and say "please"; voice messages, speak with a calm, yet firm voice; body messages, use good eye contact and avoid threatening gestures such as finger pointing. Lori's helper asks her to complete an assertive request self-monitoring log after each request to her parents (see Table 11.2). In particular, the helper asks Lori to record how she uses targeted sub-skills.

Helper Skills for Assisting Self-Monitoring

Since self-monitoring tends to take place outside sessions, helper skills for assisting clients' self-monitoring overlap with those for assigning homework. Below are some ways helpers can assist clients to monitor themselves and to develop self-monitoring skills.

Offer reasons for self-monitoring. Clients are not in the habit of systematically recording observations about how they act. You need motivate them to do so. You may make explanatory remarks like "Counting how many times you perform a behavior daily, not only indicates how severe your problem is, but also gives us a baseline against which to measure your progress in dealing with it" or "Systematically writing down how you send verbal, voice, and action messages each time you make a behavior change request provides us with information we need to build your skills."

Train clients in discrimination and recording. Thoresen and Mahoney (1974) observe, "Individuals are not naturally accurate self-observers. Training in the discrimination and recording

Table 11.2 Lori's log for monitoring assertive requests

Lori's Assertive Request Skills

Verbal messages: Make "I" statements, say "please."
Voice messages: Speak calmly and firmly.
Body messages: Use good eye contact, avoid threatening gestures.

Date and Situation	How I Acted		
	Verbal Skills	**Voice Skills**	**Body Skills**
1.			
2.			
3.			
4.			
5.			
6.			
7.			
8.			

of behavior is essential" (p. 63). Clients require clarity, not only about what to record, but also about how to record it. In addition, clients need to become aware of any tendencies they have to misperceive or selectively perceive their actions (for instance, being more inclined to notice skills weaknesses than skills strengths).

Design simple and clear recording logs. Always supply the log yourself. Do not expect clients to make up their own logs. They may not do so in the first place and, if they do, they may get them wrong. Simple recording systems enhance comprehension and recording accuracy.

Use reward skills. Reward clients with interest and praise when they fill in logs. This guideline is based on the basic behavioral principle that actions that are rewarding are more likely to be repeated. Furthermore, always reward clients by debriefing when they finish self-monitoring tasks.

Encourage clients to evaluate self-monitoring information. When clients share self-monitoring logs with you, use this as a basis for their self-exploration and evaluation. When debriefing, assist them to understand the meaning of the information they have collected. However, do not do their work for them. After helping ends, you are not going to be around to assess the implications of their frequency counts and self-monitoring logs. You need to train them in how to do this for themselves.

Use other skills-building strategies. Do not expect clients to develop action skills on the basis of self-observation alone. They are likely to require other interventions (for example, behavior rehearsals) to develop action skills. Furthermore, they must work and practice to acquire and maintain skills.

CONDUCT ACTION SKILLS REHEARSALS AND ROLE-PLAYS

Learning any skill generally requires repeated performances of targeted behaviors. Rehearsals may take place immediately after initial coached performance of skills or later, both as clients apply targeted skills in their daily lives and as they seek further assistance during helping.

Methods of Rehearsal

Various methods of rehearsing action skills include the following.

Live rehearsal Live rehearsals can take place both within and outside helping sessions. For instance, the skills of progressive muscular relaxation can be rehearsed within and outside interviews. Bandura's participant modeling approach is an example of live rehearsal within helping sessions. Here helpers use rehearsal and practice with clients who have repeated trials in graded steps with such stimuli as snakes (Bandura, 1976; Jeffrey, 1976). Helpers assist clients to perform and rehearse feared actions by allowing them to use response aids (for instance, gloves for those afraid of snakes or furry animals).

Live rehearsals can take place outside helpers' offices, with or without helpers present. For instance, in working with agoraphobic clients, helpers might rehearse targeted skills by taking them into real-life anxiety-evoking settings. Much live rehearsal takes place without helpers. Sometimes such rehearsal takes place in private (for instance, practicing public speaking with a cassette recorder or in front of a mirror). On other occasions, clients may rehearse skills in "sheltered environments" (for example, with cooperative friends or relatives). On still other occasions, clients rehearse skills by using them in real-life situations. Here, using skills in less difficult situations may be a rehearsal for later, more difficult ones.

Role-play In role-plays, clients rehearse action skills in simulated (pretend) situations involving one or more others. Most often helpers play the part of the other person, but sometimes clients switch roles. Examples of role-playing to rehearse action skills include rehearsing job interview skills, discussing vocational choices with parents, phoning to ask for a date, and expressing appreciation to employees.

Role-play with accompanying self-talk An addition to role-play is to train clients in the accompanying self-talk. For instance, before Mario proceeds with action role-plays on discussing vocational choices with his parents, his helper rehearses him in calming and coaching self-talk. During the role-plays, Mario's helper responds as a parent in different ways (for instance, either being accepting or raising objections). With each variation, Mario verbalizes appropriate self-talk.

Visualized rehearsal Visualized rehearsal, also known as *imaginal* or *covert* rehearsal, is a form of mental rehearsal involving images. The images in visualized rehearsal are usually of actual rather than role-played scenes. As such, visualized rehearsals are often stepping stones to transferring skills to live situations. Clients imagine themselves actually asking girls for dates or discussing their vocational choices with parents. Clients can also imagine themselves using calming and coaching self-talk. Often helpers assign visualized rehearsal as homework.

Skills for Assisting Rehearsal

Many helper skills for assisting clients in rehearsing action skills overlap with those of coaching (for example, giving clear instructions, breaking tasks down, and using feedback skills). Here my focus is on action role-plays of actual situations where clients require the targeted skills. Following are some helper skills for role-play rehearsals.

Present a rationale. Some clients may find the idea of role-playing off-putting. For example, they may be self-conscious about their acting skills. You may need to offer a rationale to clients to ease anxieties and help motivate them. Here is a rationale for using role-play rehearsal with a client, Darren, who gets excessively angry when his teenage daughter Virginia comes home late.

> **Helper:** Darren, I think it would be helpful if we role-played how you might use your new skills to cope better with Virginia next time she comes home late. I realize it may seem artificial acting the scene here. However, role-playing gives us the chance to rehearse different ways you might behave—your words, voice messages, and body messages—so that you are better prepared for the real event. It is safer to make mistakes here where it doesn't count. There is no substitute for learning by doing. What do you think about this approach?

Set the scene. Elicit information about the physical setting of proposed scenes, what other characters are involved, and how they behave. If you are to role-play someone, say Virginia, collect sufficient information about Virginia's verbal, voice, and body messages so that you can get into the role. Depending on what sort of office you have, you may be able to move the furniture around to create a stage (for instance, a family living room).

Assess current action skills. Usually, you spend time well if you conduct assessment role-plays in which clients demonstrate how they currently act in problem situations. You can elicit much relevant information about nonverbal communication that may not be apparent if clients only talk about how they act. Assessment role-plays can also review how clients think in the real-life situations.

Formulate changed actions. Collaborate with clients to formulate new and better ways of acting that use targeted lifeskills and still feel comfortable for clients. Facilitate clients' suggestions before making your own. You may ask, "How do you think you might use your new skills to behave differently in the situation?" Together with clients, you can generate and review alternative scripts. Also review appropriate voice and body messages. As part of this process, you can demonstrate appropriate action skills. In addition, review with clients how to cope with different responses by others.

Rehearse changed actions.   Once clients are reasonably clear in their new roles, and helpers understand their "parts," trial enactments or rehearsals take place. Avoid trying to do too much—or anything really difficult—too soon. You may allow role-plays to run their course; alternatively, you may intervene at one or more points along the way to provide feedback and coaching. Rehearsal role-plays are dry runs of how to use action skills in specific situations. Video feedback may be used as part of coaching both during and after role-plays. You may need a number of rehearsals to build clients' skills. Some of these role-plays may involve responding in different ways to clients. For example, clients asking for dates by phone may get accepted, postponed, or rejected in separate role-plays.

Role reversal and mirroring are psychodrama techniques that you could use (Blatner, 1989; Moreno, 1959). In role reversal, you get clients to play the other person in interactions. Role reversals force clients to get into another's internal viewpoint. With mirroring, you mirror back clients' verbal, voice, and body messages. Clients see themselves as others experience them.

Rehearse thinking skills.   You may rehearse clients' thinking skills alongside their action skills. For example, you can rehearse clients in the calming and coaching dimensions of appropriate self-talk to accompany new action skills. In addition, you can rehearse clients in other thinking skills relevant to targeted action skills. For instance, rehearsing visualizing restful scenes can accompany rehearsing relaxing by means of progressive muscular relaxation.

Process role-plays.   Processing involves spending time dealing with the clients' thoughts and feelings that were generated by role-plays. Together you can discuss learnings from them and make plans to transfer rehearsed skills outside. You can ask clients processing questions like "How were you feeling in that role play?," "How well do you think you used your skills in that rehearsal?," "What have you learned in that role-play to use outside?," and "What difficulties do you anticipate in implementing your changed behavior and how can you overcome them?" After processing the previous role-play, helpers and clients may move on to the next role-play either with the same or another problem situation.

TIME-TABLE ACTIVITIES

Helpers can work with clients to make a time table for desired activities and to build clients' skills in this area. How helpers assist in scheduling activities varies according to clients' needs.

Areas for Time-Tabling

Following are some areas in which time tables may assist clients to perform desired activities and build action skills. Table 11.3 shows a blank weekly time table that can serve numerous purposes.

Time-tabling daily activities Beck and his colleagues (Beck & Emery, 1985; Beck, Rush, Shaw, & Emery, 1979) stress the usefulness of developing daily activity schedules for clients who are immobilized by depression and anxiety. Helpers and clients collaborate to plan specific activities for one day at a time. These planned activities are recorded on a weekly time table, with days represented by columns and hours represented by rows. As clients develop skills and confidence, they can do their own activity scheduling, with the last activity for each day being the scheduling of the following day. To ease pressure, you can instruct clients to state what, rather than how much, they will accomplish and to realize that it is OK not to complete all activities—the important thing is to try.

Time-tabling minimum goals Some clients get extremely anxious over performing certain tasks and then engage in avoidance behavior. For instance, Alison is a college student who is very distressed because she is not studying. She has lost all sense of control over her work. One approach to Alison is to assist her to make a time table of some minimum goals that she feels prepared to commit herself to keeping before the next session. Her minimum goals may be as little as three half-hour study periods during the week. For each study period, Alison needs to write down time, task, and place. This does not mean that she cannot spend more time studying if she wishes. With certain highly anxious clients, helpers need to be very sensitive to avoid becoming just another source of pressure. The idea of scheduling minimum goals is to show clients that they can succeed in achieving modest targets instead of having to achieve large goals. Later on, Alison may increase her study periods.

Time-tabling to create personal space Many clients need time-table skills to help them prioritize and create personal space.

Table 11.3 Weekly time table

Date							
Time	**Mon.**	**Tues.**	**Wed.**	**Thurs.**	**Fri.**	**Sat.**	**Sun.**
6:00							
7:00							
8:00							
9:00							
10:00							
11:00							
12:00							
1:00							
2:00							
3:00							
4:00							
5:00							
6:00							
7:00							
8:00							
9:00							
10:00							
11:00							

Such clients include: housewives trying to stop being at everyone's beck and call; stressed executives needing to create family and relaxation time; depressed people needing to schedule more pleasant activities; and students needing to plan their study time so that they know when they can say yes rather than no to requests to go out. Helpers can assist clients to define personal space goals and to allocate time accordingly.

Time-tabling to keep contracts Clients make commitments to perform certain activities to themselves, to helpers, and to third parties (for instance, their spouses). You can assist clients to develop skills of keeping commitments by getting them to make a time table that shows when they are going to carry out these activities. For instance, Allen is a teenager who has been resisting doing any of the household chores. He finally decides he is prepared to mow the lawn each week. Allen may be more likely to keep this commitment if he time-tables when he is going to perform this task.

Time-tabling homework Certain homework activities lend themselves to a time table (for instance, practicing progressive muscular relaxation or planning an activity schedule for the next day). Other homework activities do not lend themselves so easily to regular scheduling, but are more likely to be performed if clients create a time table. For instance, Jim's homework includes developing an effective resume, a task he has avoided. Jim is more likely to complete this task and to develop resume-making skills if he blocks out specific periods of time to do it properly.

Some Skills for Working with Time Tables

As shown above, many reasons exist why helpers and clients use time tables. Below are some helper skills for using time tables to develop action skills.

Provide time tables. Give clients time tables. Do not expect clients to have easy access to made-up time tables or to make the effort to develop their own.

Offer reasons for time tables. For some clients, the need to schedule activities and goals is obvious. Other clients require an explanation. You may need to confront certain clients who insufficiently acknowledge the negative consequences of their failure to create a time table.

Be sensitive to anxieties and resistances.   Time tables can
be very threatening to highly anxious clients—they may
feel they are failures if they don't do as agreed. Be very
sensitive to how much pressure a time table creates for
vulnerable clients. Some clients may play time-table
games; either consciously or unconsciously they have little
intention of achieving goals.

Do not overdo.   Even with less vulnerable clients, helpers may
overdo the time table. Clients can spend too much time scheduling activities and too little time carrying them out.

Review progress.   At the next session, check with clients on
progress in adhering to scheduled activities and on any difficulties experienced.

Work with thinking skills.   Often the reasons clients do not ad-
here to time tables reflect faulty thinking skills (for instance,
perfectionist rules about achievement). Identify and work with
interfering thinking skills weaknesses.

Help clients to develop time-tabling skills.   Always work closely
with clients regarding what goes in the time table. Aim to help
them develop time-table skills so that you can gradually withdraw from assisting them.

PLAN SUB-GOALS AND
SEQUENCE GRADED TASKS

When helpers attempt to develop clients' action skills, planning
sub-goals and sequencing graded tasks overlap. Helpers may
plan sub-goals in two main ways.

Sequencing Sub-Skills

When assisting clients to learn complex skills, you can break the
skills down into their component parts. Then decide in what
order you wish to train each component. For example, Lori and
her helper have the overall goal of being able to make assertive
requests to her parents. However, Lori's helper decides during
their sessions to focus on verbal messages first, voice messages
second, and body messages third. To date, there appears little
research on how helpers can best sequence sub-skills.

Sequencing Graded Tasks

Sequencing graded tasks is sometimes called graded task assignment (Beck, Rush, Shaw, & Emery, 1979) or setting proximal sub-goals (Bandura, 1986). A useful distinction is that between setting distant and proximal (nearer) goals. The research evidence is equivocal regarding the effectiveness of setting distant goals (Bandura, 1986; Whelan, Mahoney, & Meyers, 1991). More certain appears the desirability of setting proximal goals or sub-goals (Bandura, 1986; Stock & Cervone, 1990). Bandura observes that "sub-goals provide present guides and inducements for action, while sub-goal attainments produce efficacy information and self-satisfactions that sustain one's efforts along the way" (Bandura, 1986, p. 475).

The following is an example of sequencing graded tasks to develop action skills.

Russ is a shy college student with an action skills goal of developing his dating skills. Together Russ and his helper draw up a sequence of graded tasks that Russ thinks he can complete before their next session.

1. *Say hello to the girls in my class when I see them on campus.*
2. *Sit down in the student union with a group of classmates of both sexes and join in the conversation.*
3. *Sit next to a girl in my class and initiate a very brief conversation in which I ask her what she thinks about the class.*
4. *Sit next to a girl in class and hold a slightly longer conversation in which I make a personal disclosure at least once.*

Near the start of the next session, Russ and his helper review progress in attaining each task. The helper facilitates Russ in sharing thoughts and feelings about progress. The helper emphasizes that Russ is achieving his sub-goals as a result of his willingness to take risks, his effort, and his skill. As a result of feedback that Russ both gets from others and gives himself about his growing skills, the helper and he develop further graded tasks for the next between-session period. At progress reviews, the helper rewards Russ for working to develop his skills whether or not he is successful. For instance, when Russ eventually asks a girl for a date, the helper rewards him for effort even if she refuses. The helper encourages Russ to view as learning experiences all attempts to attain graded tasks.

Skills for Sequencing and Reviewing Graded Tasks

Following are some helper skills for sequencing and reviewing graded tasks.

Relate graded tasks to targeted skills.   Always make links between tasks and skills. The purpose of graded tasks is not only to
assist clients to manage specific problems, but also to help them
develop specific skills. You can encourage clients to view graded
tasks as ways of developing their skills for handling not only
immediate but also future problems.

Sequence graded tasks in collaboration with clients.   Work with
clients to assess whether they feel willing and able to work on
graded tasks. Discuss with them the tasks that are important for
them. When sequencing tasks, go at a comfortable pace. Start
with small steps that clients think they can achieve. Be prepared
to build in intermediate steps if clients think the progression of
tasks is too steep. As depicted in Figure 11.1, graded tasks should
be stepping stones for clients to develop skills and confidence.

Encourage realistic evaluation of skills.   Before clients attempt
graded tasks, encourage them to assess what skills they need to

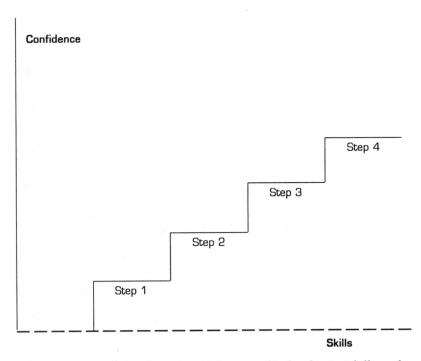

Figure 11.1   Graded tasks as stepping stones for developing skills and
confidence

attain them. Also, when reviewing progress, assist clients to evaluate use of targeted skills.

Encourage clients to view themselves as practitioner-researchers. To avoid connotations of failure, encourage clients to view attempting each graded task as an experiment in which they gain valuable information about themselves. Even if unsuccessful, attempting tasks provides useful learning experiences about how clients think, feel, and act.

Pay attention to feelings and thoughts. Facilitate clients in sharing their feelings and thoughts about attempting graded tasks. Work with clients' thinking skills weaknesses as necessary.

Assist clients to own successes. Encourage clients, not only to acknowledge their successes, but also to realize that success results from willingness to take risks, from skills, and from effort.

Sequence new and different tasks as appropriate. In collaboration with clients, sequence either easier or more difficult tasks as necessary.

Encourage homework and practice. Though some graded tasks are performed within helping sessions, most are performed outside. Where feasible, encourage clients to rehearse and practice graded tasks before trying them. Repeated success experiences with specific tasks consolidates clients' skills and confidence.

ASSIST CLIENTS TO GENERATE AND EVALUATE ALTERNATIVE ACTIONS AND ACTION SKILLS

Many clients act in repetitive ways as if they had no choice. In Chapter 10, I discussed helping clients to stop, think, generate, evaluate, and choose the best-fit perception. Here I shift the focus to helping clients generate and assess alternative actions and action skills. Clients' thinking skills weaknesses provide many blocks to considering alternative actions (for instance, spouses who continually externalize blame to partners are likely not only to think but also to act rigidly). In such instances, helpers need to work with relevant thinking skills as well as with action skills. On other occasions, clients may simply have developed a style of acting where they either do not consider alternatives at all, do not consider enough of them, or do not consider them in skills terms. Following are some examples.

Miguel, 11, thinks that the only way to act when he feels angry with another boy is to punch him.

Harriet, 32, criticizes her children vehemently whenever they leave their rooms untidy.

Frances, 58, longs for a phone call from her son Bennie. When Bennie finally calls, Frances starts complaining that he did not call sooner.

Helper Skills for Assisting Clients to Generate and Assess Alternative Actions and Action Skills

Following are some helper skills for helping clients generate and assess alternative actions and action skills.

Assist clients to define goals.   In these examples you could work with Miguel, Harriet, and Frances to clarify what they wanted from their overall relationships with peers, children, and son, respectively. Then you could assist them in stating appropriate goals for specific situations (for example, feeling provoked by another boy, getting frustrated over untidy rooms, and feeling hurt by lack of a phone call).

Train clients in appropriate self-talk.   Assist clients to become aware that they always have choices in how they act. They do not have to act out their first idea of how to behave. Instead they can instruct themselves to say, "Stop. Think. What are my goals? What are alternative ways to attain them, and what action skills do I need?"

Maintain a skills focus.   Help clients to analyze their behavior in skills terms. It is insufficient to think of alternative actions without also thinking of the skills entailed in such actions. For instance, if Harriet decides that her best course of action is to sit down and talk to her children, she still needs to work on the verbal, voice, and body message skills of doing this effectively.

Assist clients to generate alternatives.   In addition to rewarding listening, following are some helper skills for assisting clients to generate alternatives.

1. *Use questions.* Here are some questions that helpers might ask: "What are your options for how you act?" and "What action skills do you need to attain your goal?"

2. *Confront.* Helpers can ask questions that encourage clients to confront themselves (for example, "Is your present way of acting likely to help you attain your goals?" or "How is your current behavior helping you?"). Helpers may also confront directly: "The course of action you propose seems contrary to your goals. Are there any other approaches?"

3. *Assist brainstorming.* Helpers can loosen clients' thinking by getting them to brainstorm options. Two rules for brainstorming are (1) quantity is good, and (2) suspend evaluation of ideas until later. Encourage clients to generate options before suggesting options yourself.

4. *Assist exploring opposite ways of acting.* Sometimes, though not always, clients gain valuable insights by exploring ways of acting opposite to their current intentions. For instance, the spouse who is going to give his wife a piece of his (angry) mind might explore taking a conciliatory approach to her.

Assist clients to evaluate alternatives.   Assist clients to evaluate the consequences for themselves and others of alternative actions. When evaluating different courses of action, helpers and clients need to pay close attention not only to what is done but also to how it is done. As a result of evaluating alternatives, clients should choose the best-fit course of action that is most likely to help them attain their goals.

Support clients in implementing best-fit actions and action skills.   Support clients as they implement their chosen actions in real life. For instance, you can work with them to identify and develop relevant skills for their best-fit actions. Furthermore, offer support and encouragement to clients as they develop skills for generating and evaluating alternative actions outside helping.

USE ACTION SKILLS EXPERIMENTS

A major concern of all effective helpers is how best to help clients take the risks of changing their behaviors. Another major concern is how best to help them transfer trained skills outside of helping. Action skills experiments provide an excellent way to approach both concerns. Clients, in conjunction with helpers, develop hypotheses about the consequences of using outside helping the skills they learned inside. Then clients implement the skills and evaluate the consequences of their changed behavior. An advantage of viewing changing action skills in experimental terms is that it helps clients to be detached about what they do (and its results). When experiments do not work out quite as planned, clients do not have to think they failed. Rather, each experiment is a learning experience that gathers information useful for developing action skills.

Often experiments simultaneously focus on changing both thinking and action skills. For instance, Kevin wants to increase his skills at showing affection to his girlfriend Tanya. An experiment focused solely on action skills might target Kevin's skills at sending verbal, voice, and body messages of affection. An experiment focused solely on thinking skills might target Kevin's skills of coping self-talk before, during, and after he sends affection messages. An experiment focused on both action and thinking skills would target both how Kevin sends affection messages to Tanya and his use of coping self-talk. In this section, for the sake of simplicity, I focus on changing action skills experiments.

Steps in Action Skills Experiments

Experiments focus on the use of targeted skills in specific situations or relationships. There are six main steps in designing, conducting, and evaluating action skills experiments.

1. *Assess.* Helpers and clients assess clients' action skills strengths and weaknesses in problem situations.
2. *Formulate changed action skills.* Helpers and clients work out how to behave differently in certain situations by using better action skills. They pay attention to voice and body messages as well as to verbal messages
3. *Make an "If . . . then . . ." statement.* The "If" part of the statement relates to clients' rehearsing, practicing, and then using their changed action skills. The "then" part of the statement indicates the specific consequences they predict will follow from using their changed skills.
4. *Rehearse and practice.* Possibly with assistance from helpers, clients need to rehearse and practice changed action skills to have a reasonable chance of implementing them properly.
5. *Try out changed action skills.* Clients implement changed action skills in actual problem situations.
6. *Evaluate.* Initially clients should evaluate their use of changed action skills on their own. This evaluation should focus on questions like "How well did I use my changed action skills?," "What were the positive and negative consequences of using the targeted skills, for myself and for

others?," "Have my predictions been confirmed or negated?," and "Do I want to use my changed action skills in the future?" Afterwards helpers can assist clients in processing the learnings from their experiments.

DESIGNING AN ACTION SKILLS EXPERIMENT

Following is an illustrative outline for an experiment in which Kevin uses targeted action skills in how he expresses affection to Tanya.

What Happens When I Use My Action Skills for Expressing Affection to Tanya

Part A: Assessment

1. For a period of a week, monitor on a worksheet how I send affection messages to Tanya. Focus on strengths and weaknesses in each of the following sub-skills of expressing affection: verbal, voice, body, touch, and action messages. Use the following column headings on my worksheet.

Date and Situation	Expressing Affection Messages

2. List all the positive thoughts and feelings that I either fail to or inadequately convey in our relationship.

_____

_____

_____

_____

3. Based on the answers to questions 1 and 2 above, assess my action skills strengths and weaknesses in sending affection messages to Tanya. Use the following column headings.

Expressing Affection Skills Strengths	Expressing Affection Skills Weaknesses

Part B: Make an "If . . . Then . . ." Statement

Make an "If . . . then . . ." statement along the lines of:

"If I use the following changed action skills (specify) to express affection to Tanya during the next week, then these specific consequences [for instance, (a) I will feel better about myself for being honest, and (b) Tanya will feel and act more positively toward me] are likely to follow."

If _____

_____

then

(a) _____

(b) _____

(c) _____

(d) _____

Part C: Try Out and Evaluate My Action Skills

During the upcoming week, try out my changed action skills in expressing affection to Tanya. What are the positive and negative consequences for myself and Tanya? Have my predictions been confirmed or negated? Have I learned anything useful from this experiment? If so, what?

_____

_____

_____

_____

_____

_____

_____

USE EXERCISES AND GAMES

Exercises are structured activities designed with a specific learning purpose. The training manual that accompanies this book contains numerous exercises designed to build your lifeskills helping skills. Whether for children or adults, exercises involving play are called *games*. Helpers may assist clients to develop action skills, thinking skills, and action skills with accompanying self-talk by using exercises and games. Clients may use these materials both within sessions and as homework assignments.

There are two main sources of exercises and games: You can use other people's or make up your own. Using the relationship skills area as an example, existing sources of exercises include those in Egan's *You and Me* (1977), Johnson's *Reaching Out* (1990), my *Human Relationships: A Skills Approach* (Nelson-Jones, 1990b), and Pfeiffer and his associates' series of structured exercises, *The* (date) *Annual Developing Human Resources* (Pfeiffer, Goodstein, & Jones, 1972–1992).

Other people's material may not be appropriate either for the clientele or for specific individuals with whom you work. If so, you may need to construct some exercises. Such exercises are particularly cost effective if they can be used repeatedly. For instance, helpers who work with clients, many of whom have relationship difficulties, might often use exercises on making assertive requests to change others' behaviors. I encourage you not only to use existing material, but also to tap your creativity in designing learning material tailor-made to your clients and needs.

Designing Exercises

Following are guidelines for designing exercises and games.

Set clear, specific, and relevant goals. Clients should be clear about the targeted skills they are expected to work on in the exercise. Helpers should present and demonstrate these skills before asking clients to do the exercises.

Emphasize take-home skills. Exercises should be highly practical and focused on learning by doing. Avoid vague exercises unrelated to the development of specific take-home skills. Many beginning trainees have difficulty putting sufficient practical emphasis into their exercises.

Make written instructions available. Ensure that clients are clear about and remember an exercise's instructions. Written instructions, as contrasted with verbal instructions, lessen the chance of error when clients perform exercises.

Demonstrate the exercise.   Demonstrate the exercises after giving instructions and before asking clients to perform them. Such demonstrations go beyond demonstrating skills or sub-skills to show how to do the exercise.

Coach and provide feedback.   Where necessary, coach clients on how to do the exercise.

Process the experience.   When clients have completed the exercise, give them the opportunity to share their thoughts and feelings about it. Ensure that clients understand the main learnings from the exercise.

Pilot the exercise.   If possible, pilot your exercise to see if it works. If necessary, refine the exercise or even discard it and try again.

ASSIST CLIENTS TO USE SELF-REWARD

Helpers may choose to use reinforcement or reward to help develop action skills. Helper-administered rewards include praise, encouragement, smiles, and nods. However, ultimately clients have to learn to perform targeted action skills independent of your rewards. Clients may also influence and administer their own rewards. Approaches using helper-administered and client-administered rewards are based on operant conditioning (Skinner, 1953, 1969). The word *operant* emphasizes the fact that behavior operates on the environment to produce consequences as well as being influenced by (or contingent upon) the responses produced by that environment. Where clients find responses rewarding, the probability of their using the action skills again increases, and vice versa.

Basic Concepts

Here, I use the everyday word *reward* in preference to the more technical term *reinforcement*. Reward better suits the language of self-helping. Following are some basic reward concepts.

1. *Positive reward*: Providing positive rewards entails presenting stimuli that increase the probability of responses occurring (for example, money

increases the probability of work responses). Positive rewards can be verbal, material, and imaginal.

2. *Negative reward:* Negative reward also increases the probability of a response's occurring through removing something from the situation (for example, removing teachers from classrooms increases the probability of pupils' talking).

3. *Contingencies of reward:* To consider adequately the contingencies or circumstances involved in the provision of rewards, take into account: (a) the occasion upon which a response occurs, (b) the response itself, and (c) the rewarding consequences.

4. *Schedules of reward:* Basically there are three reward schedules: (a) reward each response, (b) do not reward any response, and (c) intermittently reward responses. Intermittent rewards can be very powerful (for instance, in sustaining gambling behavior).

5. *Self-reward:* Here clients influence how they act by administering their own rewards.

6. *Prompting and fading:* Prompts are verbal, physical, or environmental cues that direct clients' attention to desired actions. Fading entails progressively eliminating prompts.

7. *Shaping:* Action skills may be shaped by rewarding successive approximations to targeted goals.

8. *Covert conditioning:* Using clients' imaginations to provide consequences of varying degrees of reward.

Assist Clients to Identify Suitable Rewards

In many instances, clients find that using targeted action skills is intrinsically rewarding and also brings about rewards from others. For instance, clients developing appreciation skills may enjoy using compliments skills, both to give pleasure and to receive it. On other occasions clients may need to strengthen their motivation by giving themselves rewards. The basic idea in using self-reward to develop action skills is that clients make the administration of rewards contingent upon occurrence of target behaviors (Watson & Tharp, 1989). Rewards should be accessible and potent (Cormier & Cormier, 1985). Consequently, you may need to assist clients in identifying suitable rewards. There are several ways of helping clients identify rewards, including: asking them; getting them to monitor what they find rewarding; asking others who know them (though here you must be sensitive to confidentiality); observing them; and asking them to fill out reward questionnaires.

MacPhillamy and Lewinsohn's Pleasant Events Schedule is an example of a questionnaire to identify rewards (Lewinsohn,

Munoz, Youngren, & Zeiss, 1986; MacPhillamy & Lewinsohn, 1982). The questionnaire consists of 320 pleasing events. Respondents rate each item on three-point scales for frequency and pleasantness during the previous month. The authors believe that one way to combat clients' feelings of depression is to encourage them to participate in more rewarding activities. Illustrative pleasant events include: being with happy people, thinking about friends, breathing clean air, listening to music, reading a good book, petting and necking, eating good meals, being seen as sexually attractive, seeing beautiful scenery, and visiting friends.

For children, pictures may portray rewards. An example is Daley's reinforcement menu for finding effective rewards for 8-year-old to 11-year-old mentally retarded children (Daley, 1969). Daley enclosed 22 high-probability rewarding activities drawn in color in a single book (the "menu") with one activity per page. Children identified rewarding activities from the menu book.

Assist Clients to Deliver Self-Rewards

Helpers can assist clients in knowing how to deliver positive self-rewards. There are two main categories of reward that clients can give themselves: external and internal.

1. *External rewards:* External rewards includes: (1) giving the self new rewards that are outside the client's everyday life (for example, a new item of clothing or a special event), and (2) initial denial of some pleasant everyday experience to be enjoyed later following completion of a desired action. Kanfer and Gaelick (1986) observe that, wherever possible, a positive self-reward should be relevant to the target behavior (for instance, clients achieving weight-loss goals might buy slimmer fitting clothes).
2. *Internal reward:* Internal rewards include self-talk statements like "That's great," "I did it," or "Well done" that clearly indicate the client's satisfaction at performing a sub-goal or goal. Clients can also use their imaginations to visualize significant others praising their efforts.

Work with clients to determine the precise conditions for administering rewards to themselves. In making positive self-reward plans, several considerations may be pertinent: identification of rewards, sequencing of graded steps in developing action skills, and clear connections between achievement and reward.

It is best for clients to reward themselves immediately after performing targeted action skills or sub-skills.

Helpers may encourage clients to draw up personal contracts that specify the relationship between administering positive self-rewards and developing targeted action skills. Alternatively, you and your clients may draw up contracts between yourselves. Such bilateral contracts are a transitional phase in plans aimed at developing clients' self-helping skills.

Not all clients like self-reward plans or follow them. Some clients consider the use of self-reward too mechanical. Also, you may introduce self-reward ideas too soon, before clients are sufficiently motivated to change. You need to assess how well clients accept the idea of self-reward and their motivation for change. Often you also need to intervene with clients' thinking skills weaknesses that hinder change.

ASSIST CLIENTS TO MODIFY
THEIR ENVIRONMENTS

In addition to helping clients use self-reward, you can assist them in modifying their environments to overcome action skills weaknesses and develop action skills strengths. Clients can modify environments to influence action skills prior to their execution.

Helpers can assist clients to develop *stimulus control* skills (Thoresen & Mahoney, 1974). With stimulus control, clients learn to use presence or absence of environmental prompts to influence behavior. Stimulus control can be used both to develop strengths and modify weaknesses. An example of the use of stimulus control to enhance an action skills strength is that of students who specify a place that they only use for study. Examples of stimulus control to help overcome an action skills weakness were developed for Terry, who has a goal of losing 25 pounds by the end of the next three months. Ways in which Terry modifies her environment to influence her eating skills weakness include: putting food out of sight and easy reach, equipping her refrigerator with a time lock, and keeping only as much food in the house as can be consumed in a short period of time. In addition, Terry tries to control her environment by associating with people who are counting calories and interested in exercise.

Terry's helper also encourages her to engage in *stimulus narrowing*. Stimulus narrowing involves reducing the number of stimuli associated with her eating skills weakness. Terry agrees it is a good idea to eat only in the dining room and, where feasible, only in the presence of certain family members.

USE HELPER'S AIDES AND HELP CLIENTS TO OBTAIN SUPPORT

As a helper, you may use third parties to develop clients' action skills and also assist clients to identify and use third parties to support change attempts.

Using Helper's Aides

Reasons why helpers enlist others as aides include pressure of work and the opportunity to extend interventions into clients' home environments. Helpers may use a variety of people as aides: teachers, parents, paraprofessionals, supervisors, and friends. Following are two examples.

Janie, age 8, is referred by her teacher Felicity to Dorothy, the school counselor, because she is very shy and does not participate in class. As part of Janie's treatment plan, Dorothy enlists Felicity's help both to ask questions that draw Janie out and to reward her when she participates in class. In addition, Dorothy asks Felicity to monitor any changes in how well Janie relates to the other children on the playground.

Rachel, 21, volunteers to be a student paraprofessional "companion therapist" in a program to support anorexic and bulemic fellow students undergoing professional treatment at the university counseling service (Lenihan & Kirk, 1990). Rachel undergoes a 25-hour training program. She then maintains daily personal or phone contact with her allocated client. In addition, she engages in such activities as joint exercise, walking, and lunching. Rachel also helps her client monitor nutrition and assists with meal planning and shopping.

Following are skills needed in selecting and using helper's aides.

1. *Identify suitable aides.* Carefully select and screen helper's aides. They have the potential to do both harm and good.
2. *Obtain client permission.* Clients need to accept the potential usefulness of helper's aides if they are to work with them. With adults, helpers always need to obtain clients' permission to discuss their behavior with nonprofessional third parties. It is sometimes inappropriate to obtain children's per-

mission (for instance, in the example of Janie's teacher helping her).

3. *Involve aides in planning interventions.* Helper's aides such as teachers, parents, and supervisors may have special knowledge of how best to support clients in developing action skills. Furthermore, if consulted, aides may be more motivated to participate in treatment plans than if they think plans are imposed on them.

4. *Train aides.* Some helper's aides work with many different clients. Where this is the case, effort put into training them may reap rich rewards. Even where aides work with single clients, it is essential that they understand their roles and can competently carry them out.

5. *Support and debrief aides.* Keep in touch with aides and make sure that they perform their functions as agreed. Give aides the opportunity to share thoughts and feelings about clients and about their contribution to helping. Where necessary, revise agreements on how your aides should assist.

6. *Withdraw helper's aide assistance.* Clients need to learn how to perform action skills without the others' assistance. Consider how best to withdraw your aides' assistance. One option is to withdraw all assistance at once. Another option is to progressively withdraw (fade) assistance.

Help Clients Identify and Use Supports

Helpers may need to raise some clients' awareness about the importance of identifying and using supports and of lessening contact with unsupportive people. Helpers and clients can work together to identify people in home environments to support their efforts to develop targeted skills. For example, university students with study skills weaknesses can seek out sympathetic faculty members to help them develop specific skills (for instance, how to write term papers or prepare for tests). Unemployed people can approach friends and relatives, who may not only offer them emotional support but also be sources for job leads. Women working on developing assertion skills can seek out women's groups, where they may find other women with similar objectives. Teachers who feel burned out can associate with colleagues who are relatively happy with their lot, rather than those perpetually complaining. Furthermore, they can develop self-care skills by engaging in pleasant activities with people unconnected to education.

An inverse approach to support is for helpers and clients to identify unsympathetic or counterproductive people. Clients are then left with various choices: getting such people to accept, if not support, their efforts to change; seeing less of them; or stopping seeing them. If these people are family members, avoiding them altogether may be difficult, especially if the client is financially dependent. Here, helpers and clients may discuss damage-control strategies. Often clients *can* choose their friendship and membership groups. For example, if juvenile delinquents want to develop action skills that integrate them into the wider community, they may need to change the company they keep (Sarason, 1976).

 ## CHAPTER HIGHLIGHTS

- Action skills interventions require adequate assessments of clients' action skills weaknesses.
- Helpers and clients may focus on action skills before, after, or simultaneously with thinking skills.
- Helpers require relationship skills to support inside-session and outside-session development of action skills.
- Skills for managing clients' resistances to working on action skills include: working through thinking blocks; presenting skills clearly; using reward; arranging for early success; understanding and anticipating difficulties; confronting; and encouraging clients to view themselves as practitioner-researchers.
- Diaries and journals, frequency charts, and recording logs are methods of client self-monitoring.
- Skills for assisting client self-monitoring include: offering reasons; training clients in discrimination and recording; designing simple and clear logs; using reward; and encouraging clients to evaluate information.
- Methods for rehearsing action skills include live rehearsal, role-play, role-play with accompanying self-talk, and visualized.
- Skills for conducting role-play rehearsals include: presenting rationales; setting scenes; assessment; formulating changed actions; rehearsing; and processing.
- Helpers and clients may use time tables to: schedule daily activities; set minimum goals; create personal space; keep contracts; and perform homework.
- When assisting time-tabling, always provide the time tables and be sensitive to clients' anxieties and resistances.
- Helpers may plan sub-goals either by sequencing sub-skills or by sequencing graded tasks. Where possible, sequence graded tasks with clients.

- Helpers can assist clients to be more flexible in how they act by helping them develop skills of generating and evaluating alternatives and choosing the best-fit actions and action skills.
- Action skills experiments encourage clients to try out new skills. Six steps in action skills experiments are: (1) assess; (2) formulate changed action skills; (3) make an "If . . . then . . ." statement; (4) rehearse and practice; (5) try out changed actions; and (6) evaluate.
- Helpers may either use other people's exercises and games or design their own. Exercises and games should emphasize development of practical take-away skills.
- Helpers can assist clients to use self-reward by helping them to identify suitable rewards and reward themselves contingent on performance of targeted skills.
- Stimulus control (using or discarding prompts that influence behavior) is a useful client skill for modifying environments.
- Helpers may use third parties as aides. Select aides carefully and train and support them.
- Helpers can also train clients to identify and use supports in their home environments.

❀ ❀ ❀   **CHAPTER TWELVE**   ❀ ❀ ❀

HOW TO FOCUS ON FEELINGS

We know too much and feel too little.
— Bertrand Russell

CHAPTER QUESTIONS

❀ *Why is it important to focus on feelings?*

❀ *What is the helper's role when focusing on feelings?*

❀ *What interventions can helpers use to assist clients to experience, explore, and accurately label feelings?*

❀ *What interventions can helpers use to develop clients' skills of expressing feelings?*

❀ *What interventions can helpers use to develop clients' skills of managing feelings?*

Focusing on feelings involves helping clients learn to live with their underlying animal nature so that it works *for* them rather than against them. All clients' problems involve feelings one way or another. This chapter builds on the previous chapters by showing how to focus on clients' feelings by intervening with their thinking skills and action skills.

REASONS FOR FOCUSING ON FEELINGS

Many different reasons exist for why helpers, clients, and others need to pay attention to focusing on feelings. First, many clients require catharsis. *Catharsis* involves getting relief through purging oneself of emotions which, if allowed to persist, might interfere with fulfillment and even survival. For example, some clients have had their integrity consistently attacked by inadequate and manipulative parents. They may come to helping, while still young or later on, with a backlog of insufficiently expressed hatred, resentment, and self-pity. Initially, a main task of helping may be to assist clients to experience and release hatred in order to use the emotional energy invested in it for more constructive purposes.

Second, how clients experience, express, and manage feelings affects physical health. Emotions that are not adequately handled may be *somatized*—that is, clients may feel physically stressed and fatigued or even ill. They may fall prey to psychophysical disorders such as eczema, muscle cramps, tension headaches, asthma, heart attacks, hypertension, peptic ulcers, chronic gastritis, and disturbances in urination or menstruation.

A third reason for focusing on feelings involves the desirability of lifting unwanted inhibitions and repressions. Clients' families of origin have differing values about what feelings are safe to experience (Laing, 1969; Rogers, 1951, 1957, 1961, 1980; Satir, 1972). Cultural and sex-role conditioning further influences how people feel. Fourth, and closely related to lifting unwanted repressions, is the need for many clients to get more in touch with wants and wishes. Clients' wants and wishes stimulate both their initial motivation to act and how persistent they are.

Developing a sense of identity is a fifth reason for focusing on feelings. In varying degrees, many clients lack a clear sense of identity. People's feelings, their unique valuing of what transpires in their lives, can allow a healthy sense of continuity and sameness. People with an effective sense of identity are centered in their unique capacity for responsiveness. They are always in the process of identity formation, yet this making and remaking of themselves is a process of renewal in accord with, rather than violating, the core of their beings.

Providing a base for effective relating provides a sixth reason for focusing on feelings. Clients require the ability to send and receive feelings messages accurately. Furthermore, they need to be able both to experience and express pro-social feelings. A final reason for focusing on feelings is that clients require help in managing feelings that are both self-defeating and often destructive of others (for instance, anxiety, hatred, depression and shyness). Furthermore, in times of crisis, clients can require assistance in handling feelings experienced as overwhelming (for instance, panic).

The area of feelings is complex. I have subdivided it into three main areas: experiencing feelings, expressing feelings, and managing negative feelings. Figure 12.1 depicts the interrelationships between these areas.

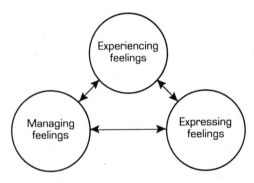

Figure 12.1   Interrelationship between experiencing, expressing, and managing feelings

HELPERS AS FEELINGS EDUCATORS

Broadly speaking, helpers can take two main approaches to clients' feelings. First, there is the facilitative approach. Here you use helping relationship skills to facilitate clients in experiencing, disclosing, and exploring feelings. You assume that if clients truly experience their significant feelings and self-actualizing drives they think rationally and act appropriately. Second, there is the training approach. Here you use training skills to assist clients to make better choices in how they feel. The facilitative approach emphasizes experiencing feelings; the training approach emphasizes expressing and managing feelings. Rogers' person-centered therapy and cognitive-behavioral therapy are prime examples of the facilitative and training approaches, respectively.

Lifeskills helping draws on both facilitative and training approaches to feelings. Helpers, as psychological educators, need to assist clients, not only to get in touch with their animal nature, but also to use what distinguishes them from lower animals— their capacity for reason and thinking—to regulate and manage that nature. As depicted in Figure 12.2, lifeskills helpers flexibly use both helping relationship and training skills to assist clients to experience, express, and manage feelings.

Areas of client's feelings	Helper skills	
	Relationship skills	Training skills
Experiencing	✔	✔
Expressing	✔	✔
Managing	✔	✔

Figure 12.2 Helper skills that assist clients to experience, express, and manage feelings

What skills do clients require to experience, express, and manage feelings? Since feelings represent the human's animal nature, I prefer not to use the term "feeling skills." Instead clients require *feelings-related skills* to help manage problematic feelings. Figure 12.3 depicts how clients require both thinking and action skills to fully develop their potential for using their animal nature to support rather than to oppress themselves and others.

Areas of client's feelings	Client skills	
	Thinking skills	Action skills
Experiencing	✔	✔
Expressing	✔	✔
Managing	✔	✔

Figure 12.3 Client skills for experiencing, expressing, and managing feelings

Assist Clients to Own Responsibility for Feelings

Clients are responsible not only for their thoughts and actions but also for their feelings. Whatever other interventions you use for clients' problematic feelings, always work on the assumption that clients are responsible for feelings. Following are three examples of clients' needing to assume more responsibility for feelings.

Experiencing feelings: Arnold, 17, sees his school counselor to decide what university and program he should apply to. Arnold has few ideas of his own and relies mainly on others' thoughts and feelings about what he should do.

Expressing feelings: Fran, 27, is in a relationship that is heading for the rocks. She has great difficulty expressing both positive and negative feelings to her boyfriend Jay.

Managing feelings: Dora, 43, is the principal of an urban school with major staff morale and discipline problems. Over the past few weeks, Dora has been getting increasingly tense, anxious, and depressed about her work and life.

Responsibility for feelings has various dimensions (for instance, "How can I get in touch with my feelings?," "Who or what creates my feelings?," and "What can I do about my feelings?"). Assist clients to see that they have choices about how they feel. Though past and present circumstances may influence how clients feel, such circumstances do not *create* how they feel. Also, assist clients to see that they have choices both in how they express feelings and how they react to others' feelings. Go beyond making them aware that they are responsible for their feelings and feelings choices. Clients need to know how to do it. They require relevant thinking and action skills for assuming effective responsibility for their feelings, both now and in the future.

Assist Clients to Experience Feelings

Experiencing feelings has at least three dimensions. First, clients need the actual sensation of experiencing feelings rather than blocking them off or distorting them. Second, clients require skills to explore feelings and follow feelings trails to see where they lead. Third, clients require skills to label feelings accurately. Following are some interventions to assist clients to experience, explore, and label feelings.

Offer Reasons for Focusing on Feelings

You may help some clients if you legitimize the importance of focusing on feelings. How you do this depends upon the needs of individual clients. Let's take the example of Arnold, the 17-year-old whose school counselor discovers that he relies on others' thoughts and feelings to guide his choice of university and major. If you were the school counselor you would have a number of choices, albeit not mutually exclusive ones. First, you can keep using rewarding listening skills in the hope that Arnold becomes more inner- than outer-directed. Second, you can confront him along the lines of "Arnold, you seem to be saying a lot about what your parents and teachers want for you, but I'm wondering what *you* think and feel about *your* choice of university and program?" (Note the emphasis on *you* and *your*.) Third, you can suggest to Arnold that he take an occupational interest inventory to assist self-exploration. Fourth, you can offer Arnold reasons for acknowledging his own feelings more fully.

> **School Counselor:** Arnold, you seem to say a lot about what your parents and teachers want for you. However, I get the impression that you inadequately attend to *your* feelings about what *you* want to do. Though they are not the only source, your feelings can provide you with a rich source of information about what might be the right choices for you. Learning to acknowledge and listen to your feelings is a skill. If you inadequately listen to your feelings, you risk making choices that you may later regret. I think you need to develop skills of focusing more on your feelings. What do you think?

Offering reasons for focusing on feelings may lead to a discussion with clients about how much they think they are in touch with feelings and their fears about expressing them. As an intervention for aiding emotional responsiveness, it needs to be accompanied by other interventions. However, offering reasons may accelerate some clients in taking feelings more seriously as a basis for future feelings work.

Focus on Thinking Skills

Helpers can assist clients to develop thinking skills conducive to expressing feelings. Following are thinking skills weaknesses that block experiencing feelings. I refer you to Chapters 9 and 10 for how to develop clients' thinking skills.

Own responsibility for choosing.   Already I have stressed the importance of helping clients to realize that they have choices in how they feel, including how they experience feelings and what feelings they experience. Emery (1982) uses the term "choice-ability" for people's ability to choose how they feel.

Use coping self-talk.   Clients can talk to themselves in ways that enhance their capacity to get in touch with feelings. They may make calming self-statements like "Relax," "Calm down," or "Take a deep breath." They may also make coaching self-statements like "Let's clear a space to truly get in touch with what I feel," "Remember, my feelings are important and I need to spend time getting in touch with them," or "Don't rush into a decision, let's feel and think this one through." Often clients can combine calming and coaching self-statements: "Relax. Take time to get in touch with how I feel about this."

Choose realistic personal rules.   Many clients have personal rules that get in the way of experiencing feelings. Samples of such rules are:

> "I must never have strong feelings."
> "Women should not acknowledge feelings of ambition."
> "Men should be strong and silent."
> "Boys must feel competitive rather than cooperative."
> "Religious people should always pay attention to others' feelings, rather than to their own."
> "People should not have strong sexual feelings because sex is dirty."
> "I must never acknowledge that I care for others and for the welfare of the human race."

Helpers can assist clients to become aware of rules unhelpful to experiencing feelings and dispute and reformulate them into more realistic rules.

Choose how you perceive.   Clients have much more choice in how they feel than most realize. Helpers can assist clients to make links between how they perceive and how they feel. Clients can develop skills of not restricting themselves to the first feeling they experience. Instead they can generate and evaluate alternative perceptions, which in turn lead to alternative feelings. Clients can then choose the best-fit perceptions and feelings. Sometimes helpers can assist clients' "choice-ability" by getting them to explore feelings opposite to how they say they feel. For instance, clients may get more in touch with what they truly feel by exploring feelings of love toward someone they say they hate. Also, helpers may assist clients in feeling less negative about themselves and others. Searching for positive assets in self and others is one way to do this.

Attribute cause accurately. Helpers can assist clients to attribute causes of feelings accurately. For instance, depressed clients may attribute the cause of all negative events to themselves (Beck, 1991; Beck, Rush, Shaw, & Emery, 1979). Other clients may project negative feelings about themselves onto others (for instance, jealous clients being hypersensitive about others' jealousy). Many clients externalize the cause of their feelings onto others (for instance, "It's all his fault" or "She made me feel that way").

Predict realistically. Disorders of prediction permeate how people experience negative—and fail to experience positive—feelings. Distorted predictions play a large part in depression (Abramson, Seligman, & Teasdale, 1978; Bandura, 1986, 1989; Beck, 1991; Beck, Riskind, Brown, & Steer, 1988). Unrealistic predictions of physical or psychological danger are systematic biases in processing information of patients suffering from anxiety disorders (Beck & Weishaar, 1989). Many who feel shy predict that they will be rejected. Other clients require help in containing feelings of optimism (for instance, manic clients or clients who do not take health risks seriously enough).

Set realistic goals. Clients with unrealistic goals set themselves up to feel anxious about attaining them and depressed if unsuccessful. Clients setting proximal or short-range goals enhance their motivation and feelings of self-efficacy (Bandura, 1986).

Use visualizing skills. Helpers can both elicit feelings and enhance many clients' experience of past feelings by asking them to visualize situations in which they occurred. You can also use visualizing to help clients experience feelings about the future (for instance, in regard to getting married or moving). Furthermore, you may enhance feelings of competence by getting clients to visualize themselves performing competently.

Make decisions rationally. Helpers can educate clients in the importance of listening to feelings when making decisions. You can assist clients' awareness of when feelings interfere with realistic decisions (for instance, being impulsive or excessively vigilant). Furthermore, you can assist clients to experience and explore feelings of commitment or lack of commitment toward implementing decisions.

Prevent and manage problems and alter problematic skills. Helpers
can assist clients to listen to their early warning signals, either to
prevent or to manage problems. For instance, early tuning into
feelings of stress may prevent more serious stress-related problems. You can also assist clients to see that experiencing and
labeling feelings accurately is an important part of the process of
managing problems and altering problematic skills.

Use Rewarding Listening

In Chapter 4, I presented 10 skills for being a rewarding
listener. Again I emphasize the importance of rewarding listening, particularly to help thaw clients whose experiencing
of feelings is being (or has been) significantly frozen by adverse family-of-origin circumstances.

How can rewarding listening help clients get in touch with
and experience feelings? Rewarding listening allows clients
permission to experience their separateness and uniqueness,
rather than being the way others want them to be. The
affirmation helpers provide with their time, attention, and understanding can increase clients' sense of worth and lower anxiety and defensiveness. Being sensitively responded to, clients
gain practice at listening to themselves, valuing their own experience, and—increasingly—identifying and labeling it accurately. Rewarding listening gives clients the psychological space
to delve deeper into the meanings and nuances of their feelings.
It assists clients to identify wants and wishes and to distinguish
what comes from them and from others. Furthermore, empathic
helpers provide clients with secure bases from which they can
act in the world, gain new experiences, come back and discuss
them, and know that they will be understood. Though rewarding
listening skills are not always sufficient, or quick enough, for
helping clients get in touch with feelings, they are invariably
necessary. However, there are limits to the pace at which clients
out of touch with feelings can work. Consequently, another facet
of rewarding listening is showing sensitivity to clients' comfort
zones.

Train Clients in Inner Listening

So far I have emphasized the need for helpers to be rewarding
listeners to clients. However clients also need to develop skills of
being rewarding listeners to themselves. They need to experience, become aware of, explore, and label their own feelings.
Assuming clients have a moderate degree of insight, you can
impart inner listening as a self-helping skill.

Following are elements of inner listening training.

Offer reasons for focusing on inner listening. You can assist clients to realize that this is a useful skill for understanding both themselves and others. Clarify what you mean by experiencing feelings, exploring them, and labeling them accurately.

Stress creating sufficient time and psychological space. To practice inner listening, clients must give it sufficient priority in their lives. This may mean either that they spend a certain amount of time alone with themselves each day or make sure to clear a space when something bothers them or needs deciding.

Explain and demonstrate the skill. Much of the rewarding listening material in Chapter 4 is relevant here, but with modification. For instance, the concept of internal viewpoint in this context becomes that of getting inside your own, rather than another's, internal viewpoint. In inner empathy, it is vital that clients tune in to feelings. They should flow with them, try to understand their messages, and label them accurately. You may help clients to understand the skill if you demonstrate by verbalizing your feelings and associated thoughts as you attempt to listen to yourself.

Coach and assign homework. Coach clients to ensure that they understand the skill of inner listening. Assigning homework acts as a bridge between training and clients' relying on their own resources.

Eugene Gendlin and Fritz Perls are two writers who have stressed the need for inner listening and awareness. Gendlin (1962) developed a method termed *focusing* to help people change and live from a deeper place than just thoughts and feelings. In focusing, people clear a space and make contact with a special kind of internal bodily awareness called a "felt sense." When people get in touch with this "felt sense," there can be both a perceived physical shift in their bodies and a different perspective on problems.

Perls, the founder of gestalt therapy, developed a technique he called *focal awareness.* Perls (1973) observed: "The basic sentence with which we ask our patients to begin therapy and which we retain throughout its course—not only in words, but in spirit—is the simple phrase 'Now I am aware'" (p. 65). When using focal awareness, Perls asked clients to concentrate and become aware of their body language, breathing, voice quality, and emotions, as much as of any pressing thoughts. He aimed to make clients aware not only that they had interrupted their contact with themselves but also of how they did this. Helpers may impart both focusing and focal awareness as self-helping skills.

Use Feelings Questions

Helpers can use feelings questions to encourage clients to experience and share feelings. Beware of allowing clients to talk about feelings distantly rather than experiencing them. Another danger of this use of questions is that clients will respond to helpers rather than getting in touch with themselves. However, if skillfully used, feelings questions can give clients useful practice at listening to and becoming more aware of their feelings. Feelings questions and cues include:

"How do you feel about that?"
"I'm wondering what the emotional impact of that is on you."
"Could you describe your feelings more fully?"
"I'm hearing that you're feeling . . . ?"
"You seem to have conflicting feelings. On the one hand . . . , on the other hand. . . ."

Be Authentic and Appropriately Self-Disclose

The ability of helpers to be real is very important for assisting clients to experience feelings. Rogers (1957, 1975) uses terms like *congruence* and *genuineness*. Existential psychologists use terms like *presence* and *authenticity* (May, 1958; Bugental, 1981). Bugental views presence as consisting of an intake side called accessibility, allowing what happens in situations to affect you, and an output side called expressiveness, making available some of the content of your subjective awareness without editing. If you are alive and present in relating to clients, you demonstrate experiencing feelings and create the climate for them to do so too. Some research suggests that female helpers experience and express feelings more than male helpers (Maracek & Johnson, 1980). Mintz and O'Neil (1990) observe that research studies "suggest that female therapists may form more effective therapeutic alliances and be more affectively oriented than are male therapists" (p. 384).

Clients may perceive helpers who are able to experience and express feelings as disclosing involvement. Showing such involvement may make it easier for clients to experience feelings. Helpers who appropriately disclose personal information may also help clients access their experiencing (for instance, feminist helpers with women clients, gay helpers with gay clients, and former drug addicts with substance-abuse clients).

Confront Inauthenticity

Helpers can use their here-and-now experiencing as guides to whether clients communicate what they really think and feel. Clients may wear masks and play roles that interfere with their experiencing and expressing what they truly feel. Such roles include playing the clown, playing stupid, or playing helpless. Helpers may make clients aware of such tendencies (for example, "I get the impression that whenever you get close to your deeper feelings, you use humor to avoid revealing them"). Helpers can also confront clients who externalize feelings onto others.

> **Client:** Judy and Joan feel pretty angry with the way we are taught.
> **Helper:** I'm wondering whether focusing on Judy's and Joan's anger is a way of protecting yourself from acknowledging that you too feel angry with your teachers and are capable of angry feelings.

Helpers can also confront inconsistencies between verbal, voice, and body messages. For instance, "You say you don't feel hurt by his behavior, yet you speak with a sad tone of voice and your eyes seem weepy."

Raise Consciousness

Helpers can use consciousness raising as a means of improving clients' capacities for experiencing and expressing feelings. In Western countries, there are few who do not need to become more in tune with feelings. Mostly, helpers use consciousness raising to raise awareness levels of specific subgroups (for instance, women, men, gays, and various ethnic and cultural minorities). Intervening to raise clients' consciousness of social, sex-role, and cultural conditioning can beneficially affect how they experience feelings in two main ways. First, you can assist clients to overcome negative feelings (for instance, low self-esteem and guilt) attached to their minority status. Second, you can encourage subgroups to respond to the range of feelings inherent in being human (for example, encourage women to experience and express ambition and assertion, and men to express vulnerability and affection).

Teach Sensate Focus

Relatively few helpers specialize in sexual problems. Nevertheless, many have occasion to assist clients in experiencing and expressing sensuality. Insufficient sexual responsiveness takes many forms and may have multiple causes. Often it is part of a broader pattern of inadequate relationship skills. However, some clients may have good relationship skills in other areas, yet require specific assistance in acknowledging and exploring sensuality. Such difficulties may be independent of having specific sexual dysfunctions (for instance, premature ejaculation).

Masters and Johnson (1970) developed the technique of sensate focus to help couples feel and think sensuously. Sensate focus acknowledges the importance of touch in stimulating and experiencing sexual responsiveness. Partners are asked to time their periods of sensate focus for when they feel a natural sense of warmth and compatibility. They are only to continue for as long as it is pleasurable. Both partners need to be naked and have a minimum of physical fatigue and tension. Avoiding specifically sexual stimulation, including genitals and breasts, the "giving" partner massages and fondles the "getting" partner to give pleasure. The rules of sensate focus for receiving partners are that they have to protect pleasuring partners from causing discomfort or initiating sex. Receiving partners need not comment either verbally or nonverbally on their experiencing, unless such expression is completely spontaneous. Giving partners are committed, not only to giving pleasure, but also to acknowledging their sensations in giving pleasure, exploring another's body by touch, and receiving pleasurable reactions. After a time, partners exchange roles.

Sensate focus aims to give partners time, space, and permission to respond sensually without feeling that they have to go on to intercourse. Kaplan (1974) observes that, though most couples experience positive reactions to sensate focus, some individuals experience very little reaction and others do have negative reactions. She points out that these negative reactions may indicate deeper inhibitions concerning sexual responsiveness and suggests how to treat them. Helpers require sensitivity in following up clients' reactions to sensate focus.

Use Role-Play Methods

In Chapter 11, I discussed role-play as a method of rehearsing action skills. Role-plays can also be used to allow clients to experience and express feelings. Role-play methods can be powerful ways of releasing and exploring feelings in various kinds of personal relationships—be they past, present, or future. This unburdening may in turn generate further self-exploration and deeper understandings of underlying feelings. Clients may play both people in a relationship, either by visualizing with eyes closed or by switching chairs as they play each part. Alternatively, helpers may play one of the parts in the relationship (for example, a parent, spouse, boyfriend, or girlfriend). In role-reversal, both helpers and clients switch roles. In addition, helpers may heighten clients' awareness by mirroring clients' feeling-related verbal, voice, and body messages. After (or during) role-plays, you can assist clients to experience, articulate, and explore feelings uncovered by and associated with what happened.

Encourage Action

Frequently clients cannot fully experience and explore feelings until they take the risks of acting. For example, there are limits to which clients can know how much they like or dislike any activity or person if they have no firsthand contact with them. Already I have stressed the role of rewarding listening in enabling clients to feel that helpers are secure bases from which to take the risks of exploratory behavior and action skills experiments. In addition, Chapter 11 specified interventions for developing clients' action skills.

Assist Clients to Express Feelings

Expressing feelings well requires clients to be skilled at experiencing, exploring, and accurately labeling their feelings. When clients reveal feelings they put themselves very much on the line. Some feelings are difficult for most clients to express, especially when they do not feel safe with another person (for example, worthlessness, incompetence, and unattractiveness). Some feelings may be more difficult for female clients to express, though male clients may have difficulty expressing them too (for example, ambition, leadership, and assertion). Some feelings may be more difficult for male than female clients to express, though again differences exist within each sex. Such feelings include vulnerability, sensitivity, and affection. Many clients find it difficult to express specific feelings well (for instance, anger). Within the context of supportive relationships, helpers assisting clients to express feelings need to focus on both thinking and action skills.

Focus on Thinking Skills

Here I illustrate some possible thinking skills that may interfere with, or assist, appropriate expression of feelings. Thinking skills weaknesses that block experiencing of feelings overlap with those hindering appropriate expression of feelings. Again, I refer you to Chapters 9 and 10 for how to work with clients' thinking skills.

Own responsibility for choosing.   Assist clients to know that they always have choices in how to express feelings. Also, help clients to identify where their specific thinking and action skills choice points are.

Use coping self-talk.   In addition to calming themselves down, clients can develop skills of coaching themselves through sequences of choices involved in skilled expression of feelings. For example, clients feeling strongly about obtaining promotions might use the following self-statements before and during interviews with their bosses: "Stay calm. Remember to be polite and state my case in the positive. Speak firmly and make good eye contact."

Choose realistic personal and relationship rules.   Many personal and relationship rules interfere with appropriate expression of feelings. Following are examples.

Unrealistic Personal Rules

"I must have approval all the time."
"I must always express feelings smoothly."
"Men must not cry."

Unrealistic Relationship Rules

"We must never have conflict in our relationship."
"Wives must always be sexually available to husbands."
"Children should be seen and not heard."

Choose how you perceive.   Many clients need to develop skills that allow their feelings toward others to be based on more accurate perceptions, so that the feelings they express are what they truly feel. Once clients are in touch with their feelings, they still require flexibility in perceiving various action skills options for expressing them.

Attribute cause accurately.   Without realizing it, some clients may wait for others to make the first move in expressing feelings (for example, "I cannot express positive feelings about her until she expresses positive feelings about me"). Helpers may need to assist clients to take an active rather than a passive stance to expressing feelings.

Predict realistically.   Many clients do not express certain feelings either well or at all because they make false predictions. For instance, many shy clients are reluctant to initiate social contacts for fear of rejection. Clients in relationships may be unwilling to bring up differences because of catastrophic predictions about the consequences. Also, these catastrophic predictions may cause them either to under-react or to over-react when they eventually do discuss differences.

Set realistic goals.   Clients may possess unrealistic goals about what feelings to express to whom, and when. For instance, insecure teenagers with unclear or unrealistic goals may come on too strong too soon with their boyfriends or girlfriends. Another example is that of males who, when learning to be more emotionally expressive, avoid being discouraged by early set-backs because they realize that developing these skills can take time.

Use visualizing skills.   Clients can use visualizing skills to rehearse how to express feelings appropriately. Furthermore, they can visualize themselves attaining their goals if they use good expressing feelings skills. Clients can also visualize the negative consequences of using poor expressing feelings skills.

Focus on Action Skills

Helpers can assist clients to develop the action skills of expressing feelings. (See Chapters 9 and 11 for how to do this.) When assisting clients to express feelings, always pay attention to verbal, voice, and body messages. You may also focus on touch and action messages. Let me illustrate different action messages for showing caring skills (Nelson-Jones, 1990b). Needless to say, clients need to be sensitive to what others perceive as caring messages.

Verbal messages   Verbal messages of caring include statements like "I love you," "I care for you," and "I want to help you." Clients may also pay compliments. Furthermore, clients can show caring if they use good verbal skills when listening (for instance, accurate reflective responses).

Voice messages   If clients' voice messages are wrong, they negate their verbal messages. Characteristics of caring voice messages include warmth and expressiveness. Clients' voices should convey kindness and interest rather than harshness and disinterest.

Body messages   When clients send caring verbal messages, their gaze, eye contact, body orientation, and facial expressions all need to demonstrate interest and concern for the other person. Similarly, clients need to show good attending and listening body message skills when others share problems with them.

Touch messages   Touch can be a wonderful way to express caring. Clients can express caring by a hug, a half-embrace, an arm over the shoulder, a touch on the arm, or a hand on top of 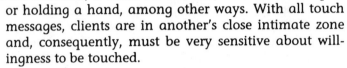 or holding a hand, among other ways. With all touch messages, clients are in another's close intimate zone and, consequently, must be very sensitive about willingness to be touched.

Action messages   Action messages indicating caring include: making the other person a cup of tea or coffee in the morning; being prepared to do your share of the household chores; giving birthday cards and presents; initiating pleasant events, such as going out to dinner; showing affection through flowers, poems, and other spontaneous gifts; and being available to help out in times of need (Argyle & Henderson, 1985).

Assist Clients to Manage Feelings

Many clients come to helping to find release from painful and negative feelings. Often clients lack confidence in themselves. In addition, they are subject to feelings like excessive anger, depression, and anxiety. In reality, feelings tend to overlap (for instance, clients can be simultaneously depressed, anxious, and excessively angry). Furthermore, success in managing one of these feelings better is likely to enhance self-esteem and, hence, aid in handling the others better too. Clients may use skills learned for managing one feeling for managing other feelings. Here, rather than cover a range of feelings, I use anger, depression, and anxiety to show how to approach developing clients' skills of managing feelings. The discussion of pertinent thinking and action skills is illustrative rather than comprehensive. In practice, skills redefinitions of clients' managing feelings problems should be tailor-made to their particular skills weaknesses and circumstances. Always use supportive relationship skills when assisting clients to manage feelings.

Managing Anger

Clients should identify and manage anger rather than attempt to rid themselves of it altogether. Anger can have positive uses. It can be a signal indicating something is wrong and requires attention. It can be an energizer, helping clients to take appro-

Table 12.1 Illustrative thinking and action skills for managing anger

Thinking Skills	Action Skills
Owning responsibility for anger Possessing realistic personal rules Perceiving provocations accurately Using coping self-talk Using visualizing	Assertion (expressing anger; requesting behavior changes) Handling aggressive criticism Using relaxation Managing stress Helping one another

priate action. In some instances, anger may also be a purge. After expressing it, clients may calm down and be more rational. Part of managing anger is to be able to experience, explore and accurately label angry feelings. Table 12.1 shows some further skills for managing anger, each of which I discuss in turn.

Thinking Skills

1. *Owning responsibility for anger:* Clients have choices in how they experience, express, and manage anger. Until they own responsibility for their anger, they will have insufficient motivation to develop the skills to manage it effectively.
2. *Possessing realistic personal rules:* Ellis (1977) regards childish demandingness as the central thinking skills weakness in anger. Clients make "mustabatory" demands on themselves (for instance, "I must never make mistakes"), on others (for instance, "Others should always agree with me" or "Others must never criticize me"), and on the environment (for instance, "The world should always be the way I want it to be" and "I should never have hassles").
3. *Perceiving provocations accurately:* Clients need to develop skills of not jumping to superficial negative conclusions about others. Beck (1988) observes of relationship difficulties that much of the friction is due to misunderstandings stemming from differences in perspective and not from meanness or selfishness.
4. *Using coping self-talk:* Simple self-instructions like "Calm down" and "Cool it" can often give clients more time and space to get feelings under control (Goldstein & Keller, 1987). Clients can also use longer self-statements such as "I can handle this situation if I don't let my pride get in the way" (Novaco, 1977; Meichenbaum, 1983).
5. *Using visualizing:* Clients can use visualization in many ways to manage anger. They can visually rehearse how to express

angry feelings appropriately. They can relax themselves by visualizing restful scenes. Also, they can use visualization to perceive others' perspectives more accurately.

Action Skills

1. *Being assertive:* Skills for expressing anger assertively include using "I" statements, avoiding provocative voice messages like screaming, and avoiding threatening body messages like finger jabbing. Clients also need to develop skills of requesting others to alter their behaviors before, rather than after, becoming thoroughly fed up with the behavior (Alberti & Emmons, 1990; Nelson-Jones, 1990b).

2. *Handling aggressive criticism:* Clients have numerous choices, other than impulsive knee-jerk reactions, in dealing with aggressive criticism. For instance, they can tell themselves to relax, calm down, and breathe more slowly until they feel more under control. They can also choose from a number of verbal strategies (for example, reflecting another's anger, or partly agreeing with another's point and then making their own, or asking another to be more specific about what they've done to upset them). Clients may also back off now and react to criticism at a later date—either requesting or, on their own initiative, taking a "cooling off" period.

3. *Using relaxation:* Clients can develop skills of muscular and visual relaxation to manage anger (Deffenbacher, McNamara, Stark, & Sabadell, 1990; Deffenbacher, Story, Brandon, Hogg, & Hazaleus, 1988). I describe relaxation skills later in this chapter.

4. *Managing stress:* Frequently, inability to handle life's stresses makes clients prone to anger. As well as using muscular and visual relaxation, clients may manage stress better if they develop adequate recreational outlets, actively look after their health, and develop adequate support networks. Since much stress is internally generated, helpers and clients also need to review relevant thinking skills.

5. *Helping one another:* Clients can develop skills of working with their partners to help each other manage anger. Relevant action skills for clients are: disciplining themselves to watch their tongues; expressing anger assertively; showing an awareness of what partners experience before, during, and after they receive clients' expressions of anger; and using rewarding listening and questioning skills to help partners express angry feelings that they may have difficulty acknowledging or getting out into the open. When helping

one another to manage anger, partners need to possess realistic relationship rules (for instance, "When either of us expresses anger in our relationship, it is a signal to explore our own thoughts, feelings, and actions, and not just those of the other person").

Managing Depression

Often helpers work with clients who feel depressed. Depressed clients can be very sensitive to the quality of the helping relationship. Experiencing difficulty in affirming themselves, they seek affirmation from outside. You require good relationship skills—both initially, when clients may feel dependent on you, and later, as they develop skills for emotional independence. Table 12.2 presents some common thinking skills and action skills for managing depression.

Thinking Skills

1. *Possessing realistic personal rules:* Clients can create and sustain their depressed feelings when striving to attain and failing to live up to unrealistic rules (Ellis, 1989; Hewitt & Dyke, 1986). Unrealistic rules that can lead to depression include "I must be perfect" and "I must always gain others' approval."
2. *Perceiving others and self accurately:* Beck (1991) observes of his cognitive theory of depression: "Of all the hypotheses, pervasiveness of negative thinking in all forms of depression, symptomatic or syndromatic, has been the most uniformly supported . . ." (p. 372). Depressed clients tend to jump to negative conclusions about how others perceive them. They are also skilled at blocking out positive information about themselves (Beck, 1991; Beck, Rush, Shaw, & Emery, 1979).
3. *Attributing cause accurately:* Depressed clients can over-emphasize their responsibility for negative events (Beck, Rush, Shaw & Emery, 1979). Depressed clients may also attribute

Table 12.2 Thinking and action skills for managing depression

Thinking Skills	Action Skills
Possessing realistic personal rules	Relationship skills (initiating contact; self-disclosing)
Perceiving others and self accurately	Assertion skills (setting limits and saying no)
Attributing cause accurately	
Predicting realistically	Pleasant activities skills

the causes of negative events, not only as more due to themselves, but also as more due to stable and global causes than
warranted (Petersen, Villanova & Raps, 1985; Seligman,
Abramson, Semmel, & von Baeyer, 1979).

4. *Predicting realistically:* Depressed clients tend to predict the
   future negatively. They are more prone to feelings of hopelessness (Beck, Rush, Shaw, & Emery, 1979), helplessness
   (Abramson, Seligman, & Teasdale, 1978), and perceived self-
   inefficacy (Bandura, 1986) than non-depressed people.

Depressed clients may have good skills in specific areas, but
under-rate them. The following discussion assumes their action
skills genuinely require development.

Action Skills

1. *Relationship skills:* Many depressed clients are lonely because
   they have insufficient (as well as insufficiently high) quality
   social contacts. Initiating contact and appropriately self-disclosing are among the relationship skills such clients may
   need to develop.

2. *Assertion skills:* Frequently depressed clients lower their self-
   esteem through inability to use assertion skills. For instance,
   clients who do not stand up for themselves may feel doubly
   bad. First, they have the outer negative consequences of having to do extra work, pay extra money, or whatever else
   follows from their lack of assertion. Second, they have the
   inner negative consequences of feeling bad about their
   nonassertion.

3. *Pleasant activities skills:* Lewinsohn and his colleagues (1986)
   state: "If you feel depressed, it is very likely that you are not
   involved in many pleasant activities" (p. 73). Depressed clients can develop skills of identifying activities they find rewarding (MacPhillamy & Lewinsohn, 1982). Then they can
   develop and implement plans to participate more in them.
   As the old adage says: "A little of what you fancy does you
   good."

Managing Anxiety

Anxiety is a normal survival mechanism. However, many, if not
most, clients suffer from excessive or debilitating anxieties that
interfere with happiness and fulfillment. Again, you need to
offer such clients a good helping relationship. Many anxious
clients are threatened by meeting new people, including helpers.
Also, clients can become anxious when talking about their anxi-

eties. Assisting clients to develop skills of managing anxiety invariably involves focusing on how they think.

Sometimes anxious clients have good action skills, but let their anxieties get in the way of manifesting them. For instance, some students perform well when tests do not count, but poorly when they count. Some otherwise good-to-passing students have poor test-taking skills. Here it can be important to focus on action skills as well as on thinking skills. Table 12.3 shows some common thinking skills for managing anxiety. The requisite action skills are less easy to list, since they vary with clients' problems. For example, clients require different action skills for attending job interviews than for developing intimacy.

Thinking Skills

1. *Using coping self-talk:* Anxious clients engage in much anxious self-talk (Beck, Epstein, Brown, & Steer, 1988; Kendall & Hollon, 1989). Their anxiety symptoms are signals for telling themselves that they cannot cope or do anything right. In social situations, their self-talk may be about making fools of themselves. Often clients with panic disorders tell themselves that a vital system (for instance, cardiovascular or "nervous") may collapse (Beck & Weishaar, 1989).

2. *Possessing realistic personal rules:* Anxious clients tend to have personal rules that engender both fear of failure and self-devaluation (Ellis, 1962, 1989). Making perfectionist demands on self and others is a central characteristic of such rules.

3. *Perceiving self and others accurately:* Anxious clients over-emphasize the degree of threat in situations. They selectively perceive what might go wrong and insufficiently perceive what might go right. In addition, anxious clients underestimate both their ability to cope and also the supports available to them (Beck & Emery, 1985; Beck & Weishaar, 1989).

Table 12.3 Thinking and action skills for managing anxiety

Thinking Skills	Action Skills
Using coping self-talk	Skills required for specific situations
Possessing realistic personal rules	
Perceiving self and others accurately	Relaxation skills
Predicting realistically	
Setting realistic goals	
Using visualizing	

Defensiveness, in which clients deny or distort aspects of themselves they find threatening, is another way that anxiety interferes with perception.

4. *Predicting realistically:* The predictions of anxious clients exaggerate dangers and risks. Such clients worry about the future and their ability to cope with it. They live out my tongue-in-cheek definition of the future as "anxiety about living in the context of anxiety about dying" (Nelson-Jones, 1990a, p. 97).

5. *Setting realistic goals:* Some anxious clients set goals that are too low, to protect themselves from failure. Many anxious clients set goals that are too high and become fearful about achieving them. The goals of other clients are realistically attainable, if they can manage anxiety better.

6. *Using visualizing:* Most anxious clients experience negative visual images prior to and concurrent with anxiety attacks (Beck, Laude, & Bohnert, 1974). Clients may have poor skills for using visualizing both to relax and to rehearse action skills.

Action Skills

1. *Skills required for specific situations:* Anxiety may either be the cause of poor action skills, their consequence, or a mixture of the two. Some clients may have good action skills, but experience difficulty implementing them under pressure. Other clients may need to develop specific skills (for instance, at public speaking, asking for a date, driving a car, managing a company, policing an angry crowd, and so on). Their increased competence in these skills lowers anxiety.

2. *Relaxation skills:* Many anxious clients have poor relaxation skills. They engage in insufficient pleasurable and relaxing activities. In addition, they may have poor muscular and mental relaxation skills.

Relaxation Skills

Helpers can train clients in muscular and mental relaxation skills (Bernstein & Borkovec, 1973; Jacobson, 1929, 1976; Wolpe, 1982). Impart these as self-helping rather than as helper-offered skills. Clients may use relaxation skills, not only for managing anxiety, but also for dealing with problems such as tension headaches, hypertension, and insomnia. Relaxation skills may be used alone or as part of more complex skills—for instance, systematic desensitization (Deffenbacher & Suinn, 1988; Goldfried & Davison, 1976; Wolpe, 1982).

Progressive muscular relaxation skills Progressive muscular re-laxation refers to the progressive cultivation of the relaxation response (Jacobson, 1929, 1976). Tell clients that the first step in physically relaxing themselves is to find a quiet space where they will be uninterrupted. They may use a bed, a recliner chair, or a comfortable chair with a headrest. If possible, they should wear loose-fitting, comfortable clothing, and remove items such as glasses and shoes. Their arms should be either by their sides or on the arms of chairs. Their legs should be uncrossed and their eyes closed.

Progressive muscular relaxation involves clients in tensing and relaxing various muscle groups. You can demonstrate how clients should go through a five-step tension-relax cycle for each muscle group (Bernstein & Borkovec, 1973). These steps are (1) *focus*—focus attention on a particular muscle group; (2) *tense*—tense the muscle group; (3) *hold*—maintain the tension for 5–7 seconds; (4) *release*—release the tension in the muscle group; and (5) *relax*—spend 20–30 seconds focusing on letting go of tension and further relaxing the muscle groups.

Table 12.4, which you may give to clients as a handout, lists the various muscle groupings and self-instructions for tensing them. For clients' homework, either provide them with copies of existing relaxation cassettes or make them afresh. However, later encourage clients to make their own self-instructional cassettes. Having said this, it remains uncertain how much home-relax-ation cassettes enhance treatment outcome (Hoelscher, Lichstein, Fischer, & Hegerty, 1987).

Give relaxation instructions in a calm and soothing voice. In step 5 of the cycle, use repetition to enhance relaxation (for instance: "Your forehead feels increasingly calm and relaxed . . . calm and relaxed . . . calm and relaxed"). When relaxing, clients observe their body posture and breathing as a check on how relaxed they are. Also, ask them how relaxed they feel and whether there are any muscle groupings requiring further atten-tion. If so, spend extra time relaxing these muscles. You can end relaxation sessions by counting backwards from five to one and, when you get to one, asking clients to wake up feeling pleas-antly relaxed as though from a peaceful sleep.

Inform clients that progressive muscular relaxation requires practice to gain its full benefits. When learning, they should practice daily for at least 15 minutes. Ask clients whether they anticipate any obstacles to practice, such as finding a quiet place, and help them to devise strategies for dealing with them. Evidence exists that clients who monitor their relaxation practice are more likely to continue doing it (Tasto & Hinkle, 1973).

Table 12.4 Tensing self-instructions for progressive muscular relaxation

Muscle Group	Tensing Self-Instructions*
Right hand and forearm	Clench my right fist and tense the muscles in my lower arm.
Right biceps	Bend my right arm at the elbow and flex my biceps by tensing the muscles of my upper right arm.
Left hand and forearm	Clench my left fist and tense the muscles in my lower arm.
Left biceps	Bend my left arm at the elbow and flex my biceps by tensing the muscles of my upper left arm.
Forehead	Lift my eyebrows as high as possible.
Eyes, nose, and upper cheeks	Squeeze my eyes tightly shut and wrinkle my nose.
Jaw and lower cheeks	Clench my teeth and pull the corners of my mouth firmly back.
Neck and throat	Pull my chin down hard toward my chest yet resist having it touch my chest.
Chest and shoulders	Pull my shoulder blades together and take a deep breath.
Stomach	Tighten the muscles in my stomach as though someone were about to hit me there.
Right thigh	Tense the muscles of my right upper leg by pressing the upper muscle down and the lower muscles up.
Right calf	Stretch my right leg and pull my toes toward my head.
Right foot	Point and curl the toes of my right foot and turn it inward.
Left thigh	Tense the muscles of my left upper leg by pressing the upper muscle down and the lower muscles up.
Left calf	Stretch my left leg and pull my toes toward my head.
Left foot	Point and curl the toes of my left foot and turn it inward.

*With left-handed people, tensing instructions for the left side of the body should come before those for the right.

Table 12.5 Relaxation homework monitoring log

Date	Time, Place, Length	Comments
Oct. 3	6 P.M., living room at home 15–20 minutes	Started off feeling tense after a day at work. Tensed and relaxed 16 muscle groups. At first, thoughts about work interfered with relaxation. Ended feeling deeply relaxed.

Consequently, ask clients to keep logs monitoring homework practice. Table 12.5 shows an entry in such a log.

Brief muscular relaxation skills Brief muscular relaxation skills aim to induce deep relaxation with less time and effort. When clients are proficient in full progressive muscular relaxation, you can introduce such skills. Brief relaxation skills are useful both in helping sessions and in homework. Following are two examples.

1. *Sequential brief relaxation:* Here you can first instruct clients, and then get them to tell themselves, the following instructions focused on tensing and relaxing in turn four composite muscle groupings.

   I'm going to count to 10 in units of two. After each unit of two I will instruct you to tense and relax a muscle grouping. One, two . . . focus on your leg and feet muscles . . . tense, and hold the tension in these muscles for five seconds . . . release . . . relax and enjoy the sensations of the tension flowing from your legs and feet. Three, four . . . take a deep breath and focus on your chest, shoulder, and stomach muscles . . . tense, and hold the tension in these muscles for five seconds . . . release . . . relax and enjoy the sensations of the tension flowing from your chest, shoulders, and stomach. Five, six . . . focus on your face, neck, and head muscles . . . tense, and hold the tension in these muscles for five seconds . . . release . . . relax and enjoy the sensations of the tension flowing from your face, neck, and head. Seven, eight . . . focus on your arm and hand muscles . . . tense, and hold the tension in these muscles for five seconds . . . release . . . relax and enjoy the sensations of the tension flowing from your arms and hands. Nine, ten . . . focus on all the muscles in your body . . . tense all the muscles in your body together and hold for five seconds . . . release . . . relax and enjoy the sensations of the tension leaving your whole body as your relaxation gets deeper and deeper . . . deeper and deeper . . . deeper and deeper.

2. *Simultaneous brief relaxation:* As at the end of the previous example, instruct clients to tense all muscle groupings simultaneously. You can say:

When I give the signal, I would like you to close your eyes very tightly, take a deep breath, and simultaneously tense your arm muscles, your face, neck, and throat muscles, your chest, shoulder, and stomach muscles, and your leg and foot muscles. Now take a deep breath and tense all your muscles . . . hold for five seconds . . . release and relax as quickly and deeply as you can.

Mental relaxation skills Often clients visualize restful scenes at the end of progressive muscular relaxation. Such a scene might be "lying in a lush green meadow on a warm, sunny day, feeling a gentle breeze, watching the clouds." Clients can visualize such scenes independent of muscular relaxation.

Systematic Desensitization

Progressive muscular relaxation forms an important part of systematic desensitization. Consider intervening with systematic desensitization when clients have specific anxieties and phobias, rather than general tension. The originator of systematic desensitization, Joseph Wolpe, presents a version that involves three elements: (1) training in deep muscular relaxation; (2) the construction around themes of hierarchies of anxiety-evoking situations; and (3) helpers asking clients, when relaxed, to imagine items from the hierarchies (Wolpe, 1958, 1982). Wolpe's "reciprocal inhibition" (or counter-conditioning) explanation is that the pairing of anxiety-evoking stimuli with the relaxation response brings about a lessening of the anxiety response, in effect weakening the bond between anxiety-evoking stimuli and anxiety responses. Other explanations exist for systematic desensitization's effectiveness. Increasingly helpers present it as a self-control skill (Goldfried & Davison, 1976), thus emphasizing *coping* with anxiety rather than mastering it.

Introduce systematic desensitization.   Offer reasons for using systematic desensitization. Presumably, your client has some anxiety management skills weaknesses for which desensitization seems the preferred intervention. Briefly explain all three elements. Stress learning desensitization as a coping skill. Having already discussed muscular relaxation skills, I now turn to hierarchy construction skills.

Construct hierarchies. Hierarchies are lists of stimuli centered around themes and ordered according to the amount of anxiety they evoke. Table 12.6 illustrates a hierarchy for a client with debilitating anxiety about math tests. Following are hierarchy construction skills.

1. *Identify suitable themes.* Precedence needs to be given to themes or areas most debilitating to clients.
2. *Generate items around themes.* Assist clients to generate items around one or more themes. Items need to be described so that clients can imagine them. Sources for hierarchy items include information gathered during assessment, homework involving self-monitoring, and suggestions from clients and you. You can ask clients to write items on index cards to make for ease of ordering.
3. *Rank items to make hierarchies.* Ranking items involves clients' rating those for each theme on a subjective anxiety scale and ordering them accordingly. A common way to check the anxiety-evoking potential of items is to say zero represents

Table 12.6 Hierarchy for client with math test anxiety

Rank	Rating	Item
1	5	Thinking about a math test when revising at my desk 1 month before
2	10	Thinking about a math test when revising at my desk 3 weeks before
3	15	Thinking about a math test when revising at my desk 2 weeks before
4	20	Thinking about a math test when revising at my desk 1 week before
5	25	Thinking about a math test the night before
6	30	Waking up the morning of the math test
7	40	Driving my car on the way to the math test
8	50	Waiting outside the test room
9	60	Going into the test room
10	70	Sitting down at my desk in the test room
11	80	Looking at the math test paper for the first time
12	90	Sitting in the test room looking at everybody else working hard
13	100	Having a panic attack during the math test

no anxiety and 100 is the maximum anxiety possible for that theme. In general, avoid gaps of over 10 units on the subjective anxiety scale. If necessary, generate intervening items. During treatment, remain flexible; you and your clients may need to reorder, reword, or generate further items.

4. *Check clients' ability to imagine items.* A basic assumption of systematic desensitization is that clients are capable of imagining hierarchy items or scenes. Check your clients' ability to imagine items. Some clients imagine items better if they describe them aloud. Also, you may provide fuller descriptions of items.

Present hierarchy items. A desensitization session starts with relaxing clients. When assured clients are deeply relaxed, present items along the lines of "Now I want you to imagine you are sitting at your desk revising for a math test 1 month before the test. . . ." Start with the least anxiety-evoking item and ask clients to raise their index finger if experiencing anxiety. If they experience no anxiety, ask them to switch the item off and go back to feeling pleasantly relaxed. After 30–50 seconds you can ask clients to imagine the item again. If this causes no anxiety, withdraw the item, possibly spend further time relaxing clients, and move on to the next item.

If clients indicate anxiety with an item, you have two main choices. First, you can withdraw the item immediately, relax the client again, and then present the item a second time. Second, and preferable for developing self-helping skills, you can both instruct clients to continue imagining the item and encourage them to relax away their anxiety by using calming and coaching self-talk and taking slow deep breaths (Goldfried, 1971; Goldfried & Davison, 1976; Meichenbaum, 1977). If clients repeatedly experience anxiety with an item, intersperse less threatening items.

Systematic desensitization assumes that once a low anxiety-evoking item (for example, 10 units) ceases to stimulate anxiety, all other hierarchy items become less anxiety-evoking by 10 units. Thus the 100-unit item becomes 90 units, and so on. Consequently, you only present weak anxiety-evoking items to clients.

Keep a record of all item presentations and their outcomes. Wolpe's (1982) desensitization sessions last 15–30 minutes. Initially, he may present a total of 8–10 items, possibly from different hierarchies. In later sessions, he may make as many as 30–50 presentations. Goldfried and Davison (1976) suggest covering from 2 to 5 items each session. You can also cassette-record items, and get clients to work through them as a homework assignment.

Encourage clients, when preparing for or facing anxiety-evoking situations in daily life, to develop self-helping skills of relaxing away tensions, taking slow and deep breaths, and using calming and coaching self-talk. Where appropriate, give clients homework logs to monitor their use of self-helping skills.

In vivo desensitization Two kinds of considerations may make in vivo (real-life, rather than visualized) desensitization the preferred intervention. First, clients may have difficulty imagining items. However, items for real-life desensitization need to be readily accessible. Second, where items are readily accessible, your intervention should be more powerful than if you work with visualized items. For instance, you may relax clients with public-speaking anxiety at the start of each session, then over a number of sessions have them give short talks in front of increasing numbers of people. You can introduce answering questions into the hierarchy to make for increased difficulty and real-lifeness. Many visualized desensitization considerations—such as using relaxation, constructing hierarchies, and the level of anxiety within which to present items—still apply to in vivo desensitization.

Use of Medication

When assisting clients to manage feelings, many helpers require familiarity with *psychotropic* drugs (drugs that act on the mind). You find difficulty assessing how clients feel unless you take into account the effects of any medication they are on. Also, if medication seems advisable, you need to refer clients to physicians. Furthermore, if working with clients on medication, you may need to discuss appropriate dosage and side effects with physicians or look them up in a reference source. In addition, clients themselves may wish to discuss their use of medication. Though you need to be careful not to go out of your depth, your clients may feel reassured if you can conduct an informed discussion.

All psychotropic drugs have possible toxic or unwanted side effects (Burns, 1980; Ponterotto, 1985). For instance, even minor tranquilizers can affect some clients with drowsiness, lessened muscular coordination, lowered sex urge, and dependency. A drug like lithium carbonate, used for mania and depression (bipolar disorder) is highly toxic and requires close medical monitoring. The levels of dosage—both amounts and frequency—are considerations for physicians prescribing drugs and for helpers working with clients on drugs. If you require information about drugs, you can ask physicians or look it up in the latest editions of regularly updated reference sources.

You may need to explore your and your clients' attitudes towards using drugs. Some helpers have prejudices against any use of drugs and, sometimes, against the medical profession. Other helpers, like some clients, may treat medication as a crutch. Clients' attitudes toward psychotropic drugs vary from viewing taking them as personal weakness to willing dependence on them. Though it is sometimes difficult to achieve, aim for clients to become psychologically self-reliant in managing feelings, including taking as little medication as possible. However, on occasion, using medication may be appropriate—for instance, with seriously disturbed clients (American Psychiatric Association, 1987) or those requiring relief in crises. As helping progresses, you may be able to wean clients off drugs, possibly by smaller and less frequent dosages. For quick-acting drugs, another option is to recommend that clients only use them in emergencies.

 ## CHAPTER HIGHLIGHTS

- Reasons for assisting clients to focus on feelings include: catharsis, improved health, lifting inhibitions and repressions, getting more in touch with wants and wishes, developing a sense of identity, providing a base for effective relating, and managing unwanted feelings.
- Helpers are feelings educators who use relationship and training skills to assist clients to experience, express, and manage feelings.
- Helpers should always assume that clients are responsible for their feelings and that they need to show clients how to implement this responsibility.
- Helpers can assist clients to experience feelings by: offering reasons for focusing on feelings; focusing on thinking skills; using rewarding listening; training clients in inner listening; using feelings questions; being authentic and appropriately self-disclosing; confronting inauthenticity; raising consciousness; teaching sensate focus; using role-play methods; and encouraging action.
- Thinking skills for expressing feelings include using coping self-talk, perceiving others accurately, and predicting realistically.

- Action skills for expressing feelings include proficiency in sending relevant verbal, voice, body, touch, and action messages.
- Thinking skills for managing anger include owning responsibility for anger, possessing realistic personal rules, perceiving provocations accurately, using coping self-talk, and using visualizing.
- Action skills for managing anger include those for assertion, handling aggressive criticism, relaxing, managing stress, and helping one another.
- Thinking skills for managing depression center on overcoming a negative outlook and include possessing realistic personal rules, perceiving self and others accurately, attributing cause accurately, and predicting realistically.
- Action skills for managing depression include relationship skills, such as initiating contact and self-disclosing; assertion skills; and pleasant activities skills.
- Thinking skills for managing anxiety center on overcoming an excessive sense of danger and include using coping self-talk, possessing realistic personal rules, perceiving self and others accurately, predicting realistically, setting realistic goals, and using visualizing.
- Action skills for managing anxiety include relaxation and the skills required for competent performance in specific situations.
- Relaxation skills may be used on their own or as part of more complex interventions like systematic desensitization. Relaxation skills include progressive muscular relaxation, brief muscular relaxation, and mental relaxation.
- Present systematic desensitization as a self-helping coping skill. In addition to training in progressive muscular relaxation, systematic desensitization includes constructing hierarchies around anxiety-evoking themes and getting clients to imagine hierarchy items when relaxed.
- Many helpers require knowledge of psychotropic drugs—drugs that work on the mind. All such drugs have unwanted side effects. Helpers may need to explore their own and clients' attitudes towards using medication.

STAGE

5

END AND CONSOLIDATE
SELF-HELPING SKILLS

The final stage of the lifeskills helping model focuses on how to end and consolidate self-helping skills. Chapter 13 looks at various ways helpers can assist clients to maintain and develop skills for the future. The chapter also focuses on further tasks and skills in the ending stage, including evaluating helping skills.

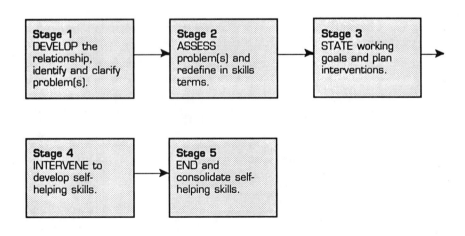

Stage 1
DEVELOP the relationship, identify and clarify problem(s).

→

Stage 2
ASSESS problem(s) and redefine in skills terms.

→

Stage 3
STATE working goals and plan interventions.

→

Stage 4
INTERVENE to develop self-helping skills.

→

Stage 5
END and consolidate self-helping skills.

CHAPTER THIRTEEN

HOW TO END AND CONSOLIDATE SELF-HELPING SKILLS

Courage is the self-affirmation of being in
    spite of the fact of nonbeing.

                           —Paul Tillich

We must combine the toughness of the
    serpent and the softness of a dove, a
    tough mind and a tender heart.

                  —Martin Luther King

CHAPTER QUESTIONS

❀ *What is the relationship between consolidating self-helping skills and ending?*

❀ *How can consolidating self-helping skills be defined?*

❀ *How can helpers focus on how clients think to consolidate self-helping skills?*

❀ *What can helpers do throughout the lifeskills helping model to enhance consolidation?*

❀ *What are different formats for ending helping?*

❀ *When should helping end?*

❀ *What are tasks and skills for the ending stage?*

❀ *How can helpers evaluate their helping skills?*

Stage 5 of the lifeskills helping model addresses the questions of how to end helping, and also of how to assist clients to continue using trained lifeskills after helping. Following are examples of helping outcomes that were not lasting.

Abdul, 24, sought help because he was worried about compulsively engaging in AIDS risk behavior. Two months after helping ended, Abdul had resumed his high-risk sexual practices.

Last year, after some sessions with her school counselor, Denise, 17, was able to cope much better with test anxiety. Again this year Denise's work suffers because she gets anxious at the thought of tests.

Sharone, 39, is a single mom with two teenage boys. Two years ago, Sharone received help to improve her parent-adolescent conflict skills in relation to her oldest boy, Jude. Sharone now experiences similar difficulties with her second son, Dave, three years younger than Jude.

For 20 years Nancy, 43, has been smoking off and mostly on. Whenever Nancy, either independently or with professional help, tries to give up smoking, she always relapses soon afterwards.

With the assistance of a helper, Han, a 51-year old-widower, started gaining confidence about going into social situations. A year after treatment, Han is back to being an unhappy "loner."

A central assumption of the lifeskills helping approach is that clients require skills, not just for managing current problems, but also for coping with future problems. Problems tend to repeat themselves if clients fail to correct underlying skills weaknesses. You can approach the ending stage of the lifeskills helping model in two ways. First, throughout helping, recognize that you must plan for its end (Teyber, 1989). Furthermore, remember that the "train-and-hope" approach to the maintenance and transfer of treatment gains is unreliable (Goldstein & Keller, 1987; Kazdin, 1989; Martin, 1990; Nemeroff & Karoly, 1991; Stokes & Osnes, 1989). Consequently, systematically attend to developing clients' lifeskills for afterwards. Recognize that, in addition to consolidating trained skills as self-helping skills, there are special tasks and skills attached to helping's final session or sessions.

Throughout this book, I use the term *self-helping skills* in preference to "self-help" skills. Self-helping, more than self-help, connotes the ongoing need for former clients to assume responsibility for maintaining and developing lifeskills worked on during helping. *Generalization, maintenance, transfer,* and *development* are four terms, albeit overlapping, for understanding what consolidating trained lifeskills as self-helping skills means (Kazdin, 1989; Nemeroff & Karoly, 1991; Skinner, 1953).

1. *Generalization:* Generalization signifies that targeted thinking skills and action skills carry over or generalize to conditions other than those included in helping. Clients apply targeted lifeskills flexibly in regard to other situations and stimuli.
2. *Maintenance:* Maintenance (resistance to extinction) refers to the extension of behavior changes after helping. Maintenance is not always consistent. Clients can suffer lapses, but over time still maintain skills. The opposite of maintenance is going back to baseline or worse.
3. *Transfer:* Transfer (transfer of training to outside helping) contains elements of both generalization and maintenance. Clients not only maintain behavior changes but also adapt them to new situations and settings.
4. *Development:* When helping ends, some former clients not only maintain, but develop targeted skills to higher levels. Such people assume responsibility for shifting the balance of strengths and weaknesses in one or more skills areas still further in the direction of strengths.

WORK WITH CLIENTS' THINKING SKILLS

Though insufficiently emphasized in the helping literature (Kazdin, 1989; Stokes & Osnes, 1989), assisting clients to consolidate trained skills as self-helping skills requires paying close attention to how they think. Even in brief helping, you may make it easier for clients to retain skills by influencing thinking. In longer-term helping, you have considerably more scope. For instance, your and your clients' work during helping on combating perfectionist rules is relevant, not only to managing problems in the short term, but also in the long term. In longer-term helping, you can spend more time specifically addressing issues of maintenance and preventing relapses. Last but not least, you have more opportunity to impart to clients the lifeskills helping conceptual framework.

Impart the Lifeskills Helping Conceptual Framework

Helpers can assist clients to approach specific problems and problematic skills within the context of the overall lifeskills helping conceptual framework outlined in Chapter 1. There are degrees to which this is feasible. In short-term helping, all you may be able to do is to structure the contact in skills terms, provide a skills redefinition of a problem, and offer one or more brief interventions to develop and maintain skills. In longer-term helping, you can go further. For instance, you can emphasize that problems can repeat themselves both horizontally (across people and situations) and vertically (over time). Consequently, effective helping needs to be based on a psychological education conceptual framework that builds and maintains clients' skills. When working with clients in the early stages of the model, you can help them to understand, not only how they initially acquired lifeskills weaknesses, but also—more importantly—how they sustain them now. During the intervention and ending stages, you can impart a psychological education viewpoint concerning the processes of developing and maintaining skills strengths. Ultimately lifeskills helping is about self-helping throughout life. If you provide truly elegant treatment, you educate clients to adopt a lifeskills approach to all situations in their lives. You move beyond treating specific problems and problematic skills weaknesses to provide them with a philosophy of living.

Following are some thinking skills that can contribute to clients' maintaining and developing lifeskills.

Owning Responsibility for Choosing

A basic assumption of lifeskills helping is that clients are personally responsible for making choices conducive to their survival, happiness, and fulfillment. Stress the importance for clients of choosing to maintain lifeskills. Unlike certain medical conditions, there is no concept of cure. Rather, clients face choices, often daily, in which they can either use or fail to use targeted lifeskills.

Self-Instructing

Ensure that clients understand the sequences of choices in targeted skills well enough to instruct and coach themselves. For example, when demonstrating assertion skills, you can demonstrate self-instruction too. Furthermore, you can get clients to summarize self-instructions either during helping sessions or as homework. Also, you can get clients to write self-instructions down or put them on cassette. Where skills are complex, helpers can instruct clients in the main rules guiding effective enactment—for example, communication rules for couples (Stuart, 1980). Often clients need to practice to retain self-instructions.

Using Coping Self-Talk

Clients can use coping self-talk skills before, during, and after difficult situations requiring them to implement additional skills (for example, speaking in public, or job interviews). If necessary, they can make up cue cards to remind themselves of appropriate self-talk. Clients can also use coping self-talk to 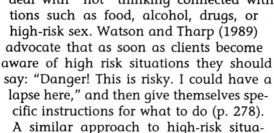 deal with "hot" thinking connected with temptations such as food, alcohol, drugs, or high-risk sex. Watson and Tharp (1989) advocate that as soon as clients become aware of high risk situations they should say: "Danger! This is risky. I could have a lapse here," and then give themselves specific instructions for what to do (p. 278). A similar approach to high-risk situations is for clients to say: "Stop . . . think . . . calm down," and then instruct themselves what to do. Further instructions include telling themselves that cravings will pass, engaging in distracting activities or thoughts, and reminding themselves of the benefits of resisting "temptation" and costs of giving in. Where clients have occasional failures or lapses, they can tell themselves "these are single events, setbacks may occur, but I can hang in there" and keep working to maintain and develop skills.

Possessing Realistic Rules

Clients may require assistance in reformulating unrealistic rules about learning and maintaining lifeskills. Following are examples of unrealistic rules and more realistic reformulations.

Unrealistic rule: "Change must be easy."
Reformulation: "I have to develop new and better skills, and also unlearn bad habits. Consequently, I have to work hard to change and maintain changes, both during and after helping."

Unrealistic rule: "During and after helping I must improve all the time."
Reformulation: "Developing any skill involves mistakes, uncertainty, and setbacks. All I can do is to learn from mistakes and cope with setbacks as best possible. The important thing is to keep trying."

Unrealistic rule: "I must have helper support to maintain my skills."

Reformulation: "Learning new skills may entail a period of dependency on helpers. However, if I conscientiously apply what I've learned, I can be independent."

Unrealistic rule: "Others must support and approve of my efforts to develop skills."

Reformulation: "Though I might prefer that others approve and support me, I cannot guarantee this. What is important is that I keep my skills development goals in mind and work hard to attain them."

These are just a few unrealistic rules that clients might possess about learning and maintaining lifeskills. You can identify, clarify, dispute, and reformulate other unrealistic rules that either you or your clients possess.

Perceiving Accurately

Assist clients to monitor and perceive skills strengths and weaknesses accurately. Clients discourage themselves if they pay disproportionate attention to setbacks rather than successes. Discouragement can also result when clients exaggerate how good they are and then fail to live up to expectations. If necessary, clients can challenge their thinking by identifying possibly inaccurate perceptions, separating fact from inference, looking for alternative perceptions and choosing the best-fit perception.

Clients can also discourage themselves if they fail to distinguish between a temporary lapse and a more permanent relapse (Watson & Tharp, 1989). When lapses occur, train clients not to commit the perceptual error of overgeneralizing them into relapses: "Since I have gone back to my old behavior once, I have permanently relapsed and can do nothing about it." Lapses should stimulate using retrieval (getting back on the track) skills rather than giving up. Clients should also beware of thinking about skills in black-and-white terms ("Either I possess a skill or I don't"). In virtually all skills areas, clients possess both strengths and weaknesses. Clients can also discourage themselves if they misperceive others' reactions. For example, they may be unnecessarily self-conscious and excessively sensitive to signs of disapproval. Furthermore, clients may become defensive when given constructive feedback.

Predicting Realistically

Predicting realistically can assist clients to maintain skills in many ways. First, clients able to predict high-risk situations can develop strategies to deal with them. Watson and Tharp (1989) observe: "A high-risk situation is one that presents a greater than usual temptation to lapse into the unwanted behavior" (p. 273). Characteristics of high-risk situations can include feeling emotionally distressed, feeling lonely, social pressure from others, and losing control under the influence of alcohol. Second, clients who predict they may have failures and lapses may feel less discouraged when they occur. Third, clients able to predict the consequences of their first post-helping failure or lapse can develop strategies for getting back on track (Marx, 1982). Fourth, clients can strengthen their resolve to maintain skills if they are able to predict benefits of continuing to use them and costs of giving them up. Fifth, clients can maintain skills if, in specific situations where realistic risk-taking is desirable, they focus on the gains of action as well as on potential losses. For example, excessively anxious clients need to develop and maintain skills of challenging and counterbalancing dangerous predictions.

Using Goal-Setting Skills

Clients need always to have the goal of at least maintaining end-of-helping skills levels. In addition, clients may have goals to develop skills still further. Such skills development goals should be specific, realistic, and possess a time frame. Helpers and clients can make plans to assist development of skills after helping. If so, remember the importance of stating sub-goals and sequencing graded tasks. Clients who set themselves unrealistic post-helping goals may even end up losing gains made during helping. Clients should always review goals in light of experience and feedback. In addition, helpers should always be sensitive to clients' commitment to attaining goals. If you sense that clients have insufficient commitment, you can share this observation and together explore the issue more fully.

Using Visualizing

Clients can use visualizing to strengthen skills strengths and prevent skills weaknesses. For instance, clients can visually rehearse and practice desired skills, possibly with accompanying self-talk. In addition, clients can visualize anticipated high-risk situations and develop strategies for coping with them. Clients can also visualize the negative consequences of engaging in, or relapsing back to, unwanted behaviors. Some clients may need to exaggerate the negative consequences to strengthen their will power (Cautela, 1967; Lazarus, 1977).

Using Self-Reward

Clients can use self-reward both to acquire and to maintain lifeskills. They can continue administering external rewards contingent on desired actions (for example, having a cup of coffee after 50 minutes of study). In addition, clients can encourage themselves with internal rewards like "Well done," "I hung in there and made it," and "I'm happy that I'm maintaining my skills." Sometimes clients can use self-reward to help them attain "natural" rewards. For instance, shy clients might encourage themselves as they continue working on skills that elicit the natural rewards of positive social interaction. Where possible, set up schedules of reward and self-reward that enable clients to shift from artificial treatment-based rewards to real-life rewards, such as approval, competence, and money (Nemeroff & Karoly, 1991).

Managing Problems

Clients can fail to maintain lifeskills because of problems in targeted skills areas. In addition, problems in other areas of clients' lives can interfere with maintaining targeted skills. For example, Jacobson's (1989) study of the maintenance of treatment gains after social-learning–based marital therapy found stressful life events by far the best predictor of relapse.

Helpers and clients can view maintaining a targeted lifeskill as a problem to be managed. Accordingly, they can apply CASIE, the five-step framework for managing problems outlined in Chapter 10, to how to maintain targeted lifeskills. Following are some considerations for each of CASIE's five steps.

C = Confront, identify, and clarify my problem.   You need to assist clients to confront their problem of needing to maintain and, if possible, develop targeted lifeskills. Such confrontations take place in earlier as well as in final sessions.

A = Assess my problem and redefine it in skills terms. Maintenance redefinitions at the end of helping can be close to initial redefinitions at the start of helping. Helpers and clients predict thinking and action skills weaknesses that may interfere with retaining targeted skills. For instance, Luke, age 16, has made considerable progress in controlling his drinking. Together Luke and his helper arrive at the following skills redefinition of Luke's problem of how to maintain control of his drinking.

Thinking Skills Weaknesses	Action Skills Weaknesses
Owning responsibility for choices	Assertion skills when faced with peer pressure to drink
Using coping self-talk skills in high-risk situations	Support network skills
Having personal rules about needing approval and having lapses	Conversational skills
	Nondrinking-related pleasant activities skills
Perceiving self and progress accurately	
Preventing and managing problems	

S = State working goals and plan self-helping interventions. If clients do not know how to do so already, helpers can assist them to translate skills redefinitions into statements of working goals. Clients and helpers can plan how to attain each maintenance sub-goal. Where clients decide on working goals in the penultimate (second to last) session, they can bring suggestions for attaining them to the final session. Maintenance plans should in particular focus on developing and using appropriate thinking and action skills to deal with high-risk situations. Identify such situations and work out strategies with clients for handling them. Clients' records of how well they use skills in difficult and high-risk situations may assist in the planning. Maintenance plans should also focus on retrieval skills for dealing with failures and lapses.

GOALS

I = Implement my plan. Since clients implement maintenance plans after final sessions, both they and you have to wait and see how they perform.

E = Evaluate the consequences of implementing my plan. Helpers and clients can discuss how to measure success in maintaining targeted lifeskills. Important questions that clients can ask themselves are: "How well am I maintaining and developing my targeted thinking and action skills?," "What are the consequences for myself and others of changes in my thinking and action skills?," and "Do I need to modify my plan in light of feedback and new information?"

SKILLS FOR ENHANCING CONSOLIDATION

In addition to focusing on clients' thinking skills, helpers can use other skills at each stage of the DASIE model to help them retain trained skills.

Stage 1: Develop the Relationship, Identify and Clarify Problems

From helping's start, be mindful of clients' needs to consolidate trained skills as self-helping skills. For all stages of the model, if you provide a good helping relationship, you will lessen the likelihood of premature termination and increase the likelihood of clients' learning skills well—and hence continuing to use them. Following are some stage 1 skills relevant to clients' maintaining trained skills.

Structure for Maintenance

You may start the first session with some open-ended structuring to encourage clients to tell their stories. However, later you may make structuring comments about how you are going to work (see Chapter 5). Ideas to incorporate in structuring for maintenance include: using skills language, focusing on self-helping, emphasizing work and practice to maintain skills, and letting clients know that they can sharpen and develop skills after helping. Included among such comments may be statements like the following.

> "I would like us to collaborate in identifying thinking and action skills, not just for managing this problem, but for working on similar problems in the future."
> "The skills you learn during helping are basically self-helping skills for you to maintain and use on your own."
> "There is no concept of cure in this approach. Even after helping, you're still going to have to work to retain your skills and their benefits."
> "You can go so far during helping, but I hope your skills are good enough by the time we end to give you a sound base for sharpening and developing them afterwards."

Develop Clients' Self-Monitoring and Clarifying Problems Skills

Accurate self-monitoring is important for maintaining and developing targeted skills. Former clients who are unaware of or misperceive how they behave lack accurate information for correcting mistakes and sharpening skills. From helping's start, influence clients to be good observers of how they feel, think, and act. If you are systematic in how you collaborate with clients to identify and clarify problems, you develop their skills of self-monitoring and clarifying problems. Emphasize the importance of accurate self-monitoring for learning, maintaining, and sharpening targeted skills. Self-monitoring skills include both perceiving behavior accurately and, where appropriate, recording it systematically (for instance, on frequency charts and, later, in use of targeted skills logs).

Stage 2: Assess Problems and Redefine in Skills Terms

Helper skills for consolidating clients' self-helping skills during stage 2 include the following.

Develop Clients' Self-Assessment Skills

If you make it a joint enterprise with clients to assess how they feel, think, and act, they will probably develop better self-assessment skills than if you fail to involve them in the process. Ongoing assessment is an integral part of lifeskills helping. However, helpers need to impart assessment skills as client self-helping skills and encourage clients to engage in self-assessment during, and after, helping. It is insufficient for clients merely to self-monitor how they feel, think, and act; they need to make accurate assessments of the significance of this information for maintaining or altering behavior.

Develop Clients' Skills at Redefining Problems in Skills Terms

How you redefine problems in skills terms influences how useful this process is for assisting clients in maintaining skills. Draw them into the process by letting them know why you break down their problems into thinking skills and action skills. Check the adequacy of your skills redefinitions with them and answer questions. Especially with longer-term clients, let them know that redefining problems in skills terms is a useful self-helping skill for understanding problems, setting working goals, assessing progress, making maintenance plans, and monitoring how well they maintain and develop skills after helping. Where possible, let clients know any characteristic thinking skills weaknesses that you perceive occurring across a range of problems (for instance, possessing perfectionist rules). This gives them a start on knowing where to look when facing future problems. Also, indicate recurring action skills weaknesses (for instance, poor assertion skills are relevant to many problems).

Stage 3: State Working Goals and Plan Interventions

Following are suggestions for using stating working goals and planning interventions skills to assist clients to consolidate trained skills as self-helping skills.

Develop Clients' Skills at Stating Working Goals

If you negotiate with clients clear initial statements of working goals, you make it easier for them to maintain targeted skills. Such goals are relevant for after, as well as during, helping. Make sure clients keep records of goals statements. During helping, clear goals assist learning—and hence maintaining skills—by providing focus and motivating clients. After helping, clear goals remind clients of skills to retain and provide yardsticks for assessing progress. With clients having multiple problems, initially state working goals yourself, but later coach them as they suggest appropriate goals.

Plan Interventions to Enhance Maintenance

In Chapter 8, I distinguished between structured and open plans for developing targeted skills. Helpers may write maintenance considerations into structured plans and keep them in mind when adopting open plans. Following are some ways that helpers can enhance maintenance when planning.

1. *Maintain a skills focus.* Use skills language. Plans containing a clear skills focus assist clients to think in skills terms both during and after helping.
2. *Focus on thinking skills.* I presented such skills earlier in this chapter.
3. *Focus on self-instruction.* Plan how you can make it clear to clients how to instruct themselves through sequences of skills choices. Also, plan how to make it easier for them to remember self-instructions.
4. *Build in ongoing self-assessment.* Develop clients' awareness and skills of monitoring and assessing thinking and action skills.
5. *Allow for overlearning.* Goldstein and Keller (1987) state: "Overlearning involves the training of a skill beyond what is necessary to produce changes in behavior" (p. 116). Where

possible, train clients thoroughly in targeted skills. Strategies for overlearning include limited goals, repeated skills demonstrations, emphasizing coaching and learning-by-doing, and ensuring adequate time and supervision of homework and practice.

6. *Emphasize real-lifeness.* Emphasizing "real-lifeness" means that helpers focus on practical ways of ensuring that clients can use skills in real life as contrasted to artificial settings. Plan to tailor presentations and demonstrations to clients' real-life situations. Role-play rehearsals should resemble real interactions. Plan homework that enhances transfer of skills to home settings.

7. *Train diversely.* Stokes and Osnes (1989) state: "What has frequently been documented is the fact that focused training frequently has focused effects" (p. 345). Beware of narrow training that does not help clients to respond flexibly to new situations. For instance, if rehearsing a client in asking for a pay raise, ensure that you have trials in which the boss responds in different ways.

8. *Plan reward strategies.* Helpers can plan reward strategies that enhance maintenance (Goldstein & Keller, 1987; Nemeroff & Karoly, 1991; Stokes & Osnes, 1989). For instance, you may reward clients frequently as they initially acquire skills and then reward them intermittently as they use them. Applying reward schedules this way is called "thinning." Nemeroff and Karoly (1991) observe: "It is particularly helpful if one can ensure that the behavior being trained will come to elicit *natural* reinforcers in the real world—money, competence, approval, and so on . . ." (p. 146). In addition, prompts and reminders can be gradually withdrawn.

9. *Consider using helper's aides.* Helpers wishing to enlist third parties as aides (for instance, teachers and parents) need to plan how to do this. Be systematic about creating roles for aides, contacting them, enlisting support, and offering them appropriate training.

10. *Spend time on coping with difficult and high-risk situations.* Plan to work on issues of maintenance and relapse throughout your program. Do not leave this to the end.

11. *Allow adequate time for ending and consolidating skills.* Different formats for ending are covered later in this chapter. For instance, you may space out sessions toward the end of helping. Attend to ending issues before, as well as during, the final session. Clients need adequate time to develop maintenance plans.

Stage 4: Intervene to Develop Self-Helping Skills

Helpers who, when intervening, offer both supportive relationships and good training skills enhance clients' likelihood of maintaining skills after helping. The enhancing maintenance skills already mentioned are relevant for focusing on consolidating skills in the intervention stage. For instance, keep developing clients' self-monitoring and self-assessment skills. Also, where possible, carry out those aspects of your plans that enhance maintenance (for instance, allow for overlearning, train diversely, and emphasize real-lifeness). Here are some further enhancing maintenance skills for you.

Emphasize Homework Assignments

Both helpers and clients require a commitment to homework as a bridge between learning and maintaining skills. Homework should be a feature of all between-session periods. Homework tasks can give clients the opportunity to practice skills in diverse situations. In subsequent sessions, always review how clients performed and inquire about related thoughts and feelings. If appropriate, discuss difficulties and setbacks that clients experience and make them the focus of skills rehearsal role-plays.

Encourage Client Summaries

Throughout the intervention stage, check that clients understand targeted skills. In addition to providing summaries yourself, you can enhance learning and maintenance by periodically requesting client summaries of targeted skills. If clients can describe skills accurately, they have a good base for implementing and remembering them. If, however, clients misunderstand or make mistakes, correct them.

Use Handouts, Cassettes, and Videotapes

Providing clients with handouts, cassettes, and videotapes that clearly describe and demonstrate targeted skills can enhance maintenance. First, you assist clients in initially learning skills. Second, if clients keep the material, they can use it for revising.

Encourage Clients to Keep Helping Files

Helpers may enhance maintenance by encouraging clients to keep a helping file. Arguably it is more important for clients than for helpers to keep records. What clients call the file is up to them. The purpose of the helping file is to record important information and learnings collected during and after helping. Contents of files can include statements of working goals, plans, self-monitoring logs, handouts describing skills, homework assignments, answers to homework assignments, and so on. The helping file enhances maintenance in many ways. First, by making the effort to keep the file, clients show a commitment to maintaining targeted skills. Second, clients can use the file for revising. Third, they can use it for evaluating progress. Fourth, after helping ends, they can update the file as they keep working on targeted skills until they are firmly established in their repertoires.

Develop Clients' Identifying and Using Supports Skills

In Chapter 10, I mentioned the helper skill of assisting clients to identify and use supports as they develop skills. Many of the supports clients identify during helping should be available after helping. In addition, during helping you can encourage clients to view identifying and using supports as a useful self-helping skill. One way of using others as supports is to encourage them to give honest feedback in nonthreatening ways. Open acknowledgement by others of positive behavior changes can motivate clients to keep working. However, feedback can also be useful if it is corrective rather than confirmatory.

THE ENDING STAGE

The boundaries of the ending stage are imprecise. As implied in the previous discussion on consolidating self-helping skills, helping has its ending built into its beginning. In another sense, the ending of formal helping is the beginning of independent self-helping. Despite advocating countdowns to ending in earlier sessions, here, for the sake of simplicity, I define the ending stage as starting with the penultimate session and concluding when all scheduled contact between client and helper finishes.

Formats for Ending Helping

Following are possible formats for ending helping.

Fixed ending Helper and client may have a contract that they work for, say, 10 sessions in one or more problem and problematic skills areas. Advantages of fixed endings include lessening the chance of dependency and motivating clients to use helping to best effect. Potential disadvantages are restricting coverage of problems and thoroughness of attention to problematic skills. Sometimes external factors make for fixed endings (for instance, upcoming tests or ends of semesters).

Open ending when goals are attained   With open endings, helping concludes when helpers and clients agree that clients have obtained their objectives. Such objectives include managing a specific problem, developing skills to manage current and future problems, and, in exceptional cases, staying in helping long enough to become thoroughly grounded in the lifeskills philosophy of life.

Faded ending   Here the withdrawal of helper assistance is gradual. For example, instead of meeting weekly, the final sessions could be at biweekly or monthly intervals.

Ending with booster sessions   Booster sessions, say after 3 months, are not to teach new skills, but to check clients' progress in consolidating skills, motivate them, and help them work through difficulties in translating trained skills into home environments.

Ending with scheduled follow-up phone calls   Helpers can schedule follow-up phone calls with clients. Such phone calls perform the same functions as booster sessions. From both phone calls and booster sessions, helpers obtain feedback on how successful helping was in assisting clients to maintain skills.

Premature ending   Frequently clients leave helping before helpers think they are ready. However, what may seem premature to helpers may seem different to clients. Beck and his colleagues cite as reasons for premature termination: rapid relief of symptoms; negative reactions to the therapist, and lack of sustained improvement or relapse during treatment (Beck, Rush, Shaw & Emery, 1979). Another reason why clients leave helping is that they find their helpers' theoretical approaches, rather than their personalities, to be uncongenial. Some clients may not like the lifeskills helping approach. Helpers who clumsily handle clients' doubts about and resistances to helping increase the likelihood of premature termination. Further reasons why clients leave prematurely include pressure from significant others, laziness, defensiveness, lack of money, moving to another location, and fear of being trapped by helpers unwilling to "let go."

Helpers may consider it premature if clients leave helping feeling able to cope with immediate problems, but without having consolidated thinking and action skills for dealing with future problems. In such instances, helpers and clients can still have done useful work together. Also, former clients may now possess insights about skills needed to cope with future problems and be more inclined to seek further assistance, if needed.

When Should Helping End?

Start helper-client termination discussions before final sessions and aim for convergence either then or by the final session. Throughout helping, helpers and clients collect information relevant to termination decisions. Following are sources and kinds of relevant information.

Client self-report   Clients may perceive themselves as better able to cope with problems. They may think they have attained thinking and action skills working goals. They may feel more confident and less prone to negative emotions. They perceive they no longer require the support of helpers and can maintain skills.

Helper observation   Over a series of sessions, helpers may notice improvements in how well clients use targeted thinking skills and action skills. These observations come from various sources: the helping conversation, role-plays and other structured activities, and from probes about how clients use skills outside helping. You may observe clients feeling happier and more relaxed. They no longer have symptoms that brought them to helping (for instance, excessive anxiety). Problems that previously seemed insurmountable now seem manageable. Clients use better skills in responding to such problems. In addition, they seem to understand and use targeted skills well enough to maintain them.

Feedback from significant others   Another set of reasons for considering ending helping is "when significant others in clients' lives give clients feedback that they are different, or have changed, or make comments such as 'you never used to do that before'" (Teyber, 1989, p. 190). Sometimes feedback may come direct to you (for instance, from helper's aides, spouses, bosses, or parents).

Attainment of measurable goals   Clients can have easily measurable goals. For example, they may pass a driving test or fly in an airplane. Other examples of measurable goals include: losing a stipulated amount of weight and maintaining the loss over a given period, cutting down on smoking and maintaining the reduction, keeping off alcohol, and spending only a certain amount of money each week. Clients' goals can be both objective and subjective (for instance, making a given number of friends in a set period of time). The given number and set period are objective, whereas the definition of friends is more subjective.

If you and your clients consistently obtain positive information from all four of the above sources, your decision about when to end is easy. However, if positive changes are recent, it may pay to wait and see if clients maintain them. Also, inconsistent information, either from within or between different sources, merits further exploration.

Consolidating Self-Helping Skills in the Ending Stage

The main task of the ending stage is "the consolidation of what has been achieved in terms of some durable benefit for the interviewee" (Sullivan, 1954, p. 41). Many skills that you use in this stage build on skills you have used earlier. With clients who come for brief, focused helping, you trade off and compromise on what you can achieve in the ending stage. Following are some skills for enhancing consolidation in the ending stage.

Make Transition Statements

During helping, you may make statements indicating its finiteness (for instance, comments about developing self-helping skills for after helping). Such comments may encourage clients to make the most of sessions. You can introduce the ending stage with one or more transition statements.

> "Our next session is the final session. I think we should discuss how we can use the time we have left to help you retain and build on the skills you've learned. We could even develop a maintenance plan for you."
> "I think the agenda for this final session should mainly be how to help you later use the skills you've learned. For instance, we can review how much you've changed, where you still need to change, how you might go about it, and how you can deal with high-risk situations."

Summarize

I have stressed the need throughout helping for helper and client summaries. In the ending stage, summaries can review both main learnings and perceptions of progress. Formulating personal summaries can be a homework assignment prior to final sessions. You can also ask clients to record their summaries as reminders. Another idea is for clients to keep cassette recordings of final sessions.

Facilitate Self-Assessment and Develop Maintenance Plans

During the ending stage, continue to develop clients' self-monitoring and self-assessment skills. Helpers and clients can take a systematic approach to the problem of maintaining skills. Because you assume that clients maintain skills on their own, use the client-centered CASIE self-helping framework rather than the more helper-centered DASIE framework.

Rehearse Coping with High-Risk Situations and with Lapses

Rehearsing coping with high-risk situations and lapses should be part of structured activities during helping, and not an afterthought left until the end. Helpers and clients can rehearse thinking and action skills for implementing maintenance plans. For example, clients can role-play how to use appropriate thinking and action skills in specific high-risk situations. In addition, they can rehearse and write down appropriate self-talk for handling lapses, underachievement, and failure.

Helpers can reemphasize clients' responsibility for their lives. Therefore, when they are in difficulty, looking at the adequacy of their own thinking, acting, and use of targeted skills is the best place to start. Clients can ask themselves questions like "What are my goals and how is my behavior blocking me from attaining them?," "What are my characteristic thinking and action skills weaknesses in relation to this problem?," and "How well am I using the skills I have learned and how can I improve?" Stress the importance of clients' developing good retrieval skills and realizing that maintaining gains requires continuing effort.

Reinforce Effective Thinking Skills

Helpers can use the ending stage to reinforce the importance of clients' continuing to focus on their inner game (how they think) as well as on their outer game (how they act). Also, you can reinforce specific thinking skills conducive to maintaining targeted lifeskills. Where possible, introduce such thinking skills before the final session. During final sessions, helpers and clients can review previously presented thinking skills. They can also rehearse thinking skills for coping with specific difficult or high-risk situations.

Work with Helper's Aides

During the ending stage, helpers can contact their aides to receive assessments of clients' progress outside helping. Helpers can also work with aides to identify ways in which they can continue supporting clients once helping ends. Sometimes three-way meetings between helpers, clients, and aides are desirable. For example, at the end of a series of helping sessions designed to help an elementary school child become more outgoing, teacher, child, and school counselor might together plan how the teacher could continue supporting the child.

Explore Arrangements for Continuing Support

Self-support is the main way that clients can receive continuing support. However, given the high probability of some degree of lapse in using targeted skills, think through how clients might receive ongoing support. Following are some options.

1. *Further contact with helper:* Possibilities for further contact with helpers include scheduled booster sessions, follow-up sessions at clients' request, and either scheduled or unscheduled phone calls. You can discuss with clients how you view further contact with them.
2. *Referral for further individual helping:* Though clients may have made considerable progress with the problems and problematic skills for which they came to helping, they may still require further professional assistance. For many reasons you may decide to refer such clients to other helpers (for instance, your time may be limited, or another helper may have special expertise in an emerging problem area).
3. *Use of outside supports:* At helping's end, you can assist clients to identify and use supports for maintaining and developing targeted skills.
4. *Group helping:* Some clients might gain from joining groups in which they can practice and develop targeted skills. Peer self-help groups provide an alternative to professionally led groups. Helpers can also discuss opportunities for participating in courses or workshops run by themselves or others.

5. *Further reading and audiovisual material:* Some clients appreciate the support provided by further reading. Clients can also
listen to and watch self-helping audio-
cassettes and videotapes. On your own initiative, or by request, you can suggest
appropriate books, training manuals,
audiocassettes, and videotapes.

Further Ending-Stage Tasks and Skills

In addition to the major task of consolidating self-helping skills,
there are other tasks for the ending stage. How you handle them
varies with length of helping, the nature of problems and problematic skills, and the helper-client relationship.

Deal with Feelings

Most lifeskills helping contacts are focused and short- to medium-term. Furthermore, though the helping relationship is important, it is not the central feature of lifeskills helping. Consequently, there is less likelihood of clients' feeling angry, sad,
anxious, and abandoned than in longer-term relationship-ori-
ented therapy. In addition, clients should feel better able to cope
with problems and problematic skills as a result of helping. Ideally, they will have a sense of accomplishment and optimism.

Clients' feelings at the end of helping fall into two main categories: feelings about how they are going to fare without helpers, and feelings toward helpers and the helping process. Many
clients have feelings of ambivalence about how they will cope
after helping. On the one hand, they feel more competent; on
the other, they still have doubts about their abilities to implement skills. Helpers can facilitate open discussion of clients' feelings about the future. Looking at how best to maintain skills
also addresses the issue of clients' lingering doubts. Other clients
will feel that they can cope very well without you—one hopes it
is a sign that together you have done a good job!

Clients may also wish to share feelings about you and the
helping process. Since the helping relationship is not the main
agenda, do not get side-tracked into lengthy discussions of unfinished emotional business. Nevertheless, allow clients the opportunity to share feelings about their contact with you. You
may obtain valuable feedback about how you come across. You
may also share positive feelings with clients (for instance, "I
enjoyed working with you" or "I admire the courage with which
you face your situation").

Say Goodbye

Saying goodbye, the formal leave-taking, "should be a clean-cut, respectful finish that does not confuse that which has been done" (Sullivan, 1954, p. 216). Last impressions are important. Aim to say goodbye in a businesslike, yet friendly, way appropriate to a professional rather than a personal relationship. By ending helping sloppily, you may undo some of your influence in helping clients to maintain skills. In addition, getting your personal and professional wires crossed is not only unethical, but it can also make it more difficult to help if future need arises.

End Ethically

A number of important ethical issues surround ending helping. For example, helpers need to think through their responsibilities to clients after helping. Too much support may engender dependency, too little may fail to carry out professional obligations. Each case must be judged on its merits. Another ethical issue is what to do when you think clients have other problems on which they need to work. I suggest bringing your views tactfully to their attention. A further set of ethical issues surrounds the boundaries between personal and professional relationships. Most professional associations have ethical codes covering issues in providing helping services (for instance, American Association for Counseling and Development, 1988; American Psychological Association, 1981, 1987, 1990; Australian Psychological Society, 1986; British Association for Counselling, 1990; British Psychological Society, 1991; National Association of Social Workers, 1979; National Board for Certified Counselors, 1987).

Evaluate Your Helping Skills

By the ending stage, helpers have many sources of information for evaluating their helping skills. These sources of information include: attendance; client feedback, both intentional and unintentional; perceptions of client progress; session notes; possibly video or audio feedback; feedback from third parties; and compliance with homework tasks. Effective helpers, like good clients, evaluate their skills throughout helping. You need to make a final evaluation of your work with each client soon after helping ends—otherwise you risk forgetting valuable information. Beware of perceptual distortions when evaluating helping skills; you may be too hard or too easy on yourself. What you seek is a balanced appraisal of strengths and weaknesses. Following are some questions that you might ask yourself.

1. To what extent did the client achieve goals in relation to managing the problems that brought him or her to helping?
2. To what extent did the client achieve thinking skills working goals?
3. To what extent did the client achieve action skills working goals?
4. What is the client's likelihood of maintaining and developing targeted skills?
5. What were my strengths and weaknesses in offering a supportive helping relationship?
6. What were my strengths and weaknesses in identifying and clarifying the client's problems?
7. What were my strengths and weaknesses in assessing the client's feelings, thinking skills, and action skills?
8. What were my strengths and weaknesses in redefining the client's problems in skills terms?
9. What were my strengths and weaknesses in stating working goals?
10. What were my strengths and weaknesses in planning interventions?
11. What were my strengths and weaknesses in using speaking skills to deliver interventions?
12. What were my strengths and weaknesses in using demonstration skills to deliver interventions?
13. What were my strengths and weaknesses in using structured activities skills to deliver interventions?
14. How satisfied am I with the way I assigned and monitored between-session homework?
15. How well did I deliver each intervention that I attempted?
16. Was I sufficiently flexible in responding to emerging problems and issues during the intervention stage?
17. How satisfied am I with the way I planned and handled individual sessions during the intervention stage?
18. What strategies did I use for consolidating trained skills as self-helping skills and how effective did they seem?
19. What were my skills strengths and weaknesses in handling the ending stage?
20. How satisfied am I with the way I identified and handled ethical issues that arose during helping?
21. When working with this client, did I have adequate professional support and supervision?
22. What specifically did I learn about my helping style and skills?

23. What, if any, are my goals for improving my helping skills?
24. How can I implement any goals I have for improving my helping skills?

POSTSCRIPT

Congratulations, you have now reached the last part of the ending stage of this book. In it I presented a systematic model for assisting clients to develop and maintain lifeskills. As a helper, you have a twofold challenge: to maintain and develop both your lifeskills and your helping skills. I hope this book, with its accompanying training manual, provides a useful conceptual framework and set of skills for both tasks. May you enjoy good thinking and action skills in your personal and helping lives.

 ## CHAPTER HIGHLIGHTS

- Helpers need to systematically attend to developing clients' lifeskills for after helping.
- Generalization, maintenance, transfer, and development are important considerations for consolidating clients' self-helping skills.
- Helpers need to work with clients' thinking skills to enhance consolidation. This includes imparting the lifeskills conceptual framework.
- Stage 1 skills for enhancing consolidation of trained skills as self-helping skills include structuring for maintenance and developing clients' self-monitoring and clarifying problems skills.
- Stage 2 skills for enhancing consolidation include developing clients' skills of self-assessment and of redefining problems in skills terms.
- Stage 3 skills for enhancing consolidation focus both on developing clients' skills at stating working goals and on how to plan interventions for maintaining skills.
- Considerations in planning for consolidation include: maintaining a skills focus, focusing on thinking skills and self-instructing, building in ongoing self-assessment, allowing for overlearning, emphasizing "real-lifeness," training diversely, planning reward strategies, considering using helper's aides,

spending time on coping with difficult and high-risk situations, and allowing adequate time for ending and consolidating skills.

- When intervening in stage 4, skills for enhancing consolidation include: emphasizing homework assignments; encouraging client summaries; using handouts, cassettes, and videotapes; encouraging clients to keep helping files; and developing clients' identifying and using supports skills.
- Formats for the ending stage include: fixed ending, open ending when goals are attained, faded ending, and ending with booster sessions or scheduled follow-up phone calls. In addition, from helpers' viewpoints, clients may end helping prematurely.
- Helpers should raise the issue of ending before the final session.
- Sources of information for when to end include: client self-report, helper observation, feedback from significant others, and attainment of measurable goals.
- Stage 5 skills for enhancing consolidation include: making transition statements, summarizing, facilitating self-assessment and the development of maintenance plans, rehearsing coping with high-risk situations and with lapses, reinforcing effective thinking skills, working with helper's aides, and exploring arrangements for continuing support.
- Further ending-stage tasks and skills include: dealing with feelings, saying goodbye, ending ethically, and evaluating your helping skills.
- As a helper you have a twofold challenge: to maintain and develop both your lifeskills and your helping skills.

BIBLIOGRAPHY

Abramson, L. Y., Seligman, M. E. P., & Teasdale, J. D. (1978). Learned helplessness in humans: Critique and reformulation. *Journal of Abnormal Psychology, 87,* 49–74.

Albee, G. W. (1984). A competency model must replace a defect model. In J. M. Joffe, G. W. Albee, & L. D. Kelly (Eds.), *Readings in primary prevention of psychopathology: Basic concepts* (pp. 228–46). Hanover, NH: University Press of New England.

Alberti, R. E., & Emmons, M. L. (1990). *Your perfect right: A guide to assertive living* (6th ed.). San Luis Obispo, CA: Impact Publishers.

Allen, J. P., & Turner, E. (1990). Where diversity reigns. *American Demographics, 12* (8), 34–38.

Allport, G. W. (1955). *Becoming: Basic considerations for a psychology of personality.* New Haven: Yale University Press.

Allport, G. W., Vernon, P. E., & Lindzey, G. (1960). *A study of values.* Boston: Houghton Mifflin.

Alpert, R., & Haber, R. N. (1960). Anxiety in academic achievement situations. *Journal of Abnormal and Social Psychology, 61,* 204–215.

Amatea, E. S., Clark, J. E., & Cross, E. G. (1984). Life-styles: Evaluating a life role planning program for high school students. *Vocational Guidance Quarterly, 32,* 249–59.

American Association for Counseling and Development (1988). *Ethical standards.* Alexandria, VA: Author.

American Psychiatric Association (1987). *Diagnostic and statistical manual of mental disorders* (3rd ed.—Revised). Washington, DC: Author.

American Psychological Association (1981). Ethical principles of psychologists. *American Psychologist, 36,* 633–38.

American Psychological Association (1987). General guidelines for providers of psychological services. *American Psychologist, 42,* 724–29.

American Psychological Association (1990). Ethical principles of psychologists. *American Psychologist, 45,* 390–95.

Argyle, M. (1983). *The psychology of interpersonal behaviour* (4th ed.). Harmondsworth, England: Penguin.

Argyle, M. (1984). Some new developments in social skills training. *Bulletin of the British Psychological Society, 37,* 405–410.

Argyle, M. (1986). Rules for social relationships in four cultures. *Australian Journal of Psychology, 38,* 309–318.

Argyle, M., & Henderson, M. (1985). *The anatomy of relationships.* Harmondsworth, England: Penguin.

Arlow, J. A. (1989). Psychoanalysis. In R. J. Corsini & D. Wedding (Eds.), *Current psychotherapies* (4th ed., pp. 19–62). Itasca, IL: Peacock.

Arroba, T. (1977). Styles of decision making and their use: An empirical study. *British Journal of Guidance and Counselling, 5,* 149–58.

Australian Psychological Society (1986). *Code of professional conduct.* Melbourne: Author.

Axelson, J. A. (1985). *Counseling and development in a multicultural society.* Pacific Grove, CA: Brooks/Cole.

Bacorn, C. N., & Dixon, D. N. (1984). The effects of touch on depressed and vocationally undecided clients. *Journal of Counseling Psychology, 31,* 488–96.

Bandura, A. (1969). *Principles of behavior modification.* New York: Holt, Rinehart & Winston.

Bandura, A. (1976). Effecting change through participant modeling. In J. D. Krumboltz & C. E. Thoresen (Eds.), *Counseling methods* (pp. 248–65). New York: Holt, Rinehart & Winston.

Bandura, A.(1977). *Social learning theory.* Englewood Cliffs, NJ: Prentice-Hall.

Bandura, A. (1986). *Social foundations of thought and action: A social cognitive theory.* Englewood Cliffs, NJ: Prentice-Hall.

Bandura, A. (1989). Human agency in social cognitive theory. *American Psychologist, 44,* 1175–84.

Bandura, A., Grusec, J. E., & Menlove, F. L. (1966). Observational learning as a function of symbolization and incentive set. *Child Development, 37,* 499–506.

Barrett-Lennard, G. T. (1962). Dimensions of therapeutic response as causal factors in therapeutic change. *Psychological Monographs, 76* (Whole No. 562).

Barrett-Lennard, G. T. (1981). The empathy cycle: Refinement of a nuclear concept. *Journal of Counseling Psychology, 28,* 91–100.

Barrow, J. C., & Moore, C. A. (1983). Group interventions with perfectionist thinking. *Personnel and Guidance Journal, 61,* 612–15.

Batson, C. D. (1990). How social an animal? The human capacity for caring. *American Psychologist, 45,* 336–46.

Beck, A. T. (1976). *Cognitive therapy and the emotional disorders.* New York: New American Library.

Beck, A. T. (1978). *Depression inventory.* Philadelphia: Center for Cognitive Therapy.

Beck, A. T. (1988). *Love is never enough: How couples can overcome misunderstandings, resolve conflicts, and solve relationship problems through cognitive therapy.* New York: Harper & Row.

Beck, A. T. (1991). Cognitive therapy: A 10-year retrospective. *American Psychologist, 46,* 368–75.

Beck, A. T., & Emery, G. (1985). *Anxiety disorders and phobias: A cognitive perspective.* New York: Basic Books.

Beck, A. T., Epstein, N., Brown, G., & Steer, R. A. (1988). An inventory for measuring clinical anxiety: Psychometric properties. *Journal of Consulting and Clinical Psychology, 56,* 893–97.

Beck, A. T., Laude, R., & Bohnert, M. (1974). Ideational components of anxiety neurosis. *Archives of General Psychiatry, 31,* 319–25.

Beck, A. T., Riskind, J. H., Brown, G., & Steer, R. A. (1988). Levels of hopelessness in DSM-III disorders: A partial test of content specificity in depression. *Cognitive Therapy and Research, 12,* 459–69.

Beck, A. T., Rush, A. J., Shaw, B. F., & Emery, G. (1979). *Cognitive therapy of depression.* New York: John Wiley.

Beck, A. T., & Weishaar, M. E. (1989). Cognitive therapy. In R. J. Corsini & D. Wedding (Eds.), *Current psychotherapies* (4th ed., pp. 285–320). Itasca, IL: Peacock.

Bem, S. L. (1974). The measurement of psychological androgyny. *Journal of Consulting and Clinical Psychology, 42,* 155–62.

Bem, S. L. (1981). Gender schema theory: A cognitive account of sex typing. *Psychological Review, 88,* 354–64.

Berne, E. (1961). *Transactional analysis in psychotherapy.* New York: Grove Press.

Berne, E. (1964). *Games people play.* New York: Grove Press.

Berne, E. (1972). *What do you say after you say hello?* New York: Grove Press.

Bernstein, D. (1988). *Put it together, put it across: The craft of business presentation.* London: Cassell.

Bernstein, D. A., & Borkovec, T. D. (1973). *Progressive relaxation training: A manual for the helping professions.* Champaign, IL: Research Press.

Bianchi, S. M., & Seltzer, J. A. (1986). Life without father. *American Demographics, 8*(12), 43–47.

Blackwell, R. T., Galassi, J. P., Galassi, M. D., & Watson, T. E. (1985). Are cognitive assessment methods equal? A comparison of think aloud and thought listing. *Cognitive Therapy and Research, 9,* 399–413.

Blatner, A. (1989). Psychodrama. In R. J. Corsini & D. Wedding (Eds.), *Current psychotherapies* (4th ed., pp. 561–71). Itasca, IL: Peacock.

Bordin, E. S. (1979). The generalizability of the psychoanalytic concept of the working alliance. *Psychotherapy: Theory, Research and Practice, 16,* 252–60.

Bowlby, J. (1979). *The making and breaking of affectional bonds.* London: Tavistock.

Brammer, L. M. (1985). *The helping relationship: Process and skills* (3rd ed.). Englewood Cliffs, NJ: Prentice-Hall.

British Association for Counselling (1990). *Code of ethics and practice for counsellors.* Rugby: Author.

British Psychological Society (1991). *Code of conduct, ethical principles and guidelines.* Leicester: Author.

Bugental, J. F. T. (1981). *The search for authenticity.* New York: Irvington Publishers.

Burns, D. D. (1980). *Feeling good: The new mood therapy.* New York: New American Library.

Burns, D. D. (1989). *The feeling good handbook: Using the new mood therapy in daily life.* New York: William Morrow.

Carkhuff, R. R. (1983). *The art of helping* (5th ed.). Amherst, MA: Human Resource Development Press.

Cautela, J. R. (1967). Covert sensitization. *Psychological Reports, 20,* 459–68.

Cautela, J. R. (1976). The present status of covert modeling. *Journal of Behavior Therapy and Experimental Psychiatry, 6,* 323–26.

Christensen, C. P. (1989). Cross-cultural awareness development: A conceptual model. *Counselor Education and Supervision, 28,* 270–87.

Clark, A. J. (1991). The identification and modification of defense mechanisms in counseling. *Journal of Counseling and Development, 69,* 231–36.

Corey, G. (1990). *Theory and practice of group counseling* (3rd ed.). Pacific Grove, CA: Brooks/Cole.

Corey, G., Corey, M. S., & Callanan, P. (1988). *Issues and ethics in the helping professions* (3rd ed.). Pacific Grove, CA: Brooks/Cole.

Cormier, W. H., & Cormier, L. S. (1985). *Interviewing strategies for helpers: Fundamental skills and cognitive behavioral interventions* (2nd ed.). Pacific Grove, CA: Brooks/Cole.

Corsini, R. J. (1989). Introduction. In R. J. Corsini & D. Wedding (Eds.), *Current psychotherapies* (4th ed., pp. 1–16). Itasca, IL: Peacock.

Daley, M. F. (1969). The "reinforcement menu": Finding effective reinforcers. In J. D. Krumboltz & C. E. Thoresen (Eds.), *Behavioral counseling: Cases and techniques* (pp. 42–45). New York: Holt, Rinehart & Winston.

Davidson, F. (1988). *The art of executive firing.* Melbourne: Information Australia.

Deffenbacher, J. L., McNamara, K., Stark, R. S., & Sabadell, P. M. (1990). A comparison of cognitive-behavioral and process-oriented group counseling for general anger reduction. *Journal of Counseling and Development, 69,* 167–72.

Deffenbacher, J. L., Story, D. A., Brandon, A. D., Hogg, J. A., & Hazaleus, S. I. (1988). Cognitive and cognitive-relaxation treatments of anger. *Cognitive Therapy and Research, 12,* 167–84.

Deffenbacher, J. L., & Suinn, R. M. (1988). Systematic desensitization and the reduction of anxiety. *The Counseling Psychologist, 16,* 9–30.

DeVoe, D. (1990). Feminist and nonsexist counseling: Implications for the male counselor. *Journal of Counseling and Development, 69,* 33–36.

Dorn, N., & South, N. (1986). Developing work-related education on alcohol and drugs. *British Journal of Guidance and Counselling, 14,* 88–96.

Dusay, J. M., & Dusay, K. M. (1989). Transactional analysis. In R. J. Corsini & D. Wedding (Eds.), *Current psychotherapies* (4th ed., pp. 405–453). Itasca, IL: Peacock.

Egan, G. (1977). *You and me: The skills of communicating and relating to others.* Pacific Grove, CA: Brooks/Cole.

Egan, G. (1990). *The skilled helper: A systematic approach to effective helping* (4th ed.). Pacific Grove, CA: Brooks/Cole.

Egan, G., & Cowan, M. (1979). *People in systems: A model for development in the human-service professions and education.* Pacific Grove, CA: Brooks/Cole.

Ekman, P., Friesen, W. V., & Ellsworth, P. (1972). *Emotions in the human face.* New York: Pergamon Press.

Elliott, R. (1985). Helpful and nonhelpful events in brief counseling interviews: An empirical taxonomy. *Journal of Counseling Psychology, 32,* 307–322.

Ellis, A. (1962). *Reason and emotion in psychotherapy.* New York: Lyle Stuart.

Ellis, A. (1977). *Anger: How to live with and without it.* New York: Lyle Stuart.

Ellis, A. (1980). Overview of the clinical theory of rational-emotive therapy. In R. Grieger & J. Boyd (Eds.), *Rational-emotive therapy: A skills based approach* (pp. 1–31). New York: Van Nostrand Reinhold.

Ellis, A. (1985). *Overcoming resistance: Rational-emotive therapy with difficult clients.* New York: Springer.

Ellis, A. (1987). The impossibility of achieving consistently good mental health. *American Psychologist, 42,* 364–75.

Ellis, A. (1989). Rational-emotive therapy. In R. J. Corsini & D. Wedding (Eds.), *Current psychotherapies* (4th ed., pp. 197–238). Itasca, IL: Peacock.

Ellis, A., & Harper, R. A. (1975). *A new guide to rational living.* North Hollywood, CA: Wilshire Books.

Emery, G. (1982). *Own your own life.* New York: New American Library.

Enns, C. Z., & Hackett, G. (1990). Comparison of feminist and nonfeminist women's reactions to variants of nonsexist and feminist counseling. *Journal of Counseling Psychology, 37,* 33–40.

Erikson, E. H. (1963). *Childhood and society* (2nd ed.). New York: W. W. Norton.

Feifel, H. (1990). Psychology and death: Meaningful rediscovery. *American Psychologist, 45,* 537–43.

Fischer, R. L. (1972). *Speak to communicate: An introduction to speech.* Encino, CA: Dickenson Publishing Company.

Frankl, V. E. (1959). *Man's search for meaning.* New York: Washington Square Press.

Frankl, V. E. (1967). *Psychotherapy and existentialism.* Harmondsworth, England: Penguin Books.

Frankl, V. E. (1969). *The doctor and the soul.* Harmondsworth, England: Penguin Books.

Frankl, V. E. (1975). *The unconscious god: Psychotherapy and theology.* New York: Simon and Schuster.

Freud, S. (1936). *The problem of anxiety.* New York: W. W. Norton.

Freudenberger, H. J. (1980). *Burnout: The high cost of high achievement.* London: Arrow Books.

Gallwey, W. T. (1974). *The inner game of tennis*. London: Pan Books.

Gazda, G. M. (1989). *Group counseling: A developmental approach* (4th ed.). Boston: Allyn & Bacon.

Geldard, D. (1989). *Basic personal counselling: A training manual for counsellors*. Sydney: Prentice-Hall.

Gendlin, E. T. (1962). *Experiencing and the creation of meaning*. New York: The Free Press of Glencoe.

Gendlin, E. T. (1981). *Focusing* (2nd ed.). New York: Bantam Books.

Gilbert, T. F. (1978). *Human competence: Engineering worthy performance*. New York: McGraw-Hill.

Glasser, W. (1965). *Reality therapy: A new approach to psychiatry*. New York: Harper & Row.

Glasser, W. (1984). *Control theory: A new explanation of how we control our lives*. New York: Harper & Row.

Glick, P. C. (1984). How American families are changing. *American Demographics, 6,* 20–25.

Goddard, R. W. (1989). Use language effectively. *Personnel Journal, 68,* 32–36.

Goldfried, M. R. (1971). Systematic desensitization as training in self-control. *Journal of Consulting and Clinical Psychology, 37,* 228–34.

Goldfried, M. R., & Davison, G. C. (1976). *Clinical behavior therapy*. New York: Holt, Rinehart & Winston.

Goldstein, A. P., & Keller, H. (1987). *Aggressive behavior: Assessment and intervention*. New York: Pergamon.

Good, G. E., Dell, D. M., & Mintz, L. B. (1989). Male role and gender role conflict: Relationships to help seeking in men. *Journal of Counseling Psychology, 36,* 295–300.

Good, G. E., Gilbert, L. A., & Scher, M. (1990). Gender aware therapy: A synthesis of feminist therapy and knowledge about gender. *Journal of Counseling and Development, 68,* 376–80.

Gordon, T. (1970). *Parent effectiveness training: The tested new way to raise responsible children*. New York: Wyden.

Grieger, R. (1989). A client's guide to rational-emotive therapy (RET). In W. Dryden & P. Trower (Eds.), *Cognitive psychotherapy: Stasis and change* (pp. 99–120). London: Cassell.

Guerney, B., Stollak, G., & Guerney, L. (1971). The practicing psychologist as educator—an alternative to the medical practitioner model. *Professional Psychology, 2,* 276–82.

Hall, E. T. (1966). *The hidden dimension*. New York: Doubleday.

Hatch, E. J., & Guerney, B. (1975). A pupil relationship enhancement program. *Personnel and Guidance Journal, 54,* 103–105.

Havighurst, R. J. (1972). *Developmental tasks and education* (3rd ed.). New York: David McKay.

Henley, N. M. (1977). *Body politics: Power, sex and nonverbal communication*. Englewood Cliffs, NJ: Prentice-Hall.

Heppner, P. P., Neal, G. W., & Larsen, L. M. (1984). Problem-solving training as prevention with college students. *Personnel and Guidance Journal, 62,* 514–29.

Heppner, P. P., Rogers, M. E., & Lee, L. (1984). Carl Rogers: Reflections on his life. *Journal of Counseling and Development, 63*, 14–20.

Hewitt, P. L., & Dyke, D. G. (1986). Perfectionism, stress, and vulnerability to depression. *Cognitive Therapy and Research, 10*, 137–42.

Ho, D. Y. F. (1985). Cultural values and professional issues in clinical psychology: Implications from the Hong Kong experience. *American Psychologist, 40*, 1212–18.

Hoelscher, T. J., Lichstein, K. L., Fischer, S., & Hegerty, T. B. (1987). Relaxation treatment of hypertension: Do home relaxation tapes enhance treatment outcome? *Behavior Therapy, 18*, 33–37.

Holland, J. L. (1973). *Making vocational choices: A theory of careers.* Englewood Cliffs, NJ: Prentice-Hall.

Hopson, B., & Scally, M. (1981). *Lifeskills teaching.* London: McGraw-Hill.

Hosford, R. E., & Johnson, M. E. (1983). A comparison of self-observation, self-modeling, and practice without video feedback for improving counselor interview behaviors. *Counselor Education and Supervision, 23*, 62–70.

Hosford, R. E., Moss, C. S., & Morrell, G. (1976). The self-as-a-model technique: Helping prison inmates change. In J. D. Krumboltz & C. E. Thoresen (Eds.), *Counseling methods* (pp. 487–95). New York: Holt, Rinehart & Winston.

Hutchins, D. E., & Cole, C. G. (1986). *Helping relationships and strategies.* Pacific Grove, CA: Brooks/Cole.

Ivey, A. E. (1976). Counseling psychology, the psychoeducator model and the future. *The Counseling Psychologist, 6*, 72–75.

Ivey, A. E. (1987). Cultural intentionality: The core of effective helping. *Counselor Education and Supervision, 26*, 168–72.

Ivey, A. E. (1988). *Intentional interviewing and counseling: Facilitating client development* (2nd ed.). Pacific Grove, CA: Brooks/Cole.

Ivey, A. E., Ivey, M. B., & Simek-Downing, L. (1987). *Counseling and psychotherapy: Integrating skills, theory and practice* (2nd ed.). Englewood Cliffs, NJ: Prentice-Hall.

Jacobson, E. (1929). *Progressive relaxation.* Chicago: University of Chicago Press.

Jacobson, E. (1938). *Progressive relaxation* (2nd ed.). Chicago: University of Chicago Press.

Jacobson, E. (1976). *You must relax.* Boston: Unwin Paperbacks.

Jacobson, N. S. (1989). The maintenance of treatment gains following social learning-based marital therapy. *Behavior Therapy, 20*, 325–36.

Jacobson, N. S., Follette, V. M., Follette, W. C., Holtzworth-Munroe, A., Katt, J. L., & Schmaling, K. B. (1985). A component analysis of behavioural marital therapy: 1 year follow-up. *Behaviour Research and Therapy, 23*, 549–55.

Janis, I. L., & Mann, L. (1977). *Decision making: A psychological analysis of conflict, choice, and commitment.* New York: The Free Press.

Jeffrey, R. W. (1976). Reducing fears through participant modeling and self-directed practice. In J. D. Krumboltz & C. E. Thoresen (Eds.), *Counseling methods* (pp. 301–312). New York: Holt, Rinehart & Winston.

Johnson, D. (1990). *Reaching out: Interpersonal effectiveness and self-actualization* (4th ed.). Englewood Cliffs, NJ: Prentice-Hall.

Jones, J. M. (1990). Correspondence from Associate Professor J. M. Jones, Classics Department, University of Western Australia, dated June 2.

Kanfer, F. H., & Gaelick, L. (1986). Self-management methods. In F. H. Kanfer & A. P. Goldstein (Eds.), *Helping people change: A textbook of methods* (3rd ed., pp. 283–345). New York: Pergamon Press.

Kaplan, H. S. (1974). *The new sex therapy: Active treatment of sexual dysfunctions.* Harmondsworth, England: Penguin.

Karoly, P., & Harris, A. (1986). Operant methods. In F. H. Kanfer & A. P. Goldstein (Eds.), *Helping people change: A textbook of methods* (3rd ed., pp. 283–345). New York: Pergamon Press.

Kazdin, A. E. (1976). Developing assertive behaviors through covert modeling. In J. D. Krumboltz & C. E. Thoresen (Eds.), *Counseling methods* (pp. 475–86). New York: Holt, Rinehart & Winston.

Kazdin, A. E. (1989). *Behavior modification in applied settings* (4th ed.). Pacific Grove, CA: Brooks/Cole.

Kelly, G. A. (1955). *A theory of personality: The psychology of personal constructs.* New York: W. W. Norton.

Kendall, P. C., & Hollon, S. D. (1989). Anxious self-talk: Development of the anxious self-statements questionnaire (ASSQ). *Cognitive Therapy and Research, 13,* 81–93.

Kendall, P. C., Hollon, S. D., Beck, A. T., Hammen, C. L., & Ingram, R. E. (1987). Issues and recommendations regarding use of the Beck Depression Inventory. *Cognitive Therapy and Research, 11,* 289–99.

King, M. L. (1963). *Strength to love.* Philadelphia, PA: Fortress Press.

Kinsey, A. C., Pomeroy, W. B., & Martin, C. E. (1948). *Sexual behavior in the human male.* Philadelphia, PA: W. B. Saunders.

Kinsey, A. C., Pomeroy, W. B., Martin, C. E., & Gebhard, P. H. (1953). *Sexual behavior in the human female.* Philadelphia, PA: W. B. Saunders.

Klingman, A., Melamed, B. G., Cuthbert, M. I., & Hermecz, D. A. (1984). Effects of participant modeling on information acquisition and skill utilization. *Journal of Consulting and Clinical Psychology, 52,* 414–22.

Kluckhohn, C. (1951). Values and value orientations in the theory of action. In T. Parsons & E. A. Shils (Eds.), *Toward a general theory of action.* Cambridge, MA: Harvard University Press.

Kohlberg, L., & Gilligan, C. (1971). The adolescent as philosopher: The discovery of the self in a postconventional world. *Daedalus, 100,* 1051–86.

Kokotovic, A. M., & Tracey, T. J. (1990). Working alliance in the early phase of counseling. *Journal of Counseling Psychology, 37,* 16–21.

Kruger, A. H. (1970). *Effective speaking: A complete course.* New York: Van Nostrand Reinhold.

Krumboltz, J. D. (1988). The key to achievement: Learning to love learning. In G. R. Walz (Ed.), *Building strong school counseling programs* (pp.

1–39). Alexandria, VA: American Association for Counseling and Development.

LaFromboise, T. D., Trimble, J. E., & Mohatt, G. V. (1990). Counseling intervention and American Indian tradition: An integrative approach. *The Counseling Psychologist, 18,* 628–54.

Laing, R. D. (1969). *The politics of the family.* London: Tavistock Publications.

Lazarus, A. A. (1977). *In the mind's eye.* New York: The Guilford Press.

Lazarus, A. A. (1981). *The practice of multimodal therapy.* New York: McGraw-Hill.

Lazarus, A. A. (1989). Multimodal therapy. In R. J. Corsini & D. Wedding (Eds.), *Current psychotherapies* (4th ed., pp. 503–544). Itasca, IL: Peacock.

Lee, D. Y., & Uhlemann, M. R. (1984). Comparison of verbal responses of Rogers, Shostrom and Lazarus. *Journal of Counseling Psychology, 31,* 91–94.

Lenihan, G., & Kirk, W. G. (1990). Using student paraprofessionals in the treatment of eating disorders. *Journal of Counseling and Development, 68,* 332–35.

Lewinsohn, P. M., Munoz, R. F., Youngren, M. A., & Zeiss, A. M. (1986). *Control your depression* (rev. ed.). New York: Prentice-Hall Press.

MacPhillamy, D. J., & Lewinsohn, P. M. (1982). The Pleasant Events Schedule: Studies on reliability, validity and scale intercorrelation. *Journal of Consulting and Clinical Psychology, 50,* 363–80.

Maracek, J., & Johnson, M. (1980). Gender and the process of therapy. In A. M. Brodsky & R. Hare-Mustin (Eds.), *Women and psychotherapy: An assessment of research and practice* (pp. 67–93). New York: Guilford Press.

Martin, J. (1987). Cognitive change in clients: Cognitive-mediational models. *Counselor Education and Supervision, 26,* 192–203.

Martin, J. (1990). Confusion in psychological skills training. *Journal of Counseling and Development, 68,* 402–407.

Marx, R. (1982). Relapse prevention for managerial training: A model for maintenance of behavior change. *Academy of Management Review, 7,* 433–41.

Maslow, A. H. (1962). *Towards a psychology of being.* New York: Van Nostrand.

Maslow, A. H. (1970). *Motivation and personality* (2nd ed.). New York: Harper & Row.

Maslow, A. H. (1971). *The farther reaches of human nature.* Harmondsworth, England: Penguin Books.

Masterpasqua, F. (1989). A competence paradigm for psychological practice. *American Psychologist, 44,* 1366–71.

Masters, W. H., & Johnson, V. E. (1970). *Human sexual inadequacy.* London: J. A. Churchill.

Mathews, A. M., Gelder, M. G., & Johnston, D. W. (1981). *Programmed practice for agoraphobia: Clients' manual.* London and New York: Tavistock Publications.

May, R. (1958). Contributions of existential psychotherapy. In R. May, E. Angel, & H. F. Ellenberger (Eds.), *Existence* (pp. 37–91). New York: Basic Books.

May, R., & Yalom, I. D. (1989). Existential psychotherapy. In R. J. Corsini & D. Wedding (Eds.), *Current psychotherapies* (4th ed., pp. 363–402). Itasca, IL: Peacock.

McCarthy, P. R. (1982). Differential effects of counselor self-referent responses and counselor status. *Journal of Counseling Psychology, 29,* 125–31.

McNair, D. M., Lorr, M., & Droppleman, L. F. (1981). *EITS Manual for the Profile of Mood States.* San Diego, CA: Educational and Industrial Testing Service.

Meichenbaum, D. H. (1977). *Cognitive-behavior modification: An integrative approach.* New York: Plenum.

Meichenbaum, D. H. (1983). *Coping with stress.* London: Century Publishing.

Meichenbaum, D. H. (1985) *Stress inoculation training.* New York: Pergamon Press.

Meichenbaum, D. H. (1986). Cognitive-behavior modification. In F. H. Kanfer & A. P. Goldstein (Eds.), *Helping people change: A textbook of methods* (3rd ed., pp. 346–80). New York: Pergamon Press.

Meichenbaum, D. H., & Deffenbacher, J. L. (1988). Stress inoculation training. *The Counseling Psychologist, 16,* 69–90.

MIMS (latest edition). Middlesex, England: Haymarket Publishing. Australian *MIMS,* 100 Alexander Street, Crows Nest, NSW 2065, Australia.

Mintz, L. B., & O'Neil, J. M. (1990). Gender roles, sex, and the process of psychotherapy: Many questions and few answers. *Journal of Counseling and Development, 68,* 381–87.

Moon, J. R., & Eisler, R. M. (1983). Anger control: An experimental comparison of three behavioral treatments. *Behavior Therapy, 14,* 493–505.

Morawetz, D. (1989). Behavioral self-help treatment for insomnia: A controlled evaluation. *Behavior Therapy, 20,* 365–79.

Moreno, Z. T. (1959). A survey of psychodramatic techniques. *Group Psychotherapy, 12,* 5–14.

Morgan, C., (1984). A curricular approach to primary prevention. *Personnel and Guidance Journal, 53,* 467–69.

Mosak, H. H. (1989). Adlerian psychotherapy. In R. J. Corsini & D. Wedding (Eds.), *Current psychotherapies* (4th ed., pp. 65–116). Itasca, IL: Peacock.

Murgatroyd, S. (1985). *Counselling and helping.* London: Methuen.

National Association of Social Workers (1979). Code of ethics. In Corey, G., Corey, M. S., & Callanan, P. (1988). *Issues and ethics in the helping professions* (3rd ed., pp. 397–401). Pacific Grove, CA: Brooks/Cole.

National Board for Certified Counselors (1987). *Code of ethics.* Alexandria, VA: Author.

National Training Laboratory (1967). *Feedback and the helping relationship.* Washington, DC: NTL Institute for Applied Behavioral Sciences (mimeo).

Nelson-Jones, R. (1982). The counsellor as decision-maker: Role, treatment and responding decisions. *British Journal of Guidance and Counselling, 10,* 113–24.

Nelson-Jones, R. (1986). Toward a people centred language for counselling psychology. *The Australian Counselling Psychologist, 2,* 18–23.

Nelson-Jones, R. (1987). *Personal responsibility counseling and therapy: An integrative approach.* New York: Hemisphere.

Nelson-Jones, R. (1990a). *Thinking skills: Managing and preventing personal problems.* Pacific Grove, CA: Brooks/Cole.

Nelson-Jones, R. (1990b). *Human relationships: A skills approach.* Pacific Grove, CA: Brooks/Cole.

Nelson-Jones, R. (1992). *Group leadership: A training approach.* Pacific Grove, CA: Brooks/Cole.

Nemeroff, C. J., & Karoly, P. (1991). Operant methods. In F. H. Kanfer, & A. P. Goldstein (Eds.), *Helping people change: A textbook of methods* (4th ed., pp. 122–60). New York: Pergamon.

Novaco, R. (1977). Stress inoculation: A cognitive therapy for anger and its application to a case of depression. *Journal of Consulting and Clinical Psychology, 45,* 600–608.

Oakley, A. (1972). *Sex, gender and society.* London: Temple Smith.

Osipow, S. H., Walsh, W. B., & Tosi, D. J. (1984). A survey of counseling methods (rev. ed.). Homewood, IL: Dorsey Press.

Parloff, M. B. (1967). Goals in psychotherapy: Mediating and ultimate. In A. R. Mahrer (Ed.), *The goals of psychotherapy* (pp. 5–19). New York: Appleton-Century-Crofts.

Pease, A. (1981). *Body language: How to read others' thoughts by their gestures.* Sydney: Camel.

Perls, F. S. (1973). *The gestalt approach and eyewitness to therapy.* New York: Bantam Books.

Perry, M. A., & Furukawa, M. J. (1986). *Modeling methods.* In F. H. Kanfer & A. P. Goldstein (Eds.), *Helping people change: A textbook of methods* (3rd ed., pp. 66–110). New York: Pergamon.

Perry, W. G. (1970). *Forms of intellectual development in the college years.* New York: Holt, Rinehart and Winston.

Petersen, C., Semmel, A., von Baeyer, C., Abramson, L. Y., Metalsky, G. L., & Seligman, M. E. P. (1982). The Attributional Style Questionnaire. *Cognitive Therapy and Research, 6,* 287–99.

Petersen, C., & Villanova, P. (1988). An expanded attributional style questionnaire. *Journal of Abnormal Psychology, 97,* 87–89.

Petersen, C., Villanova, P., & Raps, C. S. (1985). Depression and attributions: Factors responsible for inconsistent results in the published literature. *Journal of Abnormal Psychology, 92,* 165–68.

Peterson, L., & Ridley-Johnson, R. (1980). Pediatric hospital response to survey on pre-hospital preparation of children. *Journal of Pediatric Psychology, 5,* 1–7.

Pfeiffer, J. W., Goodstein, L., & Jones, J. E. (1972–1992). *The (date) annual developing human resources.* San Diego, CA: University Associates.

Physicians Desk Reference (latest edition). Oradell, NJ: Medical Economics Co.

Pomales, J., Claiborn, C. D., & LaFromboise, T. D. (1986). Effects of black students' racial identity on perceptions of white counselors varying in cultural sensitivity. *Journal of Counseling Psychology, 33,* 57–61.

Ponterotto, J. G. (1985). A counselor's guide to psychopharmacology. *Journal of Counseling and Development, 64,* 109–115.

Poon, D., Nelson-Jones, R., & Caputi, P. (1991, October). *Cross cultural sensitivity and perception of counsellor characteristics and effectiveness in a white counselor–Asian client dyad.* Symposium conducted at the Annual Conference of the Australian Psychological Society, Adelaide.

Pryor, E., & Norris, D. (1983). Canada in the eighties. *American Demographics, 5,* 25–29 & 44.

Raskin, N. J., & Rogers, C. R. (1989). Person-centered therapy. In R. J. Corsini & D. Wedding (Eds.), *Current psychotherapies* (4th ed., pp. 155–94). Itasca, IL: Peacock.

Robertson, J., & Fitzgerald, L. F. (1990). The (mis)treatment of men: Effects of client gender role and life-style on diagnosis and attribution of pathology. *Journal of Counseling Psychology, 37,* 3–9.

Robey, B., & Russell, C. (1984). Trends: All Americans. *American Demographics, 6,* 32–35.

Roessler, R. T. (1988). Implementing career education: Barriers and potential solutions. *Career Development Quarterly, 37,* 95–103.

Rogers, C. R. (1951). *Client-centered therapy.* Boston: Houghton Mifflin.

Rogers, C. R. (1957). The necessary and sufficient conditions of therapeutic personality change. *Journal of Consulting Psychology, 21,* 95–103.

Rogers, C. R. (1959). A theory of therapy, personality and interpersonal relationships as developed in the client-centered framework. In S. Koch (Ed.), *Psychology: A study of science* (Study No. 1, Vol. 3, pp. 184–256). New York: McGraw-Hill.

Rogers, C. R. (1961). *On becoming a person.* Boston: Houghton Mifflin.

Rogers, C. R. (1962). The interpersonal relationship: The core of guidance. *Harvard Educational Review, 32,* 416–29.

Rogers, C. R. (1975). Empathic: An unappreciated way of being. *The Counseling Psychologist, 5*(2), 2–10.

Rogers, C. R. (1980). *A way of being.* Boston: Houghton Mifflin.

Rogoff, B., & Morelli, G. (1989). Perspectives on children's development from cultural psychology. *American Psychologist, 44,* 343–48.

Rokeach, M. (1967). *Value survey.* Palo Alto, CA: Consulting Psychologists Press.

Rokeach, M., & Ball-Rokeach, S. J. (1989). Stability and change in American value priorities, 1968–1981. *American Psychologist, 44,* 775–84.

Romano, J. L. (1984). Stress management and wellness: Reaching beyond the counselor's office. *Personnel and Guidance Journal, 62,* 533–37.

Sampson, J. P., & Krumboltz, J. D. (1991). Computer-assisted instruction: A missing link in counseling. *Journal of Counseling and Development, 69,* 395–97.

Sarason, I. G. (1976). Using modeling to strengthen the behavioral repertory of the juvenile delinquent. In J. D. Krumboltz & C. E. Thoresen (Eds.), *Counseling methods* (pp. 56–66). New York: Holt, Rinehart & Winston.

Sartre, J. P. (1956). *Being and nothingness.* New York: Philosophical Library.

Satir, V. (1972). *Peoplemaking.* Palo Alto, CA: Science and Behavior Books.

Schulman, R., Seligman, M. E. P., & Amsterdam, D. (1987). The attributional style questionnaire is not transparent. *Behaviour Research & Therapy, 25,* 391–95.

Seligman, M. E. P. (1975). *Helplessness: On depression, development and death.* San Francisco, CA: W. H. Freeman.

Seligman, M. E. P., Abramson, L. Y., Semmel, A., & von Baeyer, C. (1979). Depressive attributional style. *Journal of Abnormal Psychology, 88,* 242–47.

Shaffer, W. F. (1976). *Heuristics for the initial diagnostic interview.* Paper presented at the annual meeting of the American Psychological Association, Washington, DC.

Sichel, J., & Ellis, A. (1984). *RET self-help form.* New York: Institute for Rational-Emotive Therapy.

Skinner, B. F. (1953). *Science and human behavior.* New York: Macmillan.

Skinner, B. F. (1969). *Contingencies of reinforcement.* New York: Appleton-Century-Crofts.

Skinner, B. F. (1971). *Beyond freedom and dignity.* Harmondsworth, England: Penguin Books.

Spielberger, C. D. (1983). *Manual for the State-Trait Anxiety Inventory (Form Y).* Palo Alto, CA: Consulting Psychologists Press.

Spitzer, R. L., & Williams, J. B. W. (1984). *The initial interview: Evaluation strategies for DSM III diagnosis—Interviewer's manual.* New York: BMA Audio Cassette Publications

Sprinthall, N. A. (1980). Psychology for secondary schools: The saber-tooth curriculum revisited? *American Psychologist, 35,* 336–47.

Steiner, C. M. (1974). *Scripts people live.* New York: Bantam Books.

Stock, J., & Cervone, D. (1990). Proximal goal-setting and self-regulatory process. *Cognitive Therapy and Research, 14,* 483–98.

Stokes, T. F., & Osnes, P. G. (1989). An operant pursuit of generalization. *Behavior Therapy, 20,* 337–55.

Strong, S. R. (1968). Counseling: An interpersonal influence process. *Journal of Counseling Psychology, 15,* 215–24.

Strong, S. R. (1978). Social psychological approach to psychotherapy research. In S. L. Garfield & A. E. Bergin (Eds.), *Handbook of psychotherapy and behavior change: An empirical analysis* (2nd ed., pp. 101–135). New York: Wiley.

Stuart, R. B. (1980). *Helping couples change: A social learning approach to marital therapy.* New York: Guilford Press.

Sue, S., & Zane, N. (1987). The role of culture and cultural techniques in psychotherapy. *American Psychologist, 42,* 37–45.

Sugarman, L. (1986). *Life-span development: Concepts, theories and interventions.* London: Methuen.

Sullivan, H. S. (1953). *The interpersonal theory of psychiatry.* New York: W. W. Norton.

Sullivan, H. S. (1954). *The psychiatric interview.* New York: W. W. Norton.

Swain, R. (1984). Easing the transition: A career planning course for college students. *The Personnel and Guidance Journal, 62,* 529–32.

Swenson, C. A. (1990). How to speak to Hispanics. *American Demographics 12*(2), 40–41.

Tasto, D. L., & Hinkle, J. E. (1973). Muscle relaxation for tension headaches. *Behaviour Research and Therapy, 11,* 347–49.

Teyber, E. (1989). *Interpersonal process in psychotherapy: A guide for clinical training.* Pacific Grove, CA: Brooks/Cole.

Thoresen, C. E., & Mahoney. (1974). *Behavioral self-control.* New York: Holt, Rinehart & Winston.

Tillich, P. (1952). *The courage to be.* New Haven: Yale University Press.

Valenti, J. (1982). *Speak up with confidence: How to prepare, learn, and deliver effective speeches.* New York: William Morrow.

Waldrop, J., & Exter, T. (1990). What the 1990 census will show. *American Demographics 12*(1), 20–30.

Ward, D. E. (1984). Termination of individual counseling: Concepts and strategies. *Journal of Counseling and Development, 63,* 21–25.

Watkins, C. E. (1990). The effects of counselor self-disclosure: A research review. *The Counseling Psychologist, 18,* 477–500.

Watson, D., & Friend, R. (1969). Measurement of social-evaluative anxiety. *Journal of Consulting and Clinical Psychology, 33,* 448–57.

Watson, D. L., & Tharp, R. G. (1989). *Self-directed behavior: Self-modification for personal adjustment* (5th ed.). Pacific Grove, CA: Brooks/Cole.

Webster-Stratton, C., Hollinsworth, T., & Kolpacoff, M. (1989). The long-term effectiveness and clinical significance of three cost-effective training programs for parents with conduct-problem children. *Journal of Consulting and Clinical Psychology, 57,* 550–53.

Webster-Stratton, C., Kolpacoff, M., & Hollinsworth, T. (1988). Self-administered videotape therapy for families with conduct-problem children: Comparison with two cost-effective treatments and a control group. *Journal of Consulting and Clinical Psychology, 56,* 558–66.

Wehrenberg, S. B. (1988). Learning contracts. *Personnel Journal, 62,* 100–102.

Weiner, B., & Kukla, A. (1970). An attributional analysis of achievement motivation. *Journal of Personality and Social Psychology, 15,* 1–20.

Weinstein, N. D. (1980). Unrealistic optimism about future events. *Journal of Personality and Social Psychology, 39,* 806–820.

Weinstein, N. D. (1984). Why it won't happen to me: Perceptions of risk factors and susceptibility. *Health Psychology, 3,* 431–57.

Whelan, J. P., Mahoney, M. J., & Meyers, A. W. (1991). Performance enhancement in sport: A cognitive behavioral domain. *Behavior Therapy, 22,* 307–327.

Will, O. A. (1954). Introduction to H. S. Sullivan, *The psychiatric interview.* New York: W. W. Norton, ix–xxii.

Wilson, B. F. (1984). Marriage's melting pot. *American Demographics, 6*(7), 34–37 & 45.

Wilson, B. F., & London, K. A. (1987). Going to the chapel. *American Demographics, 9* (12), 26–31.

Wolpe, J. E. (1958). *Psychotherapy by reciprocal inhibition.* Stanford, CA: Stanford University Press.

Wolpe, J. E. (1973). *The practice of behavior therapy* (2nd ed.). New York: Pergamon Press.

Wolpe, J. E. (1982). *The practice of behavior therapy* (3rd ed.). New York: Pergamon Press.

Woolfolk, R. L., Parish, M. W., & Murphy, S. M. (1985). The effects of positive and negative imagery on motor skill performance. *Cognitive Research and Therapy, 9,* 335–41.

Yalom, I. D. (1980). *Existential psychotherapy.* New York: Basic Books.

Yalom, I. D. (1985). *The theory and practice of group psychotherapy* (3rd ed.). New York: Basic Books.

Yalom, I. D. (1989). *Love's executioner: And other tales of psychotherapy.* London: Bloomsbury.

Yamauchi, K. T. (1987). Self-help audiocassette tapes: Adjunct to psychological counseling. *Journal of Counseling and Development, 65,* 448–50.

Yeo, A. (1981). *A helping hand: Coping with personal problems.* Singapore: Times Books International.

NAME INDEX

SUBJECT INDEX

TO THE OWNER OF THIS BOOK:

I hope that you have been significantly influenced by *Lifeskills Helping*. I'd like to know as much about your experiences with the book as you care to offer. Your comments can help me make it a better book for future readers.

School: _____ Instructor: _____

School address (city, state, and zip code): _____

1. What I like most about this book is: _____

_____

_____

2. What I like least about this book is: _____

_____

_____

3. The specific topics I thought were most relevant and important: _____

_____

_____

4. Questions that occurred to me that the book ignored: _____

_____

_____

_____

_____

5. The name of the course in which I used this book: _____

_____

6. In the space below—or in a separate letter, if you care to write one—please let me know what other comments about the book you'd like to make. I welcome your suggestions!

Optional:

Your name: _____ Date: _____

May Brooks/Cole quote you, either in promotion for *Lifeskills Helping* or in future publishing ventures?

Yes: _____ No: _____

Sincerely,

Richard Nelson-Jones

FOLD HERE

‖‖‖‖

NO POSTAGE
NECESSARY
IF MAILED
IN THE
UNITED STATES

BUSINESS REPLY MAIL
FIRST CLASS   PERMIT NO. 358   PACIFIC GROVE, CA

POSTAGE WILL BE PAID BY ADDRESSEE

ATT: *Dr. Richard Nelson-Jones*

**Brooks/Cole Publishing Company
511 Forest Lodge Road
Pacific Grove, California 93950-9968**

FOLD HERE